Nicolai M. Josuttis

# C++17

# The Complete Guide

## First Edition

# C++17 - The Complete Guide

**First Edition**

Nicolai M. Josuttis

This version was published on **2020-09-26**.

© 2020 by Nicolai Josuttis. All rights reserved.

This publication is protected by copyright, and permission must be obtained from the author prior to any prohibited reproduction, storage in a retrieval system, or transmission in any form or by any means, electronic, mechanical, photocopying, recording, or likewise.

This book was typeset by Nicolai M. Josuttis using the LaTeX document processing system.

ISBN-13: 978-3-96730-017-8
ISBN-10:     3-96730-017-X

This book is available as ebook at `http://leanpub.com/cpp17`.

*To those who care
for the poor and the different*

# Contents

**Preface**    xvii
    Versions of This Book . . . . . . . . . . . . . . . . . . . . . . . . . . . . . . . . . . .    xvii
    Acknowledgments . . . . . . . . . . . . . . . . . . . . . . . . . . . . . . . . . . . . .    xix

**About This Book**    xxi
    What You Should Know Before Reading This Book . . . . . . . . . . . . . . . . . .    xxi
    Overall Structure of the Book . . . . . . . . . . . . . . . . . . . . . . . . . . . . . .    xxii
    How to Read This Book . . . . . . . . . . . . . . . . . . . . . . . . . . . . . . . . .    xxii
    Error Terminology . . . . . . . . . . . . . . . . . . . . . . . . . . . . . . . . . . . .    xxii
    The C++17 Standard . . . . . . . . . . . . . . . . . . . . . . . . . . . . . . . . . .    xxiii
    Example Code and Additional Information . . . . . . . . . . . . . . . . . . . . . .    xxiii
    Feedback . . . . . . . . . . . . . . . . . . . . . . . . . . . . . . . . . . . . . . . . .    xxiii

**Part I: Basic Language Features**    1

**1 Structured Bindings**    3
    1.1  Structured Bindings in Detail . . . . . . . . . . . . . . . . . . . . . . . . . . . . .    4
    1.2  Where Structured Bindings Can Be Used . . . . . . . . . . . . . . . . . . . . . .    7
        1.2.1  Structures and Classes . . . . . . . . . . . . . . . . . . . . . . . . . . .    8
        1.2.2  Raw Arrays . . . . . . . . . . . . . . . . . . . . . . . . . . . . . . . . .    9
        1.2.3  `std::pair`, `std::tuple`, and `std::array` . . . . . . . . . . . . . . .    9
    1.3  Providing a Tuple-Like API for Structured Bindings . . . . . . . . . . . . . . . .    11
    1.4  Afternotes . . . . . . . . . . . . . . . . . . . . . . . . . . . . . . . . . . . . . . .    19

**2 `if` and `switch` with Initialization**    21
    2.1  `if` with Initialization . . . . . . . . . . . . . . . . . . . . . . . . . . . . . . . .    21

|   |   |   |
|---|---|---|
| 2.2 | `switch` with Initialization | 23 |
| 2.3 | Afternotes | 24 |

# 3 Inline Variables — 25
| 3.1 | Motivation for Inline Variables | 25 |
|---|---|---|
| 3.2 | Using Inline Variables | 27 |
| 3.3 | `constexpr` Now Implies `inline` For Static Members | 28 |
| 3.4 | Inline Variables and `thread_local` | 29 |
| 3.5 | Afternotes | 31 |

# 4 Aggregate Extensions — 33
| 4.1 | Motivation for Extended Aggregate Initialization | 34 |
|---|---|---|
| 4.2 | Using Extended Aggregate Initialization | 34 |
| 4.3 | Definition of Aggregates | 36 |
| 4.4 | Backward Incompatibilities | 36 |
| 4.5 | Afternotes | 37 |

# 5 Mandatory Copy Elision or Passing Unmaterialized Objects — 39
| 5.1 | Motivation for Mandatory Copy Elision for Temporaries | 39 |
|---|---|---|
| 5.2 | Benefit of Mandatory Copy Elision for Temporaries | 41 |
| 5.3 | Clarified Value Categories | 42 |
| | 5.3.1 Value Categories | 42 |
| | 5.3.2 Value Categories Since C++17 | 44 |
| 5.4 | Unmaterialized Return Value Passing | 45 |
| 5.5 | Afternotes | 46 |

# 6 Lambda Extensions — 47
| 6.1 | `constexpr` Lambdas | 47 |
|---|---|---|
| | 6.1.1 Using `constexpr` Lambdas | 49 |
| 6.2 | Passing Copies of `this` to Lambdas | 50 |
| 6.3 | Capturing by `const` Reference | 53 |
| 6.4 | Afternotes | 53 |

# 7 New Attributes and Attribute Features — 55
| 7.1 | Attribute `[[nodiscard]]` | 55 |
|---|---|---|

|     | 7.2  | Attribute `[[maybe_unused]]` | 57 |
|-----|------|---|---|
|     | 7.3  | Attribute `[[fallthrough]]` | 58 |
|     | 7.4  | General Attribute Extensions | 58 |
|     | 7.5  | Afternotes | 59 |
| **8** | **Other Language Features** | | **61** |
|     | 8.1  | Nested Namespaces | 61 |
|     | 8.2  | Defined Expression Evaluation Order | 62 |
|     | 8.3  | Relaxed Enum Initialization from Integral Values | 65 |
|     | 8.4  | Fixed Direct List Initialization with `auto` | 66 |
|     | 8.5  | Hexadecimal Floating-Point Literals | 67 |
|     | 8.6  | UTF-8 Character Literals | 68 |
|     | 8.7  | Exception Specifications as Part of the Type | 69 |
|     | 8.8  | Single-Argument `static_assert` | 72 |
|     | 8.9  | Preprocessor Condition `__has_include` | 73 |
|     | 8.10 | Afternotes | 73 |

## Part II: Template Features — 75

| **9** | **Class Template Argument Deduction** | | | **77** |
|---|---|---|---|---|
|   | 9.1 | Use of Class Template Argument Deduction | | 77 |
|   |     | 9.1.1 | Copying by Default | 79 |
|   |     | 9.1.2 | Deducing the Type of Lambdas | 80 |
|   |     | 9.1.3 | No Partial Class Template Argument Deduction | 81 |
|   |     | 9.1.4 | Class Template Argument Deduction Instead of Convenience Functions | 83 |
|   | 9.2 | Deduction Guides | | 84 |
|   |     | 9.2.1 | Using Deduction Guides to Force Decay | 85 |
|   |     | 9.2.2 | Non-Template Deduction Guides | 86 |
|   |     | 9.2.3 | Deduction Guides versus Constructors | 86 |
|   |     | 9.2.4 | Explicit Deduction Guides | 87 |
|   |     | 9.2.5 | Deduction Guides for Aggregates | 88 |
|   |     | 9.2.6 | Standard Deduction Guides | 89 |
|   | 9.3 | Afternotes | | 93 |

## 10 Compile-Time `if` — 95
- 10.1 Motivation for Compile-Time `if` — 96
- 10.2 Using Compile-Time `if` — 98
  - 10.2.1 Caveats for Compile-Time `if` — 98
  - 10.2.2 Other Compile-Time `if` Examples — 101
- 10.3 Compile-Time `if` with Initialization — 103
- 10.4 Using Compile-Time `if` Outside Templates — 104
- 10.5 Afternotes — 105

## 11 Fold Expressions — 107
- 11.1 Motivation for Fold Expressions — 108
- 11.2 Using Fold Expressions — 108
  - 11.2.1 Dealing with Empty Parameter Packs — 109
  - 11.2.2 Supported Operators — 112
  - 11.2.3 Using Fold Expressions for Types — 117
- 11.3 Afternotes — 118

## 12 Dealing with String Literals as Template Parameters — 119
- 12.1 Using Strings in Templates — 119
- 12.2 Afternotes — 120

## 13 Placeholder Types like `auto` as Template Parameters — 121
- 13.1 Using `auto` for Template Parameters — 121
  - 13.1.1 Parameterizing Templates for Characters and Strings — 122
  - 13.1.2 Defining Metaprogramming Constants — 123
- 13.2 Using `auto` as Variable Template Parameter — 124
- 13.3 Using `decltype(auto)` as Template Parameter — 126
- 13.4 Afternotes — 127

## 14 Extended Using Declarations — 129
- 14.1 Using Variadic Using Declarations — 129
- 14.2 Variadic Using Declarations for Inheriting Constructors — 130
- 14.3 Afternotes — 132

# Part III: New Library Components     133

## 15 `std::optional<>`     135
- 15.1 Using `std::optional<>` . . . . . . . . . . . . . . . . . . . . . . . . . . . 135
  - 15.1.1 Optional Return Values . . . . . . . . . . . . . . . . . . . . . . 135
  - 15.1.2 Optional Arguments and Data Members . . . . . . . . . . . . . . 137
- 15.2 `std::optional<>` Types and Operations . . . . . . . . . . . . . . . . . . 139
  - 15.2.1 `std::optional<>` Types . . . . . . . . . . . . . . . . . . . . . . 139
  - 15.2.2 `std::optional<>` Operations . . . . . . . . . . . . . . . . . . . 139
- 15.3 Special Cases . . . . . . . . . . . . . . . . . . . . . . . . . . . . . . . . 146
  - 15.3.1 Optional of Boolean or Raw Pointer Values . . . . . . . . . . . . 146
  - 15.3.2 Optional of Optional . . . . . . . . . . . . . . . . . . . . . . . . 146
- 15.4 Afternotes . . . . . . . . . . . . . . . . . . . . . . . . . . . . . . . . . . 147

## 16 `std::variant<>`     149
- 16.1 Motivation for `std::variant<>` . . . . . . . . . . . . . . . . . . . . . . . 149
- 16.2 Using `std::variant<>` . . . . . . . . . . . . . . . . . . . . . . . . . . . . 150
- 16.3 `std::variant<>` Types and Operations . . . . . . . . . . . . . . . . . . . 152
  - 16.3.1 `std::variant<>` Types . . . . . . . . . . . . . . . . . . . . . . . 152
  - 16.3.2 `std::variant<>` Operations . . . . . . . . . . . . . . . . . . . . 153
  - 16.3.3 Visitors . . . . . . . . . . . . . . . . . . . . . . . . . . . . . . . 157
  - 16.3.4 Valueless by Exception . . . . . . . . . . . . . . . . . . . . . . . 162
- 16.4 Polymorphism and Heterogeneous Collections with `std::variant` . . . . . . . 162
  - 16.4.1 Geometric Objects with `std::variant` . . . . . . . . . . . . . . . 163
  - 16.4.2 Other Heterogeneous Collections with `std::variant` . . . . . . . . 165
  - 16.4.3 Comparing `variant` Polymorphism . . . . . . . . . . . . . . . . . 167
- 16.5 Special Cases with `std::variant<>` . . . . . . . . . . . . . . . . . . . . . 168
  - 16.5.1 Having Both `bool` and `std::string` Alternatives . . . . . . . . . 168
- 16.6 Afternotes . . . . . . . . . . . . . . . . . . . . . . . . . . . . . . . . . . 169

## 17 `std::any`     171
- 17.1 Using `std::any` . . . . . . . . . . . . . . . . . . . . . . . . . . . . . . . 171
- 17.2 `std::any` Types and Operations . . . . . . . . . . . . . . . . . . . . . . 174
  - 17.2.1 Any Types . . . . . . . . . . . . . . . . . . . . . . . . . . . . . . 174
  - 17.2.2 Any Operations . . . . . . . . . . . . . . . . . . . . . . . . . . . 174

|       | 17.3  | Afternotes | 177 |
|---|---|---|---|

## 18 `std::byte` — 179
- 18.1 Using `std::byte` — 179
- 18.2 `std::byte` Types and Operations — 181
  - 18.2.1 `std::byte` Types — 181
  - 18.2.2 `std::byte` Operations — 182
- 18.3 Afternotes — 184

## 19 String Views — 185
- 19.1 Differences Compared to `std::string` — 185
- 19.2 Using String Views — 186
- 19.3 Using String Views as Parameters — 186
  - 19.3.1 String View Considered Harmful — 188
- 19.4 String View Types and Operations — 192
  - 19.4.1 Concrete String View Types — 192
  - 19.4.2 String View Operations — 193
  - 19.4.3 String View Support by Other Types — 196
- 19.5 Using String Views in APIs — 196
  - 19.5.1 Using String Views instead of Strings — 197
- 19.6 Afternotes — 198

## 20 The Filesystem Library — 201
- 20.1 Basic Examples — 201
  - 20.1.1 Print Attributes of a Passed Filesystem Path — 201
  - 20.1.2 Switch Over Filesystem Types — 204
  - 20.1.3 Create Different Types of Files — 206
  - 20.1.4 Dealing with Filesystems Using Parallel Algorithms — 210
- 20.2 Principles and Terminology — 210
  - 20.2.1 General Portability Disclaimer — 210
  - 20.2.2 Namespace — 211
  - 20.2.3 Paths — 211
  - 20.2.4 Normalization — 212
  - 20.2.5 Member Function versus Free-Standing Functions — 213
  - 20.2.6 Error Handling — 214

|       |        | 20.2.7  | File Types . . . . . . . . . . . . . . . . . . . . . . . . . . . . . . . . . . . | 216 |
|-------|--------|---------|----------|-----|

|      | 20.3 | Path Operations . . . . . . . . . . . . . . . . . . . . . . . . . . . . . . . . . . . . . . | 217 |
|------|------|---------|-----|
|      |      | 20.3.1  Path Creation . . . . . . . . . . . . . . . . . . . . . . . . . . . . . . . . . | 217 |
|      |      | 20.3.2  Path Inspection . . . . . . . . . . . . . . . . . . . . . . . . . . . . . . . | 218 |
|      |      | 20.3.3  Path I/O and Conversions . . . . . . . . . . . . . . . . . . . . . . . . . . | 221 |
|      |      | 20.3.4  Conversions Between Native and Generic Format . . . . . . . . . . . | 224 |
|      |      | 20.3.5  Path Modifications . . . . . . . . . . . . . . . . . . . . . . . . . . . . . | 226 |
|      |      | 20.3.6  Path Comparisons . . . . . . . . . . . . . . . . . . . . . . . . . . . . . | 228 |
|      |      | 20.3.7  Other Path Operations . . . . . . . . . . . . . . . . . . . . . . . . . . . | 229 |
|      | 20.4 | Filesystem Operations . . . . . . . . . . . . . . . . . . . . . . . . . . . . . . . . . | 230 |
|      |      | 20.4.1  File Attributes . . . . . . . . . . . . . . . . . . . . . . . . . . . . . . . | 230 |
|      |      | 20.4.2  File Status . . . . . . . . . . . . . . . . . . . . . . . . . . . . . . . . . | 234 |
|      |      | 20.4.3  Permissions . . . . . . . . . . . . . . . . . . . . . . . . . . . . . . . . . | 235 |
|      |      | 20.4.4  Filesystem Modifications . . . . . . . . . . . . . . . . . . . . . . . . . | 237 |
|      |      | 20.4.5  Symbolic Links and Filesystem-Dependent Path Conversions . . . . . . . . . . . . . . | 241 |
|      |      | 20.4.6  Other Filesystem Operations . . . . . . . . . . . . . . . . . . . . . . . | 243 |
|      | 20.5 | Iterating Over Directories . . . . . . . . . . . . . . . . . . . . . . . . . . . . . . . | 244 |
|      |      | 20.5.1  Directory Entries . . . . . . . . . . . . . . . . . . . . . . . . . . . . . . | 246 |
|      | 20.6 | Afternotes . . . . . . . . . . . . . . . . . . . . . . . . . . . . . . . . . . . . . . . . . | 248 |

# Part IV: Library Extensions and Modifications     249

## 21 Extensions of Type Traits     251
| 21.1 | Type Traits Suffix `_v` . . . . . . . . . . . . . . . . . . . . . . . . . . . . . . . . . . . | 251 |
|------|---------|-----|
| 21.2 | New Type Traits . . . . . . . . . . . . . . . . . . . . . . . . . . . . . . . . . . . . . | 252 |
| 21.3 | Afternotes . . . . . . . . . . . . . . . . . . . . . . . . . . . . . . . . . . . . . . . . . | 257 |

## 22 Parallel STL Algorithms     259
| 22.1 | Using Parallel Algorithms . . . . . . . . . . . . . . . . . . . . . . . . . . . . . . . . | 260 |
|------|---------|-----|
|      | 22.1.1  Using a Parallel `for_each()` . . . . . . . . . . . . . . . . . . . . . . . . | 260 |
|      | 22.1.2  Using a Parallel `sort()` . . . . . . . . . . . . . . . . . . . . . . . . . . | 263 |
| 22.2 | Execution Policies . . . . . . . . . . . . . . . . . . . . . . . . . . . . . . . . . . . . | 265 |
| 22.3 | Exception Handling . . . . . . . . . . . . . . . . . . . . . . . . . . . . . . . . . . . | 266 |
| 22.4 | Benefit of Not Using Parallel Algorithms . . . . . . . . . . . . . . . . . . . . . . . | 266 |
| 22.5 | Overview of Parallel Algorithms . . . . . . . . . . . . . . . . . . . . . . . . . . . . | 267 |

|  | 22.6 | Motivation for New Algorithms for Parallel Processing . . . . . . . . . . . . . . . . . . . . . . . | 269 |
|---|---|---|---|
|  |  | 22.6.1 `reduce()` . . . . . . . . . . . . . . . . . . . . . . . . . . . . . . . . . . . . . . . . . . . . . . . | 269 |
|  | 22.7 | Afternotes . . . . . . . . . . . . . . . . . . . . . . . . . . . . . . . . . . . . . . . . . . . . . . . . . . . . . . . . . . . | 278 |

## 23 New STL Algorithms in Detail    279

  23.1 `std::for_each_n()` . . . . . . . . . . . . . . . . . . . . . . . . . . . . . . . . . . . . . . . . . . . . . 279
  23.2 New Numeric STL Algorithms . . . . . . . . . . . . . . . . . . . . . . . . . . . . . . . . . . . . . . . 281
    23.2.1 `std::reduce()` . . . . . . . . . . . . . . . . . . . . . . . . . . . . . . . . . . . . . . . . . . . 281
    23.2.2 `std::transform_reduce()` . . . . . . . . . . . . . . . . . . . . . . . . . . . . . . . . . . 283
    23.2.3 `std::inclusive_scan()` and `std::exclusive_scan()` . . . . . . . . . . . . . 287
    23.2.4 `std::transform_inclusive_scan()` and `std::transform_exclusive_scan()` 289
  23.3 Afternotes . . . . . . . . . . . . . . . . . . . . . . . . . . . . . . . . . . . . . . . . . . . . . . . . . . . . . . . . . . . 291

## 24 Substring and Subsequence Searchers    293

  24.1 Using Substring Searchers . . . . . . . . . . . . . . . . . . . . . . . . . . . . . . . . . . . . . . . . . . . . 293
    24.1.1 Using Searchers with `search()` . . . . . . . . . . . . . . . . . . . . . . . . . . . . . . 293
    24.1.2 Using Searchers Directly . . . . . . . . . . . . . . . . . . . . . . . . . . . . . . . . . . . . 295
  24.2 Using General Subsequence Searchers . . . . . . . . . . . . . . . . . . . . . . . . . . . . . . . . . 296
  24.3 Using Searcher Predicates . . . . . . . . . . . . . . . . . . . . . . . . . . . . . . . . . . . . . . . . . . . . 297
  24.4 Afternotes . . . . . . . . . . . . . . . . . . . . . . . . . . . . . . . . . . . . . . . . . . . . . . . . . . . . . . . . . . . 298

## 25 Other Utility Functions and Algorithms    299

  25.1 `size()`, `empty()`, and `data()` . . . . . . . . . . . . . . . . . . . . . . . . . . . . . . . . . . . . 299
    25.1.1 Generic `size()` Function . . . . . . . . . . . . . . . . . . . . . . . . . . . . . . . . . . . 299
    25.1.2 Generic `empty()` Function . . . . . . . . . . . . . . . . . . . . . . . . . . . . . . . . . . 301
    25.1.3 Generic `data()` Function . . . . . . . . . . . . . . . . . . . . . . . . . . . . . . . . . . 301
  25.2 `as_const()` . . . . . . . . . . . . . . . . . . . . . . . . . . . . . . . . . . . . . . . . . . . . . . . . . . . . . 302
    25.2.1 Capturing by Const Reference . . . . . . . . . . . . . . . . . . . . . . . . . . . . . . . . 302
  25.3 `clamp()` . . . . . . . . . . . . . . . . . . . . . . . . . . . . . . . . . . . . . . . . . . . . . . . . . . . . . . . . 303
  25.4 `sample()` . . . . . . . . . . . . . . . . . . . . . . . . . . . . . . . . . . . . . . . . . . . . . . . . . . . . . . . 304
  25.5 Afternotes . . . . . . . . . . . . . . . . . . . . . . . . . . . . . . . . . . . . . . . . . . . . . . . . . . . . . . . . . . . 307

## 26 Container and String Extensions    309

  26.1 Node Handles . . . . . . . . . . . . . . . . . . . . . . . . . . . . . . . . . . . . . . . . . . . . . . . . . . . . . . . 309
    26.1.1 Modifying a Key . . . . . . . . . . . . . . . . . . . . . . . . . . . . . . . . . . . . . . . . . . . 309

|     |        | 26.1.2 Moving Nodes Between Containers | 311 |
|-----|--------|----|-----|

## Contents

|        |        |        |     |
|--------|--------|--------|-----|
|        |        | 26.1.2 Moving Nodes Between Containers ........................ | 311 |
|        |        | 26.1.3 Merging Containers ................................... | 312 |
|        | 26.2   | Emplace Improvements ...................................... | 314 |
|        |        | 26.2.1 Return Type of Emplace Functions ...................... | 314 |
|        |        | 26.2.2 `try_emplace()` and `insert_or_assign()` for Maps ......... | 314 |
|        |        | 26.2.3 `try_emplace()` ..................................... | 314 |
|        |        | 26.2.4 `insert_or_assign()` ................................ | 315 |
|        | 26.3   | Container Support for Incomplete Types ........................ | 316 |
|        | 26.4   | String Improvements ........................................ | 318 |
|        | 26.5   | Afternotes .................................................. | 319 |
| **27** | **Multi-Threading and Concurrency** | | **321** |
|        | 27.1   | Supplementary Mutexes and Locks ............................. | 321 |
|        |        | 27.1.1 `std::scoped_lock` .................................. | 321 |
|        |        | 27.1.2 `std::shared_mutex` ................................. | 322 |
|        | 27.2   | `is_always_lock_free` for Atomics ............................ | 323 |
|        | 27.3   | Cache Line Sizes ........................................... | 324 |
|        | 27.4   | Afternotes .................................................. | 326 |
| **28** | **Other Small Library Features and Modifications** | | **327** |
|        | 28.1   | `std::uncaught_exceptions()` ................................. | 327 |
|        | 28.2   | Shared Pointer Improvements ................................. | 329 |
|        |        | 28.2.1 Special handling for Shared Pointers to Raw C Arrays ...... | 329 |
|        |        | 28.2.2 `reinterpret_pointer_cast` for Shared Pointers ........... | 330 |
|        |        | 28.2.3 `weak_type` for Shared Pointers ........................ | 330 |
|        |        | 28.2.4 `weak_from_this` for Shared Pointers ................... | 330 |
|        | 28.3   | Numeric Extensions ........................................ | 332 |
|        |        | 28.3.1 Greatest Common Divisor and Least Common Multiple ...... | 332 |
|        |        | 28.3.2 Three-Argument Overloads of `std::hypot()` .............. | 332 |
|        |        | 28.3.3 Mathematical Special Functions ........................ | 332 |
|        | 28.4   | `chrono` Extensions ......................................... | 334 |
|        | 28.5   | `constexpr` Extensions and Fixes .............................. | 335 |
|        | 28.6   | `noexcept` Extensions and Fixes ............................... | 336 |
|        | 28.7   | Afternotes .................................................. | 336 |

## Part V: Expert Utilities                                                339

### 29 Polymorphic Memory Resources (PMR)                                   341
    29.1 Using Standard Memory Resources . . . . . . . . . . . . . . . . . . . . . . . 342
        29.1.1 Motivating Example . . . . . . . . . . . . . . . . . . . . . . . . 342
        29.1.2 Standard Memory Resources . . . . . . . . . . . . . . . . . . . 347
        29.1.3 Standard Memory Resources in Detail . . . . . . . . . . . . . . 349
    29.2 Defining Custom Memory Resources . . . . . . . . . . . . . . . . . . . . . 355
        29.2.1 Equality of Memory Resources . . . . . . . . . . . . . . . . . . 358
    29.3 Providing Memory Resource Support for Custom Types . . . . . . . . . . 360
        29.3.1 Definition of a PMR Type . . . . . . . . . . . . . . . . . . . . . 360
        29.3.2 Using a PMR Type . . . . . . . . . . . . . . . . . . . . . . . . . 362
        29.3.3 Dealing with the Different Types . . . . . . . . . . . . . . . . . 363
    29.4 Afternotes . . . . . . . . . . . . . . . . . . . . . . . . . . . . . . . . . . . 364

### 30 `new` and `delete` with Over-Aligned Data                            365
    30.1 Using `new` with Alignments . . . . . . . . . . . . . . . . . . . . . . . . . 365
        30.1.1 Distinct Dynamic/Heap Memory Arenas . . . . . . . . . . . . . 366
        30.1.2 Passing the Alignment with the `new` Expression . . . . . . . . 367
    30.2 Implementing `operator new()` for Aligned Memory . . . . . . . . . . . . 370
        30.2.1 Implementing Aligned Allocation Before C++17 . . . . . . . . . 370
        30.2.2 Implementing Type-Specific `operator new()` . . . . . . . . . . 372
    30.3 Implementing Global `operator new()` . . . . . . . . . . . . . . . . . . . 378
        30.3.1 Backward Incompatibilities . . . . . . . . . . . . . . . . . . . . 379
    30.4 Tracking All `::new` Calls . . . . . . . . . . . . . . . . . . . . . . . . . . 380
    30.5 Afternotes . . . . . . . . . . . . . . . . . . . . . . . . . . . . . . . . . . . 383

### 31 `std::to_chars()` and `std::from_chars()`                            385
    31.1 Motivation for Low-Level Conversions between Character Sequences and Numeric Values   385
    31.2 Example Usage . . . . . . . . . . . . . . . . . . . . . . . . . . . . . . . . 386
        31.2.1 `from_chars()` . . . . . . . . . . . . . . . . . . . . . . . . . . 386
        31.2.2 `to_chars()` . . . . . . . . . . . . . . . . . . . . . . . . . . . 387
    31.3 Floating-Point Round-Trip Support . . . . . . . . . . . . . . . . . . . . . . 388
    31.4 Afternotes . . . . . . . . . . . . . . . . . . . . . . . . . . . . . . . . . . . 391

## 32 std::launder() — 393

- 32.1 Motivation for std::launder() — 393
- 32.2 How launder() Solves the Problem — 396
- 32.3 Why/When launder() Does Not Work — 397
- 32.4 Afternotes — 398

## 33 Improvements for Implementing Generic Code — 399

- 33.1 std::invoke<>() — 399
- 33.2 std::bool_constant<> — 401
- 33.3 std::void_t<> — 403
- 33.4 Afternotes — 404

# Part VI: Final General Hints — 405

## 34 Common C++17 Settings — 407

- 34.1 Value of __cplusplus — 407
- 34.2 Compatibility to C11 — 407
- 34.3 Dealing with Signal Handlers — 408
- 34.4 Forward Progress Guarantees — 408
- 34.5 Afternotes — 408

## 35 Deprecated and Removed Features — 409

- 35.1 Deprecated and Removed Core Language Features — 409
  - 35.1.1 Throw Specifications — 409
  - 35.1.2 Keyword register — 409
  - 35.1.3 Disable ++ for bool — 410
  - 35.1.4 Trigraphs — 410
  - 35.1.5 Definition/Redeclaration of static constexpr Members — 410
- 35.2 Deprecated and Removed Library Features — 410
  - 35.2.1 auto_ptr — 410
  - 35.2.2 Algorithm random_shuffle() — 410
  - 35.2.3 unary_function and binary_function — 411
  - 35.2.4 ptr_fun(), mem_fun(), and Binders — 411
  - 35.2.5 Allocator Support for std::function<> — 411
  - 35.2.6 Deprecated IOStream Aliases — 411

> 35.2.7 Deprecated Library Features .................. 412
35.3 Afternotes .................................. 412

**Glossary** 415

**Index** 417

# Preface

This book is an experiment in two ways:
- I am writing an in-depth book covering language features without the direct help of a core language expert as a co-author. However, I can ask questions and I do.
- I am publishing the book myself on Leanpub and for printing on demand. That is, this book was written step by step and I will publish new versions as soon there is a significant improvement that makes the publication of a new version worthwhile.

The good thing is:
- You get the view of the language features from an experienced application programmer—somebody who feels the pain a feature might cause and asks the relevant questions to be able to motivate and explain the design and its consequences for programming in practice.
- You can benefit from my experience with C++17 while I am still learning and writing.

However, you are also part of the experiment. So help me out: give feedback (see page xxiii) about flaws, errors, features that are not explained well, or gaps so that we all can benefit from these improvements.

## Versions of This Book

Because this book is written incrementally, the following is the history of its "releases" (newest first):
- **2019-12-20**: Various small fixes due to feedback by readers
- **2019-09-06**: Proof reading fully done and processed
- **2019-08-20**: Publication of a **first printed version** with several fixes and improvements due to feedback from readers and proof reading
- **2019-08-11**: Description of guarantees to deal with signal handlers
- **2019-08-10**: Description of compatibility to C11
- **2019-07-07**: Description of removed and deprecated features
- **2019-07-06**: String view improvements
- **2019-07-04**: Description of all shared pointers improvements
- **2019-06-28**: Various proofreading updates and minor fixes
- **2019-05-31**: Description of `chrono` extensions, `noexcept` extensions, `constexpr` extensions

- **2019-05-30**: Large quantity of fixes following feedback and reviews
- **2019-05-29**: Fix of over-aligned heap memory and more due to C++17 given training
- **2019-05-12**: Addition of "placement `delete`" for over-aligned heap memory
- **2019-05-02**: Description of the new value of **__cplusplus**
- **2019-04-26**: Description of all new type traits and **std::invoke**()
- **2019-04-24**: Description of the motivation for problems of **std::launder**()
- **2019-04-24**: **merge**() for associative/unordered containers
- **2019-04-23**: Publication of a **new electronic version** with several fixes and improvements
- **2019-04-23**: Adoption of a standard fix of `create_directory()`
- **2019-04-22**: `try_emplace()` and `insert_or_assign()` for (unordered) maps
- **2019-04-21**: `data()` for strings
- **2019-03-28**: Detailed documentation of all new (parallel) STL algorithms
- **2019-03-18**: `uncaught_exceptions()`
- **2019-03-10**: Large number of small fixes due to reader feedback
- **2019-02-14**: `accumulate()` versus `reduce()` versus `transform_reduce()`
- **2019-02-12**: `for_each_n()` algorithm
- **2019-02-12**: `sample()` algorithm
- **2019-02-11**: `clamp()` utility function
- **2019-02-03**: Execution policies and list of parallel algorithms
- **2019-02-02**: Documentation of round-trip support of `to_chars()` and `from_chars()`
- **2019-01-11**: New examples with performance measurements on parallel algorithms
- **2018-12-26**: Polymorphism with `std::variant<>`
- **2018-12-25**: Using `std::tie()` for structured bindings
- **2018-12-24**: Description of Boyer-Moore(-Horspool) searchers
- **2018-11-24**: Description of generic `size()`, `empty()`, `data()`
- **2018-10-14**: Publication of a **new electronic version** with several fixes and improvements
- **2018-08-14**: Addition of polymorphic memory resources (pmr)
- **2018-08-07**: Addition of `as_const()`
- **2018-07-15**: Filesystem library chapter fully written
- **2018-05-30**: Addition of `scoped_lock` and `shared_mutex`
- **2018-05-29**: Addition of `is_always_lock_free()` and hardware interference sizes
- **2018-05-28**: Addition of variable templates with placeholders
- **2018-05-27**: Addition of container support for incomplete types
- **2018-05-11**: Addition of node handles for associative and unordered containers
- **2018-05-11**: First full supported example of parallel algorithms on filesystems
- **2018-04-04**: Beginning of an initial introduction of (new) parallel algorithms
- **2018-04-03**: Improvements to `std::optional<>` and more about the Filesystem library
- **2018-03-15**: Publication of a **new electronic version** with a couple of small fixes
- **2018-01-12**: Publication of a **new electronic version** with several fixes and improvements

- **2018-01-11**: Addition of new attribute features
- **2018-01-03**: Addition of new attributes
- **2018-01-02**: Addition of `new` and `delete` with over-aligned data
- **2017-12-25**: Publication of a **new electronic version** with several fixes and improvements
- **2017-12-24**: Addition of exception specifications becoming part of the type
- **2017-12-23**: Addition of `u8` prefix for UTF-8 character literals
- **2017-12-22**: Addition of hexadecimal floating-point literals
- **2017-12-15**: Publication of the **first electronic version**

# Acknowledgments

First of all I would like to thank you, the C++ community, for making this book possible. The incredible design of new features, the helpful feedback, and the curiosity are the basis for the evolution of a successful language. In particular, thanks for all the issues you told me about and explained and for the feedback you gave.

I would especially like to thank everyone who reviewed drafts of this book or corresponding slides and provided valuable feedback and clarification. These reviews increased the quality of the book significantly again proving that good things need the input of many "wise guys." For this reason, so far (this list is still growing) huge thanks to Roland Bock, Marshall Clow, Matthew Dodkins, Javier Estrada, Andreas Fertig, Bartlomiej Filipek, Davis Herring, Tom Honermann, Thomas, Köppe, Daniel Krügler, Graham Haynes, Austin McCartney, Alex Nash, Billy O'Neal, Paul Reilly, Barry Revzin, Vittorio Romeo, David Sankel, Tim Song, Zachary Turner, and Tony Van Eerd.

In addition, I would like to thank everyone in the C++ community and on the C++ standards committee. In addition to all the work involved in adding new language and library features, these experts spent many, many hours explaining and discussing their work with me, and they did so with patience and enthusiasm.

Special thanks go to the LaTeX community for a great text system and to Frank Mittelbach for solving my LaTeX issues (it was almost always my fault).

And finally, many thanks go to my proofreader, Tracey Duffy, who has done a tremendous job of converting my "German English" into native English.

# About This Book

C++17 is the next evolution in modern C++ programming, which is already at least partially supported by the latest version of gcc, clang, and Visual C++. Although the move to C++17 is not as big a step as the move to C++11, C++17 contains a large number of small and valuable language and library features that again will change the way we program in C++. This applies to both application programmers and programmers who provide foundation libraries.

This book will present all the new language and library features in C++17. It will cover the motivation and context of each new feature with examples and background information. As usual for my books, the focus lies on the application of the new features in practice and the book will demonstrate how features impact day-to-day programming and how you can benefit from them in projects.

## What You Should Know Before Reading This Book

To get the most from this book, you should already be familiar with C++, ideally C++11 and/or C++14. However, you do not have to be an expert. My goal is to make the content understandable for the average C++ programmer, not necessarily knowing all details of the latest features. You should be familiar with the concepts of classes and inheritance, and you should be able to write C++ programs using components such as IOstreams and containers from the C++ standard library. You should also be familiar with the basic features of "Modern C++", such as `auto`, `decltype`, move semantics, and lambdas.

Nevertheless, I will discuss basic features and review more subtle issues as the need arises, even when such issues are not directly related to C++17. This ensures that the text is accessible to experts and intermediate programmers alike.

Note that I usually use the modern form of initialization (introduced in C++11 as *uniform initialization*) with curly braces:

```
int i{42};
std::string s{"hello"};
```

This form of initialization, which is called *list initialization*, has the advantage that it can be used with fundamental types, class types, aggregates (extended with C++17 (see Chapter 4 on page 33)), enumeration types (added with C++17 (see Section 8.3 on page 65)), and `auto` (fixed with C++17 (see Section 8.4 on page 66)) and is able to detect narrowing errors (e.g., initialization of an `int` by a floating-point value).

If the braces are empty, the default constructors of (sub)objects are called and fundamental data types are initialized with 0/`false`/`nullptr`.[1]

## Overall Structure of the Book

This book covers *all* changes to C++ introduced with C++17. This applies to both language and library features as well as both features that affect day-to-day application programming and features for the sophisticated implementation of (foundation) libraries. However, the more general cases and examples usually come first.

The different chapters are grouped, but the grouping has no deeper didactic reasoning other than that it makes sense to first introduce language features because they might be used by the following library features. In principle, you can read the chapters in any order. If features from different chapters are combined, there are corresponding cross-references.

As a result, the book contains the following parts:

- **Part I** covers the new non-template language features.
- **Part II** covers the new language features for generic programming with templates.
- **Part III** introduces the new standard library components.
- **Part IV** covers the extensions and modifications to the existing components of the standard library.
- **Part V** covers language and library features for experts such as foundation library programmers.
- **Part VI** contains some concluding general hints about C++17.

## How to Read This Book

In my experience, the best way to learn something new is to look at examples. Therefore, you will find a lot of examples throughout the book. Some are just a few lines of code illustrating an abstract concept, whereas others are complete programs that provide a concrete application of the material. The latter kind of examples will be introduced by a C++ comment describing the file containing the program code. You can find these files on the website for this book at http://www.cppstd17.com.

## Error Terminology

Note that I often talk about programming errors. If there is no special hint, the term *error* or a comment such as

    ...   // ERROR

means a compile-time error. The corresponding code should not compile (with a conforming compiler).

If I use the term *runtime error*, the program might compile but not behave correctly or result in undefined behavior (thus, it might or might not do what is expected).

---

[1] The only exception are atomic data types (type `std::atomic<>`), where even list initialization does not guarantee proper initialization. This will hopefully be fixed with C++20.

# The C++17 Standard

The original C++ standard was published in 1998 and was subsequently amended by a *technical corrigendum* in 2003, which provided minor corrections and clarifications to the original standard. This "old C++ standard" is known as C++98 or C++03.

The world of "Modern C++" began with C++11 and was extended with C++14. The international C++ standards committee now aims to issue a new standard every three years. Clearly, that leaves less time for massive additions, but it brings the changes to the broader programming community more quickly. The development of larger features, therefore, takes time and might cover multiple standards.

C++17 is just the next step. It is not a revolution, but it does bring a huge number of improvements and extensions.

At the time of writing this book, C++17 is already at least partially supported by major compilers. However, as usual, compilers differ greatly in their support of new different language features. Some will compile most or even all of the code in this book, while others may only be able to handle a significant subset. However, I expect that this problem will soon be resolved as programmers everywhere demand standard support from their vendors.

# Example Code and Additional Information

You can access all example programs and find more information about this book from its website, which has the following URL:

```
http://www.cppstd17.com
```

# Feedback

I welcome your constructive input—both negative and positive. I have worked very hard to bring you what I hope you will find to be an excellent book. However, at some point I had to stop writing, reviewing, and tweaking to "release the new revision." You may therefore find errors, inconsistencies, presentations that could be improved, or topics that are missing altogether. Your feedback gives me a chance to fix these issues, inform all readers about the changes through the book's website, and improve any subsequent revisions or editions.

The best way to reach me is by email. You will find the email address at the website for this book:

```
http://www.cppstd17.com
```

Please be sure to have the latest version of this book available (remember it is written and published incrementally) and refer to the publishing date of this version when giving feedback. The current publishing date is **2020-09-26** (you can also find it on page ii, the page directly after the cover).

Many thanks.

# Part I

# Basic Language Features

This part of the book introduces the new core language features of C++17 that are not specific for generic programming (i.e., templates). They are particularly helpful for application programmers in their day-to-day programming and therefore every C++ programmer using C++17 should know them.

Core language features specific for programming with templates are covered in Part II.

# Chapter 1
# Structured Bindings

Structured bindings allow you to initialize multiple entities with the elements or members of an object.

For example, suppose you have defined a structure of two different members:

```
struct MyStruct {
  int i = 0;
  std::string s;
};

MyStruct ms;
```

You can bind members of this structure directly to new names by using the following declaration:

```
auto [u, v] = ms;
```

Here, the *names* u and v are what are called *structured bindings*. To some extent, they *decompose* the objects passed for initialization (at some point they were called *decomposition declarations*).

Each syntax for initializations is supported:

```
auto [u2, v2] {ms};
auto [u3, v3] (ms);
```

Structured bindings are especially useful for functions that return structures or arrays. For example, consider a function that returns a structure

```
MyStruct getStruct() {
  return MyStruct{42, "hello"};
}
```

You can assign the result to two entities directly giving local names to the returned data members:

```
auto[id,val] = getStruct();  // id and val name i and s of returned struct
```

Here, id and val are names for the members i and s of the returned structure. They have the corresponding types, int and std::string, and can be used as two different objects:

```
if (id > 30) {
  std::cout << val;
}
```

3

The benefit is direct access and the ability to make the code more readable by binding the value directly to names that convey semantic meaning about their purpose.[1]

The following code demonstrates how code can improve significantly with structured bindings. To iterate over the elements of a `std::map<>` without structured bindings, you would have to program:

```
for (const auto& elem : mymap) {
  std::cout << elem.first << ": " << elem.second << '\n';
}
```

The elements are `std::pair`s of the key and value type, and as the members of a `std::pair` are `first` and `second`, you have to use these names to access the key and the value. By using structured bindings, the code becomes a lot more readable:

```
for (const auto& [key,val] : mymap) {
  std::cout << key << ": " << val << '\n';
}
```

We can use the key and value member of each element directly, using names that clearly demonstrate their semantic meaning.

## 1.1 Structured Bindings in Detail

In order to understand structured bindings, it is important to be aware that there is a hidden anonymous variable involved. The new names introduced as structured bindings refer to members/elements of this anonymous variable.

**Binding to an Anonymous Entity**

The exact behavior of an initialization

```
auto [u,v] = ms;
```

is as if we had initialized a new entity *e* with ms and let the structured bindings u and v become alias names for the members of this new object, similar to defining:

```
auto e = ms;
aliasname u = e.i;
aliasname v = e.s;
```

This means that u and v are just other names for the members of a local copy of ms. However, we do not have a name for *e*, which means that we cannot access the initialized entity directly by name. Note that u and v are not references to *e*.i and *e*.s respectively. `decltype(u)` is the type of the member i and `decltype(v)` is the type of the member s.

As a result,

```
std::cout << u << ' ' << v << '\n';
```

prints the values of *e*.i and *e*.s, which are copies of ms.i and ms.s.

---

[1] Thanks to Zachary Turner for pointing that out.

## 1.1 Structured Bindings in Detail

*e* exists as long as the structured bindings to it exist. Thus, it is destroyed when the structured bindings go out of scope.

As a consequence, unless references are used, modifying the value used for initialization has no effect on the names initialized by a structured binding (and vice versa):

```
MyStruct ms{42,"hello"};
auto [u,v] = ms;
ms.i = 77;
std::cout << u;      // prints 42
u = 99;
std::cout << ms.i;   // prints 77
```

u and ms.i also have different addresses.

When using structured bindings for return values, the same principle applies. An initialization such as

```
auto [u,v] = getStruct();
```

behaves as if we had initialized a new entity *e* with the return value of getStruct() so that the structured bindings u and v become alias names for the two members/elements of *e*, similar to defining:

```
auto e = getStruct();
aliasname u =  e.i;
aliasname v =  e.s;
```

That is, structured bindings bind to a *new* entity, which is initialized from a return value, instead of binding to the return value directly.

To the type of the anonymous entity *e* the usual layout guarantees apply. Structured bindings are aligned as the corresponding members they bind to.

### Using Qualifiers

We can use qualifiers, such as const and references. Again, these qualifiers apply to the anonymous entity *e* as a whole. Usually, the effect is similar to applying the qualifiers to the structured bindings directly, but beware that this is not always the case (see below).

For example, we can declare structured bindings to a const reference:

```
const auto& [u,v] = ms;   // a reference, so that u/v refer to ms.i/ms.s
```

Here, the anonymous entity is declared as a const reference, which means that u and v are the names of the members i and s of the initialized const reference to ms. As a consequence, any change to the members of ms affect the value of u and/or v.

```
ms.i = 77;           // affects the value of u
std::cout << u;      // prints 77
```

Declared as a non-const reference, you can even modify the members of the object/value used for initialization:

```
MyStruct ms{42,"hello"};
auto& [u,v] = ms;    // the initialized entity is a reference to ms
ms.i = 77;           // affects the value of u
std::cout << u;      // prints 77
```

```
u = 99;                    // modifies ms.i
std::cout << ms.i;         // prints 99
```

If the value used to initialize a structured bindings reference is a temporary object, as usual, the lifetime of the temporary is extended to the lifetime of the bound structure:

```
MyStruct getStruct();
...
const auto& [a,b] = getStruct();
std::cout << "a: " << a << '\n';    // OK
```

## Qualifiers Do Not Necessarily Apply to the Structured Bindings

As written, the qualifiers apply to the new anonymous entity. They do not necessarily apply to the new names introduced as structured bindings. In fact, after

```
const auto& [u,v] = ms;    // a reference, so that u/v refer to ms.i/ms.s
```

both u and v are *not* declared as being references. This only specifies that the anonymous entity *e* is a reference. u and v have the type of the members of ms, both of which, however, become const here (just as you cannot modify members of an object passed as a constant reference). With our initial declaration, this means that decltype(u) is const int and decltype(v) is const std::string.

This also makes a difference when specifying an alignment:

```
alignas(16) auto [u,v] = ms;    // align the object, not v
```

Here, we align the initialized anonymous entity and not the structured bindings u and v. This means that u as the first member is forced to be aligned to 16, while v is not.

For the same reason, structured bindings do not *decay*[2] even though auto is used. For example, if we have a structure of raw arrays:

```
struct S {
  const char x[6];
  const char y[3];
};
```

then after

```
S s1{};
auto [a, b] = s1;    // a and b get the exact member types
```

the type of a is still const char[6]. Again, the auto applies to the anonymous entity, which as a whole does not decay. This is different from initializing a new object with auto, where types decay:

```
auto a2 = a;         // a2 gets decayed type of a
```

---

[2] The term *decay* describes the type conversions when arguments are passed by value, which means that raw arrays convert to pointers, and top-level qualifiers, such as const and references, are ignored.

## 1.2 Where Structured Bindings Can Be Used

**Move Semantics**

Move semantics is supported following the rules just introduced. In the following declarations:

```
MyStruct ms = { 42, "Jim" };
auto&& [v,n] = std::move(ms);           // entity is rvalue reference to ms
```

the structured bindings v and n refer to an anonymous entity being an rvalue reference to ms, while ms still holds its value:

```
std::cout << "ms.s: " << ms.s << '\n';  // prints "Jim"
```

However, you can move assign n, which refers to ms.s:

```
std::string s = std::move(n);           // moves ms.s to s
std::cout << "ms.s: " << ms.s << '\n';  // prints unspecified value
std::cout << "n:    " << n << '\n';     // prints unspecified value
std::cout << "s:    " << s << '\n';     // prints "Jim"
```

As usual, moved-from objects are in a valid state with an unspecified value. Thus, it is fine to print the value but not to make any assumptions about what is printed.[3]

This is slightly different to initializing the new entity with the moved values of ms:

```
MyStruct ms = { 42, "Jim" };
auto [v,n] = std::move(ms);             // new entity with moved-from values from ms
```

Here, the initialized anonymous entity is a new object initialized with the moved values from ms. Therefore, ms has already lost its value:

```
std::cout << "ms.s: " << ms.s << '\n';  // prints unspecified value
std::cout << "n:    " << n << '\n';     // prints "Jim"
```

You can still move assign the value of n or assign a new value there, but this does not affect ms.s:

```
std::string s = std::move(n);           // moves n to s
n = "Lara";
std::cout << "ms.s: " << ms.s << '\n';  // prints unspecified value
std::cout << "n:    " << n << '\n';     // prints "Lara"
std::cout << "s:    " << s << '\n';     // prints "Jim"
```

## 1.2 Where Structured Bindings Can Be Used

In principle, structured bindings can be used for structures with public data members, raw C-style arrays, and "tuple-like objects:"

- For **structures and classes** where all non-static data members are public, you can bind each non-static data member to exactly one name.
- For **raw arrays**, you can bind a name to each element of the array.
- For any type, you can use a **tuple-like API** to bind names to whatever the API defines as "elements." The API roughly requires the following components for a type *type*:

---

[3] For strings, moved-from objects are usually empty, but this is *not* guaranteed.

- `std::tuple_size<`*type*`>::value` has to return the number of elements.
- `std::tuple_element<`*idx,type*`>::type` has to return the type of the *idx*th element.
- A global or member `get<`*idx*`>()` has to yield the value of the *idx*th element.

The standard library types `std::pair<>`, `std::tuple<>`, and `std::array<>` are examples of types that provide this API.

If structures or classes provide the tuple-like API, the API is used.

In all cases, the number of elements or data members has to match the number of names in the declaration of the structured binding. You cannot skip a name and you cannot use a name twice. However, you could use a very short name such as '`_`' (as some programmers prefer but others hate and which is not allowed in the global namespace), but this works only once within the same scope:

```
auto [_,val1] = getStruct();    // OK
auto [_,val2] = getStruct();    // ERROR: name _ already used
```

Nested or non-flat decomposition is not supported.

The next subsections will discuss all of these uses of structured bindings in detail.

### 1.2.1 Structures and Classes

The introductory examples of structured bindings in the sections above have already described some simple uses for structures and classes with public members. A typical application is the direct use of multiple return values returned in one data structure (e.g., see `insert()` for node handles (see Section 26.1.2 on page 312)). However, there are a few edge cases to be aware of.

Note that only limited use of inheritance is possible. All non-static data members must be members of the same class definition (thus, they must be direct members of the type or of the same unambiguous public base class):

```
struct B {
  int a = 1;
  int b = 2;
};

struct D1 : B {
};
auto [x, y] = D1{};        // OK

struct D2 : B {
  int c = 3;
};
auto [i, j, k] = D2{};     // compile-time ERROR
```

Note that you should use structured bindings on public members only if their order is guaranteed to be stable. Otherwise, if the order of `int a` and `int b` inside B changes, x and y suddenly are initialized with different values. To support this stability, C++17 defines the order of members for some standard library structures (e.g., `insert_return_type` (see Section 26.1.2 on page 312)).

Structured bindings for unions are not allowed.

## 1.2.2 Raw Arrays

The following code initializes x and y with the two elements of the raw C-style array:

```
int arr[] = { 47, 11 };
auto [x, y] = arr;     // x and y are the int elems of a copy of arr
auto [z] = arr;        // ERROR: number of elements doesn't fit
```

Note that this is one of the few places in C++ where a raw array is copied by value.

The initialization is only possible as long as the array still has a known size. For an array passed as an argument by value, this is not possible because the array *decays* to the corresponding pointer type.

Note that C++ allows us to return arrays with size by reference, so that this feature also applies to functions that return an array, provided the size of the array is part of the return type:

```
auto getArr() -> int(&)[2];    // getArr() returns reference to raw int array
...
auto [x, y] = getArr();        // x and y are the int elems of a copy of the returned array
```

You can also use structured bindings for a std::array, which uses the tuple-like API, as described in the next section.

## 1.2.3 `std::pair`, `std::tuple`, and `std::array`

The structured binding mechanism is extensible, which means that you can add support for structured bindings to any type. The standard library uses this for std::pair<>, std::tuple<>, and std::array<>.

**`std::array`**

For example, the following code initializes a, b, c, and d as alias names for the four elements of a copy of the std::array<> returned by getArray():

```
std::array<int,4> getArray();
...
auto [a,b,c,d] = getArray();   // a,b,c,d name the 4 elements of the copied return value
```

Here, a, b, c, and d are structured bindings to the elements of the std::array returned by getArray().

Write access is also supported, provided the value for initialization is not a temporary return value and we are using non-const references. For example:

```
std::array<int,4> stdarr { 1, 2, 3, 4 };
...
auto& [a,b,c,d] = stdarr;
a += 10;                       // OK: modifies stdarr[0]

const auto& [e,f,g,h] = stdarr;
e += 10;                       // ERROR: reference to constant object

auto&& [i,j,k,l] = stdarr;
i += 10;                       // OK: modifies stdarr[0]
```

```
auto [m,n,o,p] = stdarr;
m += 10;                    // OK: but modifies copy of stdarr[0]
```

However, as usual, we cannot initialize a non-`const` reference from a temporary object (prvalue):

```
auto& [a,b,c,d] = getArray();   // ERROR
```

## std::tuple

The following code initializes a, b, and c as alias names for the three elements of a copy of the `std::tuple<>` returned by `getTuple()`:

```
std::tuple<char,float,std::string> getTuple();
...
auto [a,b,c] = getTuple();      // a,b,c have types and values of returned tuple
```

That is, a gets type `char`, b gets type `float`, and c gets type `std::string`.

## std::pair

As another example, the code for dealing with the return value of calling `insert()` on an associative/unordered container

```
std::map<std::string, int> coll;
```

can be made more readable by avoiding the generic names `first` and `second` from the resulting `std::pair<>` object:

```
auto ret = coll.insert({"new",42});
if (!ret.second){
    // if insertion failed, handle error using iterator ret.first
    ...
}
```

and instead binding to names that convey semantic meaning about their purpose:

```
auto [pos,ok] = coll.insert({"new",42});
if (!ok) {
    // if insertion failed, handle error using iterator pos:
    ...
}
```

Note that in this particular case, C++17 provides a way to improve this even further using `if` with initializers (see Section 2.1 on page 22).

### Assigning New Values to Structured Bindings for `pair` and `tuple`

After declaring a structured binding, you usually cannot modify all bindings together because structured bindings can only be declared but not used together. However, you can use `std::tie()` if the value assigned can be assigned to a `std::pair<>` or a `std::tuple<>`.

That is, you can implement the following:

```cpp
std::tuple<char,float,std::string> getTuple();
...
auto [a,b,c] = getTuple();       // a,b,c have types and values of returned tuple
...
std::tie(a,b,c) = getTuple();    // a,b,c get values of next returned tuple
```

In particular, this can be used to implement a loop that deals with a returned pair of values, such as when using searchers in a loop (see Section 24.1.2 on page 295):

```cpp
std::boyer_moore_searcher bmsearch{sub.begin(), sub.end()};
for (auto [beg, end] = bmsearch(text.begin(), text.end());
     beg != text.end();
     std::tie(beg,end) = bmsearch(end, text.end())) {
  ...
}
```

## 1.3 Providing a Tuple-Like API for Structured Bindings

You can add support for structured bindings to any type by providing a *tuple-like API*, just as the standard library does for `std::pair<>`, `std::tuple<>`, and `std::array<>`.

**Enable Read-Only Structured Bindings**

The following example demonstrates how to enable structured bindings for a type `Customer`, which might be defined as follows:

*lang/customer1.hpp*

```cpp
#include <string>
#include <utility>  // for std::move()

class Customer {
 private:
  std::string first;
  std::string last;
  long val;
 public:
  Customer (std::string f, std::string l, long v)
   : first{std::move(f)}, last{std::move(l)}, val{v} {
  }
  std::string getFirst() const {
    return first;
  }
  std::string getLast() const {
    return last;
  }
```

```cpp
  long getValue() const {
    return val;
  }
};
```

We can provide a tuple-like API as follows:

*lang/structbind1.hpp*

```cpp
#include "customer1.hpp"
#include <utility>  // for tuple-like API

// provide a tuple-like API for class Customer for structured bindings:
template<>
struct std::tuple_size<Customer> {
  static constexpr int value = 3;    // we have 3 attributes
};

template<>
struct std::tuple_element<2, Customer> {
  using type = long;                 // last attribute is a long
};
template<std::size_t Idx>
struct std::tuple_element<Idx, Customer> {
  using type = std::string;          // the other attributes are strings
};

// define specific getters:
template<std::size_t> auto get(const Customer& c);
template<> auto get<0>(const Customer& c) { return c.getFirst(); }
template<> auto get<1>(const Customer& c) { return c.getLast(); }
template<> auto get<2>(const Customer& c) { return c.getValue(); }
```

Here, we define a tuple-like API for three attributes of a customer, which we essentially map to the three getters of a customer (any other user-defined mapping is possible):

- The first name as `std::string`
- The last name as `std::string`
- The value as `long`

The number of attributes is defined as a specialization of `std::tuple_size` for type `Customer`:

```cpp
template<>
struct std::tuple_size<Customer> {
  static constexpr int value = 3;    // we have 3 attributes
};
```

The types of the attributes are defined as specializations of `std::tuple_element`:

## 1.3 Providing a Tuple-Like API for Structured Bindings

```
template<>
struct std::tuple_element<2, Customer> {
  using type = long;              // last attribute is a long
};
template<std::size_t Idx>
struct std::tuple_element<Idx, Customer> {
  using type = std::string;       // the other attributes are strings
};
```

The type of the third attribute is `long`, specified as a full specialization (see Section A on page 415) for index 2. The other attributes have type `std::string` specified as a partial specialization (see Section A on page 415) (which has a lower priority than the full specialization). The types specified here are the types `decltype` yields for the structured bindings.

Finally, we define the corresponding getters as overloads of a function `get<>()` in the same namespace as type `Customer`:[4]

```
template<std::size_t> auto get(const Customer& c);
template<> auto get<0>(const Customer& c) { return c.getFirst(); }
template<> auto get<1>(const Customer& c) { return c.getLast(); }
template<> auto get<2>(const Customer& c) { return c.getValue(); }
```

In this case, we have a primary function template declaration and full specializations for all cases.

Note that all full specializations of function templates have to use the same signature (including the exact same return type). This is because we provide only specific "implementations," no new declarations. The following will not compile:

```
template<std::size_t> auto get(const Customer& c);
template<> std::string get<0>(const Customer& c) { return c.getFirst(); }
template<> std::string get<1>(const Customer& c) { return c.getLast(); }
template<> long get<2>(const Customer& c) { return c.getValue(); }
```

By using the new compile-time `if` feature (see Chapter 10 on page 95), we can combine the `get<>()` implementations into one function:

```
template<std::size_t I> auto get(const Customer& c) {
  static_assert(I < 3);
  if constexpr (I == 0) {
    return c.getFirst();
  }
  else if constexpr (I == 1) {
    return c.getLast();
  }
  else {   // I == 2
    return c.getValue();
  }
}
```

---

[4] The C++17 standard also allows us to define these `get<>()` functions as member functions, but this is probably an oversight and should not be used.

With this API, we can use structured bindings for objects of type `Customer` as follows:

*lang/structbind1.cpp*

```
#include "structbind1.hpp"
#include <iostream>

int main()
{
  Customer c{"Tim", "Starr", 42};

  auto [f, l, v] = c;

  std::cout << "f/l/v:   " << f << ' ' << l << ' ' << v << '\n';

  // modify structured bindings:
  std::string s{std::move(f)};
  l = "Waters";
  v += 10;
  std::cout << "f/l/v:   " << f << ' ' << l << ' ' << v << '\n';
  std::cout << "c:       " << c.getFirst() << ' '
            << c.getLast() << ' ' << c.getValue() << '\n';
  std::cout << "s:       " << s << '\n';
}
```

With the initialization:

```
auto [f,l,v] = c;
```

as usual, the `Customer` c is copied to a hidden anonymous entity. This entity is destroyed when the structured bindings go out of scope.

In addition, for each structured binding f, l, and v, its get<>() function is called, calling the corresponding getters of type `Customer`. Because get<>() has return type auto, the getters return copies of the members, which means that the addresses of the structured bindings differ from the address of the created copy of c. Thus, after the initialization of the structured bindings, modifying c has no effect for them (and vice versa).

Using the structured bindings is then equivalent to using the values returned by get<>(). Thus:

```
std::cout << "f/l/v:   " << f << ' ' << l << ' ' << v << '\n';
```

simply outputs the values (without calling the getters (again)). And

```
std::string s{std::move(f)};
l = "Waters";
v += 10;
std::cout << "f/l/v:   " << f << ' ' << l << ' ' << v << '\n';
```

modifies the structured bindings as initialized `std::string`s and `long`.

Therefore, the program usually has the following output:

```
f/l/v:    Tim Starr 42
f/l/v:      Waters 52
c:        Tim Starr 42
s:        Tim
```

The output of the second line depends on the value of a moved-from string, which is usually an empty string but can also have any other valid string value.

Using these structured bindings you could also iterate over the `Customer` elements of a vector:

```
std::vector<Customer> coll;
...
for (const auto& [first, last, val] : coll) {
  std::cout << first << ' ' << last << ": " << val << '\n';
}
```

Inside the loop, no customer is copied because `const auto&` is used. However, the initialization of the structured bindings calls the getters via `get<>()`, returning a copy of both the first name and the last name. Then, in the body of the loop, the value of the initialized bindings is just used without calling the getters again. And at the end of an iteration, the copied strings are destructed.

Note that `decltype` for a structured binding still yields its type, not the type of the anonymous entity behind it. This means that here, `decltype(first)` is `const std::string` and not a reference.

**Enable Structured Bindings with Write Access**

The tuple-like API can use functions that yield non-const references. This enables structured bindings with write access. Assume the class `Customer` provides an API to read and modify its members:[5]

*lang/customer2.hpp*

```
#include <string>
#include <utility>  // for std::move()

class Customer {
 private:
  std::string first;
  std::string last;
  long val;
 public:
  Customer (std::string f, std::string l, long v)
   : first{std::move(f)}, last{std::move(l)}, val{v} {
  }
  const std::string& firstname() const {
    return first;
  }
```

---

[5] This class has a bad design because the member functions give direct access to private members. However, the example demonstrates how structured bindings with write access work.

```cpp
    std::string& firstname() {
      return first;
    }
    const std::string& lastname() const {
      return last;
    }
    std::string& lastname() {
      return last;
    }
    long value() const {
      return val;
    }
    long& value() {
      return val;
    }
};
```

For read-write access, we have to overload the getters for constant and non-constant references:

*lang/structbind2.hpp*

```cpp
#include "customer2.hpp"
#include <utility>   // for tuple-like API

// provide a tuple-like API for class Customer for structured bindings:
template<>
struct std::tuple_size<Customer> {
  static constexpr int value = 3;   // we have 3 attributes
};

template<>
struct std::tuple_element<2, Customer> {
  using type = long;                // last attribute is a long
};
template<std::size_t Idx>
struct std::tuple_element<Idx, Customer> {
  using type = std::string;         // the other attributes are strings
};

// define specific getters:
template<std::size_t I> decltype(auto) get(Customer& c) {
  static_assert(I < 3);
  if constexpr (I == 0) {
    return c.firstname();
  }
  else if constexpr (I == 1) {
```

## 1.3 Providing a Tuple-Like API for Structured Bindings

```
    return c.lastname();
  }
  else {  // I == 2
    return c.value();
  }
}
template<std::size_t I> decltype(auto) get(const Customer& c) {
  static_assert(I < 3);
  if constexpr (I == 0) {
    return c.firstname();
  }
  else if constexpr (I == 1) {
    return c.lastname();
  }
  else {  // I == 2
    return c.value();
  }
}
template<std::size_t I> decltype(auto) get(Customer&& c) {
  static_assert(I < 3);
  if constexpr (I == 0) {
    return std::move(c.firstname());
  }
  else if constexpr (I == 1) {
    return std::move(c.lastname());
  }
  else {  // I == 2
    return c.value();
  }
}
```

Note that you should have all three overloads, to be able to deal with constant, non-constant, and movable objects.[6] To enable the return value to be a reference, you should use `decltype(auto)`.[7]

Again, we use the new compile-time `if` feature (see Chapter 10 on page 95), which makes the implementation simple if the getters have different return types. Without this feature, we would need full specializations again, such as:

```
template<std::size_t> decltype(auto) get(const Customer& c);
template<std::size_t> decltype(auto) get(Customer& c);
```

---

[6] The standard library provides a fourth `get<>()` overload for `const&&`, which is provided for other reasons (see https://wg21.link/lwg2485) and not necessarily to support structured bindings.

[7] `decltype(auto)` was introduced with C++14 to allow a (return) type to be deduced from the value category (see Section 5.3 on page 42) of an expression. By using this as a return type, roughly speaking, references are returned by reference, but temporaries are returned by value.

```
template<std::size_t> decltype(auto) get(Customer&& c);
template<> decltype(auto) get<0>(const Customer& c) { return c.firstname(); }
template<> decltype(auto) get<0>(Customer& c) { return c.firstname(); }
template<> decltype(auto) get<0>(Customer&& c) {
                                 return std::move(c.firstname()); }
template<> decltype(auto) get<1>(const Customer& c) { return c.lastname(); }
template<> decltype(auto) get<1>(Customer& c) { return c.lastname(); }
...
```

Again, note that the primary function template declaration and the full specializations must have the same signature (including the same return type). The following will not compile:

```
template<std::size_t> decltype(auto) get(Customer& c);
template<> std::string& get<0>(Customer& c) { return c.firstname(); }
template<> std::string& get<1>(Customer& c) { return c.lastname(); }
template<> long& get<2>(Customer& c) { return c.value(); }
```

You can now use structured bindings for read access and to modify the members of a `Customer`:

*lang/structbind2.cpp*

```
#include "structbind2.hpp"
#include <iostream>

int main()
{
  Customer c{"Tim", "Starr", 42};
  auto [f, l, v] = c;
  std::cout << "f/l/v:    " << f << ' ' << l << ' ' << v << '\n';

  // modify structured bindings via references:
  auto&& [f2, l2, v2] = c;
  std::string s{std::move(f2)};
  f2 = "Ringo";
  v2 += 10;
  std::cout << "f2/l2/v2: " << f2 << ' ' << l2 << ' ' << v2 << '\n';
  std::cout << "c:        " << c.firstname() << ' '
            << c.lastname() << ' ' << c.value() << '\n';
  std::cout << "s:        " << s << '\n';
}
```

The program has the following output:

```
f/l/v:    Tim Starr 42
f2/l2/v2: Ringo Starr 52
c:        Ringo Starr 52
s:        Tim
```

## 1.4 Afternotes

Structured bindings were first proposed by Herb Sutter, Bjarne Stroustrup, and Gabriel Dos Reis in `https://wg21.link/p0144r0` by using curly braces instead of square brackets. The finally accepted wording for this feature was formulated by Jens Maurer in `https://wg21.link/p0217r3`.

# Chapter 2

# `if` and `switch` with Initialization

The `if` and `switch` control structures now allow us to specify an initialization clause before the usual condition or selection clause.

For example, you can write:

```
if (status s = check(); s != status::success) {
  return s;
}
```

where the initialization

```
status s = check();
```

initializes `s`, which is then valid for the whole `if` statement (including the optional `else` part).

## 2.1 `if` with Initialization

Any value initialized inside an `if` statement is valid until the end of the *then* and the *else* part (if this part exists). For example:

```
if (std::ofstream strm = getLogStrm(); coll.empty()) {
  strm << "<no data>\n";
}
else {
  for (const auto& elem : coll) {
    strm << elem << '\n';
  }
}
  // strm no longer declared
```

The destructor for `strm` is called at the end of the whole `if` statement (at the end of the *else* part, if any, or at the end of the *then* part, otherwise).

Another example would be the use of a lock while performing some tasks depending on a condition:

```
if (std::lock_guard<std::mutex> lg{collMutex}; !coll.empty()) {
  std::cout << coll.front() << '\n';
}
```

which, due to class template argument deduction (see Chapter 9 on page 77), can now also be written as:

```
if (std::lock_guard lg{collMutex}; !coll.empty()) {
  std::cout << coll.front() << '\n';
}
```

In any case, this code is equivalent to:

```
{
  std::lock_guard<std::mutex> lg{collMutex};
  if (!coll.empty()) {
    std::cout << coll.front() << '\n';
  }
}
```

with the minor difference that lg is defined in the scope of the if statement so that the condition is in the same scope (*declarative region*).

Note that this feature works in the same way as the initialization statement of a traditional for loop. For the guard to be effective, the initializer needs to declare a variable with a name. Otherwise, the initialization itself is an expression that creates and immediately destroys a temporary object. As a consequence, initializing a lock guard without a name is a logical error, because the guard would no longer lock when the condition is checked:

```
if (std::lock_guard<std::mutex>{collMutex};      // runtime ERROR:
    !coll.empty()) {                              // - no longer locked
  std::cout << coll.front() << '\n';              // - no longer locked
}
```

In principle, a single _ as a name would be enough (as some programmers prefer but others hate and which is not allowed in the global namespace):

```
if (std::lock_guard<std::mutex> _{collMutex};    // OK, but...
    !coll.empty()) {
  std::cout << coll.front() << '\n';
}
```

You can have multiple declarations with optional initializations:

```
if (auto x = qqq1(), y = qqq2(); x != y) {
  std::cout << "return values " << x << " and " << y << " differ\n";
}
```

or:

```
if (auto x{qqq1()}, y{qqq2()}; x != y) {
  std::cout << "return values " << x << " and " << y << " differ\n";
}
```

As another example, consider inserting a new element into a map or unordered map. You can check whether this was successful as follows:

```
std::map<std::string, int> coll;
...
if (auto [pos,ok] = coll.insert({"new",42}); !ok) {
    // if insert failed, handle error using iterator pos:
    const auto& [key,val] = *pos;
    std::cout << "already there: " << key << '\n';
}
```

Here, we also use structured bindings (see Chapter 1 on page 3) to give both the return value and the element at the return position `pos` useful names instead of just `first` and `second`. Before C++17, the corresponding check had to be formulated as follows:

```
auto ret = coll.insert({"new",42});
if (!ret.second){
    // if insert failed, handle error using iterator ret.first
    const auto& elem = *(ret.first);
    std::cout << "already there: " << elem.first << '\n';
}
```

Note that the extension also applies to the new *compile-time* `if` feature (see Chapter 10 on page 95).

## 2.2 `switch` with Initialization

Using the `switch` statement with an initialization allows us to initialize an object/entity for the scope of the switch before formulating the condition to decide where to continue the control flow.

For example, we can initialize a filesystem path (see Section 20.2.3 on page 211) before we deal with its category:

```
namespace fs = std::filesystem;
...
switch (fs::path p{name}; status(p).type()) {
  case fs::file_type::not_found:
      std::cout << p << " not found\n";
      break;
  case fs::file_type::directory:
      std::cout << p << ":\n";
      for (const auto& e : std::filesystem::directory_iterator{p}) {
        std::cout << "- " << e.path() << '\n';
      }
      break;
  default:
      std::cout << p << " exists\n";
      break;
}
```

Here, the initialized path `p` can be used throughout the whole `switch` statement.

## 2.3 Afternotes

`if` and `switch` with initialization was first proposed by Thomas Köppe in https://wg21.link/p0305r0, initially extending only the `if` statement. The finally accepted wording was formulated by Thomas Köppe in https://wg21.link/p0305r1.

# Chapter 3
# Inline Variables

For portability and ease of integration, it often makes sense to provide classes and libraries that are entirely contained in header files. However, up to C++17, this was only possible if no global variables/objects were needed or provided by such a library.

Since C++17, you can *define* a variable/object in a header file as `inline`:

```
class MyClass {
  inline static std::string msg{"OK"};    // OK since C++17
  ...
};

inline MyClass myGlobalObj;   // OK even if included/defined by multiple CPP files
```

No further definition in one translation unit is necessary, and if this definition is used by multiple translation units, they all refer to the same unique object.

## 3.1 Motivation for Inline Variables

In C++, initializing a non-`const` static member inside the class structure is not allowed:

```
class MyClass {
  static std::string msg{"OK"};    // compile-time ERROR
  ...
};
```

Defining the variable outside the class structure is also an error if this definition is part of a header file included by multiple CPP files:

```
class MyClass {
  static std::string msg;
  ...
};
std::string MyClass::msg{"OK"};    // Link ERROR if included by multiple CPP files
```

According to the *one definition rule* (ODR), a variable or entity has to be defined in exactly one translation unit—unless the variable or entity is declared to be `inline`.

Even include guards do not help:

```
#ifndef MYHEADER_HPP
#define MYHEADER_HPP

class MyClass {
  static std::string msg;
  ...
};
std::string MyClass::msg{"OK"};    // Link ERROR if included by multiple CPP files

#endif
```

The problem is not that the header file might be included multiple times; the problem is that two different CPP files include the header so that both define `MyClass::msg`.

For the same reason, you get a link error if you define an object of your class in a header file:

```
class MyClass {
  ...
};
MyClass myGlobalObject;            // Link ERROR if included by multiple CPP files
```

**Workarounds**

For some cases, there are workarounds:

- You can initialize `static const` data members of integral and enumeration types in a `class`/`struct`:
  ```
  class MyClass {
    static const bool trace = false;    // OK, literal type
    ...
  };
  ```
  However, this is only allowed for literal types, such as fundamental integral, floating-point, or pointer types, or for classes with only constant expressions to initialize non-static data members and no user-defined or virtual destructor. In addition, you still need a definition in one translation unit once you need the location of the member (e.g., by binding it to a reference).

- You can define an inline function that returns a `static` local variable:
  ```
  inline std::string& getMsg() {
    static std::string msg{"OK"};
    return msg;
  }
  ```

- You can define a `static` member function that returns the value:
  ```
  class MyClass {
    static std::string& getMsg() {
      static std::string msg{"OK"};
  ```

```
        return msg;
    }
    ...
};
```

- You can use variable templates (since C++14):
  ```
  template<typename T = std::string>
  T myGlobalMsg{"OK"};
  ```
- You can define a class template for the static member(s):
  ```
  template<typename = void>
  class MyClassStatics
  {
    static std::string msg;
  };

  template<typename T>
  std::string MyClassStatics<T>::msg{"OK"};
  ```
  and then even derive from it:
  ```
  class MyClass : public MyClassStatics<>
  {
      ...
  };
  ```

However, all of these approaches lead to significant overhead, less readability, and/or different ways to use the global variable. In addition, the initialization of a global variable might be postponed until its first use, which disables applications in which we want to initialize objects at program start (such as when using an object to monitor the process).

## 3.2 Using Inline Variables

Now, with `inline`, you can have a single globally available object by defining it only in a header file, which might be included by multiple CPP files:

```
class MyClass {
  inline static std::string msg{"OK"};   // OK since C++17
  ...
};

inline MyClass myGlobalObj;   // OK even if included/defined by multiple CPP files
```

Formally, the `inline` used here has the same semantics as a function declared inline:
- It can be defined in multiple translation units, provided all definitions are identical.
- It must be defined in every translation unit in which it is used.

Both are given by including the definition from the same header file. The resulting behavior of the program is as if there were exactly one variable.

You can even apply this to define atomic types in header files only:

```
inline std::atomic<bool> ready{false};
```

As usual for `std::atomic`, you always have to initialize the values when you define them.

Note that you still have to ensure that types are *complete* before you can initialize them. For example, if a `struct` or `class` has a static member of its own type, the member can only be defined inline after the type declaration:

```
struct MyType {
  int value;
  MyType(int i) : value{i} {
  }
  // one static object to hold the maximum value of this type:
  static MyType max;   // can only be declared here
  ...
};
inline MyType MyType::max{0};
```

See the header file for tracking all `new` calls (see Section 30.4 on page 380) for another example of using inline variables.

## 3.3 `constexpr` Now Implies `inline` For Static Members

For static data members, `constexpr` implies `inline` now, such that since C++17, the following declaration *defines* the static data member n:

```
struct D {
  static constexpr int n = 5;   // C++11/C++14: declaration
                                // since C++17: definition
};
```

That is, it is the same as:

```
struct D {
  inline static constexpr int n = 5;
};
```

Note that before C++17, you could often have the declaration only without a corresponding definition. Consider the following declaration:

```
struct D {
  static constexpr int n = 5;
};
```

This was enough if no definition of `D::n` was needed, which was the case if `D::n` was only passed by value:

```
std::cout << D::n;          // OK (ostream::operator<<(int) gets D::n by value)
```

If `D::n` was passed by reference to a non-inlined function and/or the call was not optimized away, this was invalid. For example:

```
int twice(const int& i);

std::cout << twice(D::n);    // was often an ERROR
```

This code violated the *one definition rule* (ODR). When built with an optimizing compiler, it might have worked as expected or might have given a link error due to the missing definition. When built without any optimizations, it will almost certainly be rejected due to the missing definition of D::n.[1] Creating a pointer to the static member does even more likely result in a link error due to the missing definition (but it might still work with some compiler modes):

```
const int* p = &D::n;        // was usually an ERROR
```

As a consequence, before C++17, you had to define D::n in exactly one translation unit:

```
constexpr int D::n;          // C++11/C++14: definition
                             // since C++17: redundant declaration (deprecated)
```

Now, when built with C++17, the declaration inside the class is a definition by itself, so all examples above are now valid without the former definition. The former definition is still valid but a deprecated redundant declaration.

## 3.4 Inline Variables and `thread_local`

By using `thread_local` you can also make an inline variable unique for each thread:

```
struct ThreadData {
  inline static thread_local std::string name;    // unique name per thread
  ...
};

inline thread_local std::vector<std::string> cache;    // one cache per thread
```

As a complete example, consider the following header file:

*lang/inlinethreadlocal.hpp*

```
#include <string>
#include <iostream>

struct MyData {
  inline static std::string gName = "global";              // unique in program
  inline static thread_local std::string tName = "tls";    // unique per thread
  std::string lName = "local";                             // for each object
  ...
  void print(const std::string& msg) const {
    std::cout << msg << '\n';
    std::cout << "- gName: " << gName << '\n';
    std::cout << "- tName: " << tName << '\n';
```

---

[1] Thanks to Richard Smith for pointing that out.

```
      std::cout << "- lName: " << lName << '\n';
  }
};

inline thread_local MyData myThreadData;   // one object per thread
```

You can use it in the translation unit that contains `main()`:

*lang/inlinethreadlocal1.cpp*

```
#include "inlinethreadlocal.hpp"
#include <thread>

void foo();

int main()
{
  myThreadData.print("main() begin:");

  myThreadData.gName = "thread1 name";
  myThreadData.tName = "thread1 name";
  myThreadData.lName = "thread1 name";
  myThreadData.print("main() later:");

  std::thread t(foo);
  t.join();
  myThreadData.print("main() end:");
}
```

You can also use the header file in another translation unit that defines `foo()`, which is called in a different thread:

*lang/inlinethreadlocal2.cpp*

```
#include "inlinethreadlocal.hpp"

void foo()
{
  myThreadData.print("foo() begin:");

  myThreadData.gName = "thread2 name";
  myThreadData.tName = "thread2 name";
  myThreadData.lName = "thread2 name";
  myThreadData.print("foo() end:");
}
```

The program has the following output:

```
main() begin:
- gName: global
- tName: tls
- lName: local
main() later:
- gName: thread1 name
- tName: thread1 name
- lName: thread1 name
foo() begin:
- gName: thread1 name
- tName: tls
- lName: local
foo() end:
- gName: thread2 name
- tName: thread2 name
- lName: thread2 name
main() end:
- gName: thread2 name
- tName: thread1 name
- lName: thread1 name
```

## 3.5 Afternotes

Inline variables were motivated by David Krauss in `https://wg21.link/n4147` and first proposed by Hal Finkel and Richard Smith in `https://wg21.link/n4424`. The finally accepted wording was formulated by Hal Finkel and Richard Smith in `https://wg21.link/p0386r2`.

# Chapter 4
# Aggregate Extensions

C++ has different ways and rules to initialize objects. One approach is called *aggregate initialization*, which describes the initialization of an aggregate.[1] As introduced by C you have to use curly braces to pass multiple values for initialization:

```
struct Data {
  std::string name;
  double value;
};

Data x = {"test1", 6.778};
```

Since C++11, you no longer need te equal sign:

```
Data x{"test1", 6.778};
```

Since C++17, aggregates can have base classes, which means that for such structures, that are derived from other classes/structures, list initialization is allowed:

```
struct MoreData : Data {
  bool done;
};

MoreData y{{"test1", 6.778}, false};
```

As you can see, aggregate initialization can now be used to pass initial values to the members of the base class. The base class members count as a sub-aggregate which means that you can use nested braces to initialize these values.

However, you can also even skip nested braces:

```
MoreData y{"test1", 6.778, false};
```

This follows the general rules of initializing nested aggregates, where you use the initial values according to the order of base structures/classes and members.

---

[1] Aggregates are either arrays or simple, C-like classes that have no user-provided constructors, no private or protected non-static data members, no virtual functions, and before C++17, no base classes.

## 4.1 Motivation for Extended Aggregate Initialization

Without this feature, deriving a structure from another type disabled aggregate initialization, which meant that you had to define a constructor:

```
struct Cpp14Data : Data {
  bool done;
  Cpp14Data (const std::string& s, double d, bool b)
    : Data{s,d}, done{b} {
  }
};

Cpp14Data y{"test1", 6.778, false};
```

Now we have this ability without declaring any constructor. The feature uses the syntax of nested braces, which can be omitted if at least one value is passed:

```
MoreData x{{"test1", 6.778}, false};  // OK since C++17
MoreData y{"test1", 6.778, false};    // OK
```

Note that because this is an aggregate now, other initializations are possible:

```
MoreData u;     // OOPS: value/done are uninitialized
MoreData z{};   // OK: value/done have values 0/false
```

If this is too dangerous, use default member initializers if you can:

```
struct Data {
  std::string name;
  double value{0.0};
};

struct Cpp14Data : Data {
  bool done{false};
};
```

Alternatively, continue to provide a constructor.

## 4.2 Using Extended Aggregate Initialization

One typical application of aggregate initialization is the ability to initialize members of a C-style structure derived by a class to add additional data members or operations. For example:

```
struct Data {
  const char* name;
  double value;
};

struct CppData : Data {
  bool critical;
```

## 4.2 Using Extended Aggregate Initialization

```cpp
    void print() const {
      std::cout << '[' << name << ',' << value << "]\n";
    }
};

CppData y{{"test1", 6.778}, false};
y.print();
```

Here, the arguments in the inner braces are passed to the base type `Data`.

Note that you can skip initial values. In that case, the elements are initialized from a default member initializer or they are copy-initialized from `{}` (usually getting the default-constructed value of the type of the element or 0, `false`, or `nullptr` if the type is a fundamental data type). For example:

```cpp
CppData x1{};           // zero-initialize all elements
CppData x2{{"msg"}};    // same as {{"msg",0.0},false}
CppData x3{{}, true};   // same as {{nullptr,0.0},true}
CppData x4;             // values of fundamental types are unspecified
```

Note the difference between using empty curly braces and no braces at all:

- The definition of x1 initializes all members so that the character pointer `name` is initialized by `nullptr`, the `double value` is initialized by `0.0`, and the `bool flag` is initialized by `false`.
- The definition of x4 does not initialize any member. All members have an unspecified value.

You can also derive aggregates from non-aggregate classes. For example:

```cpp
struct MyString : std::string {
  void print() const {
    if (empty()) {
      std::cout << "<undefined>\n";
    }
    else {
      std::cout << c_str() << '\n';
    }
  }
};

MyString x{{"hello"}};
MyString y{"world"};
```

Note that this is not the usual public inheritance for polymorphism. Because `std::string` has no virtual member functions, you should be very careful and avoid mixing these two types.

You can even derive aggregates from multiple base classes and/or aggregates:

```cpp
template<typename T>
struct D : std::string, std::complex<T>
{
   std::string data;
};
```

which you could then use and initialize as follows:

```cpp
D<float> s{{"hello"}, {4.5,6.7}, "world"};      // OK since C++17
D<float> t{"hello", {4.5, 6.7}, "world"};       // OK since C++17
std::cout << s.data;                             // outputs: "world"
std::cout << static_cast<std::string>(s);        // outputs: "hello"
std::cout << static_cast<std::complex<float>>(s); // outputs: (4.5,6.7)
```

The inner initializer lists are passed to the base classes in the order of the base class declarations.

The new feature also helps in defining an overload of lambdas (see Section 14.1 on page 129) with very little code.

## 4.3 Definition of Aggregates

To summarize, since C++17, an *aggregate* is defined as
- Either an array
- Or a *class type* (`class`, `struct`, or `union`) with:
  - No user-declared or `explicit` constructor
  - No constructor inherited by a `using` declaration
  - No `private` or `protected` non-static data members
  - No `virtual` functions
  - No `virtual`, `private`, or `protected` base classes

However, there are additional constraints for aggregates to be able to *initialize* them:
- No `private` or `protected` base class members
- No `private` or `protected` constructors

See the next section for an example that fails to compile due to these additional constraints.

C++17 also introduces a new type trait `is_aggregate<>` (see Section 21.2 on page 252) to test whether a type is an aggregate:

```cpp
template<typename T>
struct D : std::string, std::complex<T> {
    std::string data;
};
D<float> s{{"hello"}, {4.5,6.7}, "world"};          // OK since C++17
std::cout << std::is_aggregate<decltype(s)>::value; // outputs: 1 (true)
```

## 4.4 Backward Incompatibilities

Note that the following example no longer compiles:

*lang/aggr14.cpp*

```cpp
struct Derived;

struct Base {
 friend struct Derived;
 private:
  Base() {
  }
};

struct Derived : Base {
};

int main()
{
  Derived d1{};    // ERROR since C++17
  Derived d2;      // still OK (but might not initialize)
}
```

Before C++17, `Derived` was not an aggregate. Thus,

```cpp
Derived d1{};
```

called the implicitly defined default constructor of `Derived`, which by default called the default constructor of the base class `Base`. Although the default constructor of the base class is `private`, calling it via the default constructor of the derived class was valid because the derived class was defined to be a `friend` class.

Since C++17, `Derived` in this example is an aggregate, with no implicit default constructor at all (the constructor is not inherited by a `using` declaration). Therefore, the initialization is an aggregate initialization, which means that the expression

```cpp
std::is_aggregate<Derived>::value
```

yields `true`.

However, you cannot use brace initialization because the base class has a `private` constructor (see the previous section). Whether the base class is a `friend` is irrelevant.

## 4.5 Afternotes

Extended aggregate initialization was first proposed by Oleg Smolsky in https://wg21.link/n4404. The finally accepted wording was also formulated by Oleg Smolsky in https://wg21.link/p0017r1.

The type trait `std::is_aggregate<>` was introduced as a US national body comment for the standardization of C++17 (see https://wg21.link/lwg2911).

# Chapter 5
# Mandatory Copy Elision or Passing Unmaterialized Objects

The topic of this chapter can be seen from two points of view:
- Technically, C++17 introduces a new rule for *mandatory copy elision* under certain conditions: the former option to eliminate the copying of temporary objects when passing or returning them by value now becomes mandatory.
- The effect of this is that we pass around the values of *unmaterialized objects* for initialization.

I will introduce this feature technically, coming later to the effect and terminology of *materialization*.

## 5.1 Motivation for Mandatory Copy Elision for Temporaries

Since the first standard, C++ has permitted the omission (*elision*) of certain copy operations even if this might impact the behavior of a program (e.g., skipping a print statement in the copy constructor). One such case is when a temporary object is used to initialize a new object. This happens especially when a temporary is passed to or returned from a function by value. For example:

```
class MyClass
{
  ...
};

void foo(MyClass param) {   // param is initialized by passed argument
  ...
}

MyClass bar() {
  return MyClass{};         // returns temporary
}
```

```
int main()
{
  foo(MyClass{});       // pass temporary to initialize param
  MyClass x = bar();    // use returned temporary to initialize x
  foo(bar());           // use returned temporary to initialize param
}
```

However, because these optimizations were not mandatory, it had to be *possible* to copy the objects by implicitly or explicitly providing a copy or move constructor. That is, although the copy/move constructor was usually not called, it had to exist. Code like this did not compile when no copy/move constructor was defined.

Thus, with the following definition of the class `MyClass`, the code above did not compile:

```
class MyClass
{
 public:
   ...
   // no copy/move constructor defined:
   MyClass(const MyClass&) = delete;
   MyClass(MyClass&&) = delete;
   ...
};
```

It was enough not to have the copy constructor, because the move constructor is only implicitly available when no copy constructor (or assignment operator or destructor) is user-declared.

The copy elision to initialize objects from temporaries is mandatory since C++17. In fact, what we will see later is that we simply pass a value for initialization as an argument or return value that is then used to *materialize* a new object.

This means that even with a definition of class `MyClass` not enabling copying at all, the example above compiles.

However, note that all other optional copy elisions are still optional and require a callable copy or move constructor. For example:

```
MyClass foo()
{
  MyClass obj;
  ...
  return obj;   // still requires copy/move support
}
```

Here, `foo()` contains a variable `obj` that has a name (which is an *lvalue* (see Section 5.3.1 on page 42) when used). Therefore, the **named** *return value optimization* (NRVO) is used, which still requires copy/move support. This would be the case even if `obj` were a parameter:

```
MyClass bar(MyClass obj)   // copy elision for passed temporaries
{
  ...
  return obj;   // still requires copy/move support
}
```

While passing a temporary (which is a *prvalue* (see Section 5.3.1 on page 42) when used) to the function is no longer a copy/move, returning the parameter requires copy/move support because the returned object has a name.

As part of this change, a couple of modifications and clarifications were made in the terminology of value categories (see Section 5.3 on page 42).

## 5.2 Benefit of Mandatory Copy Elision for Temporaries

One benefit of this feature is, of course, that better performance is now *guaranteed* when returning a value that is expensive to copy (although all major compilers did the copy elision anyway). Although move semantics helps to reduce copying costs significantly, not performing copies can still be a significant improvement (e.g., if the objects have many fundamental data types as members). This might reduce the need to use out-parameters rather than simply returning a value (provided the return value is created with the return statement).

Another benefit is the ability to now define a factory function that *always* works because it can now also return an object even when neither copying nor moving is allowed. For example, consider the following generic factory function:

*lang/factory.hpp*

```
#include <utility>

template <typename T, typename... Args>
T create(Args&&... args)
{
  ...
  return T{std::forward<Args>(args)...};
}
```

This function can now even be used for a type such as `std::atomic<>`, where neither the copy nor the move constructor is defined:

*lang/factory.cpp*

```
#include "factory.hpp"
#include <memory>
#include <atomic>

int main()
{
  int i = create<int>(42);
  std::unique_ptr<int> up = create<std::unique_ptr<int>>(new int{42});
  std::atomic<int> ai = create<std::atomic<int>>(42);
}
```

As another effect, for classes with explicitly deleted move constructors, you can now return temporaries by value and initialize objects with them:

```
class CopyOnly {
 public:
    CopyOnly() {
    }
    CopyOnly(int) {
    }
    CopyOnly(const CopyOnly&) = default;
    CopyOnly(CopyOnly&&) = delete;    // explicitly deleted
};

CopyOnly ret() {
    return CopyOnly{};    // OK since C++17
}

CopyOnly x = 42;        // OK since C++17
```

The initialization of x was invalid before C++17 because the *copy initialization* (initialization using the =) needed the conversion of 42 to a temporary and that temporary in principle needed the move constructor, although it was never called. (The fact that the copy constructor serves as a fallback for a move constructor applies only if the move constructor is *not* user-declared.)

## 5.3 Clarified Value Categories

As a side effect of the proposed change to require copy elision for temporaries when initializing new objects, some adjustments were made to *value categories*.

### 5.3.1 Value Categories

Each expression in a C++ program has a value category. In particular, the category describes what can be done with an expression.

**History of Value Categories**

Historically (taken from C), we had only *lvalue* and *rvalue*, based on an assignment:

```
x = 42;
```

where x used as an expression was an *lvalue* because it could stand on the left side of an assignment, and 42 used as an expression was an *rvalue*, because it could only stand on the right side. However, things already became more complicated with ANSI-C because an x declared as `const int` could not stand on the left side of an assignment but was still a (non-modifyable) lvalue.

Then, C++11 introduced movable objects, which from a semantic perspective, were objects for the right side of an assignment only but could be modified because an assignment operator could steal their value. For this reason, the category *xvalue* was introduced and the former category *rvalue* was renamed to *prvalue*.

## 5.3 Clarified Value Categories

**Value Categories Since C++11**

Since C++11, the value categories are as described in Figure 5.1: We have the primary categories *lvalue*, *prvalue* ("pure rvalue"), and *xvalue* ("eXpiring value"). The composite categories are: *glvalue* ("generalized lvalue," which is the union of *lvalue* and *xvalue*) and *rvalue* (the union of *xvalue* and *prvalue*).

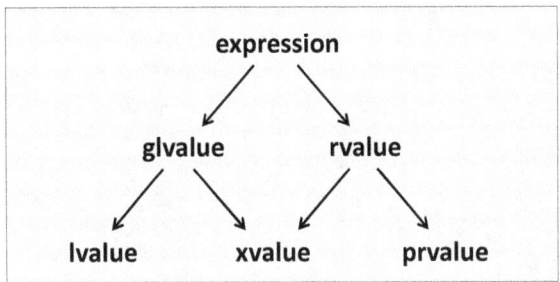

*Figure 5.1. Value categories since C++11*

Examples of **lvalues** are:
- An expression that is just the name of a variable, function, or data member (except a plain value member of an rvalue)
- An expression that is just a string literal (e.g., `"hello"`)
- The return value of a function if it is declared to return an lvalue reference (return type *Type&*)
- Any reference to a function, even when marked with `std::move()`
- The result of the built-in unary `*` operator (i.e., what dereferencing a raw pointer yields)

Examples of **prvalues** are:
- Expressions that consist of a built-in literal that is not a string literal (e.g., `42`, `true`, or `nullptr`)
- The return type of a function if it is declared to return by value (return type *Type*)
- The result of the built-in unary `&` operator (i.e., what taking the address of an expression yields)
- A lambda expression

Examples of **xvalues** are:
- The result of marking an object with `std::move()`
- A cast to an rvalue reference of an object type (not a function type)
- The returned value of a function if it is declared to return an rvalue reference (return type *Type&&*)
- A non-`static` value member of an rvalue

Roughly speaking:
- All names used as expressions are *lvalues*.
- All string literals used as expression are *lvalues*.
- All other literals (`4.2`, `true`, or `nullptr`) are *prvalues*.
- All temporaries without a name (especially objects returned by value) are *prvalues*.
- All objects marked with `std::move()` and their value members are *xvalues*.

For example:
```
class X {
};

X v;
const X c;

void f(const X&);    // accepts an expression of any value category
void f(X&&);         // accepts prvalues and xvalues only, but is a better match

f(v);                // passes a modifiable lvalue to the first f()
f(c);                // passes a non-modifiable lvalue to the first f()
f(X());              // passes a prvalue to the second f()
f(std::move(v));     // passes an xvalue to the second f()
```

It is worth emphasizing that strictly speaking, glvalues, prvalues, and xvalues are terms for expressions and *not* for values (which means that these terms are misnomers). For example, a variable itself is not an lvalue; only an expression denoting the variable is an lvalue:

```
int x = 3;    // here, x is a variable, not an lvalue
int y = x;    // here, x is an lvalue
```

In the first statement, 3 is a prvalue which initializes the variable (not the lvalue) x. In the second statement, x is an lvalue (its evaluation designates an object containing the value 3). The lvalue x is converted to a prvalue, which is what initializes the variable y.

### 5.3.2 Value Categories Since C++17

C++17 clarified the semantic meaning of value categories as described in Figure 5.2.

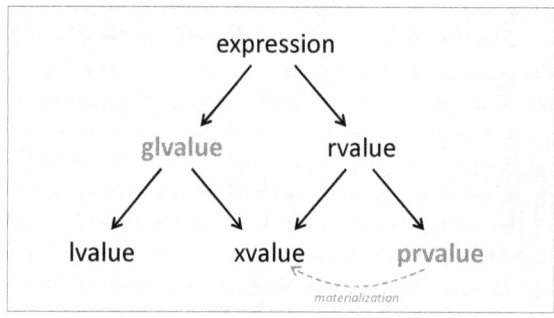

Figure 5.2. *Value categories since C++17*

The key approach for explaining value categories now is that in general, we have two kinds of expressions:
- **glvalues**: expressions for *locations* of objects or functions
- **prvalues:** expressions for *initializations*

An **xvalue** is then considered a special location, representing an object whose resources can be reused (usually because the object is near the end of its lifetime).

C++17 then introduces a new term, called *materialization* (of a temporary), for the moment a prvalue becomes a temporary object. Thus, a *temporary materialization conversion* is a prvalue-to-xvalue conversion.

Any time a prvalue validly appears where a glvalue (lvalue or xvalue) is expected, a temporary object is created and initialized with the prvalue (remember that prvalues are primarily "initializing values"), and the prvalue is replaced by an *xvalue* designating the temporary. So in the example above, strictly speaking, we have:

```
void f(const X& p);    // accepts an expression of any value category,
                       // but expects a glvalue

f(X());                // passes a prvalue materialized as xvalue
```

Because `f()` in this example has a reference parameter, it expects a glvalue argument. However, the expression `X()` is a prvalue. The "temporary materialization" rule therefore kicks in, and the expression `X()` is "converted" into an xvalue designating a temporary object initialized with the default constructor.

Note that materialization does not mean that we create a new/different object. The lvalue reference p still *binds* to both an xvalue and a prvalue, although the latter now always involves a conversion to an xvalue.

With this modification (that prvalues are no longer objects but are instead expressions that can be used to initialize objects), the required copy elision makes perfect sense because the prvalues no longer need to be movable in order to initialize a variable using assignment syntax. We simply pass an initial value around that, sooner or later, is *materialized* to initialize an object.[1]

## 5.4 Unmaterialized Return Value Passing

Unmaterialized return value passing applies to all forms of returning a temporary object (prvalue) by value:

- When we return a literal that is not a string literal:
  ```
  int f1() {     // return int by value
    return 42;
  }
  ```

- When we return a temporary object by its type or `auto`:
  ```
  auto f2() {  // return deduced type by value
    ...
    return MyType{...};
  }
  ```

- When we return a temporary object by `decltype(auto)`:
  ```
  decltype(auto) f3() {   // return temporary from return statement by value
    ...
    return MyType{...};
  }
  ```

---

[1] Thanks to Richard Smith and Graham Haynes for pointing that out.

Remember that a declaration with `decltype(auto)` operates *by value* if the expression used for initialization (here the return statement) is an expression that creates a temporary (a prvalue).

Because we return a prvalue in all these cases by value, we do not require any copy/move support at all.

## 5.5 Afternotes

The mandatory copy elision for initializations from temporaries was first proposed by Richard Smith in `https://wg21.link/p0135r0`. The finally accepted wording was also formulated by Richard Smith in `https://wg21.link/p0135r1`.

# Chapter 6
# Lambda Extensions

Lambdas, introduced with C++11, and generic lambdas, introduced with C++14, are a success story. They allow us to specify functionality as arguments, which makes it a lot easier to specify behavior right where it is needed.

C++17 allows the use of lambdas in even more places:
- In constant expressions (i.e., at compile time)
- In places where you need a copy of the current object (e.g., when calling lambdas in threads)

## 6.1 `constexpr` Lambdas

Since C++17, lambdas are implicitly `constexpr` if possible. That is, any lambda can be used in compile-time contexts provided the features it uses are valid for compile-time contexts (e.g., only literal types, no static variables, no `virtual`, no `try/catch`, no `new/delete`).

For example, you can use the result of calling a lambda that computes the square of a passed value as a compile-time argument for the declaration of the size of a `std::array<>`:

```cpp
auto squared = [](auto val) {        // implicitly constexpr since C++17
    return val*val;
};
std::array<int,squared(5)> a;        // OK since C++17 => std::array<int,25>
```

Using features that are not allowed in `constexpr` contexts disables this ability but you can still use the lambda in runtime contexts:

```cpp
auto squared2 = [](auto val) {       // implicitly constexpr since C++17
    static int calls = 0;            // OK, but disables lambda for constexpr contexts
    ...
    return val*val;
};
std::array<int,squared2(5)> a;       // ERROR: static variable in compile-time context
std::cout << squared2(5) << '\n';    // OK
```

To find out at compile time whether a lambda is valid for a compile-time context, you can declare it as `constexpr`:

```
auto squared3 = [] (auto val) constexpr {     // OK since C++17
  return val*val;
};
```

With specified return types, the syntax looks as follows:

```
auto squared3i = [] (int val) constexpr -> int {   // OK since C++17
  return val*val;
};
```

The usual rules regarding `constexpr` for functions apply: if the lambda is used in a runtime context, the corresponding functionality is performed at run time.

However, using features in a `constexpr` lambda that are not valid in a compile-time context results in a compile-time error:[1]

```
auto squared4 = [] (auto val) constexpr {
  static int calls=0;            // ERROR: static variable in compile-time context
  ...
  return val*val;
};
```

For an implicit or explicit `constexpr` lambda, the function call operator is `constexpr`. That is, the definition of

```
auto squared = [] (auto val) {      // implicitly constexpr since C++17
  return val*val;
};
```

converts into the *closure type*:

```
class CompilerSpecificName {
  public:
    ...
    template<typename T>
    constexpr auto operator() (T val) const {
      return val*val;
    }
};
```

Note that the function call operator of the generated closure type is automatically `constexpr` here. In general, since C++17, the generated function call operator is `constexpr` if either the lambda is explicitly defined to be `constexpr` or the lambda is implicitly `constexpr` (as is the case here).

Note that there is a difference between

```
auto squared1 = [] (auto val) constexpr {   // compile-time lambda calls
  return val*val;
};
```

---

[1] Features not allowed in compile-time context are, for example, `static` variables, `virtual` functions, `try` and `catch`, and `new` and `delete`.

## 6.1 constexpr Lambdas

and
```
constexpr auto squared2 = [](auto val) {   // compile-time initialization
  return val*val;
};
```
If (only) the lambda is `constexpr` it can be used at compile time, but `squared1` might be initialized at run time, which means that some problems might occur if the static initialization order matters (e.g., causing the *static initialization order fiasco*). If the (closure) object initialized by the lambda is `constexpr`, the object is initialized when the program starts but the lambda might still be a lambda that can only be used at run time (e.g., using `static` variables). Therefore, you might consider declaring:
```
constexpr auto squared = [](auto val) constexpr {
  return val*val;
};
```

### 6.1.1 Using `constexpr` Lambdas

Here is an example using `constexpr` lambdas. Assume we have a generic hash function for character sequences which is still parameterized according to the way a hash value is combined with the next character value:[2]
```
auto hashed = [](const char* str) {
  std::size_t hash = 5381;       // initial hash value
  while (*str != '\0') {
    hash = hash * 33 ^ *str++;   // combine hash value with next character
  }
  return hash;
};
```
With that lambda, we can initialize enumeration values for different strings at compile time:
```
enum Hashed { beer = hashed("beer"),
              wine = hashed("wine"),
              water = hashed("water"), ... };   // OK, compile-time hashing
```
We can also compute `case` labels at compile time:
```
switch (hashed(argv[1])) {        // runtime hashing
  case hashed("beer"):            // OK, compile-time hashing
    ...
    break;
  case hashed("wine"):
    ...
    break;
  ...
}
```

---

[2] See the djb2 algorithm at http://www.cse.yorku.ca/~oz/hash.html for the source of this algorithm.

Note that we use the lambda `hashed` in the `case` labels at compile time, but inside the `switch` expression we use it at run time.

If we initialize a container using a compile-time lambda, it becomes more likely that an optimizing compiler will compute the initial values at compile time (here, also using class template argument deduction for (see Section 9.2.6 on page 90) `std::array` (see Section 9.2.6 on page 90)):

```
std::array arr{hashed("beer"),
               hashed("wine"),
               hashed("water")};
```

You can even parameterize such a `constexpr` lambda with another `constexpr` lambda. Assume that we parameterized the lambda `hashed` according to the way a hash value is combined with the next character value:

```
auto hashed = [](const char* str, auto combine) {
  std::size_t hash = 5381;            // initial hash value
  while (*str != '\0') {
    hash = combine(hash, *str++);     // combine hash value with next character
  }
  return hash;
};
```

The lambda can then be used at compile time as follows:

```
constexpr std::size_t hv1{hashed("wine",
                          [](auto h, char c){return h*33 + c;})};
```

```
constexpr std::size_t hv2{hashed("wine",
                          [](auto h, char c){return h*33 ^ c;})};
```

Here, we initialize two different hash values for `"wine"` at compile time using different sub-algorithms for combining a hash value with the value of the next character. Both the lambda `hashed` and the passed lambdas are called at compile time.

## 6.2 Passing Copies of `this` to Lambdas

When using lambdas in non-static member functions, you have no implicit access to the object the member function is called for. That is, inside the lambda, you cannot use members of the object without capturing `this` in some form (whether you qualify the members with `this->` does not matter):

```
class C {
  private:
    std::string name;
  public:
    ...
    void foo() {
      auto l1 = [] { std::cout << name << '\n'; };         // ERROR
      auto l2 = [] { std::cout << this->name << '\n'; };   // ERROR
      ...
```

## 6.2 Passing Copies of this to Lambdas

```
    }
};
```

In C++11 and C++14, you have to pass this either by value or by reference:

```
class C {
  private:
    std::string name;
  public:
    ...
    void foo() {
      auto l1 = [this] { std::cout << name << '\n'; };   // OK
      auto l2 = [=]    { std::cout << name << '\n'; };   // OK
      auto l3 = [&]    { std::cout << name << '\n'; };   // OK
      ...
    }
};
```

However, the problem here is that even copying this captures the underlying object by reference (as only the *pointer* was copied). This can become a problem if the lifetime of the lambda exceeds the lifetime of the object upon which the member function is invoked. One critical example is when the lambda defines the task of a new thread which should use its own copy of the object to avoid any concurrency or lifetime issues. Another reason might simply be to pass a copy of the object with its current state.

A workaround has been possible since C++14 but it does not read and work well:

```
class C {
  private:
    std::string name;
  public:
    ...
    void foo() {
      auto l1 = [thisCopy=*this] { std::cout << thisCopy.name << '\n'; };
      ...
    }
};
```

For example, programmers could still accidentally use this when also using = or & to capture other objects:

```
auto l1 = [&, thisCopy=*this] {
            thisCopy.name = "new name";
            std::cout << name << '\n'; // OOPS: still the old name
          };
```

Since C++17, you can explicitly ask to capture a copy of the current object by capturing *this:

```
class C {
  private:
    std::string name;
  public:
    ...
```

```cpp
    void foo() {
      auto l1 = [*this] { std::cout << name << '\n'; };
      ...
    }
};
```

That is, the capture *this means that a *copy* of the current object is stored in the closure object defined by the lambda.

You can still combine capturing *this with other captures, as long as there is no contradiction for handling this:

```cpp
        auto l2 = [&, *this] { ... };      // OK
        auto l3 = [this, *this] { ... };   // ERROR
```

Here is a complete example:

*lang/lambdathis.cpp*

```cpp
#include <iostream>
#include <string>
#include <thread>

class Data {
  private:
    std::string name;
  public:
    Data(const std::string& s) : name(s) {
    }
    auto startThreadWithCopyOfThis() const {
        // start and return new thread using this after 3 seconds:
        using namespace std::literals;
        std::thread t([*this] {
                          std::this_thread::sleep_for(3s);
                          std::cout << name << '\n';
                      });
        return t;
    }
};

int main()
{
    std::thread t;
    {
      Data d{"c1"};
      t = d.startThreadWithCopyOfThis();
    } // d is no longer valid
    t.join();
}
```

The lambda takes a copy of *this, which means that a copy of d is passed. Therefore, it is no problem that the thread probably uses the passed object after the destructor of d was called.

If we have captured this with [this], [=], or [&], the thread would run into undefined behavior, because when printing the name in the lambda passed to the thread, the lambda would use a member of a destroyed object.

## 6.3 Capturing by `const` Reference

Using a new library utility, you can now also capture objects by const reference (see Section 25.2.1 on page 302).

## 6.4 Afternotes

`constexpr` lambdas were first proposed by Faisal Vali, Ville Voutilainen, and Gabriel Dos Reis in https://wg21.link/n4487. The finally accepted wording was formulated by Faisal Vali, Jens Maurer, and Richard Smith in https://wg21.link/p0170r1.

Capturing *this in lambdas was first proposed by H. Carter Edwards, Christian Trott, Hal Finkel Jim Reus, Robin Maffeo, and Ben Sander in https://wg21.link/p0018r0. The finally accepted wording was formulated by H. Carter Edwards, Daveed Vandevoorde, Christian Trott, Hal Finkel, Jim Reus, Robin Maffeo, and Ben Sander in https://wg21.link/p0180r3.

# Chapter 7
# New Attributes and Attribute Features

Since C++11, it has been possible to specify *attributes* (formal annotations that enable or disable warnings). With C++17, new attributes were introduced. In addition, attributes can now be used in a few more places and with some additional convenience.

## 7.1 Attribute [[nodiscard]]

The new attribute [[nodiscard]] can be used to encourage warnings by the compiler if a return value of a function is not used (however, the compiler is not required to issue a warning).

[[nodiscard]] should usually be used to signal misbehavior when return values are not used. The misbehavior might be:
- **Memory leaks**, such as not using returned allocated memory
- **Unexpected or non-intuitive behavior** such as getting different/unexpected behavior when not using the return value
- **Unnecessary overhead**, such as calling something that is a no-op if the return value is not used

Here are some examples of where using this attribute is useful:
- Functions that allocate resources that have to be released by another function call should be marked with [[nodiscard]]. A typical example would be a function to allocate memory, such as `malloc()` or the member function `allocate()` of allocators.
  
  However, note that some functions *might* return a value meaning that no compensating call is necessary. For example, programmers call the C function `realloc()` with a size of zero bytes to free memory so that the return values do not have to be saved to call `free()` later. For this reason, marking `realloc()` with [[nodiscard]] would be counterproductive.
- A good example of a function changing its behavior non-intuitively when not using the return value is `std::async()` (introduced with C++11). `std::async()` starts a functionality asynchronously in the background and returns a handle that can be used to wait for the end of the started functionality (and get access to any return value or exception). However, when the return value is not used the call becomes a synchronous call because the destructor of the unused return value is called immediately waiting for the end of the started functionality. Therefore, not using the return value silently contradicts the whole

purpose of calling `std::async()`. Compilers can warn about this when `std::async()` is marked with `[[nodiscard]]`.
- Another example is the member function `empty()`, which checks whether an object (container/string) has no elements. Programmers pretty often call this function to "empty" the container (remove all elements):

    ```
    cont.empty();
    ```

    This incorrect application of `empty()` can often be detected because it does not use the return value. Therefore, marking the member function accordingly:

    ```
    class MyContainer {
        ...
      public:
        [[nodiscard]] bool empty() const noexcept;
        ...
    };
    ```

    helps to detect such an logical error.

If for whatever reason you do not want to use a return value marked with `[[nodiscard]]` you can cast the return value to `void`:

```
(void)coll.empty();   // disable [[nodiscard]] warning
```

Note that attributes in function declarations are not inherited if the functions are overwritten:

```
struct B {
  [[nodiscard]] int* foo();
};

struct D : B {
  int* foo();
};

B b;
b.foo();              // warning
(void)b.foo();        // no warning

D d;
d.foo();              // no warning
```

Therefore, you have mark the derived member function with `[[nodiscard]]` again (unless there is a reason that not using the return value makes sense in the derived class).

As usual, you can place an attribute that applies to a function in front of all declaration specifiers or after the function name:

```
class C {
    ...
    [[nodiscard]] friend bool operator== (const C&, const C&);
    friend bool operator!= [[nodiscard]] (const C&, const C&);
```

};

Placing the attribute between `friend` and `bool` or between `bool` and `operator==` is not correct.

Although the language feature was introduced with C++17, it is not used in the standard library yet. The proposal to apply this feature there simply came too late for C++17. Therefore, one of the key motivations for this feature, adding it to the declaration of `std::async()`, has not been done yet. However, for all the examples discussed above, corresponding fixes will come with the next C++ standard (see https://wg21.link/p0600r1 proposal, accepted for C++20).

However, to make your code more portable, you should use [[nodiscard]] instead of non-portable means (such as [[gnu:warn_unused_result]] for gcc and clang or _Check_return_ for Visual C++) to mark functions accordingly.

When defining `operator new()` (see Section 30.2.2 on page 374), you should mark the functions with [[nodiscard]] as is done, for example, when defining a header file to track all calls of `new` (see Section 30.4 on page 380).

## 7.2 Attribute [[maybe_unused]]

The new attribute [[maybe_unused]] can be used to avoid warnings by the compiler for not using a name or entity.

The attribute may be applied to the declaration of a class, a type definition with `typedef` or `using`, a variable, a non-static data member, a function, an enumeration type, or an enumerator (enumeration value).

One application is to name a parameter without (necessarily) using it:

```
void foo(int val, [[maybe_unused]] std::string msg)
{
#ifdef DEBUG
  log(msg);
#endif
  ...
}
```

Another example would be to have a member without using it:

```
class MyStruct {
  char c;
  int i;
  [[maybe_unused]] char makeLargerSize[100];
  ...
};
```

Note that you cannot apply [[maybe_unused]] to a statement. Therefore, you cannot counter [[nodiscard]] with [[maybe_unused]] directly:[1]

```
[[nodiscard]] void* foo();
```

---

[1] Thanks to Roland Bock for pointing that out.

```cpp
int main()
{
  foo();                              // WARNING: return value not used
  [[maybe_unused]] foo();             // ERROR: attribute not allowed here
  [[maybe_unused]] auto x = foo();    // OK
}
```

## 7.3 Attribute [[fallthrough]]

The new attribute `[[fallthrough]]` can be used to avoid warnings by the compiler for not having a `break` statement after a sequence of one or more `case` labels inside a `switch` statement.

For example:

```cpp
void commentPlace(int place)
{
  switch (place) {
    case 1:
      std::cout << "very ";
      [[fallthrough]];
    case 2:
      std::cout << "well\n";
      break;
    default:
      std::cout << "OK\n";
      break;
  }
}
```

Here, passing the place 1 will print:

```
very well
```

using a statement of `case 1` and `case 2`.

Note that the attribute has to be used in an empty statement. It must therefore end with a semicolon.

Using the attribute as the last statement in a `switch` statement is not allowed.

## 7.4 General Attribute Extensions

The following features were enabled for attributes in general with C++17:

1. Attributes can now be used to mark namespaces. For example, you can now deprecate a namespace as follows:

```cpp
namespace [[deprecated]] DraftAPI {
  ...
```

```
    }
```
This is also possible for inline and unnamed namespaces.

2. Attributes can now be used to mark enumerators (values of enumeration types).

    For example, you can introduce a new enumeration value as a replacement of an existing (now deprecated) enumeration value as follows:
    ```
    enum class City { Berlin = 0,
                      NewYork = 1,
                      Mumbai = 2, Bombay [[deprecated]] = Mumbai,
                      ... };
    ```
    Here, both `Mumbai` and `Bombay` represent the same numeric code for a city but using `Bombay` is marked as deprecated. Note that for enumeration values, the attribute is placed *behind* the identifier.

3. For user-defined attributes, which should usually be defined in their own namespace, you can now use a `using` prefix to avoid the repetition of the attribute namespace for each attribute. That is, instead of:
    ```
    [[MyLib::WebService, MyLib::RestService, MyLib::doc("html")]] void foo();
    ```
    you can just write
    ```
    [[using MyLib: WebService, RestService, doc("html")]] void foo();
    ```
    Note that with a `using` prefix, using the namespace again is an error:
    ```
    [[using MyLib: MyLib::doc("html")]] void foo();   // ERROR
    ```

## 7.5 Afternotes

The three new attributes were first proposed by Andrew Tomazos in `https://wg21.link/p0068r0`. The finally accepted wording for the `[[nodiscard]]` attribute was formulated by Andrew Tomazos in `https://wg21.link/p0189r1`. The finally accepted wording for the `[[maybe_unused]]` attribute was formulated by Andrew Tomazos in `https://wg21.link/p0212r1`. The finally accepted wording for the `[[fallthrough]]` attribute was formulated by Andrew Tomazos in `https://wg21.link/p0188r1`.

Allowing attributes for namespaces and enumerators was first proposed by Richard Smith in `https://wg21.link/n4196`. The finally accepted wording was formulated by Richard Smith in `https://wg21.link/n4266`.

The `using` prefix for attributes was first proposed by J. Daniel Garcia, Luis M. Sanchez, Massimo Torquati, Marco Danelutto, and Peter Sommerlad in `https://wg21.link/p0028r0`. The finally accepted wording was formulated by J. Daniel Garcia and Daveed Vandevoorde in `https://wg21.link/P0028R4`.

# Chapter 8
# Other Language Features

In C++17, there are a couple of minor or small changes to the C++ core language, which are described in this chapter.

## 8.1 Nested Namespaces

Proposed in 2003 for the first time, the C++ standards committee has finally enabled to specify nested namespaces as follows:

```
namespace A::B::C {
    ...
}
```

which is equivalent to:

```
namespace A {
  namespace B {
    namespace C {
        ...
    }
  }
}
```

Note that there is no support for nesting `inline` namespaces (yet). This is simply because it is not obvious whether the `inline` applies to the last or to all namespaces (both could equally be useful).

## 8.2 Defined Expression Evaluation Order

Many code bases and C++ books contain code that looks valid according to intuitive assumptions but strictly speaking has undefined behavior. One example is finding and replacing multiple substrings in a string:[1]

```
std::string s = "I heard it even works if you don't believe";

s.replace(0,8,"").replace(s.find("even"),4,"sometimes")
                .replace(s.find("you don't"),9,"I");
```

The usual assumption is that this code is valid replacing the first 8 characters with nothing, `"even"` with `"sometimes"`, and `"you don't"` with `"I"` so that we get:

```
it sometimes works if I believe
```

However, before C++17, this outcome was not guaranteed because the `find()` calls, which return where to start with a replacement, might be performed at any time while the whole statement is being processed and before the result of this call is needed. In fact, all `find()` calls, which compute the starting indexes of the replacements, might be processed *before* any of the replacements happen, meaning that the resulting string *might* become:

```
it sometimes works if I believe
```

or might also become:

```
it sometimes workIdon't believe
it even worsometiIdon't believe
it even worsometimesf youIlieve
```

As another example, consider using the output operator to print values computed by expressions that depend on each other:

```
std::cout << f() << g() << h();
```

The usual assumption is that `f()` is called before `g()` and both are called before `h()`. However, this assumption is wrong. `f()`, `g()`, and `h()` might be called in any order, which might have surprising or even nasty effects when these calls depend on each other.

As a concrete example, up to C++17, the following code had undefined behavior:

```
i = 0;
std::cout << ++i << ' ' << --i << '\n';
```

Before C++17, it *might* have printed 1 0; but it might also have printed 0 -1 or even 0 0. Whether `i` is `int` or a user-defined type was irrelevant (for fundamental types, some compilers at least warn about this problem).

To fix all this unexpected behavior, the evaluation guarantees were refined for *some* operators so that they now specify a guaranteed evaluation order:

---

[1] A similar example is part of the motivation in the paper proposing the new feature with the comment *This code has been reviewed by C++ experts world-wide, and published (The C++ Programming Language, 4th edition.)*

## 8.2 Defined Expression Evaluation Order

- For

    *e1* [ *e2* ]
    *e1* . *e2*
    *e1* .* *e2*
    *e1* ->* *e2*
    *e1* << *e2*
    *e1* >> *e2*

    *e1* is guaranteed to be evaluated before *e2* now, so that the evaluation order is left to right.
    However, note that the evaluation order of different arguments of the same function call is still undefined. That is, in

    ```
    e1.f(a1,a2,a3)
    ```

    e1.f is guaranteed to be evaluated before a1, a2, and a3 now. However, the evaluation order of a1, a2, and a3 is still undefined.

- In all assignment operators

    *e2* = *e1*
    *e2* += *e1*
    *e2* *= *e1*
    ...

    the right-hand side *e1* is guaranteed to be evaluated before the left-hand side *e2* now.

- Finally, in new expressions like

    **new** *Type* (*e*)

    the allocation is now guaranteed to be performed before the evaluation *e*, and the initialization of the new value is guaranteed to happen before any usage of the allocated and initialized value.

All these guarantees apply to both fundamental types and user-defined types.

As a consequence, since C++17

```
std::string s = "I heard it even works if you don't believe";
s.replace(0,8,"").replace(s.find("even"),4,"always")
                .replace(s.find("don't believe"),13,"use C++17");
```

is guaranteed to change the value of s to:

```
it always works if you use C++17
```

Thus, each replacement in front of a find() expression is done before the find() expression is evaluated.

As another consequence, for the statements

```
i = 0;
std::cout << ++i << ' ' << --i << '\n';
```

the output is now guaranteed to be 1 0 for any type of i that supports these operands.

However, the undefined order for most of the other operators still exists. For example:

```
i = i++ + i;    // still undefined behavior
```

Here, the i on the right might be the value of i before or after it was incremented.

Another application of the new expression evaluation order is the function that inserts a space (see Section 11.2.1 on page 110) before passed arguments.

## Backward Incompatibilities

The new guaranteed evaluation order might impact the output of existing programs. This is not just theory. Consider, for example, the following program:

*lang/evalexcept.cpp*

```cpp
#include <iostream>
#include <vector>

void print10elems(const std::vector<int>& v) {
  for (int i=0; i<10; ++i) {
    std::cout << "value: " << v.at(i) << '\n';
  }
}

int main()
{
  try {
    std::vector<int> vec{7, 14, 21, 28};
    print10elems(vec);
  }
  catch (const std::exception& e) {     // handle standard exception
    std::cerr << "EXCEPTION: " << e.what() << '\n';
  }
  catch (...) {                          // handle any other exception
    std::cerr << "EXCEPTION of unknown type\n";
  }
}
```

Because the `vector<>` in this program has only four elements, the program throws an exception in the loop in `print10elems()` when calling `at()` as part of an output statement for an invalid index:

```cpp
std::cout << "value: " << v.at(i) << "\n";
```

Before C++17, the output could be:

```
value: 7
value: 14
value: 21
value: 28
EXCEPTION: ...
```

because `at()` was allowed to be evaluated before `"value: "` was written, so that for the wrong index, the output was skipped completely.[2]

Since C++17, the output is guaranteed to be:

```
value: 7
value: 14
value: 21
value: 28
value: EXCEPTION: ...
```

because the output of `"value: "` has to be performed before `at()` is evaluated.

## 8.3 Relaxed Enum Initialization from Integral Values

For enumerations with a fixed underlying type, since C++17, you can use an integral value of that type for direct list initialization. This applies to unscoped enumerations with a specified type and all scoped enumerations because they always have an underlying default type:

```
// unscoped enum with underlying type:
enum MyInt : char { };
MyInt i1{42};           // OK since C++17 (ERROR before C++17)
MyInt i2 = 42;          // still ERROR
MyInt i3(42);           // still ERROR
MyInt i4 = {42};        // still ERROR

// scoped enum with default underlying type:
enum class Weekday { mon, tue, wed, thu, fri, sat, sun };
Weekday s1{0};          // OK since C++17 (ERROR before C++17)
Weekday s2 = 0;         // still ERROR
Weekday s3(0);          // still ERROR
Weekday s4 = {0};       // still ERROR
```

The same applies if `Weekday` has a specified underlying type:

```
// scoped enum with specified underlying type:
enum class Weekday : char { mon, tue, wed, thu, fri, sat, sun };
Weekday s1{0};          // OK since C++17 (ERROR before C++17)
Weekday s2 = 0;         // still ERROR
Weekday s3(0);          // still ERROR
Weekday s4 = {0};       // still ERROR
```

For unscoped enumerations (`enum` without `class`) with *no* specified underlying type, you still cannot use list initialization for numeric values:

```
enum Flag { bit1=1, bit2=2, bit3=4 };
Flag f1{0};             // still ERROR
```

---

[2] This was, for example, the behavior of older GCC or Visual C++ versions.

Note also that list initialization still does not allow narrowing, which means that you cannot pass a floating-point value:

```
enum MyInt : char { };
MyInt i5{42.2};        // still ERROR
```

This feature was motivated to support the trick of defining new integral types just by defining an enumeration type that maps to an existing integral type as done here with `MyInt`. Without the feature, there is no way to initialize a new object without a cast.

In fact, since C++17, the C++ standard library also provides `std::byte` (see Chapter 18 on page 179), which uses this feature directly.

## 8.4 Fixed Direct List Initialization with `auto`

After the introduction of *uniform initialization* with braces in C++11, it turned out that there were some unfortunate and non-intuitive inconsistencies when using `auto` instead of a specific type:

```
int x{42};         // initializes an int
int y{1,2,3};      // ERROR
auto a{42};        // initializes a std::initializer_list<int>
auto b{1,2,3};     // OK: initializes a std::initializer_list<int>
```

These inconsistencies were fixed for *direct list initialization* (brace initialization without =) so that we now have the following behavior:

```
int x{42};         // initializes an int
int y{1,2,3};      // ERROR
auto a{42};        // initializes an int now
auto b{1,2,3};     // ERROR now
```

Note that this is a **breaking change** that might even silently result in a different program behavior (e.g., when printing a). Therefore, compilers that adopt this change usually also adopt it even in C++11 mode. For the major compilers, the fix was adopted for all modes with Visual Studio 2015, g++ 5, and clang 3.8.

Note also that *copy list initialization* (brace initialization with =) still has the behavior to initialize a `std::initializer_list<>` when auto is used:

```
auto c = {42};       // still initializes a std::initializer_list<int>
auto d = {1,2,3};    // still OK: initializes a std::initializer_list<int>
```

Thus, we now have another significant difference between direct initialization (without =) and copy initialization (with =):

```
auto a{42};          // initializes an int now
auto c = {42};       // still initializes a std::initializer_list<int>
```

This is one additional reason by default to prefer direct list initialization (brace initialization without =). when initializing variables and objects.

## 8.5 Hexadecimal Floating-Point Literals

C++17 standardizes the ability to specify hexadecimal floating-point literals (which some compilers supported even before C++17). This notation is especially useful when an exact floating-point representation is desired (for decimal floating-point values there is no general guarantee that the exact value exists).

For example:

*lang/hexfloat.cpp*

```
#include <iostream>
#include <iomanip>

int main()
{
  // init list of floating-point values:
  std::initializer_list<double> values {
                0x1p4,         // 16
                0xA,           // 10
                0xAp2,         // 40
                5e0,           // 5
                0x1.4p+2,      // 5
                1e5,           // 100000
                0x1.86Ap+16,   // 100000
                0xC.68p+2,     // 49.625
  };

  // print all values both as decimal and hexadecimal value:
  for (double d : values) {
    std::cout << "dec: " << std::setw(6) << std::defaultfloat << d
              << "  hex: " << std::hexfloat << d << '\n';
  }
}
```

The program defines different floating-point values by using different existing notations and the new hexadecimal floating-point notation. The new notation is a base-2 scientific notation:

- The significand/mantissa is written in hexadecimal format.
- The exponent is written in decimal format and interpreted with respect to base 2.

For example, `0xAp2` is a way to specify the decimal value 40 (10 multiplied by "2 to the power of 2"). The value could also be expressed as `0x1.4p+5`, which is 1.25 multiplied by 32 (0.4 is a hexadecimal quarter and 2 to the power of 5 is 32).

The program has the following output:

```
dec:      16  hex: 0x1p+4
dec:      10  hex: 0x1.4p+3
dec:      40  hex: 0x1.4p+5
dec:       5  hex: 0x1.4p+2
```

```
dec:         5  hex: 0x1.4p+2
dec:    100000  hex: 0x1.86ap+16
dec:    100000  hex: 0x1.86ap+16
dec:    49.625  hex: 0x1.8dp+5
```

As you can see in the example program, support for hexadecimal floating-point notation already existed for output streams using the `std::hexfloat` manipulator (available since C++11).

## 8.6 UTF-8 Character Literals

Since C++11, C++ supports the prefix u8 for UTF-8 string literals. However, the prefix was not enabled for character literals. C++17 fixes this gap, so that you can write:

```
auto c = u8'6';   // character 6 with UTF-8 encoding value
```

In C++17, the type of u8'6' is char, which might change in C++20 to char8_t, so that using auto here might be appropriate.

This way you guarantee that your character value is the value of the character '6' in UTF-8. You can use all 7-bit US-ASCII characters for which the UTF-8 code has the same value. That is, u8'6' specifies to have the correct character value for the character '6' according to 7-bit US-ASCII (and therefore also according to ISO Latin-1, ISO-8859-15, and the basic Windows character set.[3] Usually, your source code interprets characters in US-ASCII/UTF-8 anyway meaning that the prefix is not necessary. The value of c will almost always be 54 (hexadecimal 36).

To give you some background regarding where the prefix might be necessary: for character and string literals in source code, C++ standardizes the characters you can use but not their values. The values depend on the *source character set*. And when the compiler generates the code for the executable program, it uses the *execution character set*. The source character set is almost always 7-bit US-ASCII and the execution character set is usually the same; this means that in any C++ program, all character and string literals (with and without the u8 prefix) have the same value.

However, in very rare scenarios, this might not be the case. For example, on old IBM hosts, which (still) use the EBCDIC character set, the character '6' would have the value 246 (hexadecimal F6) instead. In a program using an EBCDIC character set, the value of the character c above would therefore be 246 instead of 54, and running the program on a UTF-8 encoding platform might therefore print the character ö, which is the character with the value of 246 in ISO/IEC 8859-x encodings (if available). In situations like this, the prefix might be necessary.

Note that u8 can be used only for single characters and characters that have a single byte (code unit) in UTF-8. An initialization such as:

```
char c = u8'ö';
```

is not allowed because the value of the German umlaut ö in UTF-8 is a sequence of two bytes, 195 and 182 (hexadecimal C3 B6).

As a result, both character and string literals now accept the following prefixes:

---

[3] ISO Latin-1 is formally named ISO-8859-1, while the ISO character set that was introduced to include the European Euro symbol €, ISO-8859-15, is also named ISO Latin-9 (yes, this is not a spelling error).

## 8.7 Exception Specifications as Part of the Type

- u8 for single-byte US-ASCII and UTF-8 encoding
- u for two-byte UTF-16 encoding
- U for four-byte UTF-32 encoding
- L for wide characters without specific encoding, which might have two or four bytes

## 8.7 Exception Specifications as Part of the Type

Since C++17, exception handling specifications have become part of the type of a function. That is, the following two functions now have two different types:

```
void fMightThrow();
void fNoexcept() noexcept;      // different type
```

Before C++17, both functions had the same type. One consequence is that passing a function that might throw to a function pointer guaranteeing not to throw it is now an error:[4]

```
void (*fp)() noexcept;   // pointer to function that doesn't throw
fp = fNoexcept;          // OK
fp = fMightThrow;        // ERROR since C++17
```

Passing a function that does not throw to a function pointer that does not guarantee not to throw is still valid, of course:

```
void (*fp2)();           // pointer to function that might throw
fp2 = fNoexcept;         // OK
fp2 = fMightThrow;       // OK
```

Thus, the new feature does not break programs that have not used `noexcept` for function pointers yet, but ensures that you can now no longer violate `noexcept` requirements in function pointers (which might break existing programs for a good reason).

Overloading a function name for the same signature with a different exception specification is not allowed (as it is not allowed to overload functions that differ only in their return types):

```
void f3();
void f3() noexcept;      // ERROR
```

Note that all other rules are not affected. For example, you are still not allowed to ignore a `noexcept` specification of a base class:

```
class Base {
 public:
   virtual void foo() noexcept;
   ...
};

class Derived : public Base {
 public:
```

---

[4] It seem this was an error before, but at least g++ did allow it even in pedantic mode.

```
    void foo() override;    // ERROR: does not override
    ...
};
```

Here, the member function `foo()` in the derived class has a different type so that it does not override the `foo()` of the base class. This code still does not compile. Even without the `override` specifier this code would not compile because we still cannot overload with a looser throw specification.

**Using Conditional Exception Specifications**

When using conditional noexcept specifications, the type of the functions depends on whether the condition is true or false:

```
void f1();
void f2() noexcept;
void f3() noexcept(sizeof(int)<4);    // same type as either f1() or f2()
void f4() noexcept(sizeof(int)>=4);   // different type to f3()
```

Here, the type of `f3()` depends on the type of the condition when the code is compiled:

- If `sizeof(int)` yields 4 (or more), the resulting signature is

    ```
    void f3() noexcept(false);    // same type as f1()
    ```

- If `sizeof(int)` yields a value less than 4, the resulting signature is

    ```
    void f3() noexcept(true);    // same type as f2()
    ```

Because the exception condition of `f4()` uses the negated exception condition of `f3()`, the types or `f3()` and `f4()` always differ (i.e., one of them specifies that it might throw, while the other specifies not to throw).

The "old-fashioned" empty throw specification can still be used but is deprecated since C++11:

```
    void f5() throw();    // same as void f5() noexcept but deprecated
```

Dynamic exception specifications with arguments are no longer supported (they also have been deprecated since C++11):

```
    void f6() throw(std::bad_alloc);    // ERROR: invalid since C++17
```

**Consequences for Generic Libraries**

Making `noexcept` declarations part of the type might have some consequences for generic libraries. For example, the following program was valid up to C++14 but no longer compiles with C++17:

*lang/noexceptcalls.cpp*

```
#include <iostream>

template<typename T>
void call(T op1, T op2)
{
  op1();
  op2();
```

## 8.7 Exception Specifications as Part of the Type

```
}
void f1() {
  std::cout << "f1()\n";
}
void f2() noexcept {
  std::cout << "f2()\n";
}

int main()
{
  call(f1, f2);    // ERROR since C++17
}
```

The problem is that since C++17, f1() and f2() have different types so that the compiler no longer finds a common type T for both types when instantiating the function template call().

Since C++17, you have to use two different template parameter types to ensure that this still compiles:

```
template<typename T1, typename T2>
void call(T1 op1, T2 op2)
{
  op1();
  op2();
}
```

If you want or have to overload on all possible function types, you also have to double the overloads now. This applies, for example, to the definition of the standard type trait std::is_function<>. The primary template is defined so that in general a type T is not a function:

```
// primary template (in general type T is no function):
template<typename T> struct is_function : std::false_type { };
```

The template derives from std::false_type (see Section 33.2 on page 401) so that is_function<T>::value in general yields false for any type T.

For all types that *are* functions, partial specializations exist which derive from std::true_type (see Section 33.2 on page 401) so that the member value yields true for them:

```
// partial specializations for all function types:
template<typename Ret, typename... Params>
struct is_function<Ret (Params...)> : std::true_type { };

template<typename Ret, typename... Params>
struct is_function<Ret (Params...) const> : std::true_type { };

template<typename Ret, typename... Params>
struct is_function<Ret (Params...) &> : std::true_type { };

template<typename Ret, typename... Params>
```

```
struct is_function<Ret (Params...) const &> : std::true_type { };
...
```

Before C++17, there were already 24 partial specializations because function types can have `const` and `volatile` qualifiers as well as lvalue (`&`) and rvalue (`&&`) reference qualifiers, and you need overloads for functions with a variadic list of arguments.

Now, with C++17, the number of partial specializations is doubled by adding a `noexcept` qualifier to all these partial specializations so that we have 48 partial specializations now:

```
...
// partial specializations for all function types with noexcept:
template<typename Ret, typename... Params>
struct is_function<Ret (Params...) noexcept> : std::true_type { };

template<typename Ret, typename... Params>
struct is_function<Ret (Params...) const noexcept> : std::true_type { };

template<typename Ret, typename... Params>
struct is_function<Ret (Params...) & noexcept> : std::true_type { };

template<typename Ret, typename... Params>
struct is_function<Ret (Params...) const& noexcept> : std::true_type { };
...
```

Libraries that do not implement the `noexcept` overloads might no longer compile code that uses them to pass functions or function pointers to places where `noexcept` is required.

## 8.8 Single-Argument `static_assert`

Since C++17, the previously required message argument for `static_assert()` is now optional. This means that the resulting diagnostic message is completely platform-specific. For example:

```
#include <type_traits>

template<typename T>
class C {
  // OK since C++11:
  static_assert(std::is_default_constructible<T>::value,
                "class C: elements must be default-constructible");

  // OK since C++17:
  static_assert(std::is_default_constructible_v<T>);
  ...
};
```

The new assertion without the message also uses the new type traits suffix `_v` (see Section 21.1 on page 251).

## 8.9 Preprocessor Condition `__has_include`

C++17 extends the preprocessor to allow you to check whether a specific header file could be included. For example:

```
#if __has_include(<filesystem>)
#  include <filesystem>
#  define HAS_FILESYSTEM 1
#elif __has_include(<experimental/filesystem>)
#  include <experimental/filesystem>
#  define HAS_FILESYSTEM 1
#  define FILESYSTEM_IS_EXPERIMENTAL 1
#elif __has_include("filesystem.hpp")
#  include "filesystem.hpp"
#  define HAS_FILESYSTEM 1
#  define FILESYSTEM_IS_EXPERIMENTAL 1
#else
#  define HAS_FILESYSTEM 0
#endif
```

The conditions inside `__has_include(...)` evaluate to 1 (true) if a corresponding `#include` command would be valid. Nothing else matters (e.g., the answer does not depend on whether the file was already included).

Furthermore, the fact that the file exists does not prove that it has the expected contents. It might be empty or invalid.

`__has_include` is a pure preprocessor feature. Using `__has_include` as condition in source code is not possible:

```
if (__has_include(<filesystem>) {    // ERROR
}
```

## 8.10 Afternotes

Nested namespace definitions (see Section 8.1 on page 61) were first proposed in 2003 by Jon Jagger in `https://wg21.link/n1524`. Robert Kawulak introduced a new proposal in 2014 in `https://wg21.link/n4026`. The finally accepted wording was formulated by Robert Kawulak and Andrew Tomazos in `https://wg21.link/n4230`.

The refined expression evaluation order (see Section 8.2 on page 62) was first proposed by Gabriel Dos Reis, Herb Sutter, and Jonathan Caves in `https://wg21.link/n4228`. The finally accepted wording was formulated by Gabriel Dos Reis, Herb Sutter, and Jonathan Caves in `https://wg21.link/p0145r3`.

Relaxed enum initialization (see Section 8.3 on page 65) was first proposed by Gabriel Dos Reis in `https://wg21.link/p0138r0`. The finally accepted wording was formulated by Gabriel Dos Reis in `https://wg21.link/p0138r2`.

Fixing list initialization with `auto` (see Section 8.4 on page 66) was first proposed by Ville Voutilainen in https://wg21.link/n3681 and https://wg21.link/3912. The final fix for list initialization with `auto` was proposed by James Dennett in https://wg21.link/n3681.

Hexadecimal floating-point literals (see Section 8.5 on page 67) were first proposed by Thomas Köppe in https://wg21.link/p0245r0. The finally accepted wording was formulated by Thomas Köppe in https://wg21.link/p0245r1.

The prefix for UTF-8 character literals (see Section 8.6 on page 68) was first proposed by Richard Smith in https://wg21.link/n4197. The finally accepted wording was formulated by Richard Smith in https://wg21.link/n4267.

Making exception specifications part of the function type (see Section 8.7 on page 69) was first proposed by Jens Maurer in https://wg21.link/n4320. The finally accepted wording was formulated by Jens Maurer in https://wg21.link/p0012r1.

Single-argument `static_assert` (see Section 8.8 on page 72) was accepted as proposed by Walter E. Brown in https://wg21.link/n3928.

The preprocessor clause `__has_include()` (see Section 8.9 on page 73) was first proposed by Clark Nelson and Richard Smith as part of https://wg21.link/p0061r0. The finally accepted wording was formulated by Clark Nelson and Richard Smith in https://wg21.link/p0061r1.

# Part II

# Template Features

This part of the book introduces the new language features that C++17 provides for generic programming (i.e., templates).

We start with class template argument deduction, which also impacts just the use of templates, and the later chapters provide features for programmers of generic code (function templates, class templates, and generic libraries).

# Chapter 9
# Class Template Argument Deduction

Before C++17, you always had to explicitly specify all template arguments for class templates. For example, you cannot omit the `double` here:

```
std::complex<double> c{5.1,3.3};
```

or omit the need to specify `std::mutex` here a second time:

```
std::mutex mx;
std::lock_guard<std::mutex> lg(mx);
```

Since C++17, the constraint of always having to specify the template arguments explicitly has been relaxed. By using *class template argument deduction* (CTAD), you can omit explicit definition of the template arguments if the constructor is able to *deduce* all template parameters.

For example:

- You can now declare:

    ```
    std::complex c{5.1,3.3};    // OK: std::complex<double> deduced
    ```

- You can now implement:

    ```
    std::mutex mx;
    std::lock_guard lg{mx};     // OK: std::lock_guard<std_mutex> deduced
    ```

- You can even let containers deduce element types:

    ```
    std::vector v1 {1, 2, 3}              // OK: std::vector<int> deduced
    std::vector v2 {"hello", "world"};    // OK: std::vector<const char*> deduced
    ```

## 9.1 Use of Class Template Argument Deduction

Class template argument deduction can be used whenever the arguments passed to a constructor can be used to deduce the class template parameters. The deduction supports all methods of initialization (provided the initialization itself is valid):

```
std::complex c1{1.1, 2.2};    // deduces std::complex<double>
std::complex c2(2.2, 3.3);    // deduces std::complex<double>
```

```
std::complex c3 = 3.3;      // deduces std::complex<double>
std::complex c4 = {4.4};    // deduces std::complex<double>
```

c3 and c4 can be initialized because you can initialize a `std::complex<>` by passing only one argument, which is enough to deduce the template parameter T, which is then used for both the real and the imaginary part:

```
namespace std {
  template<typename T>
  class complex {
    constexpr complex(const T& re = T(), const T& im = T());
    ...
  }
};
```

With a declaration such as

```
std::complex c1{1.1, 2.2};
```

the compiler finds the constructor

```
constexpr complex(const T& re = T(), const T& im = T());
```

as a possible function to call. For both arguments, T is double, Therefore, the compiler deduces T to be double and compiles the corresponding code for:

```
complex<double>::complex(const double& re = double(),
                         const double& im = double());
```

Note that the template parameter has to be unambiguously deducible. Thus, the following initialization does not work:

```
std::complex c5{5,3.3};    // ERROR: attempts to int and double as T
```

As usual for templates, there are no type conversions used to deduce template parameters.

Class template argument deduction for variadic templates is also supported. For example, for a `std::tuple<>` defined as:

```
namespace std {
  template<typename... Types>
  class tuple {
    public:
      constexpr tuple(const Types&...);
      ...
  };
};
```

the declaration:

```
std::tuple t{42, 'x', nullptr};
```

deduces the type of t as `std::tuple<int, char, std::nullptr_t>`.

You can also deduce non-type template parameters. For example, we can deduce template parameters for both the element type and the size from a passed initial array as follows:

# 9.1 Use of Class Template Argument Deduction

```cpp
template<typename T, int SZ>
class MyClass {
  public:
    MyClass (T(&)[SZ]) {
        ...
    }
};

MyClass mc("hello");    // deduces T as const char and SZ as six
```

Here we deduce 6 as `SZ` because the template parameter passed is a string literal with 6 characters.[1]

You can even deduce the type of lambdas used as base classes (see Section 14.1 on page 129) for overloading or deduce the type of `auto` template parameters (see Section 13.1 on page 121).

## 9.1.1 Copying by Default

If class template argument deduction could be interpreted as initializing a copy, this interpretation is preferred. For example, after initializing a `std::vector` with one element:

```cpp
std::vector v1{42};      // vector<int> with one element
```

using that vector as an initializer for another vector is interpreted as creating a copy:

```cpp
std::vector v2{v1};      // v2 also is a vector<int>
```

instead of assuming that a vector gets initialized having elements being vectors (`vector<vector<int>>`).

Again, this applies to all valid forms of initialization:

```cpp
std::vector v2{v1};              // v3 also is a vector<int>
std::vector v3(v1);              // v3 also is a vector<int>
std::vector v4 = {v1};           // v4 also is a vector<int>
auto v5 = std::vector{v1};       // v5 also is a vector<int>
```

Note that this means that there is an exception to the rule that initializations with curly braces always use the passed arguments as elements. If you pass an initializer list with a single vector argument, you create a copy of the vector. However, passing an initializer list with more than one element always deduces the type of the elements as template parameter (because this cannot be interpreted as creating a copy):

```cpp
std::vector vv{v1, v2};          // vv is vector<vector<int>>
```

This raises the question of what happens with class template argument deduction when passing variadic templates:

```cpp
template<typename... Args>
auto make_vector(const Args&... elems) {
    return std::vector{elems...};
}

std::vector<int> v{1, 2, 3};
```

---

[1] Note that passing the initial argument by reference is important here, because otherwise, according to language rules, the array passed by value decays to a pointer meaning that `SZ` cannot be deduced.

```
auto x1 = make_vector(v, v);    // vector<vector<int>>
auto x2 = make_vector(v);       // vector<int> or vector<vector<int>> ?
```

Currently, different compilers handle this differently and the issue is under discussion.

### 9.1.2 Deducing the Type of Lambdas

With class template argument deduction, we can instantiate class templates with the type of a lambda (to be precise: the *closure type* of a lambda). For example, we could provide a generic class that wraps and counts calls of an arbitrary callback:

*tmpl/classarglambda.hpp*

```cpp
#include <utility>       // for std::forward()

template<typename CB>
class CountCalls
{
  private:
    CB callback;          // callback to call
    long calls = 0;       // counter for calls
  public:
    CountCalls(CB cb) : callback(cb) {
    }
    template<typename... Args>
    decltype(auto) operator() (Args&&... args) {
      ++calls;
      return callback(std::forward<Args>(args)...);
    }
    long count() const {
      return calls;
    }
};
```

Here, the constructor, taking the callback to wrap, enables the deduction of its type as the template parameter CB. For example, we can initialize an object passing a lambda as an argument:

```cpp
CountCalls sc{[](auto x, auto y) {
                return x > y;
              }};
```

which means that the type of the sorting criterion sc is deduced as CountCalls<*TypeOfTheLambda*>. This way, we can count the number of calls for a passed sorting criterion:

```cpp
std::sort(v.begin(), v.end(),    // range
          std::ref(sc));          // sorting criterion
std::cout << "sorted with " << sc.count() << " calls\n";
```

## 9.1 Use of Class Template Argument Deduction

Here, the wrapped lambda is used as a sorting criterion. It has to be passed by reference, because otherwise, `std::sort()` uses only its own copy of the passed counter, as `std::sort()` takes the sorting criterion by value.

However, we can pass a wrapped lambda to `std::for_each()` because this algorithm (in the nonparallel version) returns its own copy of the passed callback to be able to use its resulting state:

```
auto fo = std::for_each(v.begin(), v.end(),
                        CountCalls{[](auto i) {
                            std::cout << "elem: " << i << '\n';
                        }});
std::cout << "output with " << fo.count() << " calls\n";
```

The output will be something like the following (the sorted count might vary because the implementation of `sort()` might vary):

```
sorted with 39 calls
elem: 19
elem: 17
elem: 13
elem: 11
elem: 9
elem: 7
elem: 5
elem: 3
elem: 2
output with 9 calls
```

If the counter for the calls is atomic, you could also use parallel algorithms (see Chapter 22 on page 259):

```
std::sort(std::execution::par,
          v.begin(), v.end(),
          std::ref(sc));
```

### 9.1.3 No Partial Class Template Argument Deduction

Note that, unlike function templates, class template arguments may not be partially deduced by explicitly specifying only *some* of the template arguments. Not even passing an empty list of argument with `<>` is allowed. For example:

```
template<typename T1, typename T2, typename T3 = T2>
class C
{
  public:
    C (T1 x = {}, T2 y = {}, T3 z = {}) {
        ...
    }
    ...
```

```
};

// all deduced:
C c1(22, 44.3, "hi");      // OK: T1 is int, T2 is double, T3 is const char*
C c2(22, 44.3);            // OK: T1 is int, T2 and T3 are double
C c3("hi", "guy");         // OK: T1, T2, and T3 are const char*

// only some deduced:
C<string> c4("hi", "my");  // ERROR: only T1 explicitly defined
C<> c5(22, 44.3);          // ERROR: neither T1 not T2 explicitly defined
C<> c6(22, 44.3, 42);      // ERROR: neither T1 nor T2 explicitly defined

// all specified:
C<string,string,int> c7;            // OK: T1,T2 are string, T3 is int
C<int,string> c8(52, "my");         // OK: T1 is int,T2 and T3 are strings
C<string,string> c9("a", "b", "c"); // OK: T1,T2,T3 are strings
```

Note that the third template parameter has a default value. For this reason, you do not have to explicitly specify the last type if the second type is specified.

If you are wondering why partial specialization is not supported, here is the example that caused this decision:

```
std::tuple<int> t(42, 43);   // still ERROR
```

`std::tuple` is a variadic template, so you could specify an arbitrary number of arguments. In this case, therefore, it is not clear whether specifying only one type is an error or whether this is intentional. It looks questionable at least.

Unfortunately, the inability to partially specialize means that a common unfortunate coding requirement is not solved. We still cannot easily use a lambda to specify the sorting criterion of an associative container or the hash function of an unordered container:

```
std::set<Cust> coll([](const Cust& x, const Cust& y) {  // still ERROR
                     return x.getName() > y.getName();
                });
```

We still have to specify the type of the lambda. For example:

```
auto sortcrit = [](const Cust& x, const Cust& y) {
                   return x.getName() > y.getName();
              };
std::set<Cust, decltype(sortcrit)> coll(sortcrit);      // OK
```

Specifying only the type does not work because then the container tries to create a lambda of the given type, which is not allowed in C++17, because the default constructor can be called only by the compiler. With C++20, this will be possible, provided the lambda does not capture anything.

### 9.1.4 Class Template Argument Deduction Instead of Convenience Functions

In principle, by using class template argument deduction, we can get rid of several convenience function templates that existed only to allow the deduction of class template parameters from the passed call arguments.

The obvious example is `std::make_pair()`, which avoided the need to specify the type of the passed arguments. For example, after:

```
std::vector<int> v;
```

we use:

```
auto p = std::make_pair(v.begin(), v.end());
```

instead of writing:

```
std::pair<typename std::vector<int>::iterator,
          typename std::vector<int>::iterator> p(v.begin(), v.end());
```

Here, `std::make_pair()` is no longer needed, as we can now simply declare:

```
std::pair p(v.begin(), v.end());
```

or

```
std::pair p{v.begin(), v.end()};
```

However, `std::make_pair()` is also a good example to demonstrate that sometimes the convenience functions do more than just deduce template parameters. In fact, `std::make_pair()` decays the passed argument (passing them by value in C++03 and using traits since C++11). This has the effect that the type of passed string literals (arrays of characters) are deduced as `const char*`:

```
auto q = std::make_pair("hi", "world");   // deduces pair of pointers
```

In this case, q has type `std::pair<const char*, const char*>`.

Using class template argument deduction makes things more complicated. Look at the relevant part of a simple class declaration like `std::pair`:

```
template<typename T1, typename T2>
struct Pair1 {
  T1 first;
  T2 second;
  Pair1(const T1& x, const T2& y) : first{x}, second{y} {
  }
};
```

The elements are passed by reference and according to language rules, when passing arguments of a template type by reference, the parameter type does not *decay*, which is the term for the mechanism to convert a raw array type to the corresponding raw pointer type. Therefore, when calling:

```
Pair1 p1{"hi", "world"};   // deduces pair of arrays of different size, but...
```

T1 is deduced as `char[3]` and T2 is deduced as `char[6]`. In principle, such a deduction is valid. However, we use T1 and T2 to declare the members `first` and `second`. As a consequence, they are declared as

```
char first[3];
char second[6];
```

and initializing an array from an lvalue of an array is not allowed. It is like trying to compile:

```
const char x[3] = "hi";
const char y[6] = "world";
char first[3] {x};         // ERROR
char second[6] {y};        // ERROR
```

Note that we would not have this problem when declaring the parameter to be passed by value:

```
template<typename T1, typename T2>
struct Pair2 {
  T1 first;
  T2 second;
  Pair2(T1 x, T2 y) : first{x}, second{y} {
  }
};
```

If we would create an object of this type as follows:

```
Pair2 p2{"hi", "world"};   // deduces pair of pointers
```

T1 and T2 would both be deduced as `const char*`.

However, because the constructors of class `std::pair<>` take the arguments by reference, the following initialization should normally not compile:

```
std::pair p{"hi", "world"};   // seems to deduce pair of arrays of different size, but...
```

However, it does compile because class `std::pair<>` has *deduction guides*, which we discuss in the next section.

## 9.2 Deduction Guides

You can define specific *deduction guides* to provide additional class template argument deductions or fix existing deductions defined by constructors. For example, you can define that whenever the types of a `Pair3` are deduced, the type deduction should operate as if the types had been passed by value:

```
template<typename T1, typename T2>
struct Pair3 {
  T1 first;
  T2 second;
  Pair3(const T1& x, const T2& y) : first{x}, second{y} {
  }
};

// deduction guide for the constructor:
template<typename T1, typename T2>
Pair3(T1, T2) -> Pair3<T1, T2>;
```

Here, on the left side of the `->`, we declare *what* we want to deduce. In this case, it is the creation of a `Pair3` from two objects of arbitrary types T1 and T2 passed by value. On the right side of the `->`, we define the resulting deduction. In this example, `Pair3` is instantiated with the two types T1 and T2.

## 9.2 Deduction Guides

You might argue that this is what the constructor does already. However, the constructor takes the arguments by reference, which is not the same. In general, even outside templates, arguments passed by value *decay*, while arguments passed by reference do not decay. *Decay* means that raw arrays convert to pointers and that top-level qualifiers, such as `const`, and references are ignored.

Without the deduction guide, for example, when declaring the following:

```
Pair3 p3{"hi", "world"};
```

the type of parameter x is `const char(&)[3]` and therefore T1 is `char[3]`, and the type of parameter y is `const char(&)[6]` and therefore T2 is `char[6]`.

Due to the deduction guide, the template parameters decay, which means that passed arrays or string literals decay to the corresponding pointer types. Now, when declaring the following:

```
Pair3 p3{"hi", "world"};
```

the deduction guide is used that takes the parameters by value. Therefore, both types decay to `const char*`, which is used a deduced template parameters. The declaration has the same effect as if we had declared:

```
Pair3<const char*, const char*> p3{"hi", "world"};
```

Note that the constructor still takes the arguments by reference. The deduction guide is relevant only for the deduction of the template types; it is irrelevant for the actual constructor call after the types T1 and T2 are deduced.

### 9.2.1 Using Deduction Guides to Force Decay

As the previous example demonstrates, in general, a very useful application of these overloading rules is to ensure that a template parameter T *decays* while it is deduced. Consider a typical class template:

```
template<typename T>
struct C {
  C(const T&) {
  }
  ...
};
```

Here, if we pass a string literal "hello", we pass type `const char(&)[6]` so that T is deduced as `const char[6]`:

```
C x{"hello"};    // T deduced as char[6]
```

The reason for this is that template parameter deduction does not *decay* to the corresponding pointer type when arguments are passed by reference.

With a simple deduction guide

```
template<typename T> C(T) -> C<T>;
```

we can fix this problem:

```
C x{"hello"};    // T deduced as const char*
```

The deduction guide takes its argument by value and therefore its type decays, which means that "hello" deduces T to be of type `const char*`.

For this reason, a corresponding deduction guide sounds very reasonable for any class template that has a constructor that takes an object of its template parameter by reference. The C++ standard library provides corresponding deduction guides for pairs and tuples (see Section 9.2.6 on page 89).

### 9.2.2 Non-Template Deduction Guides

Deduction guides do not have to be templates and do not have to apply to constructors. For example, implementing the following structure and deduction guide is valid:

```
template<typename T>
struct S {
  T val;
};
```

```
S(const char*) -> S<std::string>;    // map S<> for string literals to S<std::string>
```

Here, we have a deduction guide without a constructor. The deduction guide is used to deduce parameter T, but then the structure is used as if the template parameter had been specified explicitly.

For this reason, the following declarations are possible and deduce std::string as class template parameter T:

```
S s1{"hello"};          // OK, same as: S<std::string> s1{"hello"};
S s2 = {"hello"};       // OK, same as: S<std::string> s2 = {"hello"};
S s3 = S{"hello"};      // OK, both S deduced to be S<std::string>
```

All initializations are valid because the passed string literals implicitly convert to std::string

Note that aggregates need list initialization. The following deductions work, but the initializations are not allowed because no braces are used:

```
S s4 = "hello";         // ERROR: can't initialize aggregates without braces
S s5("hello");          // ERROR: can't initialize aggregates without braces
```

### 9.2.3 Deduction Guides versus Constructors

Deduction guides compete with the constructors of a class. Class template argument deduction uses the constructor/guide that has the highest priority according to overload resolution. If a constructor and a deduction guide match equally well, the deduction guide is preferred.

Consider the following definition:

```
template<typename T>
struct C1 {
  C1(const T&) {
  }
};
C1(int) -> C1<long>;
```

## 9.2 Deduction Guides

When passing an `int`, the deduction guide is used because it is preferred by overload resolution.[2] Therefore, T is deduced as `long`:

```
C1 x1{42};          // T deduced as long
```

However, if we pass a `char`, the constructor is a better match (because no type conversion is necessary), which means that we deduce T to be `char`:

```
C1 x3{'x'};         // T deduced as char
```

In overload resolution, there is no preference between call-by-value and call-by-reference. However, deduction guides are preferred for equally good matches. Therefore, it is usually fine to let the deduction guide take the argument by value (which also has the advantage of decaying (see Section 9.2.1 on page 85)).

### 9.2.4 Explicit Deduction Guides

A deduction guide can be declared as `explicit`. It is then ignored for cases where the `explicit` would disable initializations or conversions. For example, given:

```
template<typename T>
struct S {
  T val;
};

explicit S(const char*) -> S<std::string>;
```

a copy initialization (using the =) ignores the deduction guide. In this case, it means that the initialization becomes invalid:

```
S s1 = {"hello"};       // ERROR (deduction guide ignored and otherwise invalid)
```

Direct initialization or an explicit deduction on the right-hand side is still possible:

```
S s2{"hello"};          // OK, same as: S<std::string> s2{"hello"};
S s3 = S{"hello"};      // OK
S s4 = {S{"hello"}};    // OK
```

As another example, we could do the following:

```
template<typename T>
struct Ptr
{
  Ptr(T) { std::cout << "Ptr(T)\n"; }
  template<typename U>
  Ptr(U) { std::cout << "Ptr(U)\n"; }
};

template<typename T>
explicit Ptr(T) -> Ptr<T*>;
```

which would have the following effect:

---

[2] A non-template function is preferred over a template unless other aspects of overload resolution are more important.

```
Ptr p1{42};      // deduces Ptr<int*> due to deduction guide
Ptr p2 = 42;     // deduces Ptr<int> due to constructor
int i = 42;
Ptr p3{&i};      // deduces Ptr<int**> due to deduction guide
Ptr p4 = &i;     // deduces Ptr<int*> due to constructor
```

### 9.2.5 Deduction Guides for Aggregates

Deduction guides can be used in generic aggregates to enable class template argument deduction. For example, for:

```
template<typename T>
struct A {
  T val;
};
```

any attempt of class template argument deduction without a deduction guide is an error:

```
A i1{42};        // ERROR
A s1("hi");      // ERROR
A s2{"hi"};      // ERROR
A s3 = "hi";     // ERROR
A s4 = {"hi"};   // ERROR
```

You have to pass the argument for type T explicitly:

```
A<int> i2{42};
A<std::string> s5 = {"hi"};
```

However, after a deduction guide such as:

```
A(const char*) -> A<std::string>;
```

you can initialize the aggregate as follows:

```
A s2{"hi"};      // OK
A s4 = {"hi"};   // OK
```

Note that (as usual for aggregate initialization) you still need curly braces. Otherwise, type T is successfully deduced but the initialization is an error:

```
A s1("hi");      // ERROR: T is string, but no aggregate initialization
A s3 = "hi";     // ERROR: T is string, but no aggregate initialization
```

The deduction guides for `std::array` (see Section 9.2.6 on page 90) are further examples of deduction guides for aggregates.

## 9.2.6 Standard Deduction Guides

The C++ standard library introduces a couple of deduction guides with C++17.

**Deduction Guides for Pairs and Tuples**

As introduced in the motivation for deduction guides (see Section 9.1.4 on page 83), `std::pair` needs deduction guides to ensure that class template argument deduction uses the decayed type of the passed argument (see Section 9.2.1 on page 85):[3]

```
namespace std {
  template<typename T1, typename T2>
  struct pair {
    ...
    constexpr pair(const T1& x, const T2& y);   // take argument by-reference
    ...
  };

  template<typename T1, typename T2>
    pair(T1, T2) -> pair<T1, T2>;               // deduce argument types by-value
}
```

As a consequence, the declaration

```
std::pair p{"hi", "world"};     // takes const char[3] and const char[6]
```

is equivalent to:

```
std::pair<const char*, const char*> p{"hi", "world"};
```

For the variadic class template `std::tuple`, the same approach is used:

```
namespace std {
  template<typename... Types>
  class tuple {
   public:
    constexpr tuple(const Types&...);                              // take arguments by-reference
    template<typename... UTypes> constexpr tuple(UTypes&&...);
    ...
  };

  template<typename... Types>
    tuple(Types...) -> tuple<Types...>;    // deduce argument types by-value
};
```

As a consequence, the declaration:

```
std::tuple t{42, "hello", nullptr};
```

deduces the type of `t` as `std::tuple<int, const char*, std::nullptr_t>`.

---

[3] The original declaration uses `class` instead of `typename` and declared the constructors as conditionally `explicit`.

## Deduction From Iterators

To be able to deduce the type of the elements from iterators that define a range for initialization, containers have a deduction guide such as the following for `std::vector<>`:

```
// let std::vector<> deduce element type from initializing iterators:
namespace std {
  template<typename Iterator>
  vector(Iterator, Iterator)
    -> vector<typename iterator_traits<Iterator>::value_type>;
}
```

This allows, for example:

```
std::set<float> s;
std::vector v1(s.begin(), s.end());    // OK, deduces std::vector<float>
```

Note that the use of initialization with parentheses is important here. If you use curly braces:

```
std::vector v2{s.begin(), s.end()};    // BEWARE: doesn't deduce std::vector<float>
```

the two arguments are taken as elements of an initializer list (which has a higher priority according to the overload resolution rules). That is, it is equivalent to:

```
std::vector<std::set<float>::iterator> v2{s.begin(), s.end()};
```

meaning that we initialize a vector of two elements, the first referring to the first element and the second representing the position behind the last element.

On the other hand, consider:

```
std::vector v3{"hi", "world"};    // OK, deduces std::vector<const char*>
std::vector v4("hi", "world");    // OOPS: fatal runtime error
```

While the declaration of v3 also initializes the vector with two elements (both being string literals), the second causes a fatal runtime error, which hopefully causes a core dump. The problem is that string literals convert to character pointers, which are valid iterators. Thus, we pass two iterators that do *not* point to the same object. In other words: we pass an invalid range. We deduce a `std::vector<const char>`, but depending on the location of the two literals in memory, we get a `bad_alloc` exception, or we get a core dump because there is no distance at all, or we get a range of some undefined characters stored in between.

To summarize, using curly braces is always the best way to initialize the **elements** of a vector. The only exception is when a single vector is passed (where the copy constructor is preferred (see Section 9.1.1 on page 79)). When passing something else, it is better to use parentheses.

In any case, for a type with complicated constructors such as `std::vector<>` and other STL containers, **it is highly recommended** *not* **to use class template argument deduction** and instead, to specify the element type(s) explicitly.

## `std::array<>` Deduction

A more interesting example is provided by class `std::array<>`. To be able to deduce both the element type and the number of elements:

```
std::array a{42, 45, 77};              // OK, deduces std::array<int,3>
```

the following deduction guide is defined (indirectly):

## 9.2 Deduction Guides

```
// let std::array<> deduce its number of elements (must have same type):
namespace std {
  template<typename T, typename... U>
  array(T, U...)
    -> array<enable_if_t<(is_same_v<T,U> && ...), T>,
             (1 + sizeof...(U))>;
}
```

The deduction guide uses the fold expression (see Chapter 11 on page 107)

`(is_same_v<T,U> && ...)`

to ensure that the types of all passed arguments are the same.[4] Therefore, the following is not possible:

`std::array a{42, 45, 77.7};        // ERROR: types differ`

Note that an initialization with class template argument deduction works even in compile-time contexts (see Section 28.5 on page 335):

`constexpr std::array arr{0, 8, 15};   // OK, deduces std::array<int,3>`

### (Unordered) Map Deduction

The complexity involved in getting deduction guides that behave correctly can be demonstrated by the attempts to define deduction guides for containers that have key/value pairs (`map`, `multimap`, `unordered_map`, `unordered_multimap`).

The elements of these containers have type `std::pair<const` *keytype*`,` *valuetype*`>`. The `const` is necessary because the location of an element depends on the value of the key, which means that the ability to modify the key could create inconsistencies inside the container.

For this reason, the first approach in the C++17 standard for a `std::map`:

```
namespace std {
  template<typename Key, typename T,
           typename Compare = less<Key>,
           typename Allocator = allocator<pair<const Key, T>>>
  class map {
    ...
  };
}
```

was, for the following constructor:

```
      map(initializer_list<pair<const Key, T>>,
          const Compare& = Compare(),
          const Allocator& = Allocator());
```

to define the following deduction guide:

```
  namespace std {
    template<typename Key, typename T,
```

---

[4] The C++ standards committee has discussed allowing implicit type conversions but decided to be conservative here.

```
          typename Compare = less<Key>,
          typename Allocator = allocator<pair<const Key, T>>>
  map(initializer_list<pair<const Key, T>>,
      Compare = Compare(),
      Allocator = Allocator())
    -> map<Key, T, Compare, Allocator>;
}
```

All arguments are passed by value, therefore this deduction guide enabled the type of a passed comparator or allocator to decay as discussed (see Section 9.2.1 on page 85). However, we naively used the same argument types, which meant that the initializer list took a `const` key type. As a consequence, the following did not work (as Ville Voutilainen pointed out in https://wg21.link/lwg3025):

```
std::pair elem1{1,2};
std::pair elem2{3,4};
...
std::map m1{elem1, elem2};        // ERROR with original C++17 guides
```

Because `elem1` and `elem2` are deduced as `std::pair<int,int>`, the deduction guide requiring a `const` type as first type in the pair did not match. Therefore, you still had to write the following:

```
std::map<int,int> m1{elem1, elem2};   // OK
```

As a consequence, in the deduction guide, the `const` had to be removed:

```
namespace std {
  template<typename Key, typename T,
           typename Compare = less<Key>,
           typename Allocator = allocator<pair<const Key, T>>>
  map(initializer_list<pair<Key, T>>,
      Compare = Compare(),
      Allocator = Allocator())
    -> map<Key, T, Compare, Allocator>;
}
```

However, to still support the decay of the comparator and allocator, we also have to overload the deduction guide for a pair with `const` key type. Otherwise, the constructor would be used for class template argument deduction when passing a pair with a `const` key type, meaning that the deduction would differ slightly between passing pairs with `const` and non-`const` keys.

**No Deduction Guides for Smart Pointers**

Note that some places in the C++ standard library do not have deduction guides even though you might expect them to be present.

You might expect to have deduction guides for shared and unique pointers, so that instead of:

```
std::shared_ptr<int> sp{new int(7)};
```

you could just write:

```
std::shared_ptr sp{new int(7)};          // not supported
```

This does not work automatically because the corresponding constructor is a template, which means that no implicit deduction guide applies:

```
namespace std {
  template<typename T> class shared_ptr {
    public:
      ...
      template<typename Y> explicit shared_ptr(Y* p);
      ...
  };
}
```

Y is a different template parameter to T, meaning that deducing Y from the constructor does not mean that we can deduce type T. This is a feature to be able to call something like:

```
std::shared_ptr<Base> sp{new Derived(...)};
```

The corresponding deduction guide would be simple to provide:

```
namespace std{
  template<typename Y> shared_ptr(Y*) -> shared_ptr<Y>;
}
```

However, this would also mean that this guide is taken when allocating arrays:

```
std::shared_ptr sp{new int[10]};        // OOPS: would deduce shared_ptr<int>
```

As so often in C++, we run into the nasty C problem that the type of a pointer to one object and an array of objects have or decay to the same type.

This problem seems dangerous and therefore, the C++ standards committee has decided not to support it. For single objects, you still have to call:

```
std::shared_ptr<int> sp1{new int};      // OK
auto sp2 = std::make_shared<int>();     // OK
```

and for arrays:

```
std::shared_ptr<std::string> p(new std::string[10],
                               [](std::string* p) {
                                   delete[] p;
                               });
```

or, using the new feature to instantiate shared pointers for raw arrays (see Section 28.2.1 on page 329), just:

```
std::shared_ptr<std::string[]> p{new std::string[10]};
```

## 9.3 Afternotes

Class template argument deduction was first proposed in 2007 by Michael Spertus in https://wg21.link/n2332. The proposal was revisited in 2013 by Michael Spertus and David Vandevoorde in https://wg21.link/n3602. The finally accepted wording was formulated by Michael Spertus, Faisal Vali, and

Richard Smith in `https://wg21.link/p0091r3`, with modifications by Michael Spertus, Faisal Vali, and Richard Smith in `https://wg21.link/p0512r0`, by Jason Merrill in `https://wg21.link/p0620r0`, and by Michael Spertus and Jason Merrill (as a defect report against C++17) in `https://wg21.link/p702r1`.

The support for class template argument deduction in the standard library was added by Michael Spertus, Walter E. Brown, and Stephan T. Lavavej in `https://wg21.link/p0433r2` and (as a defect report against C++17) in `https://wg21.link/p0739r0`.

# Chapter 10
# Compile-Time `if`

With the syntax `if constexpr(...)`, the compiler uses a compile-time expression to decide at compile time whether to use the *then* part or the *else* part (if any) of an `if` statement. The other part (if any) is discarded, meaning that no code is generated. This does not mean that the discarded part is completely ignored though. It will be checked just like the code of unused templates.

For example:

*tmpl/ifcomptime.hpp*

```cpp
#include <string>

template <typename T>
std::string asString(T x)
{
  if constexpr(std::is_same_v<T, std::string>) {
    return x;                    // statement invalid if no conversion to string
  }
  else if constexpr(std::is_arithmetic_v<T>) {
    return std::to_string(x);    // statement invalid if x is not numeric
  }
  else {
    return std::string(x);       // statement invalid if no conversion to string
  }
}
```

By using `if constexpr` we decide at compile time whether we just return a passed string, call `to_string()` for a passed integral or floating-point value, or use a constructor to convert the passed argument to type `std::string`. The invalid calls are *discarded*, therefore the following code compiles (which would not be the case when using a regular runtime `if`):

*tmpl/ifcomptime.cpp*

```
#include "ifcomptime.hpp"
#include <iostream>

int main()
{
  std::cout << asString(42) << '\n';
  std::cout << asString(std::string("hello")) << '\n';
  std::cout << asString("hello") << '\n';
}
```

## 10.1 Motivation for Compile-Time `if`

If we used the runtime `if` in the example above, the corresponding code would *never* compile:

*tmpl/ifruntime.hpp*

```
#include <string>

template <typename T>
std::string asString(T x)
{
  if (std::is_same_v<T, std::string>) {
    return x;                        // ERROR if no conversion to string
  }
  else if (std::is_numeric_v<T>) {
    return std::to_string(x);        // ERROR if x is not numeric
  }
  else {
    return std::string(x);           // ERROR if no conversion to string
  }
}
```

This is a consequence of the rule that function templates are compiled as a whole when being instantiated. The check of the `if` condition is a runtime feature. Even if at compile-time it becomes clear that a condition must be `false`, the *then* part must be able to compile. Therefore, when passing a `std::string` or string literal, the compilation fails because the call of `std::to_string()` for the passed argument is not valid. Furthermore, when passing a numeric value, the compilation fails because the first and third return statements would be invalid.

Using the compile-time `if`, the *then* and *else* parts that cannot be used become *discarded statements*:

- When passing a `std::string` value, the *else* part of the first `if` is discarded.
- When passing a numeric value, the *then* part of the first `if` and the final *else* part are discarded.

## 10.1 Motivation for Compile-Time `if`

- When passing a string literal (i.e., type `const char*`), the *then* parts of the first and second `if` are discarded.

Therefore, on each instantiation, each invalid combination is discarded at compile-time and the code compiles successfully.

Note that a discarded statement is not ignored. Even for discarded statements, the syntax must be correct and calls that do not depend on template parameters must be valid. In fact, the first translation phase (the *definition time*) is always performed, which checks for correct syntax and the validity of all names that do not depend on template parameters. All `static_assert`s must also be valid, even in branches that are not compiled.

For example:

```
template<typename T>
void foo(T t)
{
  if constexpr(std::is_integral_v<T>) {
    if (t > 0) {
      foo(t-1);   // OK
    }
  }
  else {
    undeclared(t);    // error if not declared and not discarded (i.e., T is not integral)
    undeclared();     // error if not declared (even if discarded)
    static_assert(false, "no integral");   // always asserts (even if discarded)
  }
}
```

With a conforming compiler, this example *never* compiles for two reasons:

- Even if T is an integral type, the call of

    `undeclared();`   // *error if not declared (even if discarded)*

  in the discarded *else* part is an error if no such function is declared, because this call does not depend on a template parameter.

- The assertion

    `static_assert(false, "no integral");`   // *always asserts (even if discarded)*

  always fails even if it is part of the discarded *else* part, because again it does not depend on a template parameter. A static assertion repeating the compile-time condition would be fine:

    `static_assert(!std::is_integral_v<T>, "no integral");`

Note that some compilers (e.g., Visual C++ 2013 and 2015) do not implement or perform the two-phase translation of templates correctly. They defer most of the first phase (the *definition time*) to the second phase (the *instantiation time*), which means that invalid function calls and even some syntax errors might compile.[1]

---

[1] Visual C++ is on the way to fixing this behavior step by step, which, however, requires specific options such as `/permissive-`, because the fix might break existing code.

## 10.2 Using Compile-Time `if`

In principle, you can use the compile-time `if` like the runtime `if` provided the condition is a compile-time expression. You can also mix compile-time and runtime `if`:

```
if constexpr (std::is_integral_v<std::remove_reference_t<T>>) {
  if (val > 10) {
    if constexpr (std::numeric_limits<char>::is_signed) {
      ...
    }
    else {
      ...
    }
  }
  else {
    ...
  }
}
else {
  ...
}
```

Note that you cannot use `if constexpr` outside function bodies. Thus, you cannot use it to replace conditional preprocessor directives.

### 10.2.1 Caveats for Compile-Time `if`

Even when it is possible to use compile-time `if`, there might be some consequences that are not obvious. These are discussed in the following subsections.[2]

**Compile-Time `if` Impacts the Return Type**

Compile-time `if` might impact the return type of a function. For example, the following code always compiles but the return type might differ:

```
auto foo()
{
  if constexpr (sizeof(int) > 4) {
    return 42;
  }
  else {
    return 42u;
  }
}
```

---

[2] Thanks to Graham Haynes, Paul Reilly, and Barry Revzin for bringing all these aspects of compile-time `if` to my attention.

## 10.2 Using Compile-Time `if`

Here, because we use `auto`, the return type of the function depends on the return statements, which depend on the size of `int`:

- If the size is greater than 4, there is only one valid return statement returning 42, meaning that the return type is `int`.
- Otherwise, there is only one return statement returning 42u, meaning that the return type becomes `unsigned int`.

This way, the return type of a function with `if constexpr` might differ even more dramatically. For example, if we skip the *else* part the return type might be `int` or `void`:

```
auto foo()                              // return type might be int or void
{
  if constexpr (sizeof(int) > 4) {
    return 42;
  }
}
```

Note that this code never compiles if the runtime `if` is used here, because then both return statements are taken into account meaning that the deduction of the return type is ambiguous.

### `else` Matters Even if `then` Returns

For runtime `if` statements there is a pattern that does not apply to compile-time `if` statements: if code with return statements in both the *then* and the *else* part compiles, you can always skip the `else` in the runtime `if` statements. That is, instead of

```
if (...) {
  return a;
}
else {
  return b;
}
```

you can always write:

```
if (...) {
  return a;
}
return b;
```

This pattern does not apply to compile-time `if` because in the second form, the return type depends on two return statements instead of one, which can make a difference. For example, modifying the example above results in code that *might or might not* compile:

```
auto foo()
{
  if constexpr (sizeof(int) > 4) {
    return 42;
  }
  return 42u;
}
```

If the condition is true (the size of int is greater than 4), the compiler deduces two different return types, which is not valid. Otherwise, we have only one return statement that matters, meaning that the code compiles.

**Short-Circuit Compile-Time Conditions**

Consider the following code:

```
template<typename T>
constexpr auto foo(const T& val)
{
  if constexpr (std::is_integral<T>::value) {
    if constexpr (T{} < 10) {
      return val * 2;
    }
  }
  return val;
}
```

Here, we have two compile-time conditions to decide whether to return the passed value as it is or doubled.

This compiles for both:

```
constexpr auto x1 = foo(42);      // yields 84
constexpr auto x2 = foo("hi");    // OK, yields "hi"
```

Conditions in runtime ifs short-circuit (evaluating conditions with && only until the first false and conditions with || only until the first true). This might result in the expectation that this is also the case for compile-time if:

```
template<typename T>
constexpr auto bar(const T& val)
{
  if constexpr (std::is_integral<T>::value && T{} < 10) {
      return val * 2;
  }
  return val;
}
```

However, the condition for the compile-time if is always instantiated and must be valid as a whole, which means that passing a type that does not support <10 no longer compiles:

```
constexpr auto x2 = bar("hi");    // compile-time ERROR
```

Thus, compile-time if does *not* short-circuit the instantiations. If the validity of compile-time conditions depends on earlier compile-time conditions, you have to nest them as done in foo(). As another example, you have to write:[3]

```
if constexpr (std::is_same_v<MyType, T>) {
```

---

[3] For the discussion about this example, see:
https://groups.google.com/a/isocpp.org/forum/#!msg/std-proposals/eiBAIoynhrM/Y_iPP6aNBgAJ

```
    if constexpr (T::i == 42) {
      ...
    }
  }
```
instead of just:
```
  if constexpr (std::is_same_v<MyType, T> && T::i == 42) {
    ...
  }
```

### 10.2.2 Other Compile-Time `if` Examples

**Perfect Return of a Generic Value**

One application of compile-time `if` is the perfect forwarding of return values, where they have to be processed before they can be returned. Because `decltype(auto)` cannot be deduced for `void` when declaring a variable (as `void` is an incomplete type (see Section A on page 415)), you have to write something like the following:

*tmpl/perfectreturn.hpp*

```
#include <functional>   // for std::forward()
#include <type_traits>  // for std::is_same<> and std::invoke_result<>

template<typename Callable, typename... Args>
decltype(auto) call(Callable op, Args&&... args)
{
  if constexpr(std::is_void_v<std::invoke_result_t<Callable, Args...>>) {
    // return type is void:
    op(std::forward<Args>(args)...);
    ...  // do something before we return
    return;
  }
  else {
    // return type is not void:
    decltype(auto) ret{op(std::forward<Args>(args)...)};
    ...  // do something (with ret) before we return
    return ret;
  }
}
```

The return type declaration works for `void` but the declaration of `ret` does not, so we have to skip the use of `ret` in that case.

## Compile-Time `if` for Tag Dispatching

A typical application of compile-time `if` is tag dispatching. Before C+17, you had to provide an overload set with a separate function for each type you wanted to handle. Now, with compile-time `if`, you can put all the logic together in one function.

For example, instead of overloading the `std::advance()` algorithm:

```
template<typename Iterator, typename Distance>
void advance(Iterator& pos, Distance n) {
  using cat = std::iterator_traits<Iterator>::iterator_category;
  advanceImpl(pos, n, cat{});   // tag dispatch over iterator category
}

template<typename Iterator, typename Distance>
void advanceImpl(Iterator& pos, Distance n,
                 std::random_access_iterator_tag) {
  pos += n;
}

template<typename Iterator, typename Distance>
void advanceImpl(Iterator& pos, Distance n,
                 std::bidirectional_iterator_tag) {
  if (n >= 0) {
    while (n--) {
      ++pos;
    }
  }
  else {
    while (n++) {
      --pos;
    }
  }
}

template<typename Iterator, typename Distance>
void advanceImpl(Iterator& pos, Distance n, std::input_iterator_tag) {
  while (n--) {
    ++pos;
  }
}
```

we can now implement all behavior in one function:

```
template<typename Iterator, typename Distance>
void advance(Iterator& pos, Distance n) {
  using cat = std::iterator_traits<Iterator>::iterator_category;
```

```
      if constexpr (std::is_convertible_v<cat, std::random_access_iterator_tag>) {
        pos += n;
      }
      else if constexpr (std::is_convertible_v<cat,
                                  std::bidirectional_access_iterator_tag>) {
        if (n >= 0) {
          while (n--) {
            ++pos;
          }
        }
        else {
          while (n++) {
            --pos;
          }
        }
      }
      else {  // input_iterator_tag
        while (n--) {
          ++pos;
        }
      }
    }
```

Here, to some extent, we have a compile-time `switch`, where the different cases have to be formulated as `if constexpr` clauses. However, note one difference that might matter:[4]

- The set of overloaded functions gives you **best match** semantics.
- The implementation with compile-time `if` gives you **first match** semantics.

Another example of tag dispatching is the use of compile-time `if` for `get<>()` overloads (see Section 1.3 on page 13) to implement a structured bindings interface.

A third example is the handling of different types in a generic lambda as in `std::variant<>` visitors (see Section 16.3.3 on page 159).

## 10.3  Compile-Time `if` with Initialization

Note that the compile-time `if` can also use the new form of `if` with initialization (see Chapter 2 on page 21). For example, if there is a `constexpr` function `foo()`, you can use:

```
template<typename T>
void bar(const T x)
{
  if constexpr (auto obj = foo(x); std::is_same_v<decltype(obj), T>) {
    std::cout << "foo(x) yields same type\n";
```

---

[4] Thanks to Graham Haynes and Barry Revzin for pointing that out.

```
      ...
    }
    else {
      std::cout << "foo(x) yields different type\n";
      ...
    }
  }
```

If there is a `constexpr` function `foo()` for a passed type, you can use this code to provide different behavior depending on whether `foo(x)` yields the same type as `x`.

To decide on the value returned by `foo(x)`, you can write:

```
constexpr auto c = ... ;
if constexpr (constexpr auto obj = foo(c); obj == 0) {
  std::cout << "foo() == 0\n";
  ...
}
```

Note that `obj` has to be declared as `constexpr` for you to use its value in the condition.

## 10.4 Using Compile-Time `if` Outside Templates

`if constexpr` can be used in any function, not just in templates. All we need is a compile-time expression that yields something convertible to `bool`. However, in that case, in both the *then* and the *else* parts, all statements always have to be valid even if they are discarded.

For example, the following code will always fail to compile because the call of `undeclared()` must be valid even if `chars` are signed and the *else* part is discarded:

```
#include <limits>

template<typename T>
void foo(T t);

int main()
{
  if constexpr(std::numeric_limits<char>::is_signed) {
    foo(42);           // OK
  }
  else {
    undeclared(42);    // ALWAYS ERROR if not declared (even if discarded)
  }
}
```

The following code can never successfully compile because one of the static assertions will always fail:

```
if constexpr(std::numeric_limits<char>::is_signed) {
  static_assert(std::numeric_limits<char>::is_signed);
}
```

```
  else {
    static_assert(!std::numeric_limits<char>::is_signed);
  }
```

The (only) benefit of the compile-time `if` outside generic code is that code in the discarded statement, although it must be valid, does not become part of the resulting program, which reduces the size of the resulting executable. For example, in this program:

```
#include <limits>
#include <string>
#include <array>

int main()
{
  if (!std::numeric_limits<char>::is_signed) {
    static std::array<std::string,1000> arr1;
    ...
  }
  else {
    static std::array<std::string,1000> arr2;
    ...
  }
}
```

either `arr1` or `arr2` is part of the final executable but not both.[5]

## 10.5 Afternotes

Compile-time `if` was initially motivated by Walter Bright, Herb Sutter, and Andrei Alexandrescu in https://wg21.link/n3329 and Ville Voutilainen in https://wg21.link/n4461 by proposing a `static if` language feature. In https://wg21.link/p0128r0, Ville Voutilainen proposed the feature for the first time as `constexpr_if` (which is where the feature got its name). The finally accepted wording was formulated by Jens Maurer in https://wg21.link/p0292r2.

---

[5] This effect is also possible without `constexpr` because compilers can optimize code that is not used away. However, with `constexpr`, this is guaranteed behavior.

# Chapter 11
# Fold Expressions

Since C++17, there is a feature to compute the result of using a binary operator over *all* the arguments of a parameter pack.

For example, the following function returns the sum of all passed arguments:
```
template<typename... T>
auto foldSum (T... args) {
  return (... + args);   // ((arg1 + arg2) + arg3) ...
}
```
Note that the parentheses around the return expression are part of the fold expression and cannot be omitted.

Calling the function with
```
foldSum(47, 11, val, -1);
```
instantiates the template to perform:
```
return 47 + 11 + val + -1;
```
Calling it for
```
foldSum(std::string("hello"), "world", "!");
```
instantiates the template for:
```
return std::string("hello") + "world" + "!";
```
Also note that the order of fold expression arguments can differ and is important (and might look a bit counter-intuitive): As written,
```
(... + args)
```
results in
```
((arg1 + arg2) + arg3) ...
```
which means that the fold expression repeatedly "post-adds" things. You can also write
```
(args + ...)
```
which repeatedly "pre-adds" things, so that the resulting expression is:
```
(arg1 + (arg2 + arg3)) ...
```

## 11.1 Motivation for Fold Expressions

Fold expressions avoid the need to recursively instantiate templates to perform an operation on all parameters of a parameter pack. Before C++17, you had to implement:

```
template<typename T>
auto foldSumRec (T arg) {
  return arg;
}
template<typename T1, typename... Ts>
auto foldSumRec (T1 arg1, Ts... otherArgs) {
  return arg1 + foldSumRec(otherArgs...);
}
```

Such an implementation is not only cumbersome to write, it also stresses C++ compilers. With

```
template<typename... T>
auto foldSum (T... args) {
  return (... + args);   // arg1 + arg2 + arg3 ...
}
```

the effort reduces significantly for both the programmer and the compiler.

## 11.2 Using Fold Expressions

Given a parameter *args* and an operator *op*, C++17 allows us to write

- Either a ***unary left fold***

    ( ... *op args* )

    which expands to: ((*arg1 op arg2*) *op arg3*) *op* ...

- Or a ***unary right fold***

    ( *args op* ... )

    which expands to: *arg1 op* (*arg2 op* ... (*argN-1 op argN*))

The parentheses are required. However, the parentheses and the ellipsis (...) do not have to be separated by whitespaces.

The difference between left and right fold is important more often than expected. For example, there might be different effects even when you use operator +. With the left fold expression:

```
template<typename... T>
auto foldSumL(T... args){
  return (... + args);   // ((arg1 + arg2) + arg3) ...
}
```

the call

```
foldSumL(1, 2, 3)
```

evaluates to:

```
((1 + 2) + 3)
```

This also means that the following example compiles:

```
std::cout << foldSumL(std::string("hello"), "world", "!") << '\n';  // OK
```

Remember that operator + is defined for standard strings provided at least one operand is a `std::string`. Because the left fold is used, the call first evaluates

```
std::string("hello") + "world"
```

which returns a `std::string`, so that adding the string literal `"!"` is then also valid.

However, a call such as

```
std::cout << foldSumL("hello", "world", std::string("!")) << '\n';  // ERROR
```

will not compile because it evaluates to

```
("hello" + "world") + std::string("!")
```

and adding two string literals is not allowed.

However, if we change the implementation to:

```
template<typename... T>
auto foldSumR(T... args){
  return (args + ...);    // (arg1 + (arg2 + arg3))...
}
```

the call

```
foldSumR(1, 2, 3)
```

evaluates to:

```
(1 + (2 + 3))
```

which means that the following example no longer compiles:

```
std::cout << foldSumR(std::string("hello"), "world", "!") << '\n';  // ERROR
```

while the following call does now compile:

```
std::cout << foldSumR("hello", "world", std::string("!")) << '\n';  // OK
```

In almost all cases, evaluation from left to right is the intention. Therefore, the left fold syntax with the parameter pack at the end should usually be preferred:

```
(... + args);    // preferred syntax for fold expressions
```

### 11.2.1 Dealing with Empty Parameter Packs

If a fold expression is used with an empty parameter pack, the following rules apply:

- If operator `&&` is used, the value is `true`.
- If operator `||` is used, the value is `false`.
- If the comma operator is used, the value is `void()`.
- For all other operators, the call is ill-formed.

For all other cases (and in general), you can add an initial value: given a parameter pack *args*, an initial value *value*, and an operator *op*, C++17 also allows us to write

- Either a ***binary left fold***

    ( *value op* ... *op args* )

    which expands to: (((*value op arg1*) *op arg2*) *op arg3*) *op* ...
- Or a ***binary right fold***

    ( *args op* ... *op value* )

    which expands to: *arg1 op* (*arg2 op* ... (*argN op value*))

The operator *op* has to be the same on both sides of the ellipsis.

For example, the following definition allows you to pass an empty parameter pack when adding values:

```
template<typename... T>
auto foldSum (T... s){
  return (0 + ... + s);   // even works if sizeof...(s)==0
}
```

From a concept perspective, whether we add 0 as the first or last operand should be irrelevant:

```
template<typename... T>
auto foldSum (T... s){
  return (s + ... + 0);   // even works if sizeof...(s)==0
}
```

However, as for unary fold expressions, the different evaluation order is important more often than expected (see Section 11.2 on page 108) and the binary left fold should be preferred:

```
(val + ... + args);   // preferred syntax for binary fold expressions
```

Also, the first operand might be special, such as in this example:

```
template<typename... T>
void print (const T&... args)
{
  (std::cout << ... << args) << '\n';
}
```

Here, it is important that the first call is the output of the first passed argument to `print()`, which returns the stream to perform the other output calls. Other implementations might not compile or might even do something unexpected. For example, with

```
std::cout << (args << ... << '\n');
```

a call like `print(1)` will compile but print the value 1 left shifted by the value of '\n', which is usually 10, so that the resulting output is 1024.

Note that in this `print()` example, no whitespace separates all the elements of the parameter pack from each other. A call such as `print("hello", 42, "world")` will print:

```
hello42world
```

To separate the passed elements with spaces, you need a helper that ensures that the output of any but the first argument is extended by a leading space. This can be done, for example, with a helper function template `spaceBefore()`:

*tmpl/addspace.hpp*

## 11.2 Using Fold Expressions

```
template<typename T>
const T& spaceBefore(const T& arg) {
  std::cout << ' ';
  return arg;
}

template <typename First, typename... Args>
void print (const First& firstarg, const Args&... args) {
  std::cout << firstarg;
  (std::cout << ... << spaceBefore(args)) << '\n';
}
```

Here,

```
(std::cout << ... << spaceBefore(args))
```

is a fold expression that expands to:

```
std::cout << spaceBefore(arg1) << spaceBefore(arg2) << ...
```

Thus, for each element in the parameter pack `args`, the expression calls a helper function, that prints out a space character before returning the passed argument, writing it to `std::cout`. To ensure that this does not apply to the first argument, we add an additional first parameter that does not use `spaceBefore()`.

Note that the evaluation of the output of the parameter pack requires that all output on the left is done before `spaceBefore()` is called for the actual element. Thanks to the defined evaluation order (see Section 8.2 on page 62) of operator `<<` and function calls, this is guaranteed to work since C++17.

We can also use a lambda to define `spaceBefore()` inside `print()`:

```
template<typename First, typename... Args>
void print (const First& firstarg, const Args&... args) {
  std::cout << firstarg;
  auto spaceBefore = [](const auto& arg) {
    std::cout << ' ';
    return arg;
  };
  (std::cout << ... << spaceBefore(args)) << '\n';
}
```

However, note that by default, lambdas return objects by value, which means that this would create an unnecessary copy of the passed argument. The way to avoid that is to explicitly declare the return type of the lambda to be `const auto&` or `decltype(auto)`:

```
template<typename First, typename... Args>
void print (const First& firstarg, const Args&... args) {
  std::cout << firstarg;
  auto spaceBefore = [](const auto& arg) -> const auto& {
    std::cout << ' ';
    return arg;
  };
```

```
    (std::cout << ... << spaceBefore(args)) << '\n';
}
```
C++ would not be C++ if you were not able to combine this all in one statement:
```
template<typename First, typename... Args>
void print (const First& firstarg, const Args&... args) {
  std::cout << firstarg;
  (std::cout << ... << [](const auto& arg) -> decltype(auto) {
                        std::cout << ' ';
                        return arg;
                      }(args)) << '\n';
}
```
Nevertheless, a simpler way to implement `print()` is to use a lambda that prints both the space and the argument and then pass this to a unary fold:[1]
```
template<typename First, typename... Args>
void print(First first, const Args&... args) {
  std::cout << first;
  auto outWithSpace = [](const auto& arg) {
                        std::cout << ' ' << arg;
                      };
  (... , outWithSpace(args));
  std::cout << '\n';
}
```
By using an additional template parameter declared with `auto` (see Section 13.1.1 on page 122), we can make `print()` even more flexible so that it is parameterized for the separator to be a character, a string, or any other printable type.

## 11.2.2 Supported Operators

You can use all binary operators for fold expressions except `.`, `->`, and `[]`.

**Folded Function Calls**

Fold expressions can also be used with the comma operator, combining multiple function calls into one statement. That is, you can now simply implement:
```
template<typename... Types>
void callFoo(const Types&... args)
{
  ...
  (... , foo(args));         // calls foo(arg1), foo(arg2), foo(arg3), ...
}
```

---

[1] Thanks to Barry Revzin for pointing that out.

## 11.2 Using Fold Expressions

to call function `foo()` for all passed arguments.

Alternatively, if move semantics should be supported:

```
template<typename... Types>
void callFoo(Types&&... args)
{
  ...
  (... , foo(std::forward<Types>(args)));  // calls foo(arg1), foo(arg2), ...
}
```

To make this code safe in case the called function returns a value of a type with an overloaded comma operator, you should cast the return type to `void`:

```
template<typename... Types>
void callFoo(const Types&... args)
{
  ...
  (... , (void)foo(std::forward<Types>(args)));  // calls foo(arg1), foo(arg2), ...
}
```

Note that due to the nature of the comma operator, whether we use the left or right fold operator is usually irrelevant. The functions are always called from left to right. With

```
(foo(args) , ...);
```

the parentheses only group the calls so that the first `foo()` call is combined with the result of the next two `foo()` calls as follows:

```
foo(arg1) , (foo(arg2) , foo(arg3));
```

However, because the evaluation order of the comma operator is usually from left to right, the first call still takes place before the group of two calls inside the parentheses, while within the parentheses, the middle call still takes place before the right call.[2]

Nevertheless, as the left fold expression matches with the "native" evaluation order, again the use of left fold expressions is recommended if you use fold expressions for multiple function calls.

### Combining Hash Functions

Another example of using the comma operator for fold expressions is to combine hash values. This can be done as follows:

```
template<typename T>
void hashCombine (std::size_t& seed, const T& val)
{
  seed ^= std::hash<T>()(val) + 0x9e3779b9 + (seed<<6) + (seed>>2);
}

template<typename... Types>
```

---

[2] By overloading the comma operator, you can change its evaluation order, which might then affect the order of calls of both left and right folds.

```
std::size_t combinedHashValue (const Types&... args)
{
  std::size_t seed = 0;                  // initial seed
  (... , hashCombine(seed,args));        // chain of hashCombine() calls
  return seed;
}
```

By calling

```
combinedHashValue ("Hi", "World", 42);
```

the statement in the middle expands to:

```
hashCombine(seed,"Hi"), (hashCombine(seed,"World"), hashCombine(seed,42);
```

With these definitions, we can easily define a new hash function object for a type such as `Customer` to use it in an unordered set or as a key in an unordered map:

```
struct CustomerHash
{
  std::size_t operator() (const Customer& c) const {
    return combinedHashValue(c.getFirstname(), c.getLastname(),
                             c.getValue());
  }
};

std::unordered_set<Customer, CustomerHash> coll;
std::unordered_map<Customer, std::string, CustomerHash> map;
```

**Folded Function Calls for Base Classes**

Folded function calls can even be used in more complex expressions. For example, you can fold the comma operator to perform function calls of member functions of a variadic number of base classes:

*tmpl/foldcalls.cpp*

```
#include <iostream>

// template for variadic number of base classes
template<typename... Bases>
class MultiBase : private Bases...
{
  public:
    void print() {
      // call print() of all base classes:
      (... , Bases::print());
    }
};

struct A {
```

## 11.2 Using Fold Expressions

```
  void print() { std::cout << "A::print()\n"; }
};

struct B {
  void print() { std::cout << "B::print()\n"; }
};

struct C {
  void print() { std::cout << "C::print()\n"; }
};

int main()
{
    MultiBase<A,B,C> mb;
    mb.print();
}
```

Here,

```
template<typename... Bases>
class MultiBase : private Bases...
{
    ...
};
```

allows us to initialize objects with a variadic number of base classes:

```
MultiBase<A,B,C> mb;
```

Furthermore, with

```
(... , Bases::print());
```

a fold expression is used to expand this to call `print` for each base class. That is, the statement with the fold expression expands to the following:

```
(A::print() , B::print()) , C::print();
```

### Folded Path Traversals

You can also use a fold expression to traverse a path in a binary tree with operator `->*`. Consider the following recursive data structure:

*tmpl/foldtraverse.hpp*

```
// define binary tree structure and traverse helpers:
struct Node {
  int value;
  Node* subLeft{nullptr};
  Node* subRight{nullptr};
  Node(int i = 0)
```

```cpp
    : value{i} {
  }
  int getValue() const {
    return value;
  }
  ...
  // traverse helpers:
  static constexpr auto left = &Node::subLeft;
  static constexpr auto right = &Node::subRight;

  // traverse tree, using fold expression:
  template<typename T, typename... TP>
  static Node* traverse (T np, TP... paths) {
    return (np ->* ... ->* paths);      // np ->* paths1 ->* paths2 ...
  }
};
```

Here,

```
(np ->* ... ->* paths)
```

uses a fold expression to traverse the variadic elements of paths from np, which can be used as follows:

*tmpl/foldtraverse.cpp*

```cpp
#include "foldtraverse.hpp"
#include <iostream>

int main()
{
  // init binary tree structure:
  Node* root = new Node{0};
  root->subLeft = new Node{1};
  root->subLeft->subRight = new Node{2};
  ...
  // traverse binary tree:
  Node* node = Node::traverse(root, Node::left, Node::right);
  std::cout << node->getValue() << '\n';
  node = root ->* Node::left ->* Node::right;
  std::cout << node->getValue() << '\n';
  node = root -> subLeft -> subRight;
  std::cout << node->getValue() << '\n';
}
```

When calling

```
Node::traverse(root, Node::left, Node::right);
```

## 11.2 Using Fold Expressions

the call of the fold expression expands to:

```
root ->* Node::left ->* Node::right
```

which results in:

```
root -> subLeft -> subRight
```

### 11.2.3 Using Fold Expressions for Types

By using type traits, we can also use fold expressions to deal with template parameter packs (an arbitrary number of types passed as template parameters). For example, you can use a fold expression to find out whether a list of types is homogeneous:

*tmpl/ishomogeneous.hpp*

```cpp
#include <type_traits>

// check whether passed types are homogeneous:
template<typename T1, typename... TN>
struct IsHomogeneous {
  static constexpr bool value = (std::is_same_v<T1,TN> && ...);
};

// check whether passed arguments have the same type:
template<typename T1, typename... TN>
constexpr bool isHomogeneous(T1, TN...)
{
  return (std::is_same_v<T1,TN> && ...);
}
```

The type trait `IsHomogeneous<>` can be used, for example, as follows:

```
IsHomogeneous<int, Size, decltype(42)>::value
```

In this case, the fold expression that initializes the member `value` expands to:

```
std::is_same_v<int,MyType> && std::is_same_v<int,decltype(42)>
```

The function template `isHomogeneous<>()` can be used, for example, as follows:

```
isHomogeneous(43, -1, "hello", nullptr)
```

In this case, the fold expression that initializes the member `value` expands to:

```
std::is_same_v<int,int> && std::is_same_v<int,const char*>
  && std::is_same_v<int,std::nullptr_t>
```

As usual, operator `&&` short-circuits (aborts the evaluation after the first `false`).

The deduction guide for `std::array<>` (see Section 9.2.6 on page 90) uses this feature in the standard library.

## 11.3 Afternotes

Fold expressions were first proposed by Andrew Sutton and Richard Smith in `https://wg21.link/n4191`. The finally accepted wording was formulated by Andrew Sutton and Richard Smith in `https://wg21.link/n4295`. Support for empty sequences was later removed for operators *, +, &, and | as proposed by Thibaut Le Jehan in `https://wg21.link/p0036`.

# Chapter 12
# Dealing with String Literals as Template Parameters

Over time, the different versions of C++ relaxed the rules for what can be used as template parameters, and this happened again with C++17. Templates now can be used without having to be defined outside the current scope.

## 12.1 Using Strings in Templates

Non-type template parameters can be only constant integral values (including enumerations), pointers to objects/functions/members, lvalue references to objects or functions, or `std::nullptr_t` (the type of `nullptr`).

For pointers, before C++17, external or internal linkage was required. However, since C++17, you can have pointers with what is called "no linkage." However, you still cannot pass string literals directly. For example:

```
template<const char* str>
class Message {
  ...
};

extern const char hello[] = "Hello World!";      // external linkage
const char hello11[] = "Hello World!";           // internal linkage

void foo()
{
  Message<hello>   msg;       // OK (all C++ versions)
  Message<hello11> msg11;     // OK since C++11

  static const char hello17[] = "Hello World!";  // no linkage
```

```
    Message<hello17> msg17;      // OK since C++17

    Message<"hi"> msgError;      // ERROR
}
```

That is, since C++17, you still need two lines to pass a string literal to a template. However, you can have the first line in the same scope as the class instantiation.

This ability also solves an unfortunate constraint: While it has been possible to pass a pointer to a class template since C++11:

```
template<int* p> struct A {
};

int num;
A<&num> a;    // OK since C++11
```

It was not possible to use a compile-time function that returned the address but this is now supported:

```
int num;
...
constexpr int* pNum() {
  return &num;
}
A<pNum()> b;    // ERROR before C++17, now OK
```

## 12.2 Afternotes

Allowing constant evaluation for all non-type template arguments was first proposed by Richard Smith in https://wg21.link/n4198. The finally accepted wording was formulated by Richard Smith in https://wg21.link/n4268.

# Chapter 13

# Placeholder Types like `auto` as Template Parameters

Since C++17, you can use placeholder types (`auto` and `decltype(auto)`) as non-type template parameter types. This means that we can write generic code for non-type parameters of different types.

## 13.1 Using `auto` for Template Parameters

Since C++17, you can use `auto` to declare a non-type template parameter. For example:

```
template<auto N> class S {
  ...
};
```

This allows us to instantiate the non-type template parameter N for different types:

```
S<42>   s1;   // OK: type of N in S is int
S<'a'>  s2;   // OK: type of N in S is char
```

However, you cannot use this feature to get instantiations for types that in general are not allowed as template parameters:

```
S<2.5> s3;   // ERROR: template parameter type still cannot be double
```

We can even have a specific type as a partial specialization:

```
template<int N> class S<N> {
  ...
};
```

Even class template argument deduction (see Chapter 9 on page 77) is supported. For example:

```
template<typename T, auto N>
class A {
  public:
    A(const std::array<T,N>&) {
```

```
        }
        A(T(&)[N]) {
        }
        ...
    };
```

This class can deduce the type of T, the type of N, and the value of N:

```
A a2{"hello"};     // OK, deduces A<const char, 6> with N being std::size_t
```

```
std::array<double,10> sa1;
A a1{sa1};         // OK, deduces A<double, 10> with N being std::size_t
```

You can also qualify auto, for example, to require the type of the template parameter to be a pointer:

```
template<const auto* P> struct S;
```

Furthermore, by using variadic templates, you can parameterize templates to use a list of heterogeneous constant template arguments:

```
template<auto... VS> class HeteroValueList {
};
```

or a list of homogeneous constant template arguments:

```
template<auto V1, decltype(V1)... VS> class HomoValueList {
};
```

For example:

```
HeteroValueList<1, 2, 3> vals1;          // OK
HeteroValueList<1, 'a', true> vals2;     // OK
HomoValueList<1, 2, 3> vals3;            // OK
HomoValueList<1, 'a', true> vals4;       // ERROR
```

### 13.1.1 Parameterizing Templates for Characters and Strings

One application of this feature is to allow you to pass both a character or a string as a template parameter. For example, we can improve the way we output an arbitrary number of arguments with fold expressions (see Section 11.2.1 on page 110) as follows:

*tmpl/printauto.hpp*

```
#include <iostream>

template<auto Sep = ' ', typename First, typename... Args>
void print(const First& first, const Args&... args) {
  std::cout << first;
  auto outWithSep = [](const auto& arg) {
                    std::cout << Sep << arg;
                   };
  (... , outWithSep(args));
  std::cout << '\n';
```

## 13.1 Using auto for Template Parameters

```
}
```

We can still print the arguments, with a space being the default argument for the template parameter Sep:

```
template<auto Sep = ' ', typename First, typename... Args>
void print (const First& firstarg, const Args&... args) {
    ...
}
```

That is, we can still call:

```
std::string s{"world"};
print(7.5, "hello", s);            // prints: 7.5 hello world
```

However, by having `print()` parameterized for the separator Sep, we can now explicitly pass a different character as the first template argument:

```
print<'-'>(7.5, "hello", s);       // prints: 7.5-hello-world
```

Furthermore, due to the use of `auto`, we can even use the workaround to pass a string literal (see Chapter 12 on page 119), by declaring it as an object with no linkage:

```
static const char sep[] = ", ";
print<sep>(7.5, "hello", s);       // prints: 7.5, hello, world
```

Alternatively, we can pass a separator of any other type that can be used as a template parameter (which can make more sense than here):

```
print<-11>(7.5, "hello", s);       // prints: 7.5-11hello-11world
```

### 13.1.2 Defining Metaprogramming Constants

Another application of the `auto` feature for template parameters is to make it easier to define compile-time constants.[1] Instead of defining:

```
template<typename T, T v>
struct constant
{
    static constexpr T value = v;
};

using i = constant<int, 42>;
using c = constant<char, 'x'>;
using b = constant<bool, true>;
```

you can now just do the following:

```
template<auto v>
struct constant
{
```

---

[1] Thanks to Bryce Adelstein Lelbach for providing these examples.

```
    static constexpr auto value = v;
};

using i = constant<42>;
using c = constant<'x'>;
using b = constant<true>;
```

Instead of:

```
template<typename T, T... Elements>
struct sequence {
};

using indexes = sequence<int, 0, 3, 4>;
```

you can now just implement:

```
template<auto... Elements>
struct sequence {
};

using indexes = sequence<0, 3, 4>;
```

You can now even define compile-time objects that represent a heterogeneous list of values (something like a condensed tuple):

```
using tuple = sequence<0, 'h', true>;
```

## 13.2 Using `auto` as Variable Template Parameter

You can also use `auto` as template parameters with *variable templates*.[2] For example, the following declaration, which might occur in a header file, defines a variable template `arr` parameterized for the type of elements and both the type and value of the number of elements:

```
template<typename T, auto N> std::array<T,N> arr;
```

In each translation unit, all uses of `arr<int,10>` share the same global object, while `arr<long,10>` and `arr<int,10u>` would be different global objects (again, both can be used in all translation units).

As a full example, consider the following header file:

*tmpl/vartmplauto.hpp*

```
#ifndef VARTMPLAUTO_HPP
#define VARTMPLAUTO_HPP

#include <array>
```

---

[2] Do not confuse *variable templates*, which are templified variables, with *variadic templates*, which are templates that have an arbitrary number of parameters.

## 13.2 Using auto as Variable Template Parameter

```cpp
template<typename T, auto N> std::array<T,N> arr{};

void printArr();

#endif // VARTMPLAUTO_HPP
```

Here, one translation unit could modify the values of two different instances of this variable template:

*tmpl/vartmplauto1.cpp*
```cpp
#include "vartmplauto.hpp"

int main()
{
  arr<int,5>[0] = 17;
  arr<int,5>[3] = 42;
  arr<int,5u>[1] = 11;
  arr<int,5u>[3] = 33;
  printArr();
}
```

Another translation unit could print these two variables:

*tmpl/vartmplauto2.cpp*
```cpp
#include "vartmplauto.hpp"
#include <iostream>

void printArr()
{
  std::cout << "arr<int,5>:  ";
  for (const auto& elem : arr<int,5>) {
    std::cout << elem << ' ';
  }
  std::cout << "\narr<int,5u>: ";
  for (const auto& elem : arr<int,5u>) {
    std::cout << elem << ' ';
  }
  std::cout << '\n';
}
```

The output of the program would be:[3]

```
arr<int,5>:  17 0 0 42 0
arr<int,5u>: 0 11 0 33 0
```

---
[3] There is a bug in g++ 7 that means that these are handled as one object. This bug is fixed with g++ 8.

In the same way, you can declare a constant variable of an arbitrary type deduced from its initial value:

```
template<auto N> constexpr auto val = N;         // OK since C++17
```

and use it later, for example, as follows:

```
auto v1 = val<5>;                // v1 == 5, v1 is int
auto v2 = val<true>;             // v2 == true, v2 is bool
auto v3 = val<'a'>;              // v3 == 'a', v3 is char
```

To clarify what is happening here:

```
std::is_same_v<decltype(val<5>), int>            // yields false
std::is_same_v<decltype(val<5>), const int>      // yields true
std::is_same_v<decltype(v1), int>;               // yields true (because auto decays)
```

## 13.3 Using `decltype(auto)` as Template Parameter

You can also use the other placeholder type `decltype(auto)` (introduced with C++14) as template parameter. However, note that this type has very special rules regarding how the type is deduced. According to the rules of `decltype`, if *expressions* instead of names are passed to `decltype(auto)`, the deduction yields a type that depends on the value category (see Section 5.3 on page 42) of the expression:

- *type* for a prvalue (e.g., temporaries)
- *type&* for an lvalue (e.g., objects with names)
- *type&&* for an xvalue (e.g., objects marked with `std::move()`).

That means that you can easily deduce template parameters to become references, which might result in surprising effects.

For example:

*tmpl/decltypeauto.cpp*

```
#include <iostream>

template<decltype(auto) N>
struct S {
  void printN() const {
    std::cout << "N: " << N << '\n';
  }
};

static const int c = 42;
static int v = 42;

int main()
{
  S<c> s1;          // deduces N as const int 42
  S<(c)> s2;        // deduces N as const int& referring to c
  s1.printN();
```

```
    s2.printN();

    S<(v)> s3;      // deduces N as int& referring to v
    v = 77;
    s3.printN();    // prints: N: 77
}
```

## 13.4 Afternotes

Placeholder types for non-type template parameters were first proposed by James Touton and Michael Spertus as part of `https://wg21.link/n4469`. The finally accepted wording was formulated by James Touton and Michael Spertus in `https://wg21.link/p0127r2`.

# Chapter 14
# Extended Using Declarations

Using declarations were extended to allow a comma-separated list of names, That way using declarations can apply to parameter packs.

For example, you can now program:

```
class Base {
  public:
    void a();
    void b();
    void c();
};

class Derived : private Base {
  public:
    using Base::a, Base::b, Base::c;
};
```

Before C++17, you needed three different using declarations instead.

## 14.1 Using Variadic Using Declarations

Comma-separated using declarations allow you to generically derive all operations of the same kind from a variadic list of base classes.

A pretty cool application of this technique is to create a set of lambda overloads. By defining the following:

*tmpl/overload.hpp*

```
// "inherit" all function call operators of passed base types:
template<typename... Ts>
struct overload : Ts...
{
  using Ts::operator()...;
```

```
};
```

```
// base types are deduced from passed arguments:
template<typename... Ts>
overload(Ts...) -> overload<Ts...>;
```

you can overload two lambdas as follows:
```
auto twice = overload {
               [](std::string& s) { s += s; },
               [](auto& v) { v *= 2; }
             };
```
Here, we create an object of type `overload`, where we use a deduction guide (see Chapter 9 on page 77) to deduce the types of the lambdas as base classes of the template type `overload` and use aggregate initialization (see Chapter 4 on page 33) to initialize the subobjects for the bases classes with the copy constructor of the closure type of each lambda.

The using declaration then makes both function call operators available for type `overload`. Without the using declaration, the base classes would have two different overloads of the same member function `operator()`, which would be ambiguous.[1]

As a result, you can pass a string, which calls the first overload, or pass another type, which (provided operator `*=` is valid) uses the second overload:
```
int i = 42;
twice(i);
std::cout << "i: " << i << '\n';   // prints: 84
std::string s = "hi";
twice(s);
std::cout << "s: " << s << '\n';   // prints: hihi
```
One application of this technique are `std::variant` visitors (see Section 16.3.3 on page 161).

## 14.2  Variadic Using Declarations for Inheriting Constructors

Together with some clarifications on inheriting constructors, the following is also possible now: you can declare a variadic class template `Multi` that derives from a base class for each of its passed types:

*tmpl/using2.hpp*
```
template<typename T>
class Base {
   T value{};
  public:
   Base() {
```

---

[1] Neither clang nor Visual C++ handle the overloading of operators of base classes for different types as ambiguity, so there, `using` is not necessary. However, without a using declaration the code is not portable.

## 14.2 Variadic Using Declarations for Inheriting Constructors

```
        ...
    }
    Base(T v) : value{v} {
        ...
    }
    ...
};

template<typename... Types>
class Multi : private Base<Types>...
{
  public:
    // derive all constructors:
    using Base<Types>::Base...;
    ...
};
```

With the using declaration for all base class constructors, you derive a corresponding constructor for each type.

Now, when declaring `Multi<>` type for values of three different types:

```
using MultiISB = Multi<int,std::string,bool>;
```

you can declare objects using each one of the corresponding constructors:

```
MultiISB m1 = 42;
MultiISB m2 = std::string("hello");
MultiISB m3 = true;
```

According to the new language rules, each initialization calls the corresponding constructor for the matching base class and the default constructor for all other base classes. Thus

```
MultiISB m2 = std::string("hello");
```

calls the default constructor for `Base<int>`, the string constructor for `Base<std::string>`, and the default constructor for `Base<bool>`.

In principle, you could also enable all assignment operators in `Multi<>` by specifying:

```
template<typename... Types>
class Multi : private Base<Types>...
{
    ...
    // derive all assignment operators:
    using Base<Types>::operator=...;
};
```

## 14.3 Afternotes

Comma-separated using declarations were proposed by Robert Haberlach in `https://wg21.link/p0195r0`. The finally accepted wording was formulated by Robert Haberlach and Richard Smith in `https://wg21.link/p0195r2`.

Various core issues asked for clarification of inheriting constructors. The finally accepted wording to fix these issues was formulated by Richard Smith in `https://wg21.link/n4429`.

There is a proposal by Vicente J. Botet Escriba to add a generic `overload` function to overload lambdas but also ordinary functions and member functions. However, the paper did not make it into C++17. See `https://wg21.link/p0051r1` for details.

# Part III

# New Library Components

This part of the book introduces the new library components of C++17.

# Chapter 15
# `std::optional<>`

In programming, we often have the situation that we *might* return/pass/use an object of a certain type. That is, we could have a value of a certain type or we might not have any value at all. Therefore, we need a way to simulate semantics similar to pointers, where we can express having *no value* by using `nullptr`. The way to handle this is to define an object of a certain type with an additional Boolean member/flag that signals whether a value exists. `std::optional<>` provides such objects in a type-safe way.

Optional objects simply have internal memory for the *contained* objects plus a Boolean flag. Thus, the size is usually one byte larger than the contained object (plus a possible alignment overhead). No heap memory is allocated. The objects use the same alignment as the contained type.

However, optional objects are not just structures that add the functionality of a Boolean flag to a value member. For example, if there is no value, no constructor is called for the contained type (that way, objects that do not have a default constructor can get a default state).

As with `std::variant<>` and `std::any`, the resulting objects have value semantics. That is, copying is implemented as a *deep copy* that creates an independent object with the flag and the contained value (if there is one) in its own memory. Copying a `std::optional<>` without a contained value is cheap; copying a `std::optional<>` with a contained value is as cheap/expensive as copying the contained type/value. Move semantics is supported.

## 15.1 Using `std::optional<>`

`std::optional<>` models a nullable instance of an arbitrary type. The instance might be a member, an argument, or a return value.

### 15.1.1 Optional Return Values

The following program demonstrates some abilities of `std::optional<>` by using it as a return value:

*lib/optional.cpp*
```
#include <optional>
#include <string>
```

```
#include <iostream>

// convert string to int if possible:
std::optional<int> asInt(const std::string& s)
{
  try {
    return std::stoi(s);
  }
  catch (...) {
    return std::nullopt;
  }
}

int main()
{
  for (auto s : {"42", "  077", "hello", "0x33"} ) {
    // try to convert s to int and print the result if possible:
    std::optional<int> oi = asInt(s);
    if (oi) {
      std::cout << "convert '" << s << "' to int: " << *oi << "\n";
    }
    else {
      std::cout << "can't convert '" << s << "' to int\n";
    }
  }
}
```

The program contains a function `asInt()` to convert a passed string into an integer. However, this might not succeed. Therefore, a `std::optional<>` is used so that we can return *"no int"* instead of defining a special `int` value for this return value or throwing an exception to the caller.

Thus, we either return the result of calling `stoi()`, which initializes the return value with an `int`, or we return `std::nullopt`, signaling that we do not have an `int` value.

We could also implement the behavior as follows:

```
std::optional<int> asInt(const std::string& s)
{
  std::optional<int> ret;   // initially no value
  try {
    ret = std::stoi(s);
  }
  catch (...) {
  }
  return ret;
}
```

## 15.1.2 Using std::optional<>

In `main()`, we call this function for different strings:

```
for (auto s : {"42", " 077", "hello", "0x33"} ) {
    // convert s to int and use the result if possible:
    std::optional<int> oi = asInt(s);
    ...
}
```

For each returned `std::optional<int> oi`, we evaluate whether we have a value (by evaluating the object as a Boolean expression) and access the value by "dereferencing" the optional object:

```
if (oi) {
    std::cout << "convert '" << s << "' to int: " << *oi << "\n";
}
```

Note that for the string `"0x33"` `asInt()` yields 0 because `stoi()` does not parse the string as a hexadecimal value.

There are alternative ways to implement the handling of the return value, such as:

```
std::optional<int> oi = asInt(s);
if (oi.has_value()) {
    std::cout << "convert '" << s << "' to int: " << oi.value() << "\n";
}
```

Here, `has_value()` is used to check whether a value was returned. `value()` is used to access the value. `value()` is safer than operator `*`: it throws an exception if no value exists. Operator `*` should be used only when you are sure that the optional contains a value, otherwise your program will have undefined behavior.[1]

Note that we can improve `asInt()` (see Section 19.3 on page 187) by using the new type `std::string_view` and the new convenience function `std::from_chars()` (see Section 31.2.1 on page 386).

### 15.1.2 Optional Arguments and Data Members

Another example using `std::optional<>` is the optional passing of arguments and/or the optional setting of a data member:

*lib/optionalmember.cpp*

```
#include <string>
#include <optional>
#include <iostream>

class Name
{
  private:
    std::string first;
    std::optional<std::string> middle;
```

---

[1] Note that you might not see this undefined behavior because operator `*` yields the value at a memory location, which might (still) make sense.

```
    std::string last;
  public:
    Name (std::string f,
          std::optional<std::string> m,
          std::string l)
     : first{std::move(f)}, middle{std::move(m)}, last{std::move(l)} {
    }
    friend std::ostream& operator << (std::ostream& strm, const Name& n) {
      strm << n.first << ' ';
      if (n.middle) {
        strm << *n.middle << ' ';
      }
      return strm << n.last;
    }
};

int main()
{
    Name n{"Jim", std::nullopt, "Knopf"};
    std::cout << n << '\n';

    Name m{"Donald", "Ervin", "Knuth"};
    std::cout << m << '\n';
}
```

Class `Name` represents a name that consists of a first name, an optional middle name, and a last name. The member `middle` is defined accordingly and the constructor enables you to pass `std::nullopt` when there is no middle name. This is a different state than the middle name being the empty string.

Note that as usual for types with value semantics, the best way to define a constructor that initializes the corresponding members is to take the arguments by value and move the parameters to the members.

Note also that `std::optional<>` changes the syntactic usage of the value of the member `middle`. Using `n.middle` as a Boolean expression yields whether there is a middle name. `*n.middle` is used to access the current value (if there is one).

Another option for accessing the value is by using the member function `value_or()`, which enables you to specify a fallback value in case no value exists. For example, inside class `Name` we could also implement:

```
    std::cout << middle.value_or("");    // print middle name or nothing
```

However, in this case, we would get two spaces instead of one between the first name and the last name.

## 15.2 `std::optional<>` Types and Operations

This section describes the types and operations of `std::optional<>` in detail.

### 15.2.1 `std::optional<>` Types

In the header file `<optional>`, the C++ standard library defines class `std::optional<>` as follows:

```
namespace std {
  template<typename T> class optional;
}
```

In addition, the following types and objects are defined:

- `nullopt` of type `std::nullopt_t` as a "value" for optional objects that have no value.
- Exception class `std::bad_optional_access`, which is derived from `std::exception`, for value access without a value.

Optional objects also use the object `std::in_place` (of type `std::in_place_t`) defined in `<utility>` to initialize the value of an optional object with multiple arguments (see below).

### 15.2.2 `std::optional<>` Operations

Table *15.1* `std::optional` *Operations* lists all operations that are provided for `std::optional<>`.

| Operation | Effect |
|---|---|
| *constructors* | Creates an optional object (might or might not call constructor for contained type) |
| `make_optional<>()` | Creates an optional object initialized by the passed value(s) |
| *destructor* | Destroys an optional object |
| `=` | Assigns a new value |
| `emplace()` | Assigns a new value to the contained type |
| `reset()` | Destroys any value (makes the object empty) |
| `has_value()` | Returns whether the object has a value |
| conversion to `bool` | Returns whether the object has a value |
| `*` | Value access (undefined behavior if no value) |
| `->` | Access to member of the value (undefined behavior if no value) |
| `value()` | Value access (exception if no value) |
| `value_or()` | Value access (fallback argument if no value) |
| `swap()` | Swaps values between two objects |
| `==, !=, <, <=, >, >=` | Compares optional objects |
| `hash<>` | Function object type to compute hash values |

Table 15.1. `std::optional<>` *Operations*

**Construction**

Special constructors enable you to pass the arguments directly to the contained type.

- You can create an optional object that does not have a value. In that case, you have to specify the contained type:
    ```
    std::optional<int> o1;
    std::optional<int> o2(std::nullopt);
    ```
    This does not call any constructor for the contained type.

- You can pass a value to initialize the contained type. Due to a deduction guide (see Section 9.2 on page 84), you do not have to specify the contained type:
    ```
    std::optional o3{42};          // deduces optional<int>

    std::optional o4{"hello"};     // deduces optional<const char*>

    using namespace std::string_literals;
    std::optional o5{"hello"s};    // deduces optional<string>
    ```

- To initialize an optional object with multiple arguments, you have to pass an existing object or add `std::in_place` as the first argument (the contained type cannot be deduced):
    ```
    std::optional o6{std::complex{3.0, 4.0}};
    std::optional<std::complex<double>> o7{std::in_place, 3.0, 4.0};
    ```
    Note that the latter form avoids the creation of a temporary object. By using this form, you can even pass an initializer list plus additional arguments:
    ```
    // initialize set with lambda as sorting criterion:
    auto sc = [] (int x, int y) {
                return std::abs(x) < std::abs(y);
              };
    std::optional<std::set<int,decltype(sc)>> o8{std::in_place,
                                                 {4, 8, -7, -2, 0, 5},
                                                 sc};
    ```
    However, this works only if all initial values match the element type of the container exactly. Otherwise, you have to explicitly pass a `std::initializer_list<>`:
    ```
    // initialize set with lambda as sorting criterion:
    auto sc = [] (int x, int y) {
                return std::abs(x) < std::abs(y);
              };
    std::optional<std::set<int,decltype(sc)>> o8{std::in_place,
                                                 std::initializer_list<int>{4, 5L},
                                                 sc};
    ```

- You can copy optional objects (including type conversions) provided their underlying type supports copying:
    ```
    std::optional o9{"hello"};              // deduces optional<const char*>
    std::optional<std::string> o10{o9};     // OK
    ```

## 15.2 std::optional<> Types and Operations

However, note that if the contained type itself can be constructed from an optional object, then the construction from the optional object is preferred:[2]

```
std::optional<int> o11;
std::optional<std::any> o12{o11};   // o12 contains an any object of an empty optional int
```

Note that there is also a convenience function `make_optional<>()`, which allows an initialization with single or multiple arguments (without the need for the `in_place` argument). As usual for `make...` functions, its arguments decay:

```
auto o13 = std::make_optional(3.0);                              // optional<double>
auto o14 = std::make_optional("hello");                          // optional<const char*>
auto o15 = std::make_optional<std::complex<double>>(3.0, 4.0);
```

However, note that there is no constructor that takes a value and decides, according its value, whether to initialize an optional with a value or `nullopt`. For this, operator `?:` has to be used.[3] For example:

```
std::multimap<std::string, std::string> englishToGerman;
...
auto pos = englishToGerman.find("wisdom");
auto o16 = pos != englishToGerman.end()
           ? std::optional{pos->second}
           : std::nullopt;
```

Here, the type of `o16` is `std::optional<std::string>` due to class template argument deduction (see Chapter 9 on page 77) for `std::optional{pos->second}`. Class template argument deduction would not work for `std::nullopt` alone, but by using operator `?:`, `std::nullopt` also converts to an optional string as the common type of both alternatives.

**Accessing the Value**

To check whether an optional object has a value, you can call `has_value()` or use it in a Boolean expression:

```
std::optional o{42};

if (o) ...                  // true
if (!o) ...                 // false
if (o.has_value()) ...      // true
```

No I/O operators are defined (because there is no obvious output if the optional object has no value):

```
std::cout << o;             // ERROR
```

Pointer syntax is provided to access the value. That is, with `operator*`, you can directly access the underlying value of an optional object, while `operator->` enables access to members of the value:

```
std::optional o{std::pair{42, "hello"}};
```

---

[2] Thanks to Tim Song for pointing that out.
[3] Thanks to Roland Bock for pointing that out.

```
auto p = *o;              // initializes p as pair<int,string>
std::cout << o->first;    // prints 42
```

Note that these operators require that the optional contains a value. Using them without a value is undefined behavior:

```
std::optional<std::string> o{"hello"};

std::cout << *o;          // OK: prints "hello"
o = std::nullopt;
std::cout << *o;          // undefined behavior
```

Note that in practice, the second output will still compile and perform some output such as printing `"hello"` again, because the underlying memory for the value of the optional object was not modified. However, you cannot and should never rely on that. If you do not know whether an optional object has a value, you have to call the following instead:

```
if (o) std::cout << *o;   // OK (might output nothing)
```

Alternatively, you can use `value()`, which throws a `std::bad_optional_access` exception if there is no contained value:

```
std::cout << o.value();   // OK (throws if no value)
```

`std::bad_optional_access` is derived directly from `std::exception`.

Please note that both `operator*` and `value()` return the contained object by reference. Therefore, you have to be careful when calling these operations directly for temporary return values. For example, for a function that returns an optional string:

```
std::optional<std::string> getString();
```

it is always safe to assign any optional return value to a new object:

```
auto a = getString().value();   // OK: copy of contained object or exception
```

However, using the returned value directly (other than passing it as an argument) is a source of trouble:

```
auto b = *getString();                    // ERROR: undefined behavior if std::nullopt
const auto& r1 = getString().value();     // ERROR: reference to deleted contained object
auto&& r2 = getString().value();          // ERROR: reference to deleted contained object
```

The problem with the references is that by rule, they extend the lifetime of the return value of `value()` but *not* the lifetime of the optional object returned by `getString()`. Thus, `r1` and `r2` refer to values that no longer exist and using them results in undefined behavior.

Note that this problem easily arises when using a range-based `for` loop:

```
std::optional<std::vector<int>> getVector();
...
for (int i : getVector().value()) {   // ERROR: iterate over deleted vector
  std::cout << i << '\n';
}
```

Note that iterating over a returned non-optional vector of `int` would work. Therefore, do not blindly replace the return type of a function `foo()` with the corresponding optional type; call `foo().value()` instead.

Finally, you can ask for the value and pass a fallback value which is used if the optional object has no value. This is often the easiest way to write an optional value to a stream:

```
std::cout << o.value_or("NO VALUE");      // OK (writes NO VALUE if no value)
```

However, note that there is a subtle difference between `value()` and `value_or()` that you might want to take into account:[4] `value_or()` always returns by value, while `value()` returns by reference. This means that calls like

```
std::cout << middle.value_or("");
```

as well as

```
std::cout << o.value_or("fallback");
```

both potentially allocate memory, while a call to `value()` never does.

However, if called on a temporary object (an rvalue), `value_or()` returns the *moved* contained value by value, meaning that the contained value is not copy constructed. This is the only way to make `value_or()` work for types that are move-only, because the overload for lvalues requires the contained object to be copyable.

As a consequence, the most efficient implementation of the given example is

```
std::cout << o ? o->c_str() : "fallback";
```

instead of

```
std::cout << o.value_or("fallback");
```

Therefore, note that `value_or()` is a nice interface that makes the intention clear but could be a slightly more expensive operation.

**Comparisons**

You can use the usual comparison operators. Operands can be an optional object, an object of the contained type, and `std::nullopt`.
- If both operands are objects with a value, the corresponding operator of the contained type is used.
- If both operands are objects without a value, they are considered to be equal (`==`, `<=`, and `>=` yield `true` and all other comparisons yield `false`).
- If only one operand is an object with a value, the operand without a value is considered to be less than the other operand.

For example:

```
std::optional<int> o0;
std::optional<int> o1{42};

o0 == std::nullopt    // yields true
o0 == 42              // yields false
o0 < 42               // yields true
o0 > 42               // yields false
```

---

[4] Thanks to Alexander Brockmöller for pointing that out.

```
o1 == 42                // yields true
o0 < o1                 // yields true
```

This means that for optional objects of `unsigned int`, there is a value less than 0:

```
std::optional<unsigned> uo;
  uo < 0                // yields true
  uo < -42              // yields true
```

and for optional objects of `bool`, there is a value less than `false`:

```
std::optional<bool> bo;
  bo < false            // yields true
```

To make your code more readable, you should use

```
if (!uo.has_value())
```

instead of

```
if (uo < 0)
```

Mixed-type comparisons that use an optional object and the underlying type are supported provided the underlying types support them:

```
std::optional<int> o1{42};
std::optional<double> o2{42.0};

o2 == 42                // yields true
o1 == o2                // yields true
```

If the underlying type supports implicit type conversions, the mixed-type comparisons may also use implicit type conversions.

Note that optional Boolean or raw pointer values can result in some surprises (see Section 15.3.1 on page 146).

## Changing the Value

Assignment and `emplace()` operations exist corresponding to the initializations:

```
std::optional<std::complex<double>> o;   // has no value
std::optional ox{77};   // optional<int> with value 77

o = 42;                      // value becomes complex(42.0, 0.0)
o = {9.9, 4.4};              // value becomes complex(9.9, 4.4)
o = ox;                      // OK, because int converts to complex<double>
o = std::nullopt;            // o no longer has a value
o.emplace(5.5, 7.7);         // value becomes complex(5.5, 7.7)
```

Assigning `std::nullopt` removes the value, which calls the destructor of the contained type if there was a value before. You can get the same effect by calling `reset()`:

```
o.reset();              // o no longer has a value
```

or assigning empty curly braces:

## 15.2 std::optional<> Types and Operations

```
o = {};                    // o no longer has a value
```

Finally, we can also use `operator*` to modify the value because it yields the value by reference. However, note that this requires the existence of a value to modify:

```
std::optional<std::complex<double>> o;
*o = 42;                   // undefined behavior
...
if (o) {
  *o = 88;                 // OK: value becomes complex(88.0, 0.0)
  *o = {1.2, 3.4};         // OK: value becomes complex(1.2, 3.4)
}
```

**Move Semantics**

`std::optional<>` also supports move semantics. If you move the object as a whole, the state is copied and the contained object (if there is one) is moved. As a result, a moved-from object still has the same state but any value becomes unspecified.

However, you can also move a value into or out of the contained object. For example:

```
std::optional<std::string> os;
std::string s = "a very very very long string";
os = std::move(s);                  // OK, moves
std::string s2 = *os;               // OK, copies
std::string s3 = std::move(*os);    // OK, moves
```

Note that after the last call, `os` still has a string value, but as usual for moved-from objects, the value is unspecified. Thus, you can use it as long as you do not make any assumption about its value. You can even assign a new string value there.

Also note that some overloads ensure that temporary optionals are moved.[5] Consider a function that returns an optional string:

```
std::optional<std::string> func();
```

In this case, the following is well defined to move the value:

```
std::string s4 = func().value();    // OK, moves
std::string s5 = *func();           // OK, moves
```

This behavior is possible by providing rvalue overloads for the corresponding member functions:

```
namespace std {
  template<typename T>
  class optional {
    ...
    constexpr T& operator*() &;
    constexpr const T& operator*() const&;
    constexpr T&& operator*() &&;
```

---

[5] Thanks to Alexander Brockmöller for pointing that out.

```
            constexpr const T&& operator*() const&&;

            constexpr T& value() &;
            constexpr const T& value() const&;
            constexpr T&& value() &&;
            constexpr const T&& value() const&&;
      };
}
```
In other words, you can also do the following:
```
std::optional<std::string> os;
std::string s6 = std::move(os).value();   // OK, moves
```

**Hashing**

The hash value for an optional object is the hash value of the contained non-constant type (if there is one).
The hash value of an empty optional object evaluates to an unspecified value.

## 15.3  Special Cases

Specific optional value types can result in special or unexpected behavior.

### 15.3.1  Optional of Boolean or Raw Pointer Values

Note that using the comparison operator has different semantics to using an optional object as a Boolean value. This can become confusing if the contained type is `bool` or a pointer type. For example:
```
std::optional<bool> ob{false};    // has value, which is false
if (!ob) ...                      // yields false
if (ob == false) ...              // yields true

std::optional<int*> op{nullptr};
if (!op) ...                      // yields false
if (op == nullptr) ...            // yields true
```

### 15.3.2  Optional of Optional

In principle, you can also define an optional of an optional value:
```
std::optional<std::optional<std::string>> oos1;
std::optional<std::optional<std::string>> oos2 = "hello";
std::optional<std::optional<std::string>>
  oos3{std::in_place, std::in_place, "hello"};

std::optional<std::optional<std::complex<double>>>
```

```
ooc{std::in_place, std::in_place, 4.2, 5.3};
```
You can also assign new values even with implicit conversions:
```
oos1 = "hello";           // OK: assign new value
ooc.emplace(std::in_place, 7.2, 8.3);
```
Due to the two levels of having no value, an optional of optional enables you to have "no value" on the outside or on the inside, which can have different semantic meanings:
```
*oos1 = std::nullopt;     // inner optional has no value
oos1 = std::nullopt;      // outer optional has no value
```
This means that you have to take special care to deal with the optional value:
```
if (!oos1) std::cout << "no value\n";
if (oos1 && !*oos1) std::cout << "no inner value\n";
if (oos1 && *oos1) std::cout << "value: " << **oos1 << '\n';
```
However, from a semantic perspective, this is a type with two different states that both represent having no value. Therefore, a `std::variant<>` (see Chapter 16 on page 149) with two Boolean or `monostate` (see Section 16.2 on page 151) alternatives might be more appropriate.

## 15.4 Afternotes

Optional objects were first proposed in 2005 by Fernando Cacciola in `https://wg21.link/n1878`, referring to Boost.Optional as a reference implementation. This class was adopted as part of the Library Fundamentals TS as proposed by Fernando Cacciola and Andrzej Krzemienski in `https://wg21.link/n3793`.

The class was adopted with other components for C++17 as proposed by Beman Dawes and Alisdair Meredith in `https://wg21.link/p0220r1`.

Tony Van Eerd significantly improved the semantics for comparison operators with `https://wg21.link/n3765` and `https://wg21.link/p0307r2`. Vicente J. Botet Escriba harmonized the API with `std::variant<>` and `std::any` with `https://wg21.link/p0032r3`. Jonathan Wakely fixed the behavior for `in_place` tag types with `https://wg21.link/p0504r0`.

# Chapter 16
# `std::variant<>`

With `std::variant<>`, the C++ standard library provides a new *union* class, which, among other benefits, supports a new approach to implement polymorphism dealing with heterogeneous collections. That is, it allows us to deal with elements of different data types without the need for a common base class and pointers (raw or smart).

## 16.1 Motivation for `std::variant<>`

Adopted from C, C++ provides support for `union`s, which are objects that can be used to hold values of *one* of a list of possible types. However, there are some drawbacks with this language feature:
- Objects do not know which type of value they currently hold.
- Therefore, you cannot have non-trivial members, such as `std::string` (without specific effort).[1]
- You cannot derive from a `union`.

With `std::variant<>`, the C++ standard library provides a *closed discriminated union* (which means that there is a specified list of possible types)
- Where the type of the current value is always known
- That can hold values of any specified type
- That you can derive from

In fact, a `std::variant<>` holds a value of various *alternatives*, which usually have different types. However, two alternatives can also have the same type, which is useful if alternatives with different semantic meanings have the same type (e.g., holding two strings, which represent different database columns, so that you still know which of the columns the value represents).

---

[1] Since C++11, in principle, `union`s can have non-trivial members, but you have to implement special member functions such as the copy-constructor and destructor because you only know by programming logic which member is active.

Variants simply have internal memory for the maximum size of the underlying types plus a fixed overhead to manage which alternative is used. No heap memory is allocated.[2]

In general, variants cannot be empty unless you use a specific alternative to signal emptiness. However, in very rare cases (such as due to exceptions during the assignment of a new value of a different type), the variant can come into a state that has no value at all.

As with `std::optional<>` and `std::any`, the resulting objects have value semantics. That is, copying is implemented as a *deep copy* that creates an independent object with the current value of the current alternative in its own memory. However, copying a `std::variant<>` is slightly more expensive than copying the type/value of the current alternative, because the variant has to find out which value to copy. Move semantics is supported.

## 16.2 Using `std::variant<>`

The following example demonstrates the core abilities of `std::variant<>`:

*lib/variant.cpp*

```
#include <variant>
#include <iostream>

int main()
{
  std::variant<int, std::string> var{"hi"};   // initialized with string alternative
  std::cout << var.index() << '\n';           // prints 1
  var = 42;                                    // now holds int alternative
  std::cout << var.index() << '\n';           // prints 0
  ...
  try {
    int i = std::get<0>(var);                 // access by index
    std::string s = std::get<std::string>(var);  // access by type (throws exception here)
    ...
  }
  catch (const std::bad_variant_access& e) {  // in case a wrong type/index is used
    std::cerr << "EXCEPTION: " << e.what() << '\n';
    ...
  }
}
```

The member function `index()` can be used to find out which alternative is currently set (the first alternative has the index 0).

---

[2] This is different from Boost.Variant, where memory had to be allocated to be able to recover from exceptions during value changes.

## 16.2 Using `std::variant<>`

Initializations and assignments always use the best match to find the new alternative. If the type does not fit exactly, there might be surprises (see Section 16.5.1 on page 168).

Note that empty variants, variants with reference members, variants with C-style array members, and variants with incomplete types (see Section A on page 415) (such as void) are not allowed.[3]

There is no empty state. This means that for each constructed object, at least one constructor has to be called. The default constructor initializes the first type with the default constructor:

```
std::variant<std::string, int> var;       // => var.index() == 0, value == ""
```

If there is no default constructor defined for the first type, calling the default constructor for the variant is a compile-time error:

```
struct NoDefConstr {
  NoDefConstr(int i) {
    std::cout << "NoDefConstr::NoDefConstr(int) called\n";
  }
};

std::variant<NoDefConstr, int> v1;    // ERROR: can't default construct first type
```

The auxiliary type `std::monostate` provides the ability to deal with this situation and also provides the ability to simulate an empty state.

### `std::monostate`

To support variants where the first type has no default constructor, the C++ standard library provides a special helper type: `std::monostate`. Objects of type `std::monostate` always have the same state. Thus, they always compare to be equal. Their own purpose is to represent an alternative type so that the variant has *no value of any other type*.

That is, the struct `std::monostate` can serve as a first alternative type to make the variant type default constructible. For example:

```
std::variant<std::monostate, NoDefConstr, int> v2;  // OK
std::cout << "index: " << v2.index() << '\n';       // prints 0
```

To some extent, you can interpret the state to signal emptiness.[4]

There are various ways to check for the monostate, which also demonstrates some of the other operations you can call for variants:

```
if (v2.index() == 0) {
  std::cout << "has monostate\n";
}
if (!v2.index()) {
  std::cout << "has monostate\n";
}
if (std::holds_alternative<std::monostate>(v2)) {
```

---

[3] These features might be added later, but for C++17, there was not enough experience to support it.

[4] In principle, `std::monostate` can serve as any alternative, not just the first one. However, this alternative does not help to make the variant default constructible.

```
    std::cout << "has monostate\n";
  }
  if (std::get_if<0>(&v2)) {
    std::cout << "has monostate\n";
  }
  if (std::get_if<std::monostate>(&v2)) {
    std::cout << "has monostate\n";
  }
```

`get_if<>()` uses a *pointer* to a variant and returns a pointer to the current alternative if the current alternative is T. Otherwise it returns `nullptr`. This differs from `get<T>()`, which takes a reference to a variant and returns the current alternative by value if the provided type is correct, but throws in all other cases.

As usual, you can assign a value of another alternative and even assign the `monostate`, signaling emptiness again:

```
  v2 = 42;
  std::cout << "index: " << v2.index() << '\n';   // index: 1

  v2 = std::monostate{};
  std::cout << "index: " << v2.index() << '\n';   // index: 0
```

**Deriving From Variants**

You can derive from a variant. For example, you can define an aggregate (see Chapter 4 on page 33) that derives from a `std::variant<>` as follows:

```
  class Derived : public std::variant<int, std::string> {
  };

  Derived d = {{"hello"}};
  std::cout << d.index() << '\n';            // prints: 1
  std::cout << std::get<1>(d) << '\n';       // prints: hello
  d.emplace<0>(77);                          // initializes int, destroys string
  std::cout << std::get<0>(d) << '\n';       // prints: 77
```

## 16.3  `std::variant<>` Types and Operations

This section describes the types and operations of `std::variant<>` in detail.

### 16.3.1  `std::variant<>` Types

In the header file `<variant>`, the C++ standard library defines class `std::variant<>` as follows:

```
  namespace std {
    template<typename Types...> class variant;
  }
```

## 16.3 `std::variant<>` Types and Operations

That is, `std::variant<>` is a *variadic* class template (a feature introduced with C++11 that allows you to deal with an arbitrary number of types).

In addition, the following types and objects are defined:

- Class template `std::variant_size`
- Class template `std::variant_alternative`
- Value `std::variant_npos`
- Type `std::monostate`
- Exception class `std::bad_variant_access`, derived from `std::exception`.

Variants also use the two variable templates `std::in_place_type<>` and `std::in_place_index<>`, which have their own types `std::in_place_type_t` and `std::in_place_index_t` and are defined in the header file `<utility>`.

### 16.3.2 `std::variant<>` Operations

Table *16.1* `std::variant` *Operations* lists all operations that are provided for `std::variant<>`.

| Operation | Effect |
|---|---|
| *constructors* | Creates a variant object (might call constructor for underlying type) |
| *destructor* | Destroys a variant object |
| = | Assigns a new value |
| `emplace<T>()` | Destroys the old value and assigns a new value to the alternative with type T |
| `emplace<Idx>()` | Destroys the old value and assigns a new value to the alternative with index Idx |
| `valueless_by_exception()` | Returns whether the variant has no value due to an exception |
| `index()` | Returns the index of the current alternative |
| `swap()` | Swaps values between two objects |
| ==, !=, <, <=, >, >= | Compares variant objects |
| `hash<>` | Function object type for computing hash values |
| `holds_alternative<T>()` | Returns whether there is a value for type T |
| `get<T>()` | Returns the value for the alternative with type T |
| `get<Idx>()` | Returns the value for the alternative with index Idx |
| `get_if<T>()` | Returns a pointer to the value for the alternative with type T or `nullptr` |
| `get_if<Idx>()` | Returns a pointer to the value for the alternative with index Idx or `nullptr` |
| `visit()` | Performs an operation for the current alternative |

Table 16.1. `std::variant<>` Operations

**Construction**

By default, the default constructor of a variant calls the default constructor of the first alternative:

```
std::variant<int, int, std::string> v1;   // sets first int to 0, index()==0
```

The alternative is *value initialized*, which means that it is 0, `false`, or `nullptr` for fundamental types.

If a value is passed for initialization, the best matching type is used:

```
std::variant<long, int> v2{42};
std::cout << v2.index() << '\n';   // prints 1
```

However, the call is ambiguous if two types match equally well:

```
std::variant<long, long> v3{42};              // ERROR: ambiguous
std::variant<int, float> v4{42.3};            // ERROR: ambiguous
std::variant<int, double> v5{42.3};           // OK
std::variant<int, long double> v6{42.3};      // ERROR: ambiguous

std::variant<std::string, std::string_view> v7{"hello"};   // ERROR: ambiguous
std::variant<std::string, std::string_view, const char*> v8{"hello"};   // OK
std::cout << v8.index() << '\n';   // prints 2
```

To pass more than one value for initialization, you have to use the `in_place_type` or `in_place_index` tags:

```
std::variant<std::complex<double>> v9{3.0, 4.0};        // ERROR
std::variant<std::complex<double>> v10{{3.0, 4.0}};     // ERROR
std::variant<std::complex<double>> v11{std::in_place_type<std::complex<double>>,
                                       3.0, 4.0};
std::variant<std::complex<double>> v12{std::in_place_index<0>, 3.0, 4.0};
```

You can also use the `in_place_index` tags to resolve ambiguities or overrule priorities during the initialization:

```
std::variant<int, int> v13{std::in_place_index<1>, 77};    // init 2nd int
std::variant<int, long> v14{std::in_place_index<1>, 77};   // init long, not int
std::cout << v14.index() << '\n';   // prints 1
```

You can even pass an initializer list followed by additional arguments:

```
// initialize variant with a set with lambda as sorting criterion:
auto sc = [] (int x, int y) {
            return std::abs(x) < std::abs(y);
          };
std::variant<std::vector<int>,
             std::set<int,decltype(sc)>> v15{std::in_place_index<1>,
                                             {4, 8, -7, -2, 0, 5},
                                             sc};
```

However, this works only if all initial values match the element type of the container exactly. Otherwise you have to explicitly pass a `std::initializer_list<>`:

```
// initialize variant with a set with lambda as sorting criterion:
```

## 16.3 std::variant<> Types and Operations

```cpp
auto sc = [] (int x, int y) {
            return std::abs(x) < std::abs(y);
         };
std::variant<std::vector<int>,
             std::set<int,decltype(sc)>> v15{std::in_place_index<1>,
                                             std::initializer_list<int>{4, 5L},
                                             sc};
```

For `std::variant<>`, you cannot use class template argument deduction (see Chapter 9 on page 77) and there is no `make_variant<>()` convenience function (unlike for `std::optional<>` and `std::any`). Neither make sense, because the whole goal of a variant is to deal with multiple alternatives.

You can copy variant objects provided all alternatives supports copying:

```cpp
struct NoCopy {
  NoCopy() = default;
  NoCopy(const NoCopy&) = delete;
};

std::variant<int, NoCopy> v1;
std::variant<int, NoCopy> v2{v1};         // ERROR
```

### Accessing the Value

The usual way to access the value is to call `get<>()` or `get_if<>` for the corresponding alternative. You can pass its index or, provided a type is not used more than once, its type. Using an invalid index or invalid/ambiguous type results in a compile-time error. If the passed type or index requests the value of an alternative currently not set, a variant object throws a `std::bad_variant_exception`.

For example:

```cpp
std::variant<int, int, std::string> var;   // sets first int to 0, index()==0

auto a = std::get<double>(var);            // compile-time ERROR: no double
auto b = std::get<4>(var);                 // compile-time ERROR: no 4th alternative
auto c = std::get<int>(var);               // compile-time ERROR: int twice

try {
  auto s = std::get<std::string>(var);     // throws exception (first int currently set)
  auto i = std::get<0>(var);               // OK, i==0
  auto j = std::get<1>(var);               // throws exception (other int currently set)
}
catch (const std::bad_variant_access& e) { // in case of an invalid access
  std::cout << "Exception: " << e.what() << '\n';
}
```

There is also an API to access the value with the option to check whether it exists. You have to pass a pointer to a variant to `get_if<>()`, which then returns either a pointer to the current value or `nullptr`.

```cpp
if (auto ip = std::get_if<1>(&var); ip != nullptr) {
```

```
    std::cout << *ip << '\n';
  }
  else {
    std::cout << "alternative with index 1 not set\n";
  }
```

Here, if with initialization (see Section 2.1 on page 21) is used, which separates the initialization from the condition check.

You can also use the initialization as a condition directly:

```
  if (auto ip = std::get_if<1>(&var)) {
    std::cout << *ip << '\n';
  }
  else {
    std::cout << "alternative with index 1 not set\n";
  }
```

Another way to access the values of the different alternatives is using variant visitors (see Section 16.3.3 on page 157).

**Changing the Value**

Assignment and emplace() operations exist corresponding to the initializations:

```
  std::variant<int, int, std::string> var;   // sets first int to 0, index()==0
  var = "hello";                              // sets string, index()==2
  var.emplace<1>(42);                         // sets second int, index()==1
```

Note that operator= will directly assign the new value if the variant currently holds the matching alternative. emplace() always destroys the old value and assigns the new value.

You can also use get<>() or get_if<>() to assign a new value to the current alternative:

```
  std::variant<int, int, std::string> var;   // sets first int to 0, index()==0
  std::get<0>(var) = 77;                      // OK, because first int already set
  std::get<1>(var) = 99;                      // throws exception (other int currently set)

  if (auto p = std::get_if<1>(&var); p) {    // if second int set
    *p = 42;                                  // modify it
  }
```

Another way to modify the values of the different alternatives is using variant visitors (see Section 16.3.3 on page 157).

## 16.3 std::variant<> Types and Operations

**Comparisons**

For two variants of the same type (i.e., they have the same alternatives in the same order), you can use the usual comparison operators. The operators act according to the following rules:

- A variant with a value of an earlier alternative is less than a variant with a value with a later alternative.
- If two variants have the same alternative, the corresponding operators for the type of the alternatives are evaluated. Note that all objects of type `std::monostate` are always equal.
- Two variants with the special state `valueless_by_exception()` (see Section 16.3.4 on page 162) being true are equal. Otherwise, any variant with `valueless_by_exception()` being true is less than any other variant.

For example:

```
std::variant<std::monostate, int, std::string> v1, v2{"hello"}, v3{42};
std::variant<std::monostate, std::string, int> v4;
    v1 == v4    // COMPILE-TIME ERROR
    v1 == v2    // yields false
    v1 <  v2    // yields true
    v1 <  v3    // yields true
    v2 <  v3    // yields false

v1 = "hello";
    v1 == v2    // yields true

v2 = 41;
    v2 <  v3    // yields true
```

**Move Semantics**

`std::variant<>` also supports move semantics provided all alternatives support move semantics.

If you move the object as a whole, the state is copied and the value of the current alternative is moved. As a result, a moved-from object still has the same alternative, but any value becomes unspecified.

You can also move a value into or out of the contained object.

**Hashing**

The hash value for a variant object is enabled if and only if each member type can provide a hash value. Note that the hash value is *not* guaranteed to be the hash value of the current alternative. On some platforms it is, on some it is not.

### 16.3.3 Visitors

Another way to deal with the value of variants is to use visitors. Visitors are objects that have to unambiguously provide a function call operator for each possible type. When these objects "visit" a variant, they call the best matching function call operator for the actual value of the variant.

## Using Function Objects as Visitors

For example:

*lib/variantvisit.cpp*

```
#include <variant>
#include <string>
#include <iostream>

struct MyVisitor
{
  void operator() (int i) const {
    std::cout << "int:    " << i << '\n';
  }
  void operator() (std::string s) const {
    std::cout << "string: " << s << '\n';
  }
  void operator() (long double d) const {
    std::cout << "double: " << d << '\n';
  }
};

int main()
{
  std::variant<int, std::string, double> var(42);
  std::visit(MyVisitor(), var);   // calls operator() for int
  var = "hello";
  std::visit(MyVisitor(), var);   // calls operator() for string
  var = 42.7;
  std::visit(MyVisitor(), var);   // calls operator() for long double
}
```

The call of visit() is a compile-time error if not all possible types are supported by an operator() or if the call is ambiguous. The example here works because long double is a better match for a double value than int.

You can also use visitors to modify the value of the current alternative (but not to assign a new alternative). For example:

```
struct Twice
{
  void operator()(double& d) const {
    d *= 2;
  }
  void operator()(int& i) const {
    i *= 2;
  }
```

## 16.3 std::variant<> Types and Operations

```
        void operator()(std::string& s) const {
            s = s + s;
        }
    };

    std::visit(Twice(), var);    // calls operator() for matching type
```
Only the type matters. You cannot have different behavior for alternatives that have the same type.

Note that the function call operators in the above example should be marked as being `const` because they are *stateless* (they do not change their behavior, only the passed value).

### Using Generic Lambdas as Visitors

The easiest way to use this feature is to use a generic lambda, which is a function object for an arbitrary type:

```
    auto printvariant = [](const auto& val) {
                    std::cout << val << '\n';
                };
    ...
    std::visit(printvariant, var);
```

Here, the generic lambda defines a closure type that has the function call operator as a member template:

```
    class CompilerSpecificClosureTypeName {
      public:
        template<typename T>
        auto operator() (const T& val) const {
            std::cout << val << '\n';
        }
    };
```

Thus, the call of the lambda passed to `std::visit()` compiles if the statement in the generated function call operator is valid (i.e., calling the output operator is valid).

You can also use a lambda to modify the value of the current alternative:

```
    // double the value of the current alternative:
    std::visit([](auto& val) {
                    val = val + val;
                },
                var);
```

Or:

```
    // restore to the default value of the current alternative:
    std::visit([](auto& val) {
                    val = std::remove_reference_t<decltype(val)>{};
                },
                var);
```

You can even still handle the different alternatives differently using the compile-time `if` language feature (see Chapter 10 on page 95). For example:

```
auto dblvar = [](auto& val) {
                if constexpr(std::is_convertible_v<decltype(val),
                                                  std::string>) {
                  val = val + val;
                }
                else {
                  val *= 2;
                }
              };
...
std::visit(dblvar, var);
```

Here, for a `std::string` alternative, the call of the generic lambda instantiates its generic function call template to compute:

```
val = val + val;
```

while for other alternatives, such as `int` or `double`, the call of the lambda instantiates its generic function call template to compute:

```
val *= 2;
```

Note that care must be taken to check against the type of `val`. Here, we check whether the type is convertible to `std::string`. The check

```
if constexpr(std::is_same_v<decltype(val), std::string>) {
```

would not work because the type of `val` is declared as `int&`, `std::string&`, or `long double&`.

**Return Values in Visitors**

Function calls in visitors may return values provided they have the same return type. For example:

```
using IntOrDouble = std::variant<int, double>;

std::vector<IntOrDouble> coll { 42, 7.7, 0, -0.7};

double sum{0};
for (const auto& elem : coll) {
  sum += std::visit([] (const auto& val) -> double {
                      return val;
                    },
                    elem);
}
```

The code above will add the value of each alternative to `sum`. It would not compile without the explicit specification of the return type in the lambda, because then the return types would differ.

## 16.3 `std::variant<>` Types and Operations

**Using Overloaded Lambdas as Visitors**

By using an *overloader* for function objects and lambdas, you can also define a set of lambdas where the best match is used as a visitor.

Assume the overloader `overload` is defined as follows (see Section 14.1 on page 129):

*tmpl/overload.hpp*
```
// "inherit" all function call operators of passed base types:
template<typename... Ts>
struct overload : Ts...
{
  using Ts::operator()...;
};

// base types are deduced from passed arguments:
template<typename... Ts>
overload(Ts...) -> overload<Ts...>;
```

You can use `overload` to visit a variant by providing lambdas for each alternative:

```
std::variant<int, std::string> var(42);
...
std::visit(overload{    // calls best matching lambda for current alternative
              [](int i) { std::cout << "int: " << i << '\n'; },
              [](const std::string& s) {
                      std::cout << "string: " << s << '\n'; },
           },
           var);
```

You can also use generic lambdas. It is always the best match that is used. For example, to modify the current alternative of a variant, you can use the overload to "double" the value for strings and other types (see Section 14.1 on page 130):

```
auto twice = overload{
              [](std::string& s)  { s += s; },
              [](auto& i) { i *= 2; },
           };
```

With this overload, for string alternatives, the current value is appended, while for all other types, the value is multiplied by 2, which demonstrates the following application for a variant:

```
std::variant<int, std::string> var(42);
std::visit(twice, var);   // value 42 becomes 84
...
var = "hi";
std::visit(twice, var);   // value "hi" becomes "hihi"
```

## 16.3.4 Valueless by Exception

When you modify a variant so that it gets a new value and this modification throws an exception, the variant can get into a very special state: the variant has already lost its old but has not received its new value. For example:

```
struct S {
  operator int() { throw "EXCEPTION"; }   // any conversion to int throws
};

std::variant<double,int> var{12.2};       // initialized as double
var.emplace<1>(S{});                      // OOPS: throws while set as int
```

If this happens, then:
- `var.valueless_by_exception()` returns `true`
- `var.index()` returns `std::variant_npos`

which signals that the variant holds no value at all.

The exact guarantees are as follows:
- If `emplace()` throws, `valueless_by_exception()` might be set to `true`.
- If `operator=()` throws and the modification would not change the alternative, both `index()` and `valueless_by_exception()` keep their old state. The state of the value depends on the exception guarantees of the value type.
- If `operator=()` throws and the new value would set a different alternative, the variant *might* hold no value (`valueless_by_exception()` *might* become `true`). This depends on when exactly the exception is thrown. If it happens during a type conversion before the actual modification of the value started, the variant will still hold its old value.

Usually, this behavior should be no problem provided you no longer use the variant you tried to modify. If you still want to use a variant even though using it caused an exception, you should check its state. For example:

```
std::variant<double,int> var{12.2};       // initialized as double
try {
  var.emplace<1>(S{});                    // OOPS: throws while set as int
}
catch (...) {
  if (!var.valueless_by_exception()) {
    ...
  }
}
```

## 16.4 Polymorphism and Heterogeneous Collections with `std::variant`

`std::variant` enables a new form of polymorphism and dealing with heterogeneous (also called inhomogeneous) collections. It is a form of runtime polymorphism with a closed set of data types.

## 16.4 Polymorphism and Heterogeneous Collections with `std::variant`

The key approach is that a `variant<>` can hold values of multiple alternative types. By creating collections of variants, the collections become heterogeneous, holding values of the different alternative types. Because each variant knows which alternative it holds, and due to the visitor interface, we can program that at runtime different functions/methods are called for different types. As variants have value semantics, we do not need pointers (and the corresponding memory management) or virtual functions.

### 16.4.1 Geometric Objects with `std::variant`

For example, let us assume we have to program a system of geometric objects:

*lib/variantpoly1.cpp*

```cpp
#include <iostream>
#include <variant>
#include <vector>
#include "coord.hpp"
#include "line.hpp"
#include "circle.hpp"
#include "rectangle.hpp"

// common type of all geometric object types:
using GeoObj = std::variant<Line, Circle, Rectangle>;

// create and initialize a collection of geometric objects:
std::vector<GeoObj> createFigure()
{
  std::vector<GeoObj> f;
  f.push_back(Line{Coord{1,2},Coord{3,4}});
  f.push_back(Circle{Coord{5,5},2});
  f.push_back(Rectangle{Coord{3,3},Coord{6,4}});
  return f;
}

int main()
{
  std::vector<GeoObj> figure = createFigure();
  for (const GeoObj& geoobj : figure) {
    std::visit([] (const auto& obj) {
                 obj.draw();  // polymorphic call of draw()
               },
               geoobj);
  }
}
```

First, we define a common data type for all possible types:

```
using GeoObj = std::variant<Line, Circle, Rectangle>;
```

The three types do not need any special relationship. In fact they do not have to have a common base class, any virtual functions, and their interfaces might even differ. For example:

*lib/circle.hpp*

```
#ifndef CIRCLE_HPP
#define CIRCLE_HPP

#include "coord.hpp"
#include <iostream>

class Circle {
  private:
    Coord center;
    int rad;
  public:
    Circle (Coord c, int r)
      : center{c}, rad{r} {
    }

    void move(const Coord& c) {
      center += c;
    }

    void draw() const {
      std::cout << "circle at " << center
                << " with radius " << rad << '\n';
    }
};

#endif
```

We can now put elements of these types into a collection by creating corresponding objects and passing them by value into a container:

```
std::vector<GeoObj> createFigure()
{
  std::vector<GeoObj> f;
  f.push_back(Line{Coord{1,2},Coord{3,4}});
  f.push_back(Circle{Coord{5,5},2});
  f.push_back(Rectangle{Coord{3,3},Coord{6,4}});
  return f;
```

## 16.4 Polymorphism and Heterogeneous Collections with `std::variant`

}

This code would not be possible with polymorphism using inheritance because then the types would have to have `GeoObj` as a common base class and we would need a vector of pointers of `GeoObj` elements, and, due to using pointers, we would have to create the objects with `new` so that we have to track when to call `delete` or use smart pointers (`unique_ptr` or `shared_ptr`).

By using visitors, we can then iterate over the elements and "do the right thing" depending on the element type:

```
std::vector<GeoObj> figure = createFigure();
for (const GeoObj& geoobj : figure) {
  std::visit([] (const auto& obj) {
               obj.draw();    // polymorphic call of draw()
             },
             geoobj);
}
```

Here, `visit()` uses a generic lambda to be instantiated for each possible `GeoObj` type. That is, when compiling the `visit()` call, the lambda is instantiated and compiled as three functions:

- Compiling the code for type `Line`:

    ```
    [] (const Line& obj) {
      obj.draw();    // call of Line::draw()
    }
    ```

- Compiling the code for type `Circle`:

    ```
    [] (const Circle& obj) {
      obj.draw();    // call of Circle::draw()
    }
    ```

- Compiling the code for type `Rectangle`:

    ```
    [] (const Rectangle& obj) {
      obj.draw();    // call of Rectangle::draw()
    }
    ```

If one of these instantiations does not compile, the call of `visit()` does not compile at all. If all compiles, code is generated that, for each element type, calls the corresponding function. Note that the generated code is not an *if-else* chain. The standard guarantees that the performance of the calls does not depend on the number of alternatives.

That is, effectively, we get the same behavior as a virtual function table (with something like a local virtual function table for each `visit()`). Note that the called `draw()` functions do not have to be virtual.

If the type interfaces differ, we can use compile-time `if` (see Chapter 10 on page 95) or visitor overloading (see Section 16.3.3 on page 161) to deal with this situation (see the second example below).

### 16.4.2 Other Heterogeneous Collections with `std::variant`

As another example of using heterogeneous collections with `std::variant<>`, consider the following example:

*lib/variantpoly2.cpp*

```
#include <iostream>
#include <string>
#include <variant>
#include <vector>
#include <type_traits>

int main()
{
  using Var = std::variant<int, double, std::string>;

  std::vector<Var> values {42, 0.19, "hello world", 0.815};

  for (const Var& val : values) {
    std::visit([] (const auto& v) {
                 if constexpr(std::is_same_v<decltype(v),
                                 const std::string&>) {
                   std::cout << '"' << v << "\" ";
                 }
                 else {
                   std::cout << v << ' ';
                 }
               },
               val);
  }
}
```

Again, we define our own type for objects that represent one of multiple possible types:

    `using Var = std::variant<int, double, std::string>;`

We can also create and initialize a heterogeneous collection with them:

    `std::vector<Var> values {42, 0.19, "hello world", 0.815};`

Note that we can initialize the vector with a heterogeneous collection of elements because they all convert to the variant type. However, if we pass a `long`, the initialization would not compile because the compiler would not know whether to convert it to `int` or `double`.

When we iterate over the elements, we use visitors to call functions for them. Here, a generic lambda is used. The lambda instantiates the function call operator for the three different types the alternatives might have. To have different behavior for strings (putting quotes around their value), we use a compile-time `if` (see Chapter 10 on page 95):

```
for (const Var& val : values) {
  std::visit([] (const auto& v) {
               if constexpr(std::is_same_v<decltype(v),
                               const std::string&>) {
                 std::cout << '"' << v << "\" ";
```

## 16.4 Polymorphism and Heterogeneous Collections with `std::variant`

```
            }
            else {
              std::cout << v << ' ';
            }
          },
          val);
}
```

This means that the output becomes:

```
42 0.19 "hello world" 0.815
```

By using visitor overloading (see Section 16.3.3 on page 161), we could also implement this as follows:

```
for (const auto& val : values) {
  std::visit(overload{
                [] (const auto& v) {
                  std::cout << v << ' ';
                },
                [] (const std::string& v) {
                  std::cout << '"' << v << "\" ";
                }
              },
              val);
```

However, beware of the traps from overload resolution. There are cases where a generic lambda (i.e., a function template) is a better match than an implicit type conversion, which means that the wrong function might be called.

### 16.4.3 Comparing `variant` Polymorphism

Let us summarize the pros and cons of using `std::variant<>` for polymorphism and heterogeneous collections.

The benefits are:
- You can use any type and do not need common base types (the approach is non-intrusive)
- You do not have to use pointers for heterogeneous collections
- No need for `virtual` member functions
- Value semantics (no access of freed memory or memory leaks)
- Elements in a vector are located together (instead of distributed via pointers in heap memory)

The constraints and drawbacks are:
- Closed set of types (you have to know all alternatives at compile time)
- Elements all have the size of the biggest element type (this is an issue if element type sizes differ a lot)
- Copying elements might be more expensive

In general, I wonder whether to recommend to program polymorphism with `std::variant<>` by default because this approach is a lot safer (no pointers, meaning no `new` and `delete`) and does not require virtual functions. However, using visitors is a bit clumsy, sometimes you need reference semantics (using the same objects at multiple places), and there are scenarios where not all types are known at compile-time of all code.

Performance can also be very different. Not calling `new` and `delete` might save a lot of time. On the other hand, passing objects by value might cost a lot of time. In practice, you have to measure, which approach is faster for your code. On different platforms, I have seen significant differences in performance.

## 16.5 Special Cases with `std::variant<>`

Specific variants can result in special or unexpected behavior.

### 16.5.1 Having Both `bool` and `std::string` Alternatives

If a `std::variant<>` has both a `bool` and a `std::string` alternative, assigning string literals can produce surprises because a string literal converts better to `bool` than to `std::string`. For example:

```
std::variant<bool, std::string> v;
v = "hi";    // OOPS: sets the bool alternative
std::cout << "index: " << v.index() << '\n';
std::visit([](const auto& val) {
            std::cout << "value: " << val << '\n';
          },
          v);
```

This code snippet will have the following output:

```
index: 0
value: true
```

Thus, the string literal is interpreted as initializing the variant by the Boolean value `true` (`true` because the pointer is not 0).

There are a couple of options to "fix" the assignment here:

```
v.emplace<1>("hello");              // explicitly assign to second alternative

v.emplace<std::string>("hello");    // explicitly assign to string alternative

v = std::string{"hello"};           // make sure a string is assigned

using namespace std::literals;      // make sure a string is assigned
v = "hello"s;
```

See https://wg21.link/p0608 for further discussion of this issue.

## 16.6 Afternotes

Variant objects were first proposed in 2005 by Axel Naumann in `https://wg21.link/n4218`, referring to Boost.Variant as a reference implementation. The finally accepted wording was formulated by Axel Naumann in `https://wg21.link/p0088r3`.

Tony Van Eerd significantly improved the semantics for comparison operators with `https://wg21.link/p0393r3`. Vicente J. Botet Escriba harmonized the API with `std::optional<>` and `std::any` with `https://wg21.link/p0032r3`. Jonathan Wakely fixed the behavior for `in_place` tag types with `https://wg21.link/p0504r0`. The restriction to disallow references, incomplete types, arrays, and empty variants was formulated by Erich Keane with `https://wg21.link/p0510r0`. After C++17 was published, Mike Spertus, Walter E. Brown, and Stephan T. Lavavej fixed a minor flaw with `https://wg21.link/p0739r0`.

# Chapter 17
# `std::any`

In general, C++ is a language with type binding and type safety. Value objects are declared to have a specific type that defines which operations are possible and how the objects behave. Furthermore, the objects cannot change their type.

`std::any` is a value type that can change its type while still having type safety. That is, objects can hold values of any arbitrary type but they know which type the value has that they currently hold. There is no need to specify the possible types when declaring an object of this type.

The trick is that objects contain both the *contained* value and the type of the contained value. Because the value can have any size, the memory might be allocated on the heap. However, implementations should avoid the use of heap memory for small contained values such as `int`.

That is, if you assign a string, the object allocates memory for the value and copies the string, while also storing that fact that a string was assigned. Later, runtime checks can be done to find out which type the current value has. To use the current value with its type, an `any_cast<>` is necessary.

As for `std::optional<>` and `std::variant<>`, the resulting objects have value semantics. That is, copying is implemented as a *deep copy* that creates an independent object with the current value of the current type in its own memory. Because heap memory might be involved, copying a `std::any` is usually expensive. You should prefer to pass objects by reference or move them. Move semantics is partially supported.

## 17.1 Using `std::any`

The following example demonstrates the core abilities of `std::any`:

```
std::any a;               // a is empty
std::any b = 4.3;         // b has value 4.3 of type double
a = 42;                   // a has value 42 of type int
b = std::string{"hi"};    // b has value "hi" of type std::string

if (a.type() == typeid(std::string)) {
  std::string s = std::any_cast<std::string>(a);
  useString(s);
}
```

```
else if (a.type() == typeid(int)) {
  useInt(std::any_cast<int>(a));
}
```

You can declare a `std::any` as empty or initialized by a value of a specific type. If an initial value is passed, the type of the *contained* value gets the type of the passed value.

By using the member function `type()`, you can check the type of the contained value against the type ID of any type. If the object is empty, the type ID is `typeid(void)`.

To access the contained value, you have to cast it to its type with a `std::any_cast<>`:

```
auto s = std::any_cast<std::string>(a);
```

If the cast fails, because the object is empty or the contained type does not fit, a `std::bad_any_cast` is thrown. Therefore, without checking or knowing the type, you are better off implementing the following:

```
try {
  auto s = std::any_cast<std::string>(a);
  ...
}
catch (std::bad_any_cast& e) {
  std::cerr << "EXCEPTION: " << e.what() << '\n';
}
```

Note that `std::any_cast<>` creates an object of the passed type. If you pass `std::string` as a template argument to `std::any_cast<>`, it creates a temporary string (a prvalue), which is then used to initialize the new object s. Without such an initialization, it is usually better to cast to a reference type to avoid creating a temporary object:

```
std::cout << std::any_cast<const std::string&>(a);
```

To be able to modify the value, you need a cast to the corresponding reference type:

```
std::any_cast<std::string&>(a) = "world";
```

You can also call `std::any_cast` for the address of a `std::any` object. In that case, the cast returns a corresponding pointer if the type fits or `nullptr` if it does not:

```
auto p = std::any_cast<std::string>(&a);
if (p) {
  ...
}
```

Alternatively, using the new `if` with initialization (see Chapter 2 on page 21):

```
if (auto p = std::any_cast<std::string>(&a); p != nullptr) {
  ...
}
```

Or just:

```
if (auto p = std::any_cast<std::string>(&a)) {
  ...
}
```

To empty an existing `std::any` object, you can call:

## 17.1 Using std::any

```
a.reset();    // makes it empty
```
or:
```
a = std::any{};
```
or just:
```
a = {};
```
You can also check directly whether the object is empty:
```
if (a.has_value()) {
  ...
}
```
Note also that values are stored using their *decayed* type (arrays convert to pointers, and top-level references and const are ignored). For string literals, this means that the value type is `const char*`. To check against `type()` and use `std::any_cast<>`, you have to use exactly this type:
```
std::any a = "hello";    // type() is const char*
if (a.type() == typeid(const char*)) {                    // true
  ...
}
if (a.type() == typeid(std::string)) {                    // false
  ...
}
std::cout << std::any_cast<const char*>(a) << '\n';       // OK
std::cout << std::any_cast<std::string>(a) << '\n';       // EXCEPTION
```
These are more or less all the operations. No comparison operators are defined (which means that you cannot compare or sort objects), no hash function is defined, and no `value()` member functions are defined. Furthermore, because the type is only known at run time, no generic lambdas can be used to deal with the current value independently of its type. You always need the runtime function `std::any_cast<>` to be able to deal with the current value, which means that you need *some* type-specific code to reenter the C++ type system when dealing with values.

However, you can put `std::any` objects in a container. For example:
```
std::vector<std::any> v;

v.push_back(42);
std::string s = "hello";
v.push_back(s);

for (const auto& a : v) {
  if (auto pa = std::any_cast<const std::string>(&a); pa != nullptr) {
    std::cout << "string: " << *pa << '\n';
  }
  else if (auto pa = std::any_cast<const int>(&a); pa != nullptr) {
    std::cout << "int: " << *pa << '\n';
  }
}
```

Note that you always have to use if-else chains like this. There is no way to use a `switch` statement here.

## 17.2 `std::any` Types and Operations

This section describes the types and operations of `std::any` in detail.

### 17.2.1 Any Types

In the header file `<any>`, the C++ standard library defines class `std::any` as follows:

```
namespace std {
  class any;
}
```

That is, `std::any` is not a class template at all.

In addition, the following types and objects are defined:

- Exception class `std::bad_any_cast`, which is derived from `std::bad_cast`, which is derived from `std::exception` if type conversions fail.

`std::any` objects also use the object `std::in_place_type` (of type `std::in_place_type_t`) defined in `<utility>`.

### 17.2.2 Any Operations

Table *17.1* `std::any` *Operations* lists all operations that are provided for `std::any`.

| Operation | Effect |
|---|---|
| *constructors* | Creates an any object (might call constructor for underlying type) |
| `make_any()` | Creates an any object (passing value(s) to initialize it) |
| *destructor* | Destroys an any object |
| `=` | Assigns a new value |
| `emplace<T>()` | Assigns a new value with the type T |
| `reset()` | Destroys any value (makes the object empty) |
| `has_value()` | Returns whether the object has a value |
| `type()` | Returns the current type as `std::type_info` object |
| `any_cast<T>()` | Uses the current value as value of type T (exception/`nullptr` if other type) |
| `swap()` | Swaps values between two objects |

Table 17.1. `std::any` Operations

## 17.2 std::any Types and Operations

**Construction**

By default, a `std::any` is initialized by being empty.

```
std::any a1;        // a1 is empty
```

If a value is passed for initialization, its *decayed* type is used as the type of the contained value:

```
std::any a2 = 42;        // a2 contains value of type int
std::any a3 = "hello";   // a2 contains value of type const char*
```

To hold a type different to the type of the initial value, you have to use the `in_place_type` tags:

```
std::any a4{std::in_place_type<long>, 42};
std::any a5{std::in_place_type<std::string>, "hello"};
```

Even the type passed to `in_place_type` decays. The following declaration holds a `const char*`:

```
std::any a5b{std::in_place_type<const char[6]>, "hello"};
```

To initialize a `std::any` object with multiple arguments, you have to create the object or you can add `std::in_place_type` as the first argument (the contained type cannot be deduced):

```
std::any a6{std::complex{3.0, 4.0}};
std::any a7{std::in_place_type<std::complex<double>>, 3.0, 4.0};
```

You can even pass an initializer list followed by additional arguments:

```
// initialize a std::any with a set with lambda as sorting criterion:
auto sc = [] (int x, int y) {
            return std::abs(x) < std::abs(y);
          };
std::any a8{std::in_place_type<std::set<int,decltype(sc)>>,
            {4, 8, -7, -2, 0, 5},
            sc};
```

Note that there is also a convenience function `make_any<>()`, which can be used for single or multiple arguments (without the need for the `in_place_type` argument). You always have to explicitly specify the initialized type (it is not deduced if only one argument is passed):

```
auto a10 = std::make_any<float>(3.0);
auto a11 = std::make_any<std::string>("hello");
auto a13 = std::make_any<std::complex<double>>(3.0, 4.0);
auto a14 = std::make_any<std::set<int,decltype(sc)>>({4, 8, -7, -2, 0, 5},
                                                     sc);
```

**Changing the Value**

Corresponding assignment and `emplace()` operations exist. For example:

```
std::any a;

a = 42;        // a contains value of type int
a = "hello";   // a contains value of type const char*
```

```
a.emplace<std::string>("hello");
                    // a contains value of type std::string
a.emplace<std::complex<double>>(4.4, 5.5);
                    // a contains value of type std::complex<double>
```

**Accessing the Value**

To access the contained value, you have to cast it to its type with a `std::any_cast<>`. To cast the value to a string, you have several options:

```
std::any_cast<std::string>(a)            // yield copy of the value

std::any_cast<std::string&>(a);          // write access by reference

std::any_cast<const std::string&>(a);    // read access by reference
```

The type fits if the passed type with top-level references removed has the same type ID. If the cast fails, a `std::bad_any_cast` exception is thrown.

To avoid exception handling, you can pass the address of an `any` object. It returns `nullptr` if the cast fails because the current type does not fit:

```
if (auto sp{std::any_cast<std::string>(&a)}; sp != nullptr) {
    ...   // use *sp for write access to the value of a
}

if (auto sp{std::any_cast<const std::string>(&a)}; sp != nullptr) {
    ...   // use *sp for read access to the value of a
}
```

Note that here, casting to a reference results in a runtime error:

```
std::any_cast<std::string&>(&a);         // RUNTIME ERROR
```

**Move Semantics**

`std::any` also supports move semantics. However, note that move semantics is only supported for types that also have copy semantics. That is, **move-only types** are not supported as contained value types.

The best way to deal with move semantics might not be obvious so, this is how you should do it:

```
std::string s("hello, world!");

std::any a;
a = std::move(s);                                        // move s into a

s = std::move(std::any_cast<std::string&>(a));           // move assign string in a to s
```

Note that as usual for moved-from objects, a still has a valid but unspecified contained value after the last call. Therefore, you can use a as a string as long as you do not make any assumptions about its value.

Calling the following statement afterwards will **not** output "NIL" but rather the value of the moved-from string, which is usually empty (but might be any other value):

```
std::cout << (a.has_value() ? std::any_cast<std::string>(a) : std::string("NIL"));
```

Note that:

```
s = std::any_cast<std::string>(std::move(a));
```

also works but needs an additional move.

Directly casting to an rvalue reference does not compile:

```
s = std::any_cast<std::string&&>(a);          // compile-time error
```

Note that instead of calling

```
a = std::move(s);                              // move s into a
```

the following *might not* always work (although it is an example in the C++ standard):

```
std::any_cast<string&>(a) = std::move(s);     // OOPS: a must hold a string
```

This only works if `a` already contains a value of type `std::string`. If it does not, the cast throws a `std::bad_any_cast` exception before we move assign the new value.

## 17.3 Afternotes

Any objects were first proposed in 2006 by Kevlin Henney and Beman Dawes in `https://wg21.link/n1939` referring to Boost.Any as a reference implementation. This class was adopted as part of the Library Fundamentals TS as proposed by Beman Dawes, Kevlin Henney, and Daniel Krügler in `https://wg21.link/n3804`.

The class was adopted with other components for C++17 as proposed by Beman Dawes and Alisdair Meredith in `https://wg21.link/p0220r1`.

Vicente J. Botet Escriba harmonized the API with `std::variant<>` and `std::optional<>` with `https://wg21.link/p0032r3`. Jonathan Wakely fixed the behavior for `in_place` tag types with `https://wg21.link/p0504r0`.

# Chapter 18

# std::byte

With `std::byte`, C++17 introduces a type which represents the "natural" type of the elements of memory: bytes. `std::byte` essentially represents all the values a byte can hold but places no numeric or character interpretation on them, other than their bit-wise representation. For cases where numeric computing or character sequence are not the goal, this results in more type safety.

However, note that `std::byte` is implemented with the size of an `unsigned char`, meaning that it is not guaranteed to have 8 bits. It may be more.

## 18.1 Using `std::byte`

The following example demonstrates the core abilities of `std::byte`:

```cpp
#include <cstddef>   // for std::byte

std::byte b1{0x3F};
std::byte b2{0b1111'0000};

std::byte b3[4] {b1, b2, std::byte{1}};   // 4 bytes (last is 0)

if (b1 == b3[0]) {
  b1 <<= 1;
}

std::cout << std::to_integer<int>(b1) << '\n';   // outputs: 126
```

Here, we define two bytes with two different initial values. b2 is initialized using two features available since C++14:

- The prefix 0b enables the definition of binary literals.
- The *digit separator* ' allows you to make numeric literals more readable in source code (it can be placed between any two digits of numeric literals).

Note that list initialization (using curly braces) is the only way you can directly initialize a single value of a `std::byte` object. All other forms do not compile:

```
std::byte b1{42};         // OK (as for all enums with fixed underlying type since C++17)
std::byte b2(42);         // ERROR
std::byte b3 = 42;        // ERROR
std::byte b4 = {42};      // ERROR
```

This is a direct consequence of the fact that `std::byte` is implemented as an enumeration type, using the new way of initializing scoped enumerations with integral values (see Section 8.3 on page 65).

There is also no implicit conversion, which means that you have to initialize the byte array with an explicitly converted integral literal:

```
std::byte b5[] {1};              // ERROR
std::byte b6[] {std::byte{1}};   // OK
```

Without any initialization, the value of a `std::byte` is undefined for objects on the stack:

```
std::byte b;              // undefined value
```

As usual (except for atomics), you can force an initialization with all bits set to zero with list initialization:

```
std::byte b{};            // same as b{0}
```

`std::to_integer<>()` allows you to use a `std::byte` object as an integral value (including `bool` and `char`). Without the conversion, the output operator would not compile. Note that because it is a template, you even need the conversion fully qualified with `std::`:

```
std::cout << b1;                              // ERROR
std::cout << to_integer<int>(b1);             // ERROR (ADL doesn't work here)
std::cout << std::to_integer<int>(b1);        // OK
```

A using declaration would work too (but use it in a local scope only):

```
using std::to_integer;
...
std::cout << to_integer<int>(b1);             // OK
```

Such a conversion is also necessary to use a `std::byte` as a Boolean value. For example:

```
if (b2) ...                                   // ERROR
if (b2 != std::byte{0}) ...                   // OK
if (to_integer<bool>(b2)) ...                 // ERROR (ADL doesn't work here)
if (std::to_integer<bool>(b2)) ...            // OK
```

Because `std::byte` is defined as an enumeration type with `unsigned char` as the underlying type, its size is always 1:

```
std::cout << sizeof(b);    // always 1
```

The number of bits depends on the number of bits of the underlying type `unsigned char`, which you can find out with the standard numeric limits:

```
std::cout << std::numeric_limits<unsigned char>::digits;  // number of bits of std::byte
```

which is the same as:

```
std::cout << std::numeric_limits<std::underlying_type_t<std::byte>>::digits;
```
Most of the time it is 8, but there are platforms where this is not the case.

## 18.2 `std::byte` Types and Operations

This section describes the types and operations of `std::byte` in detail.

### 18.2.1 `std::byte` Types

In the header file `<cstddef>`, the C++ standard library defines type `std::byte` as follows:
```
namespace std {
  enum class byte : unsigned char {
  };
}
```
That is, `std::byte` is nothing but a scoped enumeration type with some supplementary bit-wise operators defined:
```
namespace std {
  ...
  template<typename IntType>
    constexpr byte  operator<< (byte b, IntType shift) noexcept;
  template<typename IntType>
    constexpr byte& operator<<= (byte& b, IntType shift) noexcept;
  template<typename IntType>
    constexpr byte  operator>> (byte b, IntType shift) noexcept;
  template<typename IntType>
    constexpr byte& operator>>= (byte& b, IntType shift) noexcept;

  constexpr byte&  operator|= (byte& l, byte r) noexcept;
  constexpr byte   operator|  (byte l, byte r) noexcept;
  constexpr byte&  operator&= (byte& l, byte r) noexcept;
  constexpr byte   operator&  (byte l, byte r) noexcept;
  constexpr byte&  operator^= (byte& l, byte r) noexcept;
  constexpr byte   operator^  (byte l, byte r) noexcept;
  constexpr byte   operator~  (byte b) noexcept;

  template<typename IntType>
    constexpr IntType to_integer (byte b) noexcept;
}
```

## 18.2.2 `std::byte` Operations

Table *18.1* `std::byte` *Operations* lists all operations that are provided for `std::byte`.

| Operation | Effect |
|---|---|
| *constructors* | Creates a byte object (value undefined with default constructor) |
| *destructor* | Destroys a byte object (nothing to be done) |
| = | Assigns a new value |
| ==, !=, <, <=, >, >= | Compares byte objects |
| <<, >>, \|, &, ^, ~ | Binary bit-operations |
| <<=, >>=, \|=, &=, ^= | Modifying bit-operations |
| to_integer<T>() | Converts a byte object into the integral type T |
| sizeof() | Yields 1 |

*Table 18.1.* `std::byte` *Operations*

### Conversion to Integral Types

Using `to_integer<>()`, you can convert a `std::byte` into any fundamental integral type (`bool`, a character type, or an integer type). This is necessary, for example, to compare a `std::byte` with a numeric value or to use it in a condition:

```
if (b2) ...                              // ERROR
if (b2 != std::byte{0}) ...              // OK
if (to_integer<bool>(b2)) ...            // ERROR (ADL doesn't work here)
if (std::to_integer<bool>(b2)) ...       // OK
```

Another example usage is std::byte I/O (see Section 18.2.2 on page 182).

`to_integer<>()` uses the rules for static casts from an `unsigned char` to the destination type. For example:

```
std::byte ff{0xFF};
std::cout << std::to_integer<unsigned int>(ff);   // 255
std::cout << std::to_integer<int>(ff);            // also 255 (no negative value)
std::cout << static_cast<int>(std::to_integer<signed char>(ff));  // -1
```

### I/O with `std::byte`

There are no input and output operators defined for `std::byte`, so you have to convert them into an integral value:

```
std::byte b;
...
std::cout << std::to_integer<int>(b);              // prints value as decimal value
std::cout << std::hex << std::to_integer<int>(b);  // prints value as hexadecimal value
```

By using a `std::bitset<>`, you can also output the value as a binary value (a sequence of bits):

## 18.2 std::byte Types and Operations

```cpp
#include <cstddef>   // for std::byte
#include <bitset>    // for std::bitset
#include <limits>    // for std::numeric_limits

std::byte b1{42};
using ByteBitset = std::bitset<std::numeric_limits<unsigned char>::digits>;
std::cout << ByteBitset{std::to_integer<unsigned>(b1)};
```

The using declaration defines a bitset type with the number of bits that std::byte has and then we create and output such an object initialized with the integral type of the byte. As a result, the value 42 is written as follows (assuming a char has 8 bits):

00101010

Again, you might use std::underlying_type_t<std::byte> instead of unsigned char to make the purpose of the using declaration clearer.

You can also use this to write the binary representation of a std::byte into a string:

```cpp
std::string s = ByteBitset{std::to_integer<unsigned>(b1)}.to_string();
```

If you already have a character sequence, you can also use std::to_chars() (see Section 31.2.2 on page 387) as follows:[1]

```cpp
#include <charconv>

int value = 42;
char str[100];
std::to_chars_result res = std::to_chars(str, str+99,
                                         std::to_integer<int>(b1), 2);
*res.ptr = '\0';   // ensure a trailing null character is behind
```

Note that this form does not write any leading 0, which means that for the value 42, the following is written:

1111110

Input is possible in a similar way: just read the value as an integral, string, or bitset value and convert it. For example, you can write an input operator that reads a byte from a binary representation as follows:

```cpp
std::istream& operator>> (std::istream& strm, std::byte& b)
{
  // read into a bitset:
  std::bitset<std::numeric_limits<unsigned char>::digits> bs;
  strm >> bs;
  // without failure, convert to std::byte:
  if (! std::cin.fail()) {
    b = static_cast<std::byte>(bs.to_ulong());   // OK
  }
  return strm;
```

---

[1] Thanks to Daniel Krügler for pointing this out.

}

Note that we have to use a `static_cast<>()` to convert the bitset converted into an unsigned long into `std::byte`. A list initialization would not work because the conversion narrows:[2]

```
b = std::byte{bs.to_ulong()};    // ERROR: narrowing
```

and we have no other way of initialization.

Again, you might use `std::from_chars()` (see Section 31.2.1 on page 386) to read from a given character sequence:

```
#include <charconv>

const char* str = "101001";
int value;
std::from_chars_result res = std::from_chars(str, str+6,    // range to read characters from
                                             value,         // value to set
                                             2);            // base
```

## 18.3 Afternotes

`std::byte` was first proposed by Neil MacIntosh passing in `https://wg21.link/p0298r0`. The finally accepted wording was formulated by Neil MacIntosh in `https://wg21.link/p0298r3`.

---

[2] With gcc/g++, narrowing initializations compile without the compiler option `-pedantic-errors`.

# Chapter 19
# String Views

With C++17, a special string class was adopted by the C++ standard library that allows us to deal with character sequences like strings without allocating memory for them: `std::string_view`. That is, objects of type `std::string_view` refer to external character sequences without owning them. Therefore, a string view object can be considered as a kind of *reference* to a character sequence.

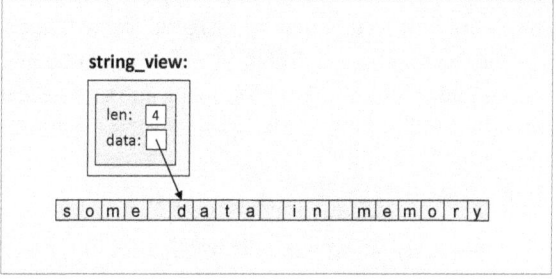

*Figure 19.1. String View Objects*

Using such a string view is cheap and fast (passing a `string_view` by value is always cheap). However, it is also potentially dangerous because, in the same way as for raw pointers, it is up to the programmer to ensure that the referred character sequence is still valid when using a `string_view`.

## 19.1 Differences Compared to `std::string`

In contrast to `std::string`, `std::string_view` objects have the following properties:
- The underlying character sequence is read-only. There is no operation that enables modification of the characters. You can only assign a new value, swap values, and shrink the view to a subset of the character sequence.
- The character sequence is not guaranteed to be null terminated. Therefore, a string view is not a *null terminated byte stream* (*NTBS*).

- The value returned by `data()` can be `nullptr`. For example, `nullptr` is returned after initializing a string view with the default constructor.
- There is no allocator support.

Due to the possible `nullptr` value and possible missing null terminator, you should always use `size()` before accessing characters via `operator[]` or `data()` (unless you know better).

## 19.2 Using String Views

There are two major applications of string views:

1. You might have allocated or mapped data with character sequences or strings and want to use this data without allocating more memory. Typical examples are the use of memory-mapped files or dealing with substrings in large texts.
2. You want to improve the performance for functions/operations that receive strings to simply process them read-only, without needing a trailing null terminator.

   A special form of this might be to deal with string literals as objects with an API similar to strings:

   ```
   std::string_view hello{"hello world"};
   ```

The first application usually means that only string views are passed around, while the programming logic has to ensure that the underlying character sequences remain valid (i.e., the mapped file content is not unmapped). You might use a string view at any time to initialize or assign its value to a `std::string`.

Beware of using string views just as "the better string." This can result in performance problems and severe runtime errors (see Section 19.3.1 on page 188). Read the following subsections carefully.

## 19.3 Using String Views as Parameters

A first example of using a string view as a read-only string is a function that prints a collection of elements with a prefix passed as a string view:

```
#include <string_view>

template<typename T>
void printElems(const T& coll, std::string_view prefix = {})
{
  for (const auto& elem : coll) {
    if (prefix.data()) {   // check against nullptr
      std::cout << prefix << ' ';
    }
    std::cout << elem << '\n';
  }
}
```

Here, just by declaring that the function will take a `std::string_view`, we might save a call to allocate heap memory compared to a function that takes a `std::string`. Details depend on whether short strings

## 19.3 Using String Views as Parameters

are passed and the short string optimization (SSO) (see Section A on page 416) is used. For example, if we declare the function as follows:

```cpp
template<typename T>
void printElems(const T& coll, const std::string& prefix = {});
```

and we pass a string literal, the call creates a temporary string, which will allocate memory on the heap unless the short string optimization is used. By using a string view instead, no allocation is needed because the string view only *refers* to the string literal.

Note that `data()` should be checked against the `nullptr` before using any unknown value of a string view. However, the check here is only necessary to avoid writing the additional space character. String views with the value `nullptr` can be used when writing to a stream but without writing characters.

Another example of using a string view as a read-only string is an improved version of the `asInt()` example of `std::optional<>` (see Section 15.1.1 on page 135), which was declared for a string parameter:

*lib/asint.cpp*

```cpp
#include <optional>
#include <string_view>
#include <charconv>     // for from_chars()
#include <iostream>

// convert string to int if possible:
std::optional<int> asInt(std::string_view sv)
{
  int val;
  // read character sequence into the int:
  auto [ptr, ec] = std::from_chars(sv.data(), sv.data()+sv.size(),
                                   val);
  // if we have an error code, return no value:
  if (ec != std::errc{}) {
    return std::nullopt;
  }
  return val;
}

int main()
{
  for (auto s : {"42", "   077", "hello", "0x33"} ) {
    // try to convert s to int and print the result if possible:
    std::optional<int> oi = asInt(s);
    if (oi) {
      std::cout << "convert '" << s << "' to int: " << *oi << "\n";
    }
    else {
      std::cout << "can't convert '" << s << "' to int\n";
```

        }
      }
    }

The fact that asInt() now takes a string view by value has significant consequences. First, it no longer makes sense to use std::stoi() to create the integer because stoi() takes a string, and creating a string from a string view is a relatively expensive operation.

Instead, we pass the range of characters to the new standard library function std::from_chars() (see Section 31.2.1 on page 386). This function takes a pair of raw character pointers for the begin and end of the characters to be converted. Note that this means that we can skip any special handling of an empty string view, where data() is nullptr and size() is 0, because the range from nullptr until nullptr+0 is a valid empty range (for any pointer type, adding 0 is supported and has no effect).

std::from_chars() returns a std::from_chars_result, which is a structure with two members, a pointer ptr to the first character that was not processed, and a std::errc ec, for which std::errc{} represents no error. Thus, after initializing ec with the ec member of the return value (using structured bindings (see Chapter 1 on page 3)), the following check returns nullopt (see Section 15.2.1 on page 139) if the conversion failed:

    if (ec != std::errc{}) {
      return std::nullopt;
    }

Using string views can also provide significant performance boosts when sorting substrings (see Section 22.1.2 on page 264).

### 19.3.1 String View Considered Harmful

Usually "smart objects" such as smart pointers are considered to be safer (or at least not more dangerous) than corresponding language features. Therefore, the impression might be that a string view, which is a kind of string reference, is safer or at least as safe as using string references. Unfortunately, this is not the case. String views are in fact more dangerous than string references or smart pointers. They behave more like raw character pointers.

**Do Not Assign Temporary Strings to String Views**

Consider declaring a function that returns a new string:

    std::string retString();

Using the return value is usually pretty safe:

- Initializing a string or an object declared with auto with the return value is safe:

        std::string s1 = retString();          // *safe*

- Initializing a string reference with the return value is, if it is possible, pretty safe as long we use the object locally because references extend the lifetime of return values to the end of their lifetime:

        std::string& s2 = retString();         // *compile-time ERROR* (const *missing*)

## 19.3 Using String Views as Parameters

```
const std::string& s3 = retString();    // s3 extends lifetime of returned string
std::cout << s3 << '\n';                // OK

auto&& s4 = retString();                // s4 extends lifetime of returned string
std::cout << s4 << '\n';                // OK
```

For a string view this safety is not given. It *neither* copies *nor* extends the lifetime of a return value:

```
std::string_view sv = retString();  // sv does NOT extend lifetime of returned string
std::cout << sv << '\n';            // RUNTIME ERROR: returned string is destroyed
```

Here, the returned string is destroyed at the end of the first statement meaning that referring to it from the string view sv is a fatal runtime error resulting in undefined behavior.

The problem is the same as when calling:

```
const char* p = retString().c_str();
```

or:

```
auto p = retString().c_str();
```

Therefore, you should also be very careful when returning a string view:[1]

```
// very dangerous:
std::string_view substring(const std::string& s, std::size_t idx = 0);

// because:
auto sub = substring("very nice", 5);  // returns view to passed temporary string
                                        // but temporary string is destroyed after the call
std::cout << sub << '\n';               // RUNTIME ERROR: tmp string s is destroyed
```

### Do Not Return String Views to Strings

It is a particularly dangerous design to let getters of string members return a string view. Therefore, you should *not* implement the following:

```
class Person {
  std::string name;
 public:
  ...
  std::string_view getName() const {   // don't do this
      return name;
  }
};
```

This is because, again, as a result, the following would become a fatal runtime error causing undefined behavior:

---

[1] See https://groups.google.com/a/isocpp.org/forum/#!topic/std-discussion/Gj5gt5E-po8 for a discussion of this example.

```
Person createPerson();

auto n = createPerson().getName();    // OOPS: deletes temporary string
std::cout << "name: " << n << '\n';   // FATAL RUNTIME ERROR
```

Again, this would not be a problem if you had `getName()` return a string by value or by reference, because then `n` would become a copy of the returned string.

**Function Templates Should Use Return Type `auto`**

Note that it is easy to accidentally assign returned strings to string views. Consider, for example, the definition of two functions that by themselves look very useful:

```
// define + for string views returning string:
std::string operator+ (std::string_view sv1, std::string_view sv2) {
    return std::string(sv1) + std::string(sv2);
}

// generic concatenation:
template<typename T>
T concat (const T& x, const T& y) {
    return x + y;
}
```

However, using them together again might easily result in a fatal runtime error:

```
std::string_view hi = "hi";
auto xy = concat(hi, hi);            // xy is std::string_view
std::cout << xy << '\n';             // FATAL RUNTIME ERROR: referred string destroyed
```

Code like that can easily be accidentally written. The real problem here is the return type of `concat()`. If you declare that its return type should be deduced by the compiler, the example above initializes xy as `std::string`:

```
// improved generic concatenation:
template<typename T>
auto concat (const T& x, const T& y) {
    return x + y;
}
```

**Do Not Use String Views in Call Chains to Initialize Strings**

Also, it is counter-productive to use string views in a chain of calls, where a string is needed inside the chain or at the end of it. For example, if you define class `Person` with the following constructor:

```
class Person {
  std::string name;
  public:
    Person (std::string_view n)    // don't do this
```

## 19.3 Using String Views as Parameters

```
    : name{n} {
    }
    ...
};
```

Passing a string literal or string you still need is fine:

```
Person p1{"Jim"};          // no performance overhead
std::string s = "Joe";
Person p2{s};              // no performance overhead
```

However, moving in a string becomes unnecessarily expensive because the passed string is first implicitly converted to a string view, which is then used to create a new string that allocates memory again:

```
Person p3{std::move(s)};   // performance overhead: broken move
```

Do not deal with `std::string_view` here. Taking the parameter by value and moving it to the member is still the best solution (unless you want to implement a couple of overloads):

```
class Person {
  std::string name;
 public:
  Person (std::string n)
    : name{std::move(n)} {
  }
  ...
};
```

Thus, if we have to create/initialize a string, creating it as soon as possible allows us to benefit from all possible optimizations the moment we pass the argument. And when we have it, we only move, which is a cheap operation.

Thus, if we initialize the string with a helper function that returns a temporary string:

```
std::string newName()
{
    ...
    return std::string{...};
}

Person p{newName()};
```

the mandatory copy elision (see Chapter 5 on page 39) will defer the materialization of a new string until the value is passed to the constructor. There we have a string named n so that we have an object with a location (a *glvalue*). The value of this object is then moved to initialize the member `name`.

### Summary of Safe Use of String Views

To summarize, **use `std::string_view` with care**, meaning that you should adjust your programming style as follows:

- Do not use string views in APIs that pass the argument to a string.
  - Do not initialize string members from string view parameters.

- No string at the end of a string view chain.
- Do not return a string view.
  - Unless it is just a forwarded input argument or you signal the danger by, for example, naming the function accordingly.
- For this reason, **function templates** should never return the type T of a passed generic argument.
  - Return `auto` instead.
- Never use a returned value to initialize a string view.
- For this reason, **do not assign** the return value of a function template that return a generic type to `auto`.

  - This means the AAA (*Almost Always Auto*) pattern is broken with string view.

If these rules are too complicated or hard to follow, do not use `std::string_view` at all (unless you know what you are doing).

## 19.4 String View Types and Operations

This section describes the types and operations of string views in detail.

### 19.4.1 Concrete String View Types

In the header file `<string_view>`, the C++ standard library provides a couple of specializations of class `basic_string_view<>`:

- Class `std::string_view` is the predefined specialization of that template for characters of type `char`:

  ```
  namespace std {
      using string_view = basic_string_view<char>;
  }
  ```

- For strings that use wider character sets, such as Unicode or some Asian character sets, three other types are predefined:

  ```
  namespace std {
      using u16string_view = basic_string_view<char16_t>;
      using u32string_view = basic_string_view<char32_t>;
      using wstring_view   = basic_string_view<wchar_t>;
  }
  ```

In the following sections, no distinction is made between these types of string views. The use and the problems are the same because all string view classes have the same interface. Therefore, "string view" means any string view type: `string_view`, `u16string_view`, `u32string_view`, and `wstring_view`. The examples in this book usually use type `string_view` because the European and Anglo-American environments are the common environments for software development.

## 19.4.2 String View Operations

Table *19.1 String View Operations* lists all operations that are provided for string views.

| Operation | Effect |
|---|---|
| *constructors* | Creates or copies a string view |
| *destructor* | Destroys a string view |
| = | Assigns a new value |
| swap() | Swaps values between two strings views |
| ==, !=, <, <=, >, >=, compare() | Compares string views |
| empty() | Returns whether the string view is empty |
| size(), length() | Returns the number of characters |
| max_size() | Returns the maximum possible number of characters |
| [], at() | Accesses a character (read-only) |
| front(), back() | Accesses the first or last character (read-only) |
| << | Writes the value to a stream |
| copy() | Copies or writes the contents to a character array |
| data() | Returns the value as nullptr or constant character array (note: no terminating null character) |
| *find functions* | Searches for a certain substring or character |
| begin(), end() | Provides iterator support (const_iterator only) |
| cbegin(), cend() | Provides constant iterator support |
| rbegin(), rend() | Provides constant reverse iterator support |
| crbegin(), crend() | Provides constant reverse iterator support |
| substr() | Returns a certain substring |
| remove_prefix() | Removes leading characters |
| remove_suffix() | Removes trailing characters |
| hash<> | Function object type to compute hash values |

Table 19.1. String View Operations

With the exception of `remove_prefix()` and `remove_suffix()`, all operations of string views are also provided for `std::string`s. However, the guarantees might differ slightly because for string views, the value returned by `data()` might be `nullptr` or might not end with a null terminator.

### Construction

You can create a string view with the default constructor, as a copy, from a raw character array (null terminated or with specified length), from a `std::string`, or as a literal with the suffix `sv`. However, note the following:

- String views created with the default constructor have `nullptr` as `data()`. Thus, there is no valid call of `operator[]`.

```
std::string_view sv;
auto p = sv.data();       // yields nullptr
std::cout << sv[0];       // ERROR: no valid character
```

- When initializing a string view with a null terminated byte stream, the resulting size is the number of characters without '\0' and using the index of the terminating null character is not valid:
  ```
  std::string_view sv{"hello"};
  std::cout << sv;              // OK
  std::cout << sv.size();       // 5
  std::cout << sv.at(5);        // throws std::out_of_range exception
  std::cout << sv[5];           // undefined behavior
  std::cout << sv.data();       // OOPS: only works because \0' is behind sv
  ```
  You can also initialize a string view with the null terminator as part of its value by passing the number of characters including the null terminator:
  ```
  std::string_view sv{"hello", 6};  // NOTE: 6 to include '\0'
  std::cout << sv.size();       // 6
  std::cout << sv.at(5);        // OK, prints the value of '\0'
  std::cout << sv[5];           // OK, prints the value of '\0'
  std::cout << sv.data();       // OK
  ```

- To create a string view from a string, an implicit conversion operator is provided in class `std::string`. Again, having the null terminator right after the last character, which is usually guaranteed for a string, is not guaranteed to exist for the string view:
  ```
  std::string s = "hello";
  std::cout << s.size();        // 5
  std::cout << s.at(5);         // throws std::out_of_range
  std::cout << s[5];            // OK, prints the value of '\0'
  std::cout << s.data();        // OK

  std::string_view sv{s};
  std::cout << sv.size();       // 5
  std::cout << sv.at(5);        // throws std::out_of_range exception
  std::cout << sv[5];           // undefined behavior
  std::cout << sv.data();       // OOPS: only works because \0' is behind sv
  ```

- Because the literal operator is defined for the suffix `sv`, you can also create a string view as follows:
  ```
  using namespace std::literals;
  auto s = "hello"sv;
  ```

Note that `std::char_traits` members were changed to be `constexpr` so that you can initialize a string view from a string literal at compile time:
```
constexpr string_view hello = "Hello World!";
```

## Null Termination

The different ways to create a string view demonstrate a remarkable aspect of string views that is important to understand: in general, the values of string views are not null terminated and can even be `nullptr`. Therefore, you should **always** check the `size()` before accessing the characters of a string view (unless you know specific things about the value).

## 19.4 String View Types and Operations

However, you *can* have two special scenarios, which can both be considered confusing:

1. You can ensure that the value of the string view is null terminated, although the null terminator is not part of the value. This is what you get when you initialize a string view from a string literal:

    ```
    std::string_view sv1{"hello"};      // '\0' is right behind the value of sv1
    ```

    Here, the state of the string view might be confusing in that it is well-defined so that it can be used as a null terminated character sequence. However, it is only well-defined because we know that the characters in the string view are followed by a null terminator which is not part of their value.

2. You can ensure that '\0' is part of the string view. For example:

    ```
    std::string_view sv2{"hello", 6};   // NOTE: 6 to make '\0' part of the value
    ```

    Here, the state of the string view might be confusing in that printing it looks like it has five characters but it states that it has six characters (the null terminator being part of the value makes it more of a binary string (view)).

The question is whether taking advantage of one of these two scenarios is good style. I tend to recommend avoiding both scenarios, but so far, C++ lacks a better alternative. It seems that we still need a string view type that guarantees that the value is null terminated (as `std::string` does) without creating its own copies of the characters. And without a better alternative, string views might be used that way. In fact, we already see proposals of functions for the C++ standard that use the return type `string_view` when returning null terminated strings (see https://wg21.link/P0555r0 for an example).

### Hashing

The C++ standard library guarantees that hash values for strings and strings views are equal.

### Modifying a String View

There are only a few operations provided for modifying a string view:

- You can assign a new value or swap the values of two string views:

    ```
    std::string_view sv1 = "hey";
    std::string_view sv2 = "world";
    sv1.swap(sv2);
    sv2 = sv1;
    ```

- You can skip leading or trailing characters (i.e., move the beginning to a character behind the first character or move the end to a character before the last character).

    ```
    std::string_view sv = "I like my kindergarten";
    sv.remove_prefix(2);
    sv.remove_suffix(8);
    std::cout << sv;    // prints: like my kind
    ```

Note that there is no support for `operator+`. Thus:

```
std::string_view sv1 = "hello";
std::string_view sv2 = "world";
auto s1 = sv1 + sv2;                                // ERROR
```

All of the operands have to be a string:
```
auto s2 = std::string(sv1) + std::string(sv2);   // OK
```
Note that there is no implicit conversion to a string because this is an expensive operation since it might allocate memory. Therefore, only the explicit conversion is possible.[2]

### 19.4.3 String View Support by Other Types

In principle, a string view could be passed wherever a string value is passed, provided the receiver only reads the value and does not need it to be null terminated (e.g., by passing the value to a C function).

However, so far, the C++ standard has only added support for the most important places:

- Strings can use or be combined with string views wherever useful:
  - You can create a string from a string view (the constructor is explicit). If the string view has no value (`data()` is `nullptr`), the string is initialized as an empty string.
  - You can now also pass a string view, where you can assign, append, insert, replace, compare, or find a string value.
  - There is also an implicit conversion from a string to a string view.
- You can pass a string view to `std::quoted`, which prints its value quoted. For example:
  ```
  using namespace std::literals;

  auto s = R"(some\value)"sv;          // raw string view
  std::cout << std::quoted(s);         // output: "some\\value"
  ```
- You can initialize, extend or compare filesystem paths (see Section 20.2.3 on page 211) with string views.

Other string view support, such as for the regex component of the C++ standard library, is still missing.

## 19.5 Using String Views in APIs

String views are cheap and each `std::string` can be used as a string view. Therefore, it looks like `std::string_view` is the better type for dealing with string parameters. Well, details matter...

First, using a `std::string_view` only makes sense if the function using the parameter has the following constraints:

- It does not expect a null terminator at the end. This is not the case when passing the parameter to a C function as a single `const char*` without its size.
- It respects the lifetime of the passed argument. Usually, this means that the receiving function uses the passed value only until it ends.
- The calling function should not deal with the owner of the underlying characters (such as deleting it, changing its value, or freeing its memory).
- It can deal with the `nullptr` as value.

---

[2] In principle, we could standardize an operation to concatenate string views yielding a new string, but so far this is not provided.

Note that overloading functions for both `std::string` and `std::string_view` might cause ambiguity errors:

```
void foo(const std::string&);
void foo(std::string_view);

foo("hello");   // ERROR: ambiguous
```

Finally, remember the caveats mentioned before (see Section 19.3.1 on page 188):
- Do not assign temporary string views to strings.
- Do not return string views.
- Do not use string views in call chains to initialize/set strings.

With this taken into account, let us go through some examples where using string views is an improvement.

### 19.5.1 Using String Views instead of Strings

Consider the following code:

```
// print time point with prefix:
void print (const std::string& prefix,
            const std::chrono::system_clock::time_point& tp)
{
  // convert to calendar time:
  auto rawtime{std::chrono::system_clock::to_time_t(tp)};
  std::string ts{std::ctime(&rawtime)};   // NOTE: not thread safe

  ts.resize(ts.size()-1);   // skip trailing newline

  std::cout << prefix << ts;
}
```

This could easily be replaced by the following:

```
void print (std::string_view prefix,
            const std::chrono::system_clock::time_point& tp)
{
  auto rawtime{std::chrono::system_clock::to_time_t(tp)};
  std::string_view ts{std::ctime(&rawtime)};   // NOTE: not thread safe

  ts.remove_suffix(1);   // skip trailing newline

  std::cout << prefix << ts;
}
```

The first and easy fix is to pass the read-only string `prefix` as a string view as long as we do not use operations that fail if there is no value or no null terminator. In this case, we print the value of the string view and this is fine. If the string view has no value (`data()` is `nullptr`), no characters are written. Note that the string view is taken by value, because copying a string view is cheap.

We can also use a string view here internally for the value returned by `ctime()`. However, we have to be careful to ensure that the value still exists as long as we use it in the string view. Thus, the value is only valid until the next call of `ctime()` or `asctime()`). Therefore, in multithreaded code, this function is a problem (which is also the case when using strings).

If the function returns the string concatenated from the prefix and the time point, the code could look as follows:

```
// convert time point with prefix to string:
std::string toString (std::string_view prefix,
                     const std::chrono::system_clock::time_point& tp)
{
  auto rawtime{std::chrono::system_clock::to_time_t(tp)};
  std::string_view ts{std::ctime(&rawtime)};   // NOTE: not thread safe

  ts.remove_suffix(1);        // skip trailing newline

  return std::string{prefix} + ts;  // unfortunately no operator + yet
}
```

Note that we cannot concatenate both string views by simply calling `operator+`. Instead, we have to convert one of the operands into a `std::string` (which unfortunately might unnecessarily allocate additional memory). If the string view has no value (`data()` is `nullptr`), the string is empty.

Another example application of string views is demonstrated when using parallel algorithms to sort according to substrings (see Section 22.1.2 on page 264): using substrings of string views:

```
sort(coll.begin(), coll.end(),
     [] (const auto& a, const auto& b) {
       return std::string_view{a}.substr(2) < std::string_view{b}.substr(2);
     });
```

is much faster than using substrings of strings:

```
sort(std::execution::par,
     coll.begin(), coll.end(),
     [] (const auto& a, const auto& b) {
       return a.substr(2) < b.substr(2);
     });
```

This is because for strings, a substring is a new string that allocates its own memory.

## 19.6  Afternotes

The first string class with reference semantics was proposed by Jeffrey Yasskin in https://wg21.link/n3334 (using the name `string_ref`). This class was adopted as part of the Library Fundamentals TS as proposed by Jeffrey Yasskin in https://wg21.link/n3921.

The class was adopted with other components for C++17 as proposed by Beman Dawes and Alisdair Meredith in https://wg21.link/p0220r1. Some modifications for better integration were added by

## 19.6 Afternotes

Marshall Clow in `https://wg21.link/p0254r2` and in `https://wg21.link/p0403r1` and by Nicolai Josuttis in `https://wg21.link/p0392r0`.

`constexpr` support was added as proposed by Antony Polukhin in `https://wg21.link/p0426r1`.

Additional fixes by Daniel Krügler are contained in `https://wg21.link/lwg2946` (which were accepted with C++20 as a defect against C++17).

# Chapter 20
# The Filesystem Library

With C++17, the Boost.Filesystem library was finally adopted as a C++ standard library. As part of this process, doing this, the library was adjusted to new language features, made more consistent with other parts of the library, cleaned up, and extended to provide some missing pieces (such as operations to compute a relative path between filesystem paths).

## 20.1 Basic Examples

Let us start with some basic examples.

### 20.1.1 Print Attributes of a Passed Filesystem Path

The following program allows us to use a passed string as a filesystem path to print some aspects of the path according to its file type:

*filesystem/checkpath1.cpp*

```
#include <iostream>
#include <filesystem>
#include <cstdlib>      // for EXIT_FAILURE

int main(int argc, char* argv[])
{
  if (argc < 2) {
    std::cout << "Usage: " << argv[0] << " <path> \n";
    return EXIT_FAILURE;
  }

  std::filesystem::path p{argv[1]};    // p represents a filesystem path (might not exist)
  if (is_regular_file(p)) {            // is path p a regular file?
    std::cout << p << " exists with " << file_size(p) << " bytes\n";
```

```
  }
  else if (is_directory(p)) {         // is path p a directory?
    std::cout << p << " is a directory containing:\n";
    for (const auto& e : std::filesystem::directory_iterator{p}) {
      std::cout << "    " << e.path() << '\n';
    }
  }
  else if (exists(p)) {               // does path p actually exist?
    std::cout << p << " is a special file\n";
  }
  else {
    std::cout << "path " << p << " does not exist\n";
  }
}
```

We first convert the passed command-line argument into a filesystem path:

```
std::filesystem::path p{argv[1]};   // p represents a filesystem path (might not exist)
```

Then, we perform the following checks:

- If the path represents an existing regular file, we print its size:

    ```
    if (is_regular_file(p)) {    // is path p a regular file?
      std::cout << p << " exists with " << file_size(p) << " bytes\n";
    }
    ```

    Calling this program as follows:

    ```
    checkpath checkpath.cpp
    ```

    will output something like:

    ```
    "checkpath.cpp" exists with 907 bytes
    ```

    Note that the output operator for paths automatically writes the path name quoted (within double quotes and backslashes are escaped by another backslash, which is an issue for Windows paths (see Section 20.1.1 on page 203)).

- If the filesystem path exists as a directory, we iterate over the files in the directory and print the paths:

    ```
    if (is_directory(p)) {       // is path p a directory?
      std::cout << p << " is a directory containing:\n";
      for (auto& e : std::filesystem::directory_iterator(p)) {
        std::cout << "    " << e.path() << '\n';
      }
    }
    ```

    Here, we use a `directory_iterator`, which provides `begin()` and `end()` in a way that allows us to iterate over `directory_entry` elements using a range-based for loop. In this case, we use the `directory_entry` member function `path()`, which yields the filesystem path of the entry.

    Calling this program as follows:

    ```
    checkpath .
    ```

## 20.1 Basic Examples

will output something like:

```
"." is a directory containing:
  "./checkpath.cpp"
  "./checkpath.exe"
  ...
```

- Finally, we check whether the passed filesystem path exists at all:

  ```
  if (exists(p)) {          // does path p actually exist?
    ...
  }
  ```

Note that due to *argument dependent lookup (ADL)*, you do not have to qualify the calls of `is_regular_file()`, `file_size()`, `is_directory()`, and `exists()`. The functions belong to namespace `std::filesystem` but are automatically looked up there because they take an argument that has a type of this namespace.

**Path Handling under Windows**

The fact that by default, paths are written quoted is an issue under Windows because the usual directory separator backslash is then always escaped and written twice. Thus, calling this program under Windows as follows:

```
checkpath C:\
```

will output something like:

```
"C:\\" is a directory containing:
  ...
  "C:\\Users"
  "C:\\Windows"
```

Writing paths quoted ensures that written file names can be read back into a program restoring the original file names. However, for standard output, this is usually not acceptable.

Therefore, a portable version also that also runs well under Windows should avoid writing paths quoted to standard output by using the member function `string()`:

*filesystem/checkpath2.cpp*

```
#include <iostream>
#include <filesystem>
#include <cstdlib>      // for EXIT_FAILURE

int main(int argc, char* argv[])
{
  if (argc < 2) {
    std::cout << "Usage: " << argv[0] << " <path> \n";
    return EXIT_FAILURE;
  }
```

```
  std::filesystem::path p{argv[1]};   // p represents a filesystem path (might not exist)
  if (is_regular_file(p)) {           // is path p a regular file?
    std::cout << '"' << p.string() << "\" exists with "
              << file_size(p) << " bytes\n";
  }
  else if (is_directory(p)) {         // is path p a directory?
    std::cout << '"' << p.string() << "\" is a directory containing:\n";
    for (const auto& e : std::filesystem::directory_iterator{p}) {
      std::cout << "  \"" << e.path().string() << "\"\n";
    }
  }
  else if (exists(p)) {               // does path p actually exist?
    std::cout << '"' << p.string() << "\" is a special file\n";
  }
  else {
    std::cout << "path \"" << p.string() << "\" does not exist\n";
  }
}
```

Now, calling this program under Windows as follows:

```
checkpath C:\
```

will output something like:

```
"C:\" is a directory containing:
  ...
  "C:\Users"
  "C:\Windows"
```

Other conversions (see Section 20.3.4 on page 224) are provided to use the generic string format or convert the string to the native encoding.

## 20.1.2  Switch Over Filesystem Types

We can still modify and improve the previous program as follows:

*filesystem/checkpath3.cpp*

```
#include <iostream>
#include <filesystem>
#include <cstdlib>      // for EXIT_FAILURE

int main(int argc, char* argv[])
{
  if (argc < 2) {
    std::cout << "Usage: " << argv[0] << " <path> \n";
    return EXIT_FAILURE;
```

```
    }

    namespace fs = std::filesystem;

    switch (fs::path p{argv[1]}; status(p).type()) {
      case fs::file_type::not_found:
        std::cout << "path \"" << p.string() << "\" does not exist\n";
        break;
      case fs::file_type::regular:
        std::cout << '"' << p.string() << "\" exists with "
                  << file_size(p) << " bytes\n";
        break;
      case fs::file_type::directory:
        std::cout << '"' << p.string() << "\" is a directory containing:\n";
        for (const auto& e : std::filesystem::directory_iterator{p}) {
          std::cout << "    " << e.path().string() << '\n';
        }
        break;
      default:
        std::cout << '"' << p.string() << "\" is a special file\n";
        break;
    }
}
```

**Namespace `fs`**

First, we do something very common: we define `fs` as a shortcut for namespace `std::filesystem`:

```
namespace fs = std::filesystem;
```

Using this namespace we initialize, for example, the path p in the `switch` statement:

```
fs::path p{argv[1]};
```

The `switch` statement is an application of the new `switch` with initialization (see Section 2.2 on page 23), where we initialize the path and provide different cases for its type:

```
switch (fs::path p{argv[1]}; status(p).type()) {
    ...
}
```

The expression `status(p).type()` creates a `file_status` for which `type()` creates a `file_type`. This way we can handle the different types directly instead of following a chain of calls like `is_regular_file()`, `is_directory()`, and so on. The type is intentionally provided in multiple steps (calling `status()` and then `type()`) so that we do not have to pay the price of operating system calls if we are not interested in all information.

Note also that an implementation-specific `file_type` might exist. For example, Windows provides the special file type `junction` (see Section 20.2.7 on page 216). However, using it is not portable.

## 20.1.3 Create Different Types of Files

After having only read-access to the filesystem, let us now give a first example of modifying it. The following program creates different kinds of files in the subdirectory `tmp`:

*filesystem/createfiles.cpp*

```cpp
#include <iostream>
#include <fstream>
#include <filesystem>
#include <cstdlib>      // for std::exit() and EXIT_FAILURE

int main ()
{
  namespace fs = std::filesystem;
  try {
    // create directories tmp/test/ (if they don't exist yet):
    fs::path testDir{"tmp/test"};
    create_directories(testDir);

    // create data file tmp/test/data.txt:
    auto testFile = testDir / "data.txt";
    std::ofstream dataFile{testFile};
    if (!dataFile) {
      std::cerr << "OOPS, can't open \"" << testFile.string() << "\"\n";
      std::exit(EXIT_FAILURE);   // exit program with failure
    }
    dataFile << "The answer is 42\n";

    // create symbolic link from tmp/slink/ to tmp/test/:
    create_directory_symlink("test", testDir.parent_path() / "slink");
  }
  catch (const fs::filesystem_error& e) {
    std::cerr << "EXCEPTION: " << e.what() << '\n';
    std::cerr << "      path1: \"" << e.path1().string() << "\"\n";
  }

  // recursively list all files (also following symlinks)
  std::cout << fs::current_path().string() << ":\n";
  auto iterOpts{fs::directory_options::follow_directory_symlink};
  for (const auto& e : fs::recursive_directory_iterator(".", iterOpts)) {
    std::cout << "  " << e.path().lexically_normal().string() << '\n';
  }
}
```

Let us also go through this program step by step.

## 20.1 Basic Examples

### Namespace `fs`

First, again, we define `fs` as the usual shortcut for namespace `std::filesystem`:

```
namespace fs = std::filesystem;
```

Using this namespace we initialize the paths for a basic subdirectory for temporary files:

```
fs::path testDir{"tmp/test"};
```

### Creating Directories

We then try to create the subdirectory:

```
create_directories(testDir);
```

By using `create_directories()`, we create all missing directories of the whole passed path (there is also `create_directory()` to create a directory only inside an existing directory).

It is not an error to perform this call if the directory already exists. However, any other problem is an error and raises a corresponding exception.

If `testDir` already exists, `create_directories()` returns `false`. Thus, you could also call:

```
if (!create_directories(testDir)) {
  std::cout << "\"" << testDir.string() << "\" already exists\n";
}
```

### Creating Regular Files

Then we create a new file `/tmp/test/data.txt` with some contents:

```
auto testFile = testDir / "data.txt";
std::ofstream dataFile{testFile};
if (!dataFile) {
  std::cerr << "OOPS, can't open \"" << testFile.string() << "\"\n";
  std::exit(EXIT_FAILURE);   // exit program with failure
}
dataFile << "The answer is 42\n";
```

Here, we use operator `/` to extend a path, which we then pass as an argument to the constructor of a file stream. As you can see, the creation of a regular file can still only be done with the existing I/O streams library. However, a new overload for the constructors is provided to allow us to directly pass a filesystem path (this also applies to functions such as `open()`).

Note that you should still always check whether the creation/opening of the file was successful. A lot of things can go wrong here (see below (see Section 20.1.3 on page 209)).

### Creating Symbolic Links

The next statement tries to create a symbolic link `tmp/slink` that refers to directory `tmp/test`:

```
create_directory_symlink("test", testDir.parent_path() / "slink");
```

Note that the first argument defines the path from the view of the link created. Thus, you have to pass "test" instead of "tmp/test" to effectively link from tmp/slink to tmp/test. If you called:

```
std::filesystem::create_directory_symlink("tmp/test", "tmp/slink");
```

you would effectively create tmp/slink as a symbolic link to tmp/tmp/test.

Note that often, calling create_symlink() instead of create_directory_symlink() also works. However, some operating systems have special handling for symbolic links to directories or perform better when they know that a file is a directory, which means that you should use create_directory_symlink() if you know that the symbolic link refers to a directory.

Finally, note that this call might fail on Windows systems and cause error handling (see Section 20.1.3 on page 210), because you might need administrator rights to create a symbolic link there.

**Recursive Directory Iteration**

Finally, we recursively list our current directory:

```
auto iterOpts = fs::directory_options::follow_directory_symlink;
for (auto& e : fs::recursive_directory_iterator(".", iterOpts)) {
  std::cout << "    " << e.path().lexically_normal().string() << '\n';
}
```

Note that we use a recursive directory iterator and pass the option follow_directory_symlink to also follow symbolic links. Therefore, we should get an output like the following on POSIX-based systems:

```
/home/nico:
    ...
    tmp
    tmp/slink
    tmp/slink/data.txt
    tmp/test
    tmp/test/data.txt
    ...
```

and an output like the following on Windows systems:

```
C:\Users\nico:
    ...
    tmp
    tmp\slink
    tmp\slink\data.txt
    tmp\test
    tmp\test\data.txt
    ...
```

Note that we use lexically_normal() when we print the path of all directory entries. If we skip that, the path of the directory entries would contain a prefix with the directory the iterator was initialized with. Thus, printing just the paths inside the loop:

```
auto iterOpts = fs::directory_options::follow_directory_symlink;
```

## 20.1 Basic Examples

```
for (auto& e : fs::recursive_directory_iterator(".", iterOpts)) {
    std::cout << "    " << e.path() << '\n';
}
```

would output the following on POSIX-based systems:

```
all files:
  ...
  "./testdir"
  "./testdir/data.txt"
  "./tmp"
  "./tmp/test"
  "./tmp/test/data.txt"
```

And on Windows, the output would be:

```
all files:
  ...
  ".\\testdir"
  ".\\testdir\\data.txt"
  ".\\tmp"
  ".\\tmp\\test"
  ".\\tmp\\test\\data.txt"
```

Thus, by calling `lexically_normal()` we yield the normalized path, which removes the leading dot for the current directory. Furthermore, as written before (see Section 20.1.1 on page 203), by calling `string()` we avoid each path being written quoted, which would be OK for POSIX-based systems (just having the name in double quotes), but would look very surprising on Windows systems (because each backslash is escaped by another backslash).

**Error Handling**

Filesystems are a source of trouble. You might not be able to perform operations due to using invalid characters for file names, not having necessary permissions, or other processes might modify the filesystem while you are dealing with it. Thus, depending on the platform and permissions, a couple of things can go wrong in this program.

For those cases not covered by return values (such as the case where the directory already exists), we catch the corresponding exception and print the general message and the first path in it:

```
try {
    ...
}
catch (const fs::filesystem_error& e) {
    std::cerr << "EXCEPTION: " << e.what() << '\n';
    std::cerr << "    path1: \"" << e.path1().string() << "\"\n";
}
```

For example, if we cannot create the directory, a message such as the following might be printed:

```
EXCEPTION: filesystem error: cannot create directory: [tmp/test]
    path1: "tmp/test"
```

If we cannot create the symbolic link because, for example, it already exists or we need special rights, you get something like the following message:

```
EXCEPTION: create_directory_symlink: Can't create a file when it already
                                    exists: "tmp\test\data.txt", "testdir"
    path1: "tmp\test\data.txt"
```

or:

```
EXCEPTION: create_directory_symlink: A required privilege is not held by
                                    the client.: "test", "tmp\slink"
    path1: "test"
```

In any case, note that the situation in a multi-user/multi-process operating system can change at any time, which means that your created directory might even be removed, renamed, or replaced by a regular file after you create it. Therefore, it is simply not possible to ensure the validity of a future request by finding out the current situation. For this reason, is the best approach it usually to try to do what you want (i.e., create a directory, open a file) and process exceptions and errors or validate the expected behavior/outcome.

However, sometimes the attempt to do something with the filesystem might work but not the way you had in mind. For example, if you want to create a file in a specific directory and a symbolic link to another directory already exists, the file is created or overwritten at an unexpected location. This might be OK (the user might have a good reason to create a symbolic link where a directory was expected), but if you want to detect that situation, you have to check for the existence of a file (see Section 20.4.1 on page 231) (which is a bit more complicated than you might think at first) before you create something.

Once again: there is no guarantee that results of filesystem checks are still valid when you process them.

## 20.1.4 Dealing with Filesystems Using Parallel Algorithms

See dirsize.cpp (see Section 22.6.1 on page 276) for another example using parallel algorithms to accumulate the size of all regular files in a directory tree.

## 20.2 Principles and Terminology

Before discussing the details of the filesystem library, we have to introduce a couple of design principles and some terminology. This is necessary because the standard covers different operating systems and maps them to a common API.

### 20.2.1 General Portability Disclaimer

The C++ Standard does not merely standardize what all possible operating systems have in common for their file systems; in many cases, the C++ Standard follows POSIX standards and requests that implementations follow POSIX as closely as possible. As long as it is reasonable, the behavior should still be there, but with

## 20.2 Principles and Terminology

some limitations. If no reasonable behavior is possible, an implementation shall report an error. Possible examples for such errors are:

- Particular characters are not valid to be used as file names
- File system elements that are not supported are created (e.g., symbolic links)

The differences between specific file systems may still be relevant:

- Case sensitivity:
  "hello.txt" and "Hello.txt" and "hello.TXT" might refer to the same (Windows) or three different files (POSIX-based).
- Absolute versus relative paths:
  On some systems, "/bin" is an absolute path (POSIX-based), while on others it is not (Windows).

### 20.2.2 Namespace

The filesystem library has its own sub-namespace filesystem inside std. It is a pretty common convention to introduce the shortcut fs for it:

```
namespace fs = std::filesystem;
```

This allows us to use fs::current_path() instead of std::filesystem::current_path().

Further code examples in this chapter will often use fs as the corresponding shortcut.

Note that you should always qualify the namespace of filesystem calls explicitly, although using *argument dependent lookup* (ADL) usually works. Not qualifying filesystem calls might sometimes result in unintended behavior (see Section 20.2.5 on page 214).

### 20.2.3 Paths

The key element of the filesystem library is a path. It is a name that represents the (potential) location of a file within a filesystem. It consists of an optional root name, an optional root directory, and a sequence of file names separated by directory separators. The path can be relative (so that the file location depends on the current working directory) or absolute.

Different formats are possible:

- A generic format, which is portable
- A native format, which is specific to the underlying file system

On POSIX-based operating systems there is no difference between the generic and the native format. On Windows, the generic format /tmp/test.txt is a valid native format in addition to \tmp\test.txt, which is also supported (thus, /tmp/test.txt and \tmp\test.txt are two native versions of the same path). On OpenVMS, the corresponding native format might be [tmp]test.txt.

Special file names exist:

- "." represents the current directory
- ".." represents the parent directory

The generic path format is as follows:

   [*rootname*] [*rootdir*] [*relativepath*]

where:

- The optional root name is implementation-specific (e.g., it can be `//host` on POSIX systems and `C:` on Windows systems)
- The optional root directory is a directory separator
- The relative path is a sequence of file names separated by directory separators

By definition, a directory separator consists of one or multiple '/' or implementation-specific preferred directory separators.

Examples of portable generic paths are:

`//host1/bin/hello.txt`

`.`

`tmp/`

`/a/b//../c`

Note that the last path refers to the same location as `/a/c` and is absolute on POSIX systems but relative on Windows systems (because the drive/partition is missing).

On the other hand, a path such as `C:/bin` is an absolute path on Windows systems (the root directory `"bin"` on the `"C"` drive/partition), but a relative path on POSIX (the subdirectory `"bin"` in the directory `"C:"`).

On Windows systems, the backslash is the implementation-specific directory separator so that the paths above can *also* be written by using the backslash as the preferred directory separator:

`\\host1\bin\hello.txt`

`.`

`tmp\`

`\a\b\..\c`

The filesystem library provides functions for converting paths between the native and generic format (see Section 20.3.4 on page 224).

A `path` might be empty. This means that there is no path defined. This is *not* necessarily the same as `"."`. What it means depends on the context.

## 20.2.4 Normalization

A path might be or can become normalized. In a normalized path:
- File names are separated only by a single preferred directory separator.
- The file name `"."` is not used unless the whole path is nothing but `"."` (representing the current directory).
- The file name does not contain `".."` file names (we do not go down and then up again) unless they are at the beginning of a relative path.
- The path only ends with a directory separator if the trailing file name is a directory with a name other than `"."` or `".."`.

Note that normalization still means that a file name ending with a directory separator is different from a file name that does not end with a separator. This is because on some operating systems, the behavior differs when it is known that the path is a directory (e.g., with a trailing separator symbolic links might be resolved).

## 20.2 Principles and Terminology

Table *20.1 Effect of Path Normalization* lists some examples for normalization on POSIX and Windows systems. Note again that on POSIX systems, `C:bar` and `C:` are just file names with a colon as part of their name and have no special meaning to specify a partition, unlike Windows.

| Path | POSIX normalized | Windows normalized |
|---|---|---|
| `foo/.///bar/../` | `foo/` | `foo\` |
| `//host/../foo.txt` | `//host/foo.txt` | `\\host\foo.txt` |
| `./f/../.f/` | `.f/` | `.f\` |
| `C:bar/../` | `.` | `C:` |
| `C:/bar/..` | `C:/` | `C:\` |
| `C:\bar\..` | `C:\bar\..` | `C:\` |
| `/./../data.txt` | `/data.txt` | `\data.txt` |
| `./././` | `.` | `.` |

Table 20.1. Effect of Path Normalization

Note that the path `C:\bar\..` remains the same when normalized on a POSIX-based system. The reason is that the backslash is not a directory separator so that the whole path is just *one* file name having with colon, two backslashes, and two dots as part of its name.

The filesystem library provides functions for both lexical normalization (see Section 20.3.3 on page 221) (not taking the filesystem into account) and filesystem-dependent normalization (see Section 20.4.5 on page 241).

### 20.2.5 Member Function versus Free-Standing Functions

The filesystem library provides several functions, which can be both member and free-standing functions. The general approach is:

- **Member functions** are **cheap**. This is because they are pure lexical operations that do not take the actual filesystem into account, meaning that no operating systems calls are necessary.
  For example:
  `mypath.is_absolute()`    *// check whether path is absolute or relative*

- **Free-standing functions** are **expensive** because they usually take the actual filesystem into account, meaning that operating systems calls are necessary.
  For example:
  `equivalent(path1, path2);`    *// true if both paths refer to the same file*

Sometimes, the filesystem library even provides the same functionality operating both lexically and by taking the actual filesystem into account:

```
std::filesystem::path fromP, toP;
...
toP.lexically_relative(fromP);   // yield lexical path from fromP to toP
relative(toP, fromP);            // yield actual path from fromP to toP
```

Due to *argument dependent lookup* (ADL), in many situations you do not have to specify the full namespace `std::filesystem` when calling free-standing filesystem functions and an argument has a filesystem-specific type. You only have to qualify the call when implicit conversions from other types are used. For example:

```
create_directory(std::filesystem::path{"tmpdir"});   // OK
remove(std::filesystem::path{"tmpdir"});             // OK
std::filesystem::create_directory("tmpdir");         // OK
std::filesystem::remove("tmpdir");                   // OK
create_directory("tmpdir");                          // ERROR
```

The last call will fail to compile because we do not pass an argument of the filesystem namespace meaning that the symbol `create_directory` is not looked up in that namespace.

However, there is a famous trap:

```
remove("tmpdir");        // OOPS: calls C function remove()
```

Depending on the header file you include (indirectly), this call might compile finding the C function `remove()`, which behaves slightly differently: it might also remove the specified file but might not remove empty directories.

Therefore, the strong recommendation is to explicitly qualify all free-standing filesystem calls. For example:

```
namespace fs = std::filesystem;
...
fs::remove("tmpdir");    // OK: calls C++ filesystem function remove()
```

## 20.2.6  Error Handling

As discussed with the second example (see Section 20.1.3 on page 209), filesystems are a source of errors. You have to take into account that necessary files might not exist, file operations might not be allowed, or operations might violate resource limits. In addition, while a program is running other processes might create, modify, or remove files meaning that advance checks are no guarantee for no errors.

The problem is that in principle, you cannot ensure ahead of time that the next filesystem operation will succeed. Any result of a check might no longer be valid when you process it. Therefore, the best approach is usually to perform one or more filesystem operations and deal with resulting exceptions or errors.

Note also that when reading/writing with regular files, by default, the I/O streams library does not throw on errors. It converts any operation into a no-op instead. Therefore, the recommendation is to at least check whether files could successfully be opened.

Because dealing with exceptions is not always appropriate (such as when you want to react directly to a failed filesystem call), the filesystem library uses a mixed approach when dealing with the filesystem:

- By default, filesystem errors are handled as exceptions.
- However, you can handle specific errors locally if you have or want to.

Therefore, filesystem operations usually have two overloads for each operation:

1. By default (without an additional error handling argument), the operations throw a `filesystem_error` exceptions on errors.
2. By passing an additional out parameter, you can get an error code on error instead.

## 20.2 Principles and Terminology

Note that in the latter case, you might still have special return values, signaling a specific error that is not handled as an exception.

**Using `filesystem_error` Exceptions**

For example, you can try to create a directory as follows:

```
if (!create_directory(p)) {           // exception on error (unless path exists)
  std::cout << p << " already exists\n";   // path exists
}
```

Here, no error code argument is passed which means that errors usually raise an exception. However, note that the special case where the directory already exists is handled by returning `false`. Thus, an exception is raised due to other problems such as missing rights to create the directory, an invalid path p, or a violation of filesystem resources (such as exceeding path length limits).

Code like this should be enclosed directly or indirectly in a `try-catch` clause, which handles an exception of type `std::filesystem::filesystem_error`:

```
try {
  ...
  if (!create_directory(p)) {           // exception on error (unless path exists)
    std::cout << p << " already exists\n";   // path exists
  }
  ...
}
catch (const std::filesystem::filesystem_error& e) {   // derived from std::exception
  std::cout << "EXCEPTION: " << e.what() << '\n';
  std::cout << "    path: " << e.path1() << '\n';
}
```

As you can see, filesystem exceptions provide the usual standard exception API to yield an implementation-specific error message with `what()`. However, the API also provides `path1()` to call if a path is involved and even `path2()` if a second path is involved.

**Using `error_code` Arguments**

The other way to call the function to create a directory is as follows:

```
std::error_code ec;
create_directory(p, ec);              // set error code on error
if (ec) {                             // if error code set (due to error)
  std::cout << "ERROR: " << ec.message() << "\n";
}
```

Afterwards, we can also check against specific error codes:

```
if (ec == std::errc::read_only_file_system) {    // if specific error code set
  std::cout << "ERROR: " << p << " is read-only\n";
}
```

Note that in this case, we still can check the return value of `create_directory()`:

```
std::error_code ec;
if (!create_directory(p, ec)) {                      // set error code on error
  std::cout << "can't create directory " << p << "\n"; // any error occurred
  std::cout << "error: " << ec.message() << "\n";
}
```

However, not all filesystem operations provide this ability (because they return some value in the normal case).

Type `error_code` was introduced with C++11, including a list of portable error conditions such as `std::errc::read_only_filesystem`. On POSIX-based systems these map to `errno` values.

## 20.2.7 File Types

Different operating systems support different file types. The standard filesystem library takes this into account. In principle, there is an enumeration type `file_type`, which is standardized to have the following values:

```
namespace std::filesystem {
  enum class file_type {
    regular, directory, symlink,
    block, character, fifo, socket,
    ...
    none, not_found, unknown,
  };
}
```

Table 20.2 `file_type` *Values* lists the meaning of these values.

| Value | Meaning |
|---|---|
| regular | Regular file |
| directory | Directory file |
| symlink | Symbolic link file |
| block | Block-special file |
| character | Character-special file |
| fifo | FIFO or pipe file |
| socket | Socket file |
| ... | Additional implementation-defined file type |
| none | The type of the file is not known (yet) |
| unknown | The file exists but the type could not be determined |
| not_found | Pseudo-type indicating the file was not found |

*Table 20.2. File Type Values*

Platforms might provide additional file type values. However, using them is not portable. For example, Windows provides the file type value `junction`, which is used for *NTFS junctions* (also called *soft links*) of the NTFS file system. These are used as links to directories located on different local volumes on the same computer.

In addition to regular files and directories, the most common other type is a symbolic link, which is a type for files that refer to another filesystem location. There might be a file at that location or there might not. Note that some operating systems and/or file systems (e.g., the FAT file system) do not support symbolic links at all. Some operating systems support them only for regular files. Note that on Windows, you need special permissions to create symbolic links, which you can do with the `mklink` command.

Character-special files, block-special files, FIFOs, and sockets come from the UNIX filesystem. Currently, all four types are not used with Visual C++.[1]

As you can see, special values exist for cases where the file does not exist or its file type is not known or detectable.

In the remainder of this chapter I use two general categories to represent a couple of file types:
- *Other files*: Files with any file type other than regular file, directory, and symbolic link. The library function `is_other()` matches this term.
- *Special files*: Files with any of the following file types: character-special files, block-special files, FIFOs, and sockets.

Together, the *special* file types plus the implementation-defined file types form the *other* file types.

## 20.3 Path Operations

There are plenty of operations that you can call to deal with filesystems. A key type for dealing with the filesystem is type `std::filesystem::path`, which can be used as an absolute or relative path of a file that might or might not exist (yet).

You can create paths, inspect them, modify them, and compare them. Because these operations usually do not take the filesystem into account (ignoring whether files exist, not following symbolic links, etc.), they are cheap to call. As a consequence, they are usually member functions (if they are neither constructors nor operators).

### 20.3.1 Path Creation

Table *20.3 Path Creation* lists the ways to create a new path object.

| Call | Effect |
| --- | --- |
| `path{`*charseq*`}` | Initializes a path from a character sequence |
| `path{`*beg,end*`}` | Initializes a path from a range |
| `u8path(`*u8string*`)` | Yields a path from a UTF-8 string |
| `current_path()` | Yields the path of the current working directory |
| `temp_directory_path()` | Yields the path for temporary files |

Table 20.3. Path Creation

---

[1] Windows pipes behave differently and are not categorized as `fifo`.

The first constructor, which takes a character sequence, represents a couple of valid ways to pass a character sequence:
- A string
- A string_view
- An array of characters ending with a null terminator
- An input iterator (pointer) to characters ending with the null terminator

Note that both `current_path()` and `temp_directory_path()` are more expensive operations because they are based on operating system calls. By passing an argument, `current_path()` can also be used to modify the current working directory (see Section 20.4.6 on page 243).

With `u8path()` you can create portable paths using UTF-8 characters. For example:

```
// initialize path p with "Köln" (German name for Cologne):
std::filesystem::path p{std::filesystem::u8path(u8"K\u00F6ln")};
...

// create directory from returned UTF-8 string:
std::string utf8String = readUTF8String(...);
create_directory(std::filesystem::u8path(utf8String));
```

## 20.3.2 Path Inspection

Table *20.4 Path Inspection* lists the functions you can call to inspect a path p. Note that these operations do not take the filesystem into account and are therefore member functions of a path.

Each path is either absolute or relative. A path is relative if it has no root directory (a root name is possible; e.g., `C:hello.txt` is a relative path under Windows).

The `has_...()` functions check whether the corresponding functions without `has_` yield a non-empty path.

Note the following:
- There is always a parent path if a root element or a directory separator is part of the path. If the path consists only of root elements (i.e., the relative path is empty), `parent_path()` yields the same path. That is, the parent path of `"/"` is `"/"`. Only the parent path of a pure file name such as `"hello.txt"` is empty.
- If a path has a file name it always has a stem.[2]
- The empty path is a relative path (yielding `false` or an empty path for all other operations besides `is_empty()` and `is_relative()`).

The result of these operations might depend on the operating system. For example, the path `C:/hello.txt`
- On Unix systems
  - Is relative
  - Has no root elements (neither a root name nor a root directory), because `C:` is just a file name

---

[2] This has changed with C++17 because before, a file name could consist of a pure extension.

## 20.3 Path Operations

| Call | Effect |
|---|---|
| `p.empty()` | Yields whether a path is empty |
| `p.is_absolute()` | Yields whether a path is absolute |
| `p.is_relative()` | Yields whether a path is relative |
| `p.has_filename()` | Yields whether a path is neither a directory nor a root name |
| `p.has_stem()` | Same as `has_filename()` (as any file name has a stem) |
| `p.has_extension()` | Yields whether a path has an extension |
| `p.has_root_name()` | Yields whether a path has a root name |
| `p.has_root_directory()` | Yields whether a path has a root directory |
| `p.has_root_path()` | Yields whether a path has a root name or a root directory |
| `p.has_parent_path()` | Yields whether a path has a parent path |
| `p.has_relative_path()` | Yields whether a path consists of more than just root elements |
| `p.filename()` | Yields the file name (or the empty path) |
| `p.stem()` | Yields the file name without extension (or the empty path) |
| `p.extension()` | Yields the extension (or the empty path) |
| `p.root_name()` | Yields the root name (or the empty path) |
| `p.root_directory()` | Yields the root directory (or the empty path) |
| `p.root_path()` | Yields the root elements (or the empty path) |
| `p.parent_path()` | Yields the parent path (or the empty path) |
| `p.relative_path()` | Yields the path without root elements (or the empty path) |
| `p.begin()` | Yields the begin of the path elements |
| `p.end()` | Yields the end of the path elements |

*Table 20.4. Path Inspection*

- Has the parent path `C:`
- Has the relative path `C:/hello.txt`
- On Windows systems
  - Is absolute
  - Has the root name `C:` and the root directory `/`
  - Has no parent path
  - Has the relative path `hello.txt`

**Path Iteration**

You can iterate over a path, which yields the elements of the path: the root name if there is one, the root directory if there is one, and all the file names. If the path ends with a directory separator, the last element is an empty file name.[3]

---

[3] Before C++17, the filesystem library implementations used . to signal a trailing directory separator. This has changed to allow us to distinguish a path ending with a separator from a path ending with a dot after the separator.

The iterator is a bidirectional iterator which means that you can decrement it. The value types of the iterators are of type path. However, two iterators iterating over the same path might *not* refer to the same path object even if they refer to the same element.

For example, consider:

```
void printPath(const std::filesystem::path& p)
{
    std::cout << "path elements of \"" << p.string() << "\":\n";
    for (std::filesystem::path elem : p) {
        std::cout << "  \"" << elem.string() << '"';
    }
    std::cout << '\n';
}
```

which has the same effect as:

```
void printPath(const std::filesystem::path& p)
{
    std::cout << "path elements of \"" << p.string() << "\":\n";
    for (auto pos = p.begin(); pos != p.end(); ++pos) {
        std::filesystem::path elem = *pos;
        std::cout << "  \"" << elem.string() << '"';
    }
    std::cout << '\n';
}
```

If this function is called as follows:

```
printPath("../sub/file.txt");
printPath("/usr/tmp/test/dir/");
printPath("C:\\usr\\tmp\\test\\dir\\");
```

the output on a POSIX-based system will be:

```
path elements of "../sub/file.txt":
  ".."  "sub"  "file.txt"
path elements of "/usr/tmp/test/dir/":
  "/"  "usr"  "tmp"  "test"  "dir"  ""
path elements of "C:\\usr\\tmp\\test\\dir\\":
  "C:\\usr\\tmp\\test\\dir\\"
```

Note that the last path is just one file name, because neither is C: a valid root name nor is the backslash a valid directory separator under POSIX-based systems.

The output on a Windows system will be:

```
path elements of "../sub/file.txt":
  ".."  "sub"  "file.txt"
path elements of "/usr/tmp/test/dir/":
  "/"  "usr"  "tmp"  "test"  "dir"  ""
path elements of "C:\usr\tmp\test\dir\":
  "C:"  "\"  "usr"  "tmp"  "test"  "dir"  ""
```

To check whether a path p ends with a directory separator, you can implement:

```
if (!p.empty() && (--p.end())->empty()) {
    std::cout << p << " has a trailing separator\n";
}
```

### 20.3.3 Path I/O and Conversions

Table *20.5 Path I/O and Conversions* lists the operations to read or write and to yield a converted path. These functions do not take the actual filesystem into account. If you have to deal with paths where symbolic links matter, you might want to use the filesystem-dependent path conversions (see Section 20.4.5 on page 241).

| Call | Effect |
|---|---|
| `strm << p` | Writes the value of a path as quoted string |
| `strm >> p` | Reads the value of a path as quoted string |
| `p.string()` | Yields the path as a `std::string` |
| `p.wstring()` | Yields the path as a `std::wstring` |
| `p.u8string()` | Yields the path as a UTF-8 string of type `std::u8string` |
| `p.u16string()` | Yields the path as a UTF-16 string of type `std::u16string` |
| `p.u32string()` | Yields the path as a UTF-32 string of type `std::u32string` |
| `p.string<...>()` | Yields the path as a `std::basic_string<...>` |
| `p.lexically_normal()` | Yields p as normalized path |
| `p.lexically_relative(p2)` | Yields the path from p2 to p (empty path if none) |
| `p.lexically_proximate(p2)` | Yields the path from p2 to p (p if none) |

Table 20.5. Path I/O and Conversions

The `lexically_...()` functions return a new path, while the other conversion functions yield a corresponding string type. None of these functions modifies the path they are called for.

For example, the following code:

```
std::filesystem::path p{"/dir/./sub//sub1/../sub2"};
std::cout  << "path:              " << p << '\n';
std::cout  << "string():          " << p.string() << '\n';
std::wcout << "wstring():         " << p.wstring() << '\n';
std::cout  << "lexically_normal(): " << p.lexically_normal() << '\n';
```

has the same output for the first three rows:

```
path:              "/dir/./sub//sub1/../sub2"
string():          /dir/./sub//sub1/../sub2
wstring():         /dir/./sub//sub1/../sub2
```

but the output for the last row depends on the directory separator. On POSIX-based systems it is:

```
lexically_normal(): "/dir/sub/sub2"
```

while on Windows it is:

```
lexically_normal(): "\\dir\\sub\\sub2"
```

## Path I/O

First, note that the I/O operators write and read paths as quoted strings. You have to convert them into a string to write them without quotes:

```
std::filesystem::path file{"test.txt"}
std::cout << file << '\n';                  // writes: "test.txt"
std::cout << file.string() << '\n';         // writes: test.txt
```

On Windows, this has even worse effects. The following code:

```
std::filesystem::path tmp{"C:\\Windows\\Temp"};
std::cout << tmp << '\n';
std::cout << tmp.string() << '\n';
std::cout << '"' << tmp.string() << "\"\n";
```

has the following output:

```
"C:\\Windows\\Temp"
C:\Windows\Temp
"C:\Windows\Temp"
```

Note that reading file names supports both forms (quoted with a leading " and non-quoted). Thus, all printed forms will be read back correctly using the standard input operator for paths:

```
std::filesystem::path tmp;
std::cin >> tmp;        // reads quoted and non-quoted paths correctly
```

## Normalization

Normalization might have more surprising outcomes when you are dealing with portable code. For example:

```
std::filesystem::path p2{"//dir\\subdir/subsubdir\\/./\\"};
std::cout << "p2:                 " << p2 << '\n';
std::cout << "lexically_normal(): " << p2.lexically_normal() << '\n';
```

has the following probably expected output on Windows systems:

```
p2:                 "//host\\dir/sub\\/./\\"
lexically_normal(): "\\\\host\\dir\\sub\\"
```

However, on POSIX-based systems, the output becomes:

```
p2:                 "//host\\dir/sub\\/./\\"
lexically_normal(): "/host\\dir/sub\\/\\"
```

The reason is that for POSIX-based systems, the backslash is neither a directory separator nor a valid character for a rootname, which means that we have an absolute path with the three file names host\dir, sub\, and \. On POSIX-based systems, there is no way to detect the backslash as a possible directory separator (neither `generic_string()` nor `make_preferred()` (see Section 20.3.4 on page 224) will help in this case). Therefore, for portable code, you should always use the generic path format when dealing with paths.

## 20.3 Path Operations

Nevertheless, it is a good approach to use `lexically_normal()` to remove the leading dot when iterating over the current directory (see Section 20.5 on page 244).

**Relative Path**

Both `lexically_relative()` and `lexically_proximate()` can be called to compute the relative path between two paths. The only difference is the behavior if there is no path, which only can happen if one path is relative and the other is absolute or the root names differ. In that case:
- `p.lexically_relative(p2)` yields the empty path if there is no relative path from p2 to p.
- `p.lexically_proximate(p2)` yields p if there is no relative path from p2 to p.

Because both operations operate lexically, the actual filesystem (which might have symbolic links) and the `current_path()` are not taken into account. If both paths are equal, the relative path is `"."`. For example:

```
fs::path{"/a/d"}.lexically_relative("/a/b/c")        // "../../d"
fs::path{"/a/b/c"}.lexically_relative("/a/d")        // "../b/c"
fs::path{"/a/b"}.lexically_relative("/a/b")          // "."
fs::path{"/a/b"}.lexically_relative("/a/b/")         // "."
fs::path{"/a/b"}.lexically_relative("/a/b\\")        // "."
fs::path{"/a/b"}.lexically_relative("/a/d/../c")     // "../b
fs::path{"a/d/../b"}.lexically_relative("a/c")       // "../d/../b"
fs::path{"a//d/..//b"}.lexically_relative("a/c")     // "../d/../b"
```

On Windows systems, we have:

```
fs::path{"C:/a/b"}.lexically_relative("c:/c/d") ;    // ""
fs::path{"C:/a/b"}.lexically_relative("D:/c/d") ;    // ""
fs::path{"C:/a/b"}.lexically_proximate("D:/c/d") ;   // "C:/a/b"
```

**Conversions to Strings**

With `u8string()` you can use the path as a UTF-8 string, which nowadays is the common format for stored data. For example:

```
// store paths as a UTF-8 string:
std::vector<std::string> utf8paths;  // std::u8string with C++20
for (const auto& entry : fs::directory_iterator(p)) {
   utf8paths.push_back(entry.path().u8string());
}
```

Note that the return value of `u8string()` will probably change from `std::string` to `std::u8string` with C++20 (the new UTF-8 string type as proposed together with `char8_t` for UTF-8 characters in https://wg21.link/p0482).[4]

---

[4] Thanks to Tom Honermann for pointing this out and the proposed change (it is really important that C++ receives real UTF-8 support).

The member template `string<>()` can be used to convert to a special string type, such as a string type that operates case insensitively:

```
struct ignoreCaseTraits : public std::char_traits<char> {
  // case-insensitively compare two characters:
  static bool eq(const char& c1, const char& c2) {
    return std::toupper(c1) == std::toupper(c2);
  }
  static bool lt(const char& c1, const char& c2) {
    return std::toupper(c1) < std::toupper(c2);
  }
  // compare up to n characters of s1 and s2:
  static int compare(const char* s1, const char* s2, std::size_t n);
  // search character c in s:
  static const char* find(const char* s, std::size_t n, const char& c);
};

// define a special type for such strings:
using icstring = std::basic_string<char, ignoreCaseTraits>;

std::filesystem::path p{"/dir\\subdir/subsubdir\\/./\\"};
icstring s2 = p.string<char,ignoreCaseTraits>();
```

Note also that you should *not* use a function `c_str()`, which is also provided, because it converts to the *native* string format, which might be a `wchar_t` so that, for example, you have to use `std::wcout` instead of `std::cout` to write it to a stream.

### 20.3.4 Conversions Between Native and Generic Format

Table *20.6 Conversions Between Native and Generic Format* lists the operations you can use to convert between the generic path format (see Section 20.2.3 on page 211) and the implementation-specific format of the actual platform.

These functions should have no effect on POSIX-based systems, where there is no difference between the native and the generic path format. Calling these functions on other platforms might matter:

- The `generic...()` path functions yield the path converted to the corresponding string format with the generic format (see Section 20.2.3 on page 211).
- `native()` yields the path using the native string encoding, which is defined by the type `std::filesystem::path::string_type`. Under Windows, this type is type `std::wstring`, which means that you have to use `std::wcout` instead of `std::cout` to directly write it to the standard output stream. New overloads allow us to pass the native string to new overloads of file streams.
- `c_str()` does the same but yields the result as a null terminated character sequence. Note that using this function is also not portable, because printing the sequence with `std::cout` does not result in the correct output on Windows. You have to use `std::wcout` there.
- `make_preferred()` replaces any directory separator except for the root name with the native directory separator. Note that this is the only function that modifies the path it is called for. Thus, strictly speak-

## 20.3 Path Operations

| Call | Effect |
|---|---|
| `p.generic_string()` | Yields the path as a generic `std::string` |
| `p.generic_wstring()` | Yields the path as a generic `std::wstring` |
| `p.generic_u8string()` | Yields the path as a generic `std::u8string` |
| `p.generic_u16string()` | Yields the path as a generic `std::u16string` |
| `p.generic_u32string()` | Yields the path as a generic `std::u32string` |
| `p.generic_string<...>()` | Yields the path as a generic `std::basic_string<...>` |
| `p.native()` | Yields the path in the native format of type `path::string_type` |
| *conversionToNativeString* | Implicit conversion to the native string type |
| `p.c_str()` | Yields the path as a character sequence in the native string format |
| `p.make_preferred()` | Replaces directory separators in p with native format inplace and yields the modified p |

Table 20.6. *Conversions Between Native and Generic Format*

ing, this function belongs to the next section of modifying path functions, but because it deals with the conversions for the native format, it is also listed here.

For example, on Windows, the following code:

```
std::filesystem::path p{"/dir\\subdir/subsubdir\\/./\\"};
std::cout  << "p:                  " << p << '\n';
std::cout  << "string():           " << p.string() << '\n';
std::wcout << "wstring():          " << p.wstring() << '\n';
std::cout  << "lexically_normal(): " << p.lexically_normal() << '\n';
std::cout  << "generic_string():   " << p.generic_string() << '\n';
std::wcout << "generic_wstring():  " << p.generic_wstring() << '\n';
// because it's Windows and the native string type is wstring:
std::wcout << "native():           " << p.native() << '\n';  // Windows!
std::wcout << "c_str():            " << p.c_str() << '\n';
std::cout  << "make_preferred():   " << p.make_preferred() << '\n';
std::cout  << "p:                  " << p << '\n';
```

has the following output:

```
p:                  "/dir\\subdir/subsubdir\\/./\\"
string():           /dir\subdir/subsubdir\/./\
wstring():          /dir\subdir/subsubdir\/./\
lexically_normal(): "\\dir\\subdir\\subsubdir\\"
generic_string():   /dir/subdir/subsubdir//.//
generic_wstring():  /dir/subdir/subsubdir//.//
native():           /dir\subdir/subsubdir\/./\
c_str():            /dir\subdir/subsubdir\/./\
make_preferred():   "\\dir\\subdir\\subsubdir\\\\.\\\\"
p:                  "\\dir\\subdir\\subsubdir\\\\.\\\\"
```

Note again:
- The native string type is not portable. On Windows it is a `wstring`, on POSIX-based systems it is a `string`, which means that you would have to use `cout` instead of `wcout` to print the result of `native()` and `c_str()`. Using `wcout` is only portable for the return value of `wstring()` and `generic_wstring()`.
- Only the call to `make_preferred()` modifies the path it is called for. All other calls leave p unaffected.

## 20.3.5 Path Modifications

Table *20.7 Path Modifications* lists the operations that allow us to modify paths directly.

| Call | Effect |
|---|---|
| `p = p2` | Assigns a new path |
| `p = sv` | Assigns a string (view) as a new path |
| `p.assign(p2)` | Assigns a new path |
| `p.assign(sv)` | Assigns a string (view) as a new path |
| `p.assign(beg, end)` | Assigns elements of the range from beg to end to the path |
| `p1 / p2` | Yields the path that appends p2 as sub-path of path p1 |
| `p /= sub` | Appends sub as sub-path to path p |
| `p.append(sub)` | Appends sub as sub-path to path p |
| `p.append(beg, end)` | Appends elements of the range from beg to end as sub-paths to path p |
| `p += str` | Appends the characters of str to path p |
| `p.concat(str)` | Appends the characters of str to path p |
| `p.concat(beg, end)` | Appends elements of the range from beg to end to path p |
| `p.remove_filename()` | Removes a trailing file name from the path |
| `p.replace_filename(repl)` | Replaces the trailing file name (if any) |
| `p.replace_extension()` | Removes any trailing file name extension |
| `p.replace_extension(repl)` | Replaces the trailing file name extension (if any) |
| `p.clear()` | Makes the path empty |
| `p.swap(p2)` | Swaps the values of two paths |
| `swap(p1, p2)` | Swaps the values of two paths |
| `p.make_preferred()` | Replaces directory separators in p with native format and yields the modified p |

Table 20.7. Path Modifications

While `+=` and `concat()` simply append new characters to a path, `/`, `/=`, and `append()` add a sub path separated with the current directory separator:

```
std::filesystem::path p{"myfile"};
p += ".git";           // p: myfile.git
p /= ".git";           // p: myfile.git/.git
p.concat("1");         // p: myfile.git/git1
p.append("1");         // p: myfile.git/git1/1
```

## 20.3 Path Operations

```
std::cout << p << '\n';
std::cout << p / p << '\n';
```

On POSIX-based systems the output is:

```
"myfile.git/.git1/1"
"myfile.git/.git1/1/myfile.git/.git1/1"
```

On Windows systems the output is:

```
"myfile.git\\.git1\\1"
"myfile.git\\.git1\\1\\myfile.git\\.git1\\1"
```

Note that appending an absolute sub-path means replacing an existing path. For example, after:

```
namespace fs = std::filesystem;
auto p1 = fs::path("/usr") / "tmp";      // path is /usr/tmp or /usr\tmp
auto p2 = fs::path("/usr/") / "tmp";     // path is /usr/tmp
auto p3 = fs::path("/usr") / "/tmp";     // path is /tmp
auto p4 = fs::path("/usr/") / "/tmp";    // path is /tmp
```

we have 4 paths referring to two different files:

- p1 and p2 are equal and refer to the file /usr/tmp (note that on Windows they are equal with p1 being /usr\tmp).
- p3 and p4 are equal and refer to the file /tmp because an absolute path was appended.

For root elements, whether a new element is assigned is also important. For example, on Windows, we have:

```
auto p1 = fs::path("usr") / "C:/tmp";    // path is C:/tmp
auto p2 = fs::path("usr") / "C:";        // path is C:
auto p3 = fs::path("C:") / "";           // path is C:
auto p4 = fs::path("C:usr") / "/tmp";    // path is C:/tmp
auto p5 = fs::path("C:usr") / "C:tmp";   // path is C:usr\tmp
auto p6 = fs::path("C:usr") / "c:tmp";   // path is c:tmp
auto p7 = fs::path("C:usr") / "D:tmp";   // path is D:tmp
```

The function `make_preferred()` converts the directory separators inside a path to the native format. For example:

```
std::filesystem::path p{"//server/dir//subdir///file.txt"};
p.make_preferred();
std::cout << p << '\n';
```

writes the following on POSIX-based platforms:

```
"//server/dir/subdir/file.txt"
```

On Windows, the output is as follows:

```
"\\\\server\\dir\\\\subdir\\\\\\file.txt"
```

Note that the leading root name is not modified because it has to consist of two slashes or backslashes. Note also that this function cannot convert backslashes into a slash on a POSIX-based system because the backslash is not recognized as a directory separator.

`replace_extension()` replaces, adds, or removes an extension:
- If the file has an extension, it is replaced.
- If the file has no extension, the new extension is added.
- If you skip the new extension or the new extension is empty, any existing extension is removed.

It does not matter whether you place a leading dot in the replacement. The function ensures that there is exactly one dot between the stem and the extension of the resulting file name. For example:

```
fs::path{"file.txt"}.replace_extension("tmp")    // file.tmp
fs::path{"file.txt"}.replace_extension(".tmp")   // file.tmp
fs::path{"file.txt"}.replace_extension("")       // file
fs::path{"file.txt"}.replace_extension()         // file
fs::path{"dir"}.replace_extension("tmp")         // dir.tmp
fs::path{".git"}.replace_extension("tmp")        // .git.tmp
```

Note that file names that are "pure extensions" (such as `.git`) do not count as extensions.[5]

## 20.3.6 Path Comparisons

Table *20.8 Path Comparisons* lists the operations you can use to compare two different paths.

| Call | Effect |
| --- | --- |
| `p1 == p2` | Yields whether two paths are equal |
| `p1 != p2` | Yields whether two paths are not equal |
| `p1 < p2` | Yields whether a path is less than another |
| `p1 <= p2` | Yields whether a path is less than or equal to another |
| `p1 >= p2` | Yields whether a path is greater than or equal to another |
| `p1 > p2` | Yields whether a path is greater than another |
| `p.compare(p2)` | Yields whether p2 is less than, equal to, or greater than p |
| `p.compare(sv)` | Yields whether p2 is less than, equal to, or greater than the string (view) sv converted to a path |
| `equivalent(p1, p2)` | Expensive path comparison taking the filesystem into account |

Table 20.8. Path Comparisons

Note that most of the comparisons do not take the filesystem into account, which means that they operate only lexically, which is cheap but may result in surprising return values:

- Using `==`, `!=` and `compare()` the following paths are all different:

```
tmp1/f
./tmp1/f
tmp1/./f
tmp1/tmp11/../f
```

---

[5] This has changed with C++17. Before C++17, the result of the last statement would have been `.tmp`.

- Only different formats for specifying a directory separator are detected. Thus, the following paths are all equal (provided the backslash is a valid directory separator):

  ```
  tmp1/f
  /tmp1//f
  /tmp1\f
  tmp1/\/f
  ```

It is only if you call `lexically_normal()` for each path that all of the paths above are equal (provided the backslash is a valid directory separator). For example:

```
std::filesystem::path p1{"tmp1/f"};
std::filesystem::path p2{"./tmp1/f"};

p1 == p2                                                    // true
p1.compare(p2)                                              // not 0
p1.lexically_normal() == p2.lexically_normal()              // true
p1.lexically_normal().compare(p2.lexically_normal())        // 0
```

If you want to take the filesystem into account so that symbolic links are handled correctly, you can use `equivalent()`. However, note that this function requires that both paths represent existing files. Thus, a generic way to compare paths as accurately as possible (which does not have the best performance) is as follows:

```
bool pathsAreEqual(const std::filesystem::path& p1,
                   const std::filesystem::path& p2)
{
  return exists(p1) && exists(p2) ? equivalent(p1, p2)
         : p1.lexically_normal() == p2.lexically_normal();
}
```

## 20.3.7 Other Path Operations

Table *20.9 Other Path Operations* lists the remaining path operations not listed yet.

| Call | Effect |
|---|---|
| `p.hash_value()` | Yields the hash value for a path |

Table 20.9. Other Path Operations

Note that only equal paths (see Section 20.3.6 on page 228) are guaranteed to have the same hash value. The following paths yield different hash values:

```
tmp1/f
./tmp1/f
tmp1/./f
tmp1/tmp11/../f
```

Therefore, you might want to normalize paths before you put them in a hash table.

## 20.4 Filesystem Operations

This section covers the more expensive filesystem operations that take the current filesystem into account.

Because these operations usually take the filesystem into account (depending behavior on whether files exist, following symbolic links, etc.), they are significantly more expensive than pure path operations As a consequence, they are usually free-standing functions.

### 20.4.1 File Attributes

There are a couple of file attributes that you can ask for when having a path. First, table *20.10 Operations for File Types* lists the functions you can call to inspect whether the file specified by a path p exists and what its overall type is (if there is one). Note that these operations do take the filesystem into account and are therefore free-standing functions.

| Call | Effect |
|---|---|
| exists(p) | Yields whether there is a file that can be accessed |
| is_symlink(p) | Yields whether the file p exists and is a symbolic link |
| is_regular_file(p) | Yields whether the file p exists and is a regular file |
| is_directory(p) | Yields whether the file p exists and is a directory |
| is_other(p) | Yields whether the file p exists and is neither regular nor a directory nor a symbolic link |
| is_block_file(p) | Yields whether the file p exists and is a block-special file |
| is_character_file(p) | Yields whether the file p exists and is a character-special file |
| is_fifo(p) | Yields whether the file p exists and is a FIFO or pipe file |
| is_socket(p) | Yields whether the file p exists and is a socket |

Table 20.10. Operations for File Types

The function for the filesystem type matches the corresponding `file_type` values (see Section 20.2.7 on page 216). However, note that these functions (except `is_symlink()`) follow symbolic links. That is, for a symbolic link to a directory, both `is_symlink()` and `is_directory()` yield `true`.

Note also that for all checks for files that are special files (see Section 20.2.7 on page 217) (no regular file, no directory, no symbolic link), `is_other()` also yields `true` according to the definition of other file types (see Section 20.2.7 on page 217).

For implementation-specific file types there is no specific convenience function, which means that for them, only `is_other()` is true (and `is_symlink()` if we have a symbolic link to such a file). You can use the file status API (see Section 20.4.2 on page 234) to check against these specific types.

To not follow symbolic links, use `symlink_status()` (see Section 20.4.2 on page 234) and call these functions for the returned `file_status` (see Section 20.4.2 on page 234) as discussed below for `exists()`.

## Check for Existence of a File

`exists()` answers the question of whether there is effectively a file to open. Thus, as just discussed, it follows symbolic links. Therefore, it yields `false` if there is a symbolic link to a non-existing file.

As a consequence, code like this does not work as expected:

```
// if not done yet, create a symbolic link to file:
if (!exists(p)) {                    // OOPS: checks if the file p refers to doesn't exist
  std::filesystem::create_symlink(file, p);
}
```

If p already exists as a symbolic link to a non-existing file, `create_symlink()` will try to create the symbolic link at the location where the symbolic link already exists and raise a corresponding exception.

Because the situation in a multi-user/multi-process filesystem can change at any time, the best approach is usually to try to perform an operation and handle the error if it fails. Thus, we can simply call the operation and handle a corresponding exception (see Section 20.2.6 on page 215) or handle an error code (see Section 20.2.6 on page 215) passed as an additional argument.

However, sometimes you need to check for the existence of a file (before performing a filesystem operation). For example, if you want to create a file at a specific location and there is already a symbolic link, the file is created or is overwritten at a (possibly) unexpected location. In that case, you should check for the existence of a file as follows:[6]

```
if (!exists(symlink_status(p))) {    // OK: checks if p doesn't exist yet (as symbolic link)
  ...
}
```

Here, we use `symlink_status()` (see Section 20.4.2 on page 234), which yields the status that does *not* follow symbolic links, to check for the existence of any file at the location of p.

## Other File Attributes

Table *20.11 Operations for File Attributes* lists a couple of free-standing functions for checking for additional file attributes.

| Call | Effect |
|---|---|
| `is_empty(p)` | Yields whether the file is empty |
| `file_size(p)` | Yields the size of a file |
| `hard_link_count(p)` | Yields the number of hard links |
| `last_write_time(p)` | Yields the timepoint of the last write to a file |

*Table 20.11. Operations for File Attributes*

Note that there is a difference between whether a path is empty and whether the file specified by a path is empty:

---

[6] Thanks to Billy O'Neal for pointing this out.

```
p.empty()     // true if path p is empty (cheap operation)
is_empty(p)   // true if file at path p is empty (filesystem operation)
```

`file_size(p)` returns the size of file p in bytes if the file exists as a regular file (on POSIX system, the value is the same as the member `st_size` of the value returned by `stat()`). For all other files, the result is implementation-defined and not portable.

`hard_link_count(p)` returns the number of times a file exists in a file system. Usually, this number is 1, but on some file systems the same file can exist at different locations in the file system (i.e., has different paths). This is different from a symbolic link where a file refers to another file. Here we have a file with a different path for accessing it directly. The file itself is only removed when the last hard link is removed.

**Dealing with the Last Modification**

`last_write_time(p)` returns the timepoint of the last modification or write access of the file. The return type is a special `time_point` type of the standard chrono library for timepoints:

```
namespace std::filesystem {
  using file_time_type = chrono::time_point<trivialClock>;
}
```

The clock type *trivialClock* is an implementation-specific clock type that reflects the resolution and range of file time values. For example, you can use it as follows:

```
void printFileTime(const std::filesystem::path& p)
{
  auto filetime = last_write_time(p);
  auto diff = std::filesystem::file_time_type::clock::now() - filetime;
  std::cout << p << " is "
            << std::chrono::duration_cast<std::chrono::seconds>(diff).count()
            << " Seconds old.\n";
}
```

which might output:

```
"fileattr.cpp" is 4 Seconds old.
```

Instead of

```
std::filesystem::file_time_type::clock::now()
```

in this example, you could also write:

```
decltype(filetime)::clock::now()
```

Note that the clock used by a filesystem timepoint is not guaranteed to be the standard `system_clock`. Therefore, there is currently no standardized support for converting the filesystem timepoint into type `time_t` to use it as absolute time in strings or output.[7] There is a workaround though. The following function "roughly" converts a timepoint of any clock into a `time_t` object:

---

[7] This will be fixed with C++20 introducing a `clock_cast`.

## 20.4 Filesystem Operations

```
template<typename TimePoint>
std::time_t toTimeT(TimePoint tp)
{
  using system_clock = std::chrono::system_clock;
  return system_clock::to_time_t(tp + (system_clock::now()
                                       - decltype(tp)::clock::now()));
}
```

The trick is to compute the time of the filesystem timepoint as a duration relative to now and then add this difference to the current time of the system clock. This function is not exact because both clocks might have different resolutions and we call now() twice at slightly different times. However, in general, this works pretty well.

For example, for a path p we can call:

```
auto ftime = std::filesystem::last_write_time(p);
std::time_t t = toTimeT(ftime);
// convert to calendar time (including skipping trailing newline):
std::string ts = std::ctime(&t);
ts.resize(ts.size()-1);
std::cout << "last access of " << p << ": " << ts << '\n';
```

which might print:

```
last access of "fileattr.exe": Sun Jun 24 10:41:12 2018
```

To format a string the way we want we can call:

```
std::time_t t = toTimeT(ftime);
char mbstr[100];
if (std::strftime(mbstr, sizeof(mbstr), "last access: %B %d, %Y at %H:%M\n",
                  std::localtime(&t))) {
  std::cout << mbstr;
}
```

which might output:

```
last access: June 24, 2018 at 10:41
```

A useful helper for converting any filesystem timepoint into a string would be:

*filesystem/ftimeAsString.hpp*

```
#include <string>
#include <chrono>
#include <filesystem>

std::string asString(const std::filesystem::file_time_type& tp)
{
  using system_clock = std::chrono::system_clock;
  auto t = system_clock::to_time_t(tp + (system_clock::now()
                                         - decltype(tp)::clock::now()));
```

```cpp
  // convert to calendar time (including skipping trailing newline):
  std::string ts = std::ctime(&t);
  ts.resize(ts.size()-1);
  return ts;
}
```

Note that `ctime()` and `strftime()` are not thread-safe and must not be called concurrently.

See section "Modify Existing Files" (see Section 20.4.4 on page 239) for the corresponding API to modify the last write access.

## 20.4.2 File Status

To avoid filesystem access, there is a special type `file_status` that can be used to hold and modify file type and permissions that are cached. This status can be set
- When asking for the file status of a specific path as listed in table *20.12 Operations for File Status*
- When iterating over a directory (see Section 20.5 on page 244)

| Call | Effect |
| --- | --- |
| status(p) | Yields the `file_status` of the file p (following symbolic links) |
| symlink_status(p) | Yields the `file_status` of p (not following symbolic links) |

Table 20.12. Operations for File Status

The difference is that if the path p resolves in a symbolic link, `status()` follows the link and prints the attributes of the file there (the status might be that there is no file), while `symlink_status(p)` prints the status of the symbolic link itself.

Table *20.13 `file_status` Operations* lists the possible calls for a `file_status` object `fs`.

One benefit of the status operations is that you can save multiple operating system calls for the same file. For example, instead of

```cpp
if (!is_directory(path)) {
  if (is_character_file(path) || is_block_file(path)) {
    ...
  }
  ...
}
```

you would be better off implementing the following:

```cpp
auto pathStatus{status(path)};
if (!is_directory(pathStatus)) {
  if (is_character_file(pathStatus) || is_block_file(pathStatus)) {
    ...
  }
  ...
}
```

## 20.4 Filesystem Operations

| Call | Effect |
|---|---|
| `exists(fs)` | Yields whether a file exists |
| `is_regular_file(fs)` | Yields whether the file exists and is a regular file |
| `is_directory(fs)` | Yields whether the file exists and is a directory |
| `is_symlink(fs)` | Yields whether the file exists and is a symbolic link |
| `is_other(fs)` | Yields whether the file exists and is neither regular nor a directory nor a symbolic link |
| `is_block_file(fs)` | Yields whether the file exists and is a block-special file |
| `is_character_file(fs)` | Yields whether the file exists and is a character-special file |
| `is_fifo(fs)` | Yields whether the file exists and is a FIFO or pipe file |
| `is_socket(fs)` | Yields whether the file exists and is a socket |
| `fs.type()` | Yields the `file_type` of the file |
| `fs.permissions()` | Yields the permissions (see Section 20.4.3 on page 235) of the file |

*Table 20.13.* `file_status` *Operations*

The other key benefit is that by using `symlink_status()`, you can check for the status of a path *without* following any symbolic link. This helps, for example, if you want to check whether any file exists (see Section 20.4.1 on page 231) at a specific path.

Because a file status does not use the operating system, no overloads to return an error code are provided.

The `exists()` and `is_...()` functions for path arguments (see Section 20.4.1 on page 230) are shortcuts for calling and checking the `type()` for a file status. For example,

    `is_regular_file(mypath)`

is a shortcut for

    `is_regular_file(status(mypath))`

which is a shortcut for

    `status(mypath).type() == file_type::regular`

### 20.4.3 Permissions

The model for dealing with file permissions is adopted from the UNIX/POSIX world. There are bits to signal read, write, and/or execute/search access for owners of the file, members of the same group, or all others. In addition, there are special bits for "set user ID on execution," "set group ID on execution," and the sticky bit (or another system-dependent meaning).

Table 20.14 *Permission Bits* lists the values of the bitmask scoped enumeration type (see Section A on page 415) `perms`, defined in namespace `std::filesystem`, which represents one or multiple permission bits.

You can ask for the current permissions and as a result, check the bits of the returned `perms` object. To combine flags, you have to use the bit operators. For example:

| Enum | Octal | POSIX | Meaning |
|---|---|---|---|
| none | 0 | | No permissions set |
| owner_read | 0400 | S_IRUSR | Read permission for the owner |
| owner_write | 0200 | S_IWUSR | Write permission for the owner |
| owner_exec | 0100 | S_IXUSR | Execute/search permission for the owner |
| owner_all | 0700 | S_IRWXU | All permissions for the owner |
| group_read | 040 | S_IRGRP | Read permission for the group |
| group_write | 020 | S_IWGRP | Write permission for the group |
| group_exec | 010 | S_IXGRP | Execute/search permission for the group |
| group_all | 070 | S_IRWXG | All permissions for the group |
| others_read | 04 | S_IROTH | Read permission for all others |
| others_write | 02 | S_IWOTH | Write permission for all others |
| others_exec | 01 | S_IXOTH | Execute/search permission for all others |
| others_all | 07 | S_IRWXO | All permissions for all others |
| all | 0777 | | All permissions for all |
| set_uid | 04000 | S_ISUID | Set user ID on execution |
| set_gid | 02000 | S_ISGID | Set group ID on execution |
| sticky_bit | 01000 | S_ISVTX | Operating-system-dependent |
| mask | 07777 | | Mask for all possible bits |
| unknown | 0xFFFF | | Permissions not known |

Table 20.14. Permission Bits

```
// if writable:
if ((fileStatus.permissions()
        & (fs::perms::owner_write | fs::perms::group_write
            | fs::perms::others_write))
    != fs::perms::none) {
    ...
}
```

A shorter (but maybe less readable) way to initialize a bitmask would be to use the corresponding octal value and relaxed enum initialization (see Section 8.3 on page 65) directly:

```
// if writable:
if ((fileStatus.permissions() & fs::perms{0222}) != fs::perms::none) {
    ...
}
```

Note that you have to put the & expressions in parentheses before comparing the outcome with a specific value. Note also that you cannot skip the comparison because there is no implicit conversion to bool for bitmask scoped enumeration types (see Section A on page 415).

As another example, to convert the permissions of a file into a string with the notation of the UNIX command ls -l, you can use the following helper function:

## 20.4 Filesystem Operations

*filesystem/permAsString.hpp*

```cpp
#include <string>
#include <chrono>
#include <filesystem>

std::string asString(const std::filesystem::perms& pm)
{
  using perms = std::filesystem::perms;
  std::string s;
  s.resize(9);
  s[0] = (pm & perms::owner_read)    != perms::none ? 'r' : '-';
  s[1] = (pm & perms::owner_write)   != perms::none ? 'w' : '-';
  s[2] = (pm & perms::owner_exec)    != perms::none ? 'x' : '-';
  s[3] = (pm & perms::group_read)    != perms::none ? 'r' : '-';
  s[4] = (pm & perms::group_write)   != perms::none ? 'w' : '-';
  s[5] = (pm & perms::group_exec)    != perms::none ? 'x' : '-';
  s[6] = (pm & perms::others_read)   != perms::none ? 'r' : '-';
  s[7] = (pm & perms::others_write)  != perms::none ? 'w' : '-';
  s[8] = (pm & perms::others_exec)   != perms::none ? 'x' : '-';
  return s;
}
```

This allows you to print the permissions of a file as part of a standard ostream command:

```cpp
std::cout << "permissions: " << asString(status(mypath).permissions())
          << '\n';
```

A possible output for a file with all permissions for the owner and read/execute permissions for all others would be:

```
permissions: rwxr-xr-x
```

However, note that the Windows ACL (Access Control List) approach does not really fit in this scheme. Therefore, when using Visual C++, writable files *always* have all read, write, and execute bits set (even if they are *not* executable files) and files with the read-only flag always have all read and executable bits set. This also impacts the API when modifying permissions portably (see Section 20.4.4 on page 240).

### 20.4.4 Filesystem Modifications

You can also modify the filesystem either by creating and deleting files or by modifying existing files.

**Create and Delete Files**

Table *20.15 Creating and Deleting Files* lists the operations for a path p to create and delete files.

There is no function for creating a regular file. This is covered by the I/O Stream standard library. For example, the following statement creates a new empty file (if it does not exist yet):

```cpp
std::ofstream{"log.txt"};
```

| Call | Effect |
|---|---|
| `create_directory(p)` | Creates a directory |
| `create_directory(p, attrPath)` | Creates a directory with attributes of `attrPath` |
| `create_directories(p)` | Creates a directory and all directories above that do not exist yet |
| `create_hard_link(to, new)` | Creates another filesystem entry `new` for the existing file `to` |
| `create_symlink(to, new)` | Creates a symbolic link from `new` to `to` |
| `create_directory_symlink(to, new)` | Creates a symbolic link from `new` to the directory `to` |
| `copy(from, to)` | Copies a file of any type |
| `copy(from, to, options)` | Copies a file of any type with `options` |
| `copy_file(from, to)` | Copies a file (but not directory or symbolic link) |
| `copy_file(from, to, options)` | Copies a file with `options` |
| `copy_symlink(from, to)` | Copies a symbolic link (`to` refers to where `from` refers) |
| `remove(p)` | Removes a file or empty directory |
| `remove_all(p)` | Removes p and recursively all files in its subtree (if any) |

*Table 20.15. Creating and Deleting Files*

The functions for creating one or more directories return whether a new directory was created. Thus, finding a directory that is already there is not an error.[8]

The `copy...()` functions do not work with special file types (see Section 20.2.7 on page 217). By default they:

- Report an error if existing files are overwritten
- Do not operate recursively
- Follow symbolic links

This default can be overwritten by the parameter `options`, which has the bitmask scoped enumeration type (see Section A on page 415) `copy_options`, defined in namespace `std::filesystem`. Table *20.16 Copy Options* lists the possible values.

When creating a symbolic link to a directory, it is better to use `create_directory_symlink()` than `create_symlink()`, because some operating systems require explicit specification that the target is a directory. Note that the first argument has to be the path that the symbolic link refers to from the view of the symbolic link. Therefore, to create a symbolic link from `sub/slink` to `sub/file.txt`, you have to call:

    std::filesystem::create_symlink("file.txt", "sub/slink");

The statement

---

[8] Initially, C++17 also specified that finding a file there that is not a directory is also not an error. This was fixed later as a defect against C++17 (see `https://wg21.link/p1164r1`).

## 20.4 Filesystem Operations

| copy_options | Effect |
|---|---|
| none | Default (value 0) |
| skip_existing | Skips overwriting existing files |
| overwrite_existing | Overwrites existing files |
| update_existing | Overwrites existing files if the new files are newer |
| recursive | Recursively copies sub-directories and their contents |
| copy_symlinks | Copies symbolic links as symbolic links |
| skip_symlinks | Ignores symbolic links |
| directories_only | Copies directories only |
| create_hard_links | Creates additional hard links instead of copies of files |
| create_symlinks | Creates symbolic links instead of copies of files (the source path must be an absolute path unless the destination path is in the current directory) |

*Table 20.16. Copy Options*

```
std::filesystem::create_symlink("sub/file.txt", "sub/slink");
```
would create a symbolic link from `sub/slink` to `sub/sub/file.txt`.

The functions for removing files have the following behavior:

- `remove()` removes a file or an empty directory. It returns `false` if there was no file/directory or it could not be removed and no exception is thrown.
- `remove_all()` removes a file or recursively a directory. It returns, as an `uintmax_t` value, how many files were removed. It returns 0 if there was no file and `uintmax_t(-1)` if an error occurred and no exception is thrown.

In both cases, symbolic links are removed rather than any file they refer to.

Note that you should always qualify `remove()` correctly when passing a string literal as an argument, because otherwise the C function `remove()` is called (see Section 20.2.5 on page 214).

**Modify Existing Files**

Table *20.17 File Modifications* list the operations for modifying existing files.

| Call | Effect |
|---|---|
| rename(old, new) | Renames and/or moves a file |
| last_write_time(p, newtime) | Changes the timepoint of the last write access |
| permissions(p, prms) | Replaces the permissions of a file with prms |
| permissions(p, prms, mode) | Modifies the permissions of a file according to mode |
| resize_file(p, newSize) | Changes the size of a regular file |

*Table 20.17. File Modifications*

`rename()` can deal with any type of file including directories and symbolic links. For symbolic links, it is the link that is renamed, not where it refers to. Note that `rename()` needs the full new path including the file name to move it to a different directory:

```
// move "tmp/sub/x" to "tmp/x":
std::filesystem::rename("tmp/sub/x", "tmp");      // ERROR
std::filesystem::rename("tmp/sub/x", "tmp/x");    // OK
```

`last_write_time()` uses the timepoint format as described in section "Dealing with the Last Modification" (see Section 20.4.1 on page 232). For example:

```
// touch file p (update last file access):
std::filesystem::last_write_time(p,
                    std::filesystem::file_time_type::clock::now());
```

`permissions()` uses the permission API format as described in section "Permissions" (see Section 20.4.3 on page 235). The optional `mode` is of the bitmask enumeration type (see Section A on page 415) `perm_options`, defined in namespace `std::filesystem`. On the one hand, it allows you to choose between `replace`, `add`, and `remove`. On the other hand, using `nofollow` it allows you to modify permissions of the symbolic links instead of the files they refer to.

For example:

```
// remove write access for group and any access for others:
permissions(mypath,
            std::filesystem::perms::group_write
            | std::filesystem::perms::others_all,
            std::filesystem::perm_options::remove);
```

Note again that Windows supports different permission concepts. Its ACL permission concept (see Section 20.4.3 on page 237) supports only two modes:

- Read, write, and execute/search for all (`rwxrwxrwx`)
- Read and execute/search for all (`r-xr-xr-x`)

To switch portably between these two modes, you have to enable or disable all three write flags together (removing one after the other does not work):

```
// portable value to enable/disable write access:
auto allWrite = std::filesystem::perms::owner_write
                | std::filesystem::perms::group_write
                | std::filesystem::perms::others_write;
// portably remove write access:
permissions(file, allWrite, std::filesystem::perm_options::remove);
```

A shorter (but maybe less readable) way to initialize `allWrite` (using relaxed enum initialization (see Section 8.3 on page 65)) would be as follows:

```
std::filesystem::perms allWrite{0222};
```

`resize_file()` can be used to reduce or extend the size of a regular file: For example:

```
// make file empty:
resize_file(file, 0);
```

## 20.4.5 Symbolic Links and Filesystem-Dependent Path Conversions

Table *20.18 Filesystem Path Conversions* lists the operations for dealing with the path of files that take the filesystem into account. This is especially important if you have to deal with symbolic links. Use pure path conversions (see Section 20.3.3 on page 221) for cheap path conversions that do not take the filesystem into account.

| Call | Effect |
| --- | --- |
| `read_symlink(symlink)` | Yields the file that an existing symbolic link refers to |
| `absolute(p)` | Yields existing p as absolute path (not following symbolic links) |
| `canonical(p)` | Yields existing p as absolute path (following symbolic links) |
| `weakly_canonical(p)` | Yields p as absolute path (following symbolic links) |
| `relative(p)` | Yields relative (or empty) path from current directory to p |
| `relative(p, base)` | Yields relative (or empty) path from base to p |
| `proximate(p)` | Yields relative (or absolute) path from current directory to p |
| `proximate(p, base)` | Yields relative (or absolute) path from base to p |

Table 20.18. Filesystem Path Conversions

Note that these functions have different behavior regarding whether the file(s) must exist, whether they normalize, and whether they follow symbolic links. Table *20.19 Filesystem Path Conversion Attributes* gives an overview of what the functions require and how they perform.

| Call | Must Exist | Normalizes | Follows Symbolic Links |
| --- | --- | --- | --- |
| `read_symlink()` | Yes | Yes | Once |
| `absolute()` | No | Yes | No |
| `canonical()` | Yes | Yes | All |
| `weakly_canonical()` | No | Yes | All |
| `relative()` | No | Yes | All |
| `proximate()` | No | Yes | All |

Table 20.19. Filesystem Path Conversion Attributes

The following function demonstrates the use and effect of most of these operations when dealing with symbolic links:

*filesystem/symlink.hpp*

```
#include <filesystem>
#include <iostream>

void testSymLink(std::filesystem::path top)
{
  top = absolute(top);          // use absolute paths as we change current path
  create_directory(top);        // make sure top exists
```

```
  current_path(top);              // so that we can change the directory to it
  std::cout << std::filesystem::current_path() << '\n';  // print path of top

  // define our sub-directories (without creating them):
  std::filesystem::path px{top / "a/x"};
  std::filesystem::path py{top / "a/y"};
  std::filesystem::path ps{top / "a/s"};

  // print some relative paths (for non-existing files):
  std::cout << px.relative_path() << '\n';           // relative path from top
  std::cout << px.lexically_relative(py) << '\n';    // to px from py: "../x"
  std::cout << relative(px, py) << '\n';             // to px from py: "../x"
  std::cout << relative(px) << '\n';                 // to px from curr. path: "a/x"

  std::cout << px.lexically_relative(ps) << '\n';    // to px from ps: "../x"
  std::cout << relative(px, ps) << '\n';             // to px from ps: "../x"

  // now create all sub-directories and the symbolic link:
  create_directories(px);                            // create "top/a/x"
  create_directories(py);                            // create "top/a/y"
  if (!is_symlink(ps)) {
    create_directory_symlink(top, ps);               // create "top/a/s" -> "top"
  }
  std::cout << "ps: " << ps << '\n'
            << " -> " << read_symlink(ps) << '\n';

  // and see the difference between lexically and filesystem relative:
  std::cout << px.lexically_relative(ps) << '\n';    // to px from ps: "../x"
  std::cout << relative(px, ps) << '\n';             // to px from ps: "a/x"
}
```

Note that we first convert a possible relative path to an absolute path because otherwise, changing the current path affects the location of the path variables. `relative_path()` (see Section 20.3.2 on page 218) and `lexically_relative()` (see Section 20.3.3 on page 221) are cheap path member functions that do not take the actual filesystem into account. Thus, they ignore symbolic links.

The free-standing function `relative()` takes the filesystem into account. As long as we do not have files yet, it acts like `lexically_relative()`. However, after creating the symbolic link ps (as *top*/a/s referring to *top*), it follows the symbolic links and gives a different result.

On POSIX systems, calling the function from the current directory "/tmp" with the argument "top" produces the following output:

```
"/tmp/top"
"tmp/top/a/x"
"../x"
"../x"
```

## 20.4 Filesystem Operations

```
"a/x"
"../x"
"../x"
ps: "/tmp/top/a/s" -> "/tmp/top"
"../x"
"a/x"
```

On Windows systems, calling the function from the current directory "C:/temp" with the argument "top" produces the following output:

```
"C:\\temp\\top"
"temp\\top\\a/x"
"..\\x"
"..\\x"
"a\\x"
"..\\x"
"..\\x"
ps: "C:\\temp\\top\\a/s" -> "C:\\temp\\top"
"..\\x"
"a\\x"
```

Note again that you need administrator rights to create symbolic links on Windows.

### 20.4.6 Other Filesystem Operations

Table *20.20 Other Operations* lists other filesystem operations not mentioned yet.

| Call | Effect |
| --- | --- |
| equivalent(p1, p2) | Yields whether p1 and p2 refer to the same file |
| space(p) | Yields information about the disk space available at path p |
| current_path(p) | Sets the path of the current working directory to p |

Table 20.20. Other Operations

The equivalent() function is discussed in the section about path comparisons (see Section 20.3.6 on page 228).

The return value of space() is the following structure:

```
namespace std::filesystem {
  struct space_info {
    uintmax_t capacity;
    uintmax_t free;
    uintmax_t available;
  };
}
```

Thus, using structured bindings (see Chapter 1 on page 3), you can print the available disk space of root as follows:

```
auto [cap, _, avail] = std::filesystem::space("/");
std::cout << std::fixed << std::precision(2)
          << avail/1.0e6 << " of " << cap/1.0e6 << " MB available\n\n";
```

The output might be, for example:

```
43019.82 of 150365.79 MB available
```

`current_path()` called for a path argument modifies the current working directory of the whole program (it therefore applies to all threads). With the following code, you can switch to another working directory and restore the old one when leaving the scope:

```
// save current path:
auto currentDir{std::filesystem::current_path()};

try {
  // change current path temporarily:
  std::filesystem::current_path(subdir);
  ...    // perform some operations
}
catch (...) {
  // restore current path on exception:
  std::filesystem::current_path(currentDir);
  throw;  // rethrow
}
// restore current path without exception:
std::filesystem::current_path(currentDir);
```

## 20.5 Iterating Over Directories

One key application of the filesystem library is to iterate over directories or all files of a filesystem (sub)tree.

The most convenient way to do this is to use a range-based `for` loop. You can iterate over all files in a directory:

```
for (const auto& e : std::filesystem::directory_iterator(dir)) {
  std::cout << e.path() << '\n';
}
```

or iterate recursively over all files in a filesystem (sub)tree:

```
for (const auto& e : std::filesystem::recursive_directory_iterator(dir)) {
  std::cout << e.path() << '\n';
}
```

The passed argument `dir` can be a `path` or anything implicitly convertible to a path (especially all forms of strings).

Note that `e.path()` yields the file name including the directory the iteration was started from. Thus, if we iterate over `"."` a file name `file.txt` becomes `./file.txt` or `.\file.txt`.

## 20.5 Iterating Over Directories

In addition, this path is written quoted to a stream, which means that the output for this file name becomes
"./file.txt" or ".\\file.txt". Thus, as discussed before in an initial example (see Section 20.1.3 on
page 208), the following loop is more portable:

```
for (const auto& e : std::filesystem::directory_iterator(dir)) {
  std::cout << e.path().lexically_normal().string() << '\n';
}
```

To iterate over the current directory, pass "." as the current directory instead of "". Passing an empty path works on Windows but is not portable.

**Directory Iterators are Ranges**

You might be surprised that you can pass an iterator to a range-based for loop because you usually need a range.

The trick is that both `directory_iterator` and `recursive_directory_iterator` are classes for which global overloads of `begin()` and `end()` are provided:

- `begin()` yields the iterator itself,
- `end()` yields the end iterator, which you can also create with the default constructor

Therefore, you can also iterate as follows:

```
std::filesystem::directory_iterator di{p};
for (auto pos = begin(di); pos != end(di); ++pos) {
  std::cout << pos->path() << '\n';
}
```

Or as follows:

```
for (std::filesystem::directory_iterator pos{p};
     pos != std::filesystem::directory_iterator{};
     ++pos) {
  std::cout << pos->path() << '\n';
}
```

**Directory Iterator Options**

When iterating over directories, you can pass values of the type `directory_options`, which are listed in table *20.21 Directory Iterator Options*. The type is a bitmask scoped enumeration type (see Section A on page 415), defined in namespace `std::filesystem`.

| directory_options | **Effect** |
|---|---|
| none | Default (value 0) |
| follow_directory_symlink | Follow symbolic links (rather than skipping them) |
| skip_permission_denied | Skip directories where permission is denied |

Table 20.21. Directory Iterator Options

The default behavior is not to follow symbolic links and to throw an exception, if you do not have enough permissions to iterate over a (sub)directory. With `skip_permission_denied`, the iteration ignores directories you are not allowed to iterate over.

*filesystem/createfiles.cpp* (see Section 20.1.3 on page 206) shows an application of the option `follow_directory_symlink`.

## 20.5.1 Directory Entries

The elements directory iterators iterate over are of the type `std::filesystem::directory_entry`. Thus, if a directory iterator is valid, `operator*()` yields that type. This means that the correct types of the range-based `for` loop are as follows:

```
for (const std::filesystem::directory_entry& e
       : std::filesystem::directory_iterator(p)) {
  std::cout << e.path() << '\n';
}
```

Directory entries contain both a path object and additional attributes such as hard link count, file status, file size, last write time, whether it is a symbolic link, and where it refers to if it is.

Note that the iterators are input iterators. This is because iterating over a directory might result in different results as directory entries might change at any time. This has to be taken into account when using directory iterators in parallel algorithms (see Section 22.6.1 on page 276).

Table *20.22 Directory Entry Operations* lists the operations you can call for a directory entry e. They are more or less the operations you can call to query file attributes (see Section 20.4.1 on page 230), get the file status (see Section 20.4.2 on page 234), check permissions (see Section 20.4.3 on page 235), and compare (see Section 20.3.6 on page 228) the paths.

`assign()` and `replace_filename()` call the corresponding modifying path operations (see Section 20.3.5 on page 226) but do not modify the files in the underlying filesystem.

**Directory Entry Caching**

Implementations are encouraged to *cache* such additional file attributes to avoid additional filesystem access when using the entries. However, implementations are not required to cache the data, which means that these usually cheap operations might become more expensive.[9]

Because all the values are usually cached, these calls are usually cheap and therefore member functions:

```
for (const auto& e : std::filesystem::directory_iterator{"."})
{
  auto t = e.last_write_time();     // usually cheap
  ...
}
```

---

[9] In fact, the beta implementation of the C++17 filesystem library in g++ v9 caches only the file type, not the file size (this might change by the time the library is released).

## 20.5 Iterating Over Directories

| Call | Effect |
|---|---|
| `e.path()` | Yields the filesystem path for the current entry |
| `e.exists()` | Yields whether the file exists |
| `e.is_regular_file()` | Yields whether the file exists and is a regular file |
| `e.is_directory()` | Yields whether the file exists and is a directory |
| `e.is_symlink()` | Yields whether the file exists and is a symbolic link |
| `e.is_other()` | Yields whether the file exists and is neither regular nor a directory nor a symbolic link |
| `e.is_block_file()` | Yields whether the file exists and is a block-special file |
| `e.is_character_file()` | Yields whether the file exists and is a character-special file |
| `e.is_fifo()` | Yields whether the file exists and is a FIFO or pipe file |
| `e.is_socket()` | Yields whether the file exists and is a socket |
| `e.file_size()` | Yields the size of a file |
| `e.hard_link_count()` | Yields the number of hard links |
| `e.last_write_time()` | Yields the timepoint of the last write to a file |
| `e.status()` | Yields the status (see Section 20.4.2 on page 234) of the file p |
| `e.symlink_status()` | Yields the file status (see Section 20.4.2 on page 234) (following symbolic links) p |
| `e1 == e2` | Yields whether the two entry paths are equal |
| `e1 != e2` | Yields whether the two entry paths are not equal |
| `e1 < e2` | Yields whether an entry path is less than another |
| `e1 <= e2` | Yields whether an entry path is less than or equal to another |
| `e1 >= e2` | Yields whether an entry path is greater than or equal to another |
| `e1 > e2` | Yields whether an entry path is greater than another |
| `e.assign(p)` | Replaces the path of e with p and updates all entry attributes |
| `e.replace_filename(p)` | Replaces the file name of the current path of e with p and updates all entry attributes |
| `e.refresh()` | Updates all cached attributes for this entry |

Table 20.22. Directory Entry Operations

Whether cached or not, in a multi-user or multi-process operating system, all these iterations might yield data about files that is no longer valid. File contents and therefore sizes might change, files might be removed or replaced (thus, even file types might change), and permissions might be modified.

In that case, you can request a refresh of the data a directory entry holds:

```
for (const auto& e : std::filesystem::directory_iterator{"."})
{
    ...            // data becomes old
    e.refresh();   // refresh cache data for the file
    if (e.exists()) {
        auto t = e.last_write_time();
        ...
```

        }
    }

Alternatively, you might always ask for the current situation:

```
for (const auto& e : std::filesystem::directory_iterator{"."})
{
    ...           // data becomes old
    if (exists(e.path())) {
        auto t = last_write_time(e.path());
        ...
    }
}
```

## 20.6  Afternotes

The filesystem library was developed under the lead of Beman Dawes for many years as a Boost library. In 2014, for the first time it became a formal beta standard, the *File System Technical Specification* (see https://wg21.link/n4100).

With https://wg21.link/p0218r0 the *File System Technical Specification* was adopted as part of the standard library as proposed by Beman Dawes. Support for computing relative paths was added by Beman Dawes, Nicolai Josuttis, and Jamie Allsop in https://wg21.link/p0219r1. A couple of minor fixes were added as proposed by Beman Dawes in https://wg21.link/p0317r1, by Nicolai Josuttis in https://wg21.link/p0392r0, by Jason Liu and Hubert Tong in https://wg21.link/p0430r2, and especially by the members of the filesystem small group (Beman Dawes, S. Davis Herring, Nicolai Josuttis, Jason Liu, Billy O'Neal, P.J. Plauger, and Jonathan Wakely) in https://wg21.link/p0492r2.

After C++17 was released https://wg21.link/p1164r1 by Nicolai Josuttis fixed the behavior of `make_directory()` as a defect against C++17.

# Part IV

# Library Extensions and Modifications

This part of the book introduces extensions and modifications to existing library components with C++17.

# Chapter 21

# Extensions of Type Traits

C++17 extends the general abilities to use type traits (standard type functions) and introduces some new type traits.

## 21.1 Type Traits Suffix _v

Since C++17, you can use the suffix `_v` for all type traits that yield a value (just like you can use the suffix `_t` for all type traits that yield a type). For example, for any type T, you can now write:

```
std::is_const_v<T>         // since C++17
```

instead of

```
std::is_const<T>::value    // since C++11
```

This applies to all type traits. The approach is that a corresponding variable template is defined for each standard type trait. For example:

```
namespace std {
  template<typename T>
  constexpr bool is_const_v = is_const<T>::value;
}
```

Such a type trait can be used to formulate Boolean conditions which you can use at runtime:

```
if (std::is_signed_v<char>) {
  ...
}
```

However, because type traits are evaluated at compile time, you can also use the result at compile time (e.g., in a compile-time `if` (see Chapter 10 on page 95) statement):

```
if constexpr (std::is_signed_v<char>) {
  ...
}
```

Another application is to support different instantiations of templates:

```
// primary template for class C<T>
template<typename T, bool = std::is_pointer_v<T>>
class C {
  ...
};

// partial specialization for pointer types:
template<typename T>
class C<T, true> {
  ...
};
```

Here, class C provides a special implementation for pointer types.

The suffix _v can also be used if type traits yield a non-Boolean value, such as `std::extent<>`, which yields the size of the dimension of a raw array:

```
int a[5][7];
std::cout << std::extent_v<decltype(a)> << '\n';    // prints 5
std::cout << std::extent_v<decltype(a),1> << '\n';  // prints 7
```

## 21.2 New Type Traits

Table *21.1 New Type Traits* lists the new type traits introduced with C++17.

In addition, `is_literal_type<>` and `result_of<>` are deprecated since C++17.

The following paragraphs discuss these traits in detail.

### Type Trait is_aggregate<>

`std::is_aggregate<T>::value`

yields whether *T* is an aggregate type (see Section 4.3 on page 36):

```
template<typename T>
struct D : std::string, std::complex<T> {
    std::string data;
};

D<float> s{{"hello"}, {4.5,6.7}, "world"};              // OK since C++17
std::cout << std::is_aggregate<decltype(s)>::value;     // outputs: 1 (true)
```

## 21.2 New Type Traits

| Trait | Effect |
|---|---|
| `is_aggregate<T>` | Is aggregate type |
| `is_swappable<T>` | Can call `swap()` for this type |
| `is_nothrow_swappable<T>` | Can call `swap()` for this type and that operation cannot throw |
| `is_swappable_with<T,T2>` | Can call `swap()` for these two types with specific value category |
| `is_nothrow_swappable_with<T,T2>` | Can call `swap()` for these two types with specific value category and that operation cannot throw |
| `has_unique_object_representations<T>` | Any two objects with same value have same representation in memory |
| `is_invocable<T,Args...>` | Can be used as callable for *Args*... |
| `is_nothrow_invocable<T,Args...>` | Can be used as callable for *Args*... without throwing |
| `is_invocable_r<RT,T,Args...>` | Can be used as callable for *Args*... returning *RT* |
| `is_nothrow_invocable_r<RT,T,Args...>` | Can be used as callable for *Args*... returning *RT* without throwing |
| `invoke_result<T,Args...>` | Result type if used as callable for *Args*... |
| `conjunction<B...>` | Logical *and* for Boolean traits *B*... |
| `disjunction<B...>` | Logical *or* for Boolean traits *B*... |
| `negation<B>` | Logical *not* for Boolean trait *B* |
| `is_execution_policy<T>` | Is execution policy (see Section 22.2 on page 265) type |

Table 21.1. New Type Traits

**Type Traits `is_swappable<>` and `is_swappable_with<>`**

```
std::is_swappable<T>::value
std::is_nothrow_swappable<T>::value
std::is_swappable_with<T1,T2>::value
std::is_nothrow_swappable_with<T1,T2>::value
```

yield true if

- Lvalues of type T can be swapped, or
- Values of value category and of type T1 and T2 can be swapped

(with the guarantee that no exception is thrown using the `nothrow` form).

Note that `is_swappable<>` and `is_nothrow_swappable<>` check in general whether you can swap values of a specified type (checking the operation for lvalues). In contrast, `is_swappable_with<>` and `is_nothrow_swappable_with<>` take the value category into account. That is,

    `is_swappable_v<int>`                *// yields true*

is equivalent to

    `is_swappable_with_v<int&,int&>`      *// yields true (equivalent)* while:

```
is_swappable_with_v<int,int>      // yields false
```

yields false because you cannot call `std::swap(42, 77)`.

For example:

```
is_swappable_v<std::string>       // yields true
is_swappable_v<std::string&>      // yields true
is_swappable_v<std::string&&>     // yields true
is_swappable_v<void>              // yields false
is_swappable_v<void*>             // yields true
is_swappable_v<char[]>            // yields false

is_swappable_with_v<std::string, std::string>     // yields false
is_swappable_with_v<std::string&, std::string&>   // yields true
is_swappable_with_v<std::string&&, std::string&&> // yields false
```

### Type Trait `has_unique_object_representations<>`

std::**has_unique_object_representations**<*T*>::value

yields true if any two objects of type T have the same object representation in memory. That is, two identical values are always represented using the same sequence of byte values.

Objects with this property can produce a reliable hash value by hashing the associated byte sequence (there is no risk that some bits not participating in the object value might differ from one case to another).

### Type Traits `is_invocable<>` and `is_invocable_r<>`

```
std::is_invocable<T,Args...>::value
std::is_nothrow_invocable<T,Args...>::value
std::is_invocable_r<Ret,T,Args...>::value
std::is_nothrow_invocable_r<Ret,T,Args...>::value
```

yield true if you can use T as a callable for `Args...` returning a value convertible to type Ret (with the guarantee that no exception is thrown). That is, we can use these traits to test whether we can call (directly or via `std::invoke()` (see Section 33.1 on page 399)) a callable of type T for arguments of type `Args...` and use the return value as type Ret.

For example, given:

```
struct C {
  bool operator() (int) const {
    return true;
  }
};
```

we get the following results:

```
std::is_invocable<C>::value           // false
std::is_invocable<C,int>::value       // true
```

## 21.2 New Type Traits

```
std::is_invocable<int*>::value                              // false
std::is_invocable<int(*)()>::value                          // true

std::is_invocable_r<bool,C,int>::value                      // true
std::is_invocable_r<int,C,long>::value                      // true
std::is_invocable_r<void,C,int>::value                      // true
std::is_invocable_r<char*,C,int>::value                     // false
std::is_invocable_r<long,int(*)(int)>::value                // false
std::is_invocable_r<long,int(*)(int),int>::value            // true
std::is_invocable_r<long,int(*)(int),double>::value         // true
```

### Type Trait `invoke_result<>`

std::**invoke_result**<*T, Args...*>::type

yields the return type of using T as the type of a callable for Args.... That is, we can use this trait to get the return type obtained when we call (directly or via std::invoke() (see Section 33.1 on page 399)) a callable of type T for arguments of type Args......

The trait replaces `result_of<>`, which should no longer be used.

For example:

```
std::string foo(int);

using T1 = std::invoke_result_t<decltype(foo), int>;    // T1 is std::string

struct ABC {
  virtual ~ABC() = 0;
  void operator() (int) const {
  }
};

using T2 = typename std::invoke_result<ABC, int>::type;  // T2 is void
```

### Logical Operations for Boolean Type Traits

Table *21.2 Type Traits to Combine Other Type Traits* lists the type traits that are provided to logically combine or apply Boolean type traits (almost all standard type traits that yield a value).

| Traits | Effect |
|---|---|
| `conjunction<B...>` | Logical **and** for Boolean traits B... |
| `disjunction<B...>` | Logical **or** for Boolean traits B... |
| `negation<B>` | Logical **not** for Boolean trait B |

Table 21.2. Type Traits to Combine Other Type Traits

One application is the definition of new type traits by logically combining existing type traits. For example, you can easily define a trait that checks whether a type is "a pointer" (a raw pointer, a member pointer, or the null pointer):

```
template<typename T>
struct IsPtr
  : std::disjunction<std::is_null_pointer<T>,
                     std::is_member_pointer<T>,
                     std::is_pointer<T>>
{
};
```

We can now use this new trait, for example, in a compile-time `if` expression (see Chapter 10 on page 95):

```
template<typename T>
void foo(T x)
{
  if constexpr(IsPtr<T>) {
    ...  // handle as pointer
  }
  else {
    ...  // handle as no pointer
  }
}
```

As another example, we could define a type trait that checks whether a specific type is an integral or enumeration type, but not a `bool`:

```
template<typename T>
struct IsIntegralOrEnum
  : std::conjunction<std::disjunction<std::is_integral<T>,
                                      std::is_enum<T>>,
                     std::negation<std::is_same<T, bool>>>
{
};
```

Here, we roughly compute

```
(is_integral<T> || is_enum<T>) && !is_same<T,bool>
```

One benefit is that `std::conjunction<>` and `std::disjunction<>` *short-circuit* Boolean evaluations, which means that they stop the evaluation after the first `false` for *conjunction* or first `true` for *disjunction*. This saves compile time but can even help to make traits valid.[1]

For example, if incomplete types are used as follows:

```
struct X {
  X(int);   // converts from int
};
struct Y;   // incomplete type
```

---

[1] Thanks to Howard Hinnant for pointing this out.

the following static assertion fails because `is_constructible` results in undefined behavior for incomplete types (some compilers accept this code though):

```
// undefined behavior:
static_assert(std::is_constructible<X,int>{}
              || std::is_constructible<Y,int>{},
        "can't init X or Y from int");
```

Instead, the static assertion is guaranteed not to fail using `std::disjunction`, because the evaluation stops after `is_constructible<X,int>` yields `true`:

```
// OK:
static_assert(std::disjunction<std::is_constructible<X, int>,
                               std::is_constructible<Y, int>>{},
        "can't init X or Y from int");
```

## 21.3 Afternotes

Variable templates for standard type traits were first proposed in 2014 by Stephan T. Lavavej in `https://wg21.link/n3854`. They were finally adopted as part of the Library Fundamentals TS as proposed by Alisdair Meredith in `https://wg21.link/p0006r0`.

The type trait `std::is_aggregate<>` was introduced as a US national body comment for the standardization of C++17 (see `https://wg21.link/lwg2911`).

The `is_swappable` trait family was first proposed by Andrew Morrow in `https://wg21.link/n3619`. The finally accepted wording was formulated by Daniel Krügler in `https://wg21.link/p0185r1`.

`std::has_unique_object_representations<>` was first proposed under the name `is_contiguous_layout` by Michael Spencer in `https://wg21.link/p0258r0`. The finally accepted wording was formulated by Michael Spencer in `https://wg21.link/p0258r2`.

The `is_invocable` trait family was first proposed by Agustin Berge in `https://wg21.link/n4446`. Together with `std::invoke_result_t<>` the finally accepted wording was formulated by Daniel Krügler, Pablo Halpern, and Jonathan Wakely in `https://wg21.link/p0604r0`.

The logical operations for Boolean type traits were first proposed by Jonathan Wakely in `https://wg21.link/p0013r0`. The finally accepted wording was formulated by Jonathan Wakely in `https://wg21.link/p0013r1`.

# Chapter 22
# Parallel STL Algorithms

To benefit from modern multi-core architectures, the C++17 standard library introduces the ability to allow STL standard algorithms to run using multiple threads to deal with different elements in parallel.

Many algorithms were extended by a new first argument to specify whether and how to run the algorithm in parallel threads (the old way without this argument is, of course, still supported). In addition, some supplementary algorithms were introduced that specifically support parallel processing.

## A Simple Timer Helper

For the examples here in this chapter, sometimes we need a timer to measure the speed of the algorithms. For this, we use a simple helper class, which initializes a timer and provides `printDiff()` to print consumed milliseconds and reinitialize the timer:

*lib/timer.hpp*

```
#ifndef TIMER_HPP
#define TIMER_HPP

#include <iostream>
#include <string>
#include <chrono>

/*****************************************
 * timer to print elapsed time
 *****************************************/

class Timer
{
  private:
    std::chrono::steady_clock::time_point last;
  public:
```

```
    Timer()
     : last{std::chrono::steady_clock::now()} {
    }
    void printDiff(const std::string& msg = "Timer diff: ") {
      auto now{std::chrono::steady_clock::now()};
      std::chrono::duration<double, std::milli> diff{now - last};
      std::cout << msg << diff.count() << "ms\n";
      last = std::chrono::steady_clock::now();
    }
};

#endif // TIMER_HPP
```

## 22.1 Using Parallel Algorithms

Let us start with some example programs, demonstrating the ability to allow existing algorithms to run in parallel and use new parallel algorithms.

### 22.1.1 Using a Parallel `for_each()`

Here is a first, very simple example of running the standard algorithm `for_each()` in parallel:

*lib/parforeach.cpp*

```
#include <vector>
#include <iostream>
#include <algorithm>
#include <numeric>
#include <execution>     // for the execution policy
#include <cmath>         // for sqrt()
#include "timer.hpp"

int main()
{
  int numElems = 1000;

  struct Data {
    double value;   // initial value
    double sqrt;    // parallel computed square root
  };

  // initialize numElems values without square root:
  std::vector<Data> coll;
  coll.reserve(numElems);
```

## 22.1 Using Parallel Algorithms

```
  for (int i=0; i<numElems; ++i) {
    coll.push_back(Data{i * 4.37, 0});
  }

  // parallel computation of square roots:
  for_each(std::execution::par,
           coll.begin(), coll.end(),
           [](auto& val) {
             val.sqrt = std::sqrt(val.value);
           });
}
```

As you can see, using the parallel algorithms is in principle pretty easy:
- Include header `<execution>`
- Call the algorithms the way you would usually call algorithms with an additional first argument, which will often simply be `std::execution::par`.

In this case, we use the standard algorithm `for_each()` to compute the square root of the members `value` of all elements in the passed vector `coll`. Due to the additional first parameter `std::execution::par`, we request that the algorithm runs in parallel mode:

```
#include <algorithm>
#include <execution>
...
for_each(std::execution::par,
         coll.begin(), coll.end(),
         [](auto& val) {
           val.sqrt = std::sqrt(val.value);
         });
```

As usual, `coll` might be any range here. However, note that all parallel algorithms require the iterators to be at least forward iterators (we iterate through the same elements in different threads, which makes no sense if the iterators would not iterate over the same values).

The way the algorithms run in parallel is implementation-specific. And of course, using multiple threads might not always be faster, because starting and dealing with multiple threads also takes time.

**Performance Benefits**

To find out how to run and whether, and when it is worth running this algorithm in parallel, let us modify the example as follows:

*lib/parforeachloop.cpp*

```
#include <vector>
#include <iostream>
#include <algorithm>
#include <numeric>
#include <execution>    // for the execution policy
```

```cpp
#include <cstdlib>      // for atoi()
#include "timer.hpp"

int main(int argc, char* argv[])
{
  // initialize numElems from command line (default: 1000)
  int numElems = 1000;
  if (argc > 1) {
    numElems = std::atoi(argv[1]);
  }

  struct Data {
    double value;    // initial value
    double sqrt;     // parallel computed square root
  };

  // initialize numElems values without square root:
  std::vector<Data> coll;
  coll.reserve(numElems);
  for (int i=0; i<numElems; ++i) {
    coll.push_back(Data{i * 4.37, 0});
  }

  // loop to make measurements mature:
  for (int i{0}; i < 5; ++i) {
    Timer t;
    // sequential execution:
    for_each(std::execution::seq,
             coll.begin(), coll.end(),
             [](auto& val) {
               val.sqrt = std::sqrt(val.value);
             });
    t.printDiff("sequential: ");

    // parallel execution:
    for_each(std::execution::par,
             coll.begin(), coll.end(),
             [](auto& val) {
               val.sqrt = std::sqrt(val.value);
             });
    t.printDiff("parallel:    ");
    std::cout << '\n';
  }
}
```

## 22.1 Using Parallel Algorithms

The key modifications are:
- Via command line, we can pass how many values we operate on.
- We use the class `Timer` (see Section 22 on page 259) to measure the duration of calling the algorithms.
- We perform multiple measurements in a loop to make the durations more mature.

The result depends significantly on the hardware, C++ compiler, and C++ library used. On my laptop (using Visual C++ on an Intel i7 with 2 cores and hyper-threading), we get the following results:
- With 100 elements, the sequential algorithm is significantly (more than 10 times) faster. That is because starting and managing the threads takes too much time and is not worth it for a few elements.
- With 10,000 elements we are close to break even.
- With 1,000,000 elements the parallel execution is around three times faster.

Again, that is not general proof of where and when parallel algorithms are worthwhile, but it demonstrates that even for non-trivial numeric operations, it can be worth using them.

The key is that using parallel algorithms is worthwhile for:
- Long operations
- Many many elements

For example, using a parallel version of the algorithm `count_if()`, counting the number of even elements in a vector of ints was never worth it, not even with 1,000,000,000 elements:

```
auto num = std::count_if(std::execution::par,      // execution policy
                         coll.cbegin(), coll.cend(), // range
                         [](int elem){              // criterion
                           return elem % 2 == 0;
                         });
```

In fact, for a simple algorithm with a fast predicate (as in this example), running in parallel probably never pays off. To justify using a parallel algorithm, something should happen with each element that takes significant time and is independent of the processing of the other elements.

However, you cannot predict anything because it is up to the implementer of the C++ standard library when and how to use parallel threads. In fact, you cannot control how many threads are used and the implementation might decide to use multiple threads only with a certain number of elements.

Measure with the typical scenarios on your target platform(s).

### 22.1.2 Using a Parallel `sort()`

Sorting is another example where parallel algorithms can help. Because sorting criteria are used significantly more than once for each element, you can save significant time.

Consider the initialization of a vector of strings as follows:

```
std::vector<std::string> coll;
for (int i=0; i < numElems / 2; ++i) {
  coll.emplace_back("id" + std::to_string(i));
  coll.emplace_back("ID" + std::to_string(i));
}
```

That is, we create a vector of elements that start with "id" or "ID" followed by an integral number:

```
id0 ID0 id1 ID1 id2 ID2 id3 ... id99 ID99 id100 ID100 ...
```

As usual, we can sort the elements sequentially as follows:

```
sort(coll.begin(), coll.end());
```

This can now be done by explicitly passing a "sequential" execution policy:

```
sort(std::execution::seq,
     coll.begin(), coll.end());
```

Passing sequential execution as a parameter can be useful if the decision whether to run sequentially or in parallel is taken at runtime and you do not want to have different function calls.

Requesting parallel sorting instead is easy:

```
sort(std::execution::par,
     coll.begin(), coll.end());
```

Note that there is also another parallel execution policy:

```
sort(std::execution::par_unseq,
     coll.begin(), coll.end());
```

I will explain the difference later.

So again, the question is, (when) is using parallel sorting better? On my laptop with only 10,000 strings, you could see that the parallel sorting took half the time of sequential sorting. And even sorting 1000 strings was slightly better with parallel execution.

**Combining with Other Improvements**

Note that further modifications might give you more or additional benefits. For example, if we sort just by the numbers, using substrings without the two leading characters, we could use string operations inside the predicate and again see a two-fold improvement with parallel execution:

```
sort(std::execution::par,
     coll.begin(), coll.end(),
     [] (const auto& a, const auto& b) {
       return a.substr(2) < b.substr(2);
     });
```

However, substr() is a pretty expensive member function for strings because it creates and returns a new temporary string. By using class string_view (see Chapter 19 on page 185), we see a three-fold improvement even with sequential execution:

```
sort(coll.begin(), coll.end(),
     [] (const auto& a, const auto& b) {
       return std::string_view{a}.substr(2) < std::string_view{b}.substr(2);
     });
```

We can easily combine using parallel algorithms and string views:

```
sort(std::execution::par,
     coll.begin(), coll.end(),
     [] (const auto& a, const auto& b) {
       return std::string_view{a}.substr(2) < std::string_view{b}.substr(2);
     });
```

As a result, we become faster by a factor of up to 10 compared to a sequential execution with `string`'s `substr()` members:

```
sort(coll.begin(), coll.end(),
     [] (const auto& a, const auto& b) {
       return a.substr(2) < b.substr(2);
     });
```

## 22.2 Execution Policies

You can pass different *execution policies* to parallel STL algorithms as the first argument. They are defined in header `<execution>`. Table *22.1 Execution Policies* lists the standardized *execution policies*.

| Policy | Meaning |
| --- | --- |
| `std::execution::seq` | Sequential execution |
| `std::execution::par` | Parallel sequenced execution |
| `std::execution::par_unseq` | Parallel unsequenced (vectorized) execution |

*Table 22.1. Execution Policies*

Let us discuss the execution policies in detail:

- **Sequential execution** with `seq`

    This means that, as with the non-parallel algorithms, the current thread of execution executes the necessary operations sequentially element by element. Using this policy should behave like using the non-parallel way of calling algorithms that do not accept any execution policy at all. However, with the parallel algorithms that take this argument, additional constraints might apply, such as `for_each()` not returning any value or all iterators having to be at least forward iterators.

    This policy is provided to allow you to request sequential execution by just passing a different argument instead of using a different signature. However, note that parallel algorithms with this policy might behave slightly differently (see Section 22.4 on page 266) to corresponding non-parallel algorithms.

- **Parallel sequenced execution** with `par`

    This means that multiple threads might sequentially execute the necessary operations for the elements. When an algorithm starts the execution of the necessary operations, it finishes this execution before it deals with other elements.

    In contrast to `par_unseq`, this ensures that no problems or deadlocks occur when processing a first specific step for one element requires the call of a following step for this element before the same thread performs the first specific step with another element.

- **Parallel unsequenced execution** with `par_unseq`

    This means that multiple threads might execute the necessary operations for multiple elements without the guarantee of one thread executing all steps for the element without switching to other elements. In particular, this enables vectorized execution, where a thread might first perform the first step of an execution for multiple elements before it executes the next step.

Parallel unsequenced execution needs special support from the compiler/hardware to detect where and how operations can be vectorized.[1]

All execution policies are `constexpr` objects of a corresponding new unique class in namespace `std` (`sequenced_policy`, `parallel_policy`, and `parallel_unsequenced_policy`). The new type trait `std::is_execution_policy<>` is provided to support generic programming that needs special handling of template parameters that are execution policies.

## 22.3 Exception Handling

All parallel algorithms call `std::terminate()` whenever element access functions exit via an uncaught exception.

Note that this also applies if the sequential execution policy is chosen. If this is not acceptable, using the non-parallel version of an algorithm might be the better choice.

Note also that parallel algorithms might still throw. If they fail to acquire temporary memory resources for parallel execution, they can throw `std::bad_alloc`. However, nothing else may be thrown.

## 22.4 Benefit of Not Using Parallel Algorithms

With the ability to call parallel algorithms and the fact that they even provide a sequential execution policy, the question might arise as to whether we still need the non-parallel algorithms.

However, besides backward compatibility, using a non-parallel algorithm might provide significant benefits:

- Input and output iterators can be used.
- Algorithms do not `terminate()` on exceptions.
- Algorithms may avoid side effects due to an unintended use of elements.
- Algorithms might provide additional functionality, such as `for_each()` returning the passed callable to be able to deal with its resulting state.

---

[1] For example, if a CPU supports registers of 512 bits, a compiler might perform computations by loading eight 64-bit values or four 128-bit values into a register simultaneously and performing multiple computations with them in parallel.

## 22.5 Overview of Parallel Algorithms

Table *22.2 STL Algorithms with Unrestricted Parallelization* lists the algorithms that are standardized to support parallel processing without any modification.

Table *22.3 STL Algorithms Without Parallelization* lists the algorithms that do not support parallel processing.

| Algorithms with Unrestricted Parallelization |
|---|
| `find_end()`, `adjacent_find()` |
| `search()`, `search_n()` except with "searcher" (see Chapter 24 on page 293) |
| `swap_ranges()` |
| `replace()`, `replace_if()` |
| `fill()` |
| `generate()` |
| `remove()`, `remove_if()`, `unique()` |
| `reverse()`, `rotate()` |
| `partition()`, `stable_partition()` |
| `sort()`, `stable_sort()`, `partial_sort()` |
| `is_sorted()`, `is_sorted_until()` |
| `nth_element()` |
| `inplace_merge()` |
| `is_heap()`, `is_heap_until()` |
| `min_element()`, `max_element()`, `min_max_element()` |

*Table 22.2. STL Algorithms with Unrestricted Parallelization*

| Algorithms Without Parallelization |
|---|
| `accumulate()` |
| `partial_sum()` |
| `inner_product()` |
| `search()` with "searcher" (see Chapter 24 on page 293) |
| `copy_backward()` `move_backward()` |
| `sample()`, `shuffle()` |
| `partition_point()` |
| `lower_bound()`, `upper_bound()`, `equal_range()` |
| `binary_search()` |
| `is_permutation()`, |
| `next_permutation()`, `prev_permutation()` |
| `push_heap()`, `pop_heap()`, `make_heap()`, `sort_heap()` |

*Table 22.3. STL Algorithms Without Parallelization*

Note that for `accumulate()`, `partial_sum()`, and `inner_product()`, new parallel algorithms are provided with relaxed requirements (which is motivated below):
- To run `accumulate()` in parallel, use `reduce()` (see Section 23.2.1 on page 281) or `transform_reduce()` (see Section 23.2.2 on page 283).
- To run `partial_sum()` in parallel, use the ...`scan() algorithms` (see Section 23.2.3 on page 287).
- To run `inner_product()` in parallel, use `transform_reduce()` (see Section 23.2.2 on page 285).

Table 22.4 *STL Algorithms with Restricted Parallelization* lists the algorithms that are standardized to support parallel processing with some modifications.

| Algorithms | Restriction |
|---|---|
| `for_each()` | Return type void and forward iterators |
| `for_each_n()` | Forward iterators (NEW) |
| `all_of()`, `any_of()`, `none_of()` | Forward iterators |
| `find()`, `find_if()`, `find_if_not()` | Forward iterators |
| `find_first_of()` | Forward iterators |
| `count()`, `count_if()` | Forward iterators |
| `mismatch()` | Forward iterators |
| `equal()` | Forward iterators |
| `is_partitioned()` | Forward iterators |
| `partial_sort_copy()` | Forward iterators |
| `includes()` | Forward iterators |
| `lexicographical_compare()` | Forward iterators |
| `fill_n()` | Forward iterators |
| `generate_n()` | Forward iterators |
| `reverse_copy()` | Forward iterators |
| `rotate_copy()` | Forward iterators |
| `copy()`, `copy_n()`, `copy_if()` | Forward iterators |
| `move()` | Forward iterators |
| `transform()` | Forward iterators |
| `replace_copy()`, `replace_copy_if()` | Forward iterators |
| `remove_copy()`, `remove_copy_if()` | Forward iterators |
| `unique_copy()` | Forward iterators |
| `partition_copy()` | Forward iterators |
| `merge()` | Forward iterators |
| `set_union()`, `set_intersection()` | Forward iterators |
| `set_difference()`, `set_symmetric_difference()` | Forward iterators |
| `inclusive_scan()`, `exclusive_scan()` | Forward iterators (NEW) |
| `transform_inclusive_scan()`, `transform_exclusive_scan()` | Forward iterators (NEW) |

Table 22.4. *STL Algorithms with Restricted Parallelization*

## 22.6　Motivation for New Algorithms for Parallel Processing

Some supplementary algorithms were introduced to handle the parallel processing of standard algorithms available since C++98.

### 22.6.1　`reduce()`

For example, `reduce()` was introduced as a parallel form of `accumulate()`, which "accumulates" all elements (you can define which operation performs the "accumulation"). For example, consider the following use of `accumulate()`:

*lib/accumulate.cpp*

```cpp
#include <iostream>
#include <vector>
#include <numeric>     // for accumulate()

void printSum(long num)
{
  // create coll with num sequences of 1 2 3 4:
  std::vector<long> coll;
  coll.reserve(num * 4);
  for (long i=0; i < num; ++i) {
    coll.insert(coll.end(), {1, 2, 3, 4});
  }

  auto sum = std::accumulate(coll.begin(), coll.end(),
                             0L);
  std::cout << "accumulate(): " << sum << '\n';
}

int main()
{
  printSum(1);
  printSum(1000);
  printSum(1000000);
  printSum(10000000);
}
```

We compute the sum of all elements, which outputs:

```
accumulate(): 10
accumulate(): 10000
accumulate(): 10000000
```

## Parallelization for Associative and Commutative Operations

This program can be parallelized by switching to `reduce()`:

*lib/parreduce.cpp*

```cpp
#include <iostream>
#include <vector>
#include <numeric>      // for reduce()
#include <execution>

void printSum(long num)
{
  // create coll with num sequences of 1 2 3 4:
  std::vector<long> coll;
  coll.reserve(num * 4);
  for (long i=0; i < num; ++i) {
    coll.insert(coll.end(), {1, 2, 3, 4});
  }

  auto sum = std::reduce(std::execution::par,
                         coll.begin(), coll.end(),
                         0L);
  std::cout << "reduce():      " << sum << '\n';
}

int main()
{
  printSum(1);
  printSum(1000);
  printSum(1000000);
  printSum(10000000);
}
```

With the same output, the program might now run faster or slower (depending on whether starting multiple threads is supported and takes more or less time than the time we save by running the algorithm in parallel).

The operation used here is +, which is commutative and associative, meaning that the order of adding the integral elements is irrelevant.

## Parallelization for Non-Commutative Operations

However, for floating-point values the order makes a difference, which the following program demonstrates:

*lib/parreducefloat.cpp*

```cpp
#include <iostream>
```

## 22.6 Motivation for New Algorithms for Parallel Processing

```cpp
#include <vector>
#include <numeric>
#include <execution>

void printSum(long num)
{
  // create coll with num sequences of 0.1 0.3 0.0001:
  std::vector<double> coll;
  coll.reserve(num * 4);
  for (long i=0; i < num; ++i) {
    coll.insert(coll.end(), {0.1, 0.3, 0.00001});
  }

  auto sum1 = std::accumulate(coll.begin(), coll.end(),
                              0.0);
  std::cout << "accumulate(): " << sum1 << '\n';
  auto sum2 = std::reduce(std::execution::par,
                          coll.begin(), coll.end(),
                          0.0);
  std::cout << "reduce():     " << sum2 << '\n';
  std::cout << (sum1==sum2 ? "equal\n" : "differ\n");
}

#include<iomanip>

int main()
{
  std::cout << std::setprecision(20);
  printSum(1);
  printSum(1000);
  printSum(1000000);
  printSum(10000000);
}
```

Here we use both `accumulate()` and `reduce()` and compare the results. A possible output is:

```
accumulate(): 0.40001
reduce():     0.40001
equal
accumulate(): 400.01
reduce():     400.01
differ
accumulate(): 400010
reduce():     400010
differ
```

```
accumulate(): 4.0001e+06
reduce():     4.0001e+06
differ
```

Although the results look the same, they sometimes differ. This is a possible consequence of adding floating-point values in a different order.

If we change the precision of printing floating-point values:

```
std::cout << std::setprecision(20);
```

we can see that the resulting values are slightly different:

```
accumulate(): 0.40001000000000003221
reduce():     0.40001000000000003221
equal
accumulate(): 400.01000000000533419
reduce():     400.01000000000010459
differ
accumulate(): 400009.99999085225863
reduce():     400009.9999999878346
differ
accumulate(): 4000100.0004483023658
reduce():     4000100.0000019222498
differ
```

Because there is no specification of if, when, and how parallel algorithms are used, the result might look the same on some platforms (up to a certain number of elements).

For further details about `reduce()`, see its reference section (see Section 23.2.1 on page 281).

**Parallelization for Non-Associative Operations**

Let us now change the operation to accumulate values by always adding the square of each value:

*lib/accumulate2.cpp*

```
#include <iostream>
#include <vector>
#include <numeric>    // for accumulate()

void printSum(long num)
{
  // create coll with num sequences of 1 2 3 4:
  std::vector<long> coll;
  coll.reserve(num * 4);
  for (long i=0; i < num; ++i) {
    coll.insert(coll.end(), {1, 2, 3, 4});
  }
```

## 22.6 Motivation for New Algorithms for Parallel Processing

```cpp
  auto squaredSum = [] (auto sum, auto val) {
                       return sum + val * val;
                     };
  auto sum = std::accumulate(coll.begin(), coll.end(),
                             0L,
                             squaredSum);
  std::cout << "accumulate(): " << sum << '\n';
}

int main()
{
  printSum(1);
  printSum(1000);
  printSum(1000000);
  printSum(10000000);
}
```

Here, we pass a lambda that, for each value, takes the current sum and adds the square of the new value:

```cpp
  auto squaredSum = [] (auto sum, auto val) {
                       return sum + val * val;
                     };
```

Using `accumulate()` the output looks fine:

```
accumulate(): 30
accumulate(): 30000
accumulate(): 30000000
accumulate(): 300000000
```

However, let us switch to parallel processing with `reduce()`:

*lib/parreduce2.cpp*

```cpp
#include <iostream>
#include <vector>
#include <numeric>       // for reduce()
#include <execution>

void printSum(long num)
{
  // create coll with num sequences of 1 2 3 4:
  std::vector<long> coll;
  coll.reserve(num * 4);
  for (long i=0; i < num; ++i) {
    coll.insert(coll.end(), {1, 2, 3, 4});
  }
```

```
  auto squaredSum = [] (auto sum, auto val) {
                     return sum + val * val;
                   };

  auto sum = std::reduce(std::execution::par,
                         coll.begin(), coll.end(),
                         0L,
                         squaredSum);
  std::cout << "reduce():     " << sum << '\n';
}

int main()
{
  printSum(1);
  printSum(1000);
  printSum(1000000);
  printSum(10000000);
}
```

The output might become something like this:

```
reduce():     30
reduce():     30000
reduce():     -425251612
reduce():     705991074
```

Yes, the result might *sometimes* be wrong. The problem is that the operation is not associative. If we apply this operation to the elements 1; 2, and 3, we might first compute 0+1*1 and 2+3*3. However, when we then combine the intermediate result we square 3 again, by essentially computing:

(0+1*1) + (2+3*3) * (2+3*3)

But why are the results sometimes correct? Well, it seems that on this platform, `reduce()` only runs in parallel with a certain number of elements. And that's absolutely standard-conforming. Therefore, use test cases with enough elements to detect problems like this.

The solution to this problem is to use another new algorithm, `transform_reduce()`. It separates the modification we want to perform with each element (which is one thing we can parallelize) and the accumulation of the results provided it is commutative (which is the other thing we can parallelize).

*lib/partransformreduce.cpp*

```
#include <iostream>
#include <vector>
#include <numeric>      //for transform_reduce()
#include <execution>
#include <functional>
```

## 22.6 Motivation for New Algorithms for Parallel Processing

```cpp
void printSum(long num)
{
  // create coll with num sequences of 1 2 3 4:
  std::vector<long> coll;
  coll.reserve(num * 4);
  for (long i=0; i < num; ++i) {
    coll.insert(coll.end(), {1, 2, 3, 4});
  }

  auto sum = std::transform_reduce(std::execution::par,
                                   coll.begin(), coll.end(),
                                   0L,
                                   std::plus{},
                                   [] (auto val) {
                                     return val * val;
                                   });
  std::cout << "transform_reduce(): " << sum << '\n';
}

int main()
{
  printSum(1);
  printSum(1000);
  printSum(1000000);
  printSum(10000000);
}
```

When calling `transform_reduce()`, we pass

- The execution policy to (allow us to) run this in parallel
- The range of the values to deal with
- 0L as the initial value of the outer accumulation
- The operation + as operation of the outer accumulation
- A lambda to process each value before the accumulation

`transform_reduce()` will probably be by far the most important parallel algorithm because we often modify values before we combine them (also called the *map reduce* principle).

For further details about `transform_reduce()`, see its reference section (see Section 23.2.2 on page 283).

## `transform_reduce()` for Filesystem Operations

Here is a another example of running `transform_reduce()` in parallel:

*lib/dirsize.cpp*

```cpp
#include <vector>
#include <iostream>
#include <numeric>      // for transform_reduce()
#include <execution>    // for the execution policy
#include <filesystem>   // filesystem library
#include <cstdlib>      // for EXIT_FAILURE

int main(int argc, char* argv[])
{
  // root directory is passed as command line argument:
  if (argc < 2) {
    std::cout << "Usage: " << argv[0] << " <path> \n";
    return EXIT_FAILURE;
  }
  std::filesystem::path root{argv[1]};

  // init list of all file paths in passed file tree:
  std::vector<std::filesystem::path> paths;
  try {
    std::filesystem::recursive_directory_iterator dirpos{root};
    std::copy(begin(dirpos), end(dirpos),
              std::back_inserter(paths));
  }
  catch (const std::exception& e) {
    std::cerr << "EXCEPTION: " << e.what() << std::endl;
    return EXIT_FAILURE;
  }

  // accumulate size of all regular files:
  auto sz = std::transform_reduce(
                   std::execution::par,              // parallel execution
                   paths.cbegin(), paths.cend(),     // range
                   std::uintmax_t{0},                // initial value
                   std::plus<>(),                    // accumulate ...
                   [](const std::filesystem::path& p) { // file size if regular file
                     return is_regular_file(p) ? file_size(p)
                                               : std::uintmax_t{0};
                   });
  std::cout << "size of all " << paths.size()
            << " regular files: " << sz << '\n';
}
```

First, we recursively collect all filesystem paths (see Section 20.2.3 on page 211) in the directory given as command-line argument:

```
std::filesystem::path root{argv[1]};

std::vector<std::filesystem::path> paths;
std::filesystem::recursive_directory_iterator dirpos{root};
std::copy(begin(dirpos), end(dirpos),
          std::back_inserter(paths));
```

Note that because we might pass an invalid path, possible (filesystem) exceptions are caught.

Then, we iterate over a collection of the filesystem paths to accumulate their sizes if they are regular files:

```
auto sz = std::transform_reduce(
              std::execution::par,                     // parallel execution
              paths.cbegin(), paths.cend(),            // range
              std::uintmax_t{0},                       // initial value
              std::plus<>(),                           // accumulate ...
              [](const std::filesystem::path& p) {    // file size if regular file
                return is_regular_file(p) ? file_size(p)
                                          : std::uintmax_t{0};
              });
```

The new standard algorithm `transform_reduce()` operates as follows:

- The last argument is applied to each element. Here, the passed lambda is called for each path element and queries its size if it is a regular file.
- The second to last argument is the operation that combines all the sizes. Because we want to accumulate the sizes, we use the standard function object `std::plus<>`.
- The third to last argument is the initial value for the operation that combines all the sizes. The type of this value is the return type of the function. We convert 0 to the type of the return value of `file_size()`, `std::uintmax_t`. Otherwise, if we simply passed 0, we would narrow the result to `int`. Thus, if the list of paths is empty, the whole call returns 0.

Note that asking for the size of a file is a pretty expensive operation because it requires an operating system call. Therefore, using an algorithm that calls this transformation (from path to size) in parallel with multiple threads in any order and computes the sum pays off quite quickly. First measurements demonstrate a clear win (up to doubling the speed of the program).

Note also that you cannot pass the paths the directory iterator iterates over directly to the parallel algorithm, because directory iterators are input iterators, while the parallel algorithms require forward iterators.

Finally, note that `transform_reduce()` is defined in the header file `<numeric>` instead of `<algorithm>` (just like `accumulate()`, it counts as a numeric algorithm).

## 22.7 Afternotes

Parallelizing the STL algorithms was first proposed in 2012 by Jared Hoberock, Michael Garland, Olivier Giroux, Vinod Grover, Ujval Kapasi, and Jaydeep Marathe in `https://wg21.link/n3408`. It became a formal beta standard, the *Technical Specification for C++ Extensions for Parallelism* (see `https://wg21.link/n3850`). Additional algorithms were added by Jared Hoberock, Grant Mercer, Agustin Berge, and Harmut Kaiser in `https://wg21.link/n4276`. With `https://wg21.link/p0024r2`, the *Technical Specification for C++ Extensions for Parallelism* was adopted to the standard library as proposed by Jared Hoberock. The handling of exceptions was accepted as proposed by JF Bastien and Bryce Adelstein Lelbach in `https://wg21.link/p0394r4`.

# Chapter 23
# New STL Algorithms in Detail

C++17 introduces a few new STL algorithms. The main reason for this is to support parallelization (see Chapter 22 on page 259), but you can also use these algorithms sequentially.

## 23.1 `std::for_each_n()`

As part of the parallel STL algorithms (see Chapter 22 on page 259), a new algorithm `for_each_n()` was proposed, which is also available in the traditional non-parallel form. Similarly for `copy_n()`, `fill_n()`, and `generate_n()`, an integral parameter is required to specify for how many elements of the passed range the passed callable is called.

```
InputIterator
for_each_n (ExecutionPolicy&& pol,   // optional
            InputIterator beg,
            Size count,
            UnaryProc op)
```

- Calls *op(elem)* for the first *count* elements in the range starting with *beg*.
- Returns the position after the last element for which *op()* was called.
- The caller must ensure that the range starting with *beg* contains enough elements.
- Any return value of the passed *op* is ignored.
- If no execution policy is passed, `for_each_n()` guarantees that the passed callable is called for each element in order.
- If the first optional execution policy (see Section 22.2 on page 265) is passed:
  - There is no guaranteed order for using the operator *op* for all elements.
  - It is up to the caller to ensure that parallel calls of the operations do not result in a data race.
  - The iterators must be forward iterators.
- Complexity: linear (*count* calls of *op()*).

For example:

*lib/foreachn.cpp*

```cpp
#include <iostream>
#include <vector>
#include <string>
#include <algorithm>   // for for_each_n()

int main()
{
  // initialize a vector of 10,000 string values:
  std::vector<std::string> coll;
  for (int i=0; i < 10000; ++i) {
    coll.push_back(std::to_string(i));
  }

  // modify first 5 elements:
  for_each_n(coll.begin(), 5,
             [] (auto& elem) {
                elem = "value" + elem;
             });

  // print first 10 elements:
  for_each_n(coll.begin(), 10,
             [] (const auto& elem) {
                std::cout << elem << '\n';
             });
}
```

After initializing a vector with plenty of string values (`value0`, `value1`, ...), we first modify the first five strings:

```cpp
for_each_n(coll.begin(), 5,
           [] (auto& elem) {
              elem = "value" + elem;
           });
```

and then print the first 10 strings:

```cpp
for_each_n(coll.begin(), 10,
           [] (const auto& elem) {
              std::cout << elem << '\n';
           });
```

Thus, the program has the following output:

```
value0
value1
value2
value3
value4
5
6
7
8
9
```

## 23.2 New Numeric STL Algorithms

This section lists the new STL algorithms defined in the header file `<numeric>`. Note that the motivation of these new algorithms was discussed before (see Section 22.6 on page 269).

### 23.2.1 `std::reduce()`

```
typename iterator_traits<InputIterator>::value_type
reduce (ExecutionPolicy&& pol,    // optional
        InputIterator beg, InputIterator end)

T
reduce (ExecutionPolicy&& pol,    // optional
        InputIterator beg, InputIterator end,
        T initVal)

T
reduce (ExecutionPolicy&& pol,    // optional
        InputIterator beg, InputIterator end,
        T initVal,
        BinaryOp op)
```

- The first two forms compute and return the sum of all elements in the range [*beg*,*end*) with an initial value. Thus, after the initialization:

    *result* = *initialValue*

    the following is called for each element:

    *result* = *result* + *elem*

    - For the first form, the initial value is the "value-initialized default value" of the element types (default constructed value or equivalent value for 0, 0.0, `false`, `nullptr`).
    - For the second form, the initial value is *initVal*.

- Thus, for the values

    a1 a2 a3 a4 ...

  the forms compute and return:

    *initVal* + a1 + a2 + a3 + ...

- The third form computes and returns the result of calling *op* for *initVal* and all elements in the range [*beg,end*]. In particular, it calls the following for each element:

    *result* = *op*(*result*, *elem*)

  Thus, for the values

    a1 a2 a3 a4 ...

  the form computes and returns:

    *initVal op* a1 *op* a2 *op* a3 *op* ...

- If the range is empty (*beg==end*), all forms return the initial value.
- *op* must not modify the passed arguments.
- Complexity: linear (*numElems* calls of operator + or *op*(), respectively).
- The algorithm is the parallel (see Chapter 22 on page 259) version of `std::accumulate()` called for associative (see Section 22.6.1 on page 270) operations. If the first optional execution policy (see Section 22.2 on page 265) is passed:
    - There is no guaranteed order for using the operator *op*, which means that *op* must be commutative (see Section 22.6.1 on page 270) and associative (see Section 22.6.1 on page 270).
    - It is up to the caller to ensure that parallel calls of the operations do not result in a data race.
    - The iterators must be forward iterators.

For example, the following program:

*lib/reduce.cpp*

```
#include <array>
#include <iostream>
#include <numeric>

int main()
{
  std::array coll{3, 1, 7, 5, 4, 1, 6, 3};

  // process sum of elements
  std::cout << "sum: "
      << std::reduce(coll.cbegin(), coll.cend())   // range
      << '\n';

  // process sum of elements with initial value:
  std::cout << "sum: "
      << std::reduce(coll.cbegin(), coll.cend(),   // range
                     0)                             // initial value
```

## 23.2 New Numeric STL Algorithms

```
            << '\n';
    // process product of elements
    std::cout << "product: "
        << std::reduce (coll.cbegin(), coll.cend(),   // range
                        1LL,                          // initial value
                        std::multiplies{})            // operation
        << '\n';

    // process product of elements (use 0 as initial value)
    std::cout << "product: "
        << std::reduce (coll.cbegin(), coll.cend(),   // range
                        0,                            // initial value
                        std::multiplies{})            // operation
        << '\n';
}
```

has the following output:

```
sum: 30
sum: 30
product: 7560
product: 0
```

See the motivation for parallel algorithms for a more detailed motivation (see Section 22.6.1 on page 269) for this algorithm.

### 23.2.2 std::transform_reduce()

There are two variants of std::transform_reduce():

**std::transform_reduce() for a Single Range**

```
T
transform_reduce (ExecutionPolicy&& pol,   // optional
                  InputIterator beg, InputIterator end)
                  T initVal,
                  BinaryOp op2, UnaryOp op1)
```

- Computes and returns the combination/accumulation of all transformed elements in the range [*beg*, *end*) with the initial value *initVal*.
- Thus, for the values

    a1 a2 a3 a4 ...

    it computes and returns

$$\textit{initVal} \; op2 \; op1(a1) \; op2 \; op1(a2) \; op2 \; op1(a3) \; op2 \; ...$$

- If the range is empty (*beg==end*), it returns *initVal*.
- *op1* and *op2* must not modify the passed arguments.
- Complexity: linear (*numElems* calls of operator *op1* and *op2*).
- The algorithm is the parallel (see Chapter 22 on page 259) version of `std::accumulate()` called for non-associative (see Section 22.6.1 on page 272) operations. If the first optional execution policy (see Section 22.2 on page 265) is passed:
  - There is no guaranteed order for using the operator *op2*, which means that *op2* must be commutative (see Section 22.6.1 on page 270) and associative (see Section 22.6.1 on page 270).
  - It is up to the caller to ensure that parallel calls of the operations do not result in a data race.
  - The iterators must be forward iterators.

For example, the following program:

*lib/transformreduce1.cpp*

```cpp
#include <array>
#include <iostream>
#include <numeric>

int main()
{
  std::array coll{3, 1, 7, 5, 4, 1, 6, 3};

  auto twice = [] (int v) { return v*2; };

  // process sum of doubled values of elements:
  std::cout << "sum of doubles: "
      << std::transform_reduce(coll.cbegin(), coll.cend(),   // range
                               0,
                               std::plus{}, twice)
      << '\n';

  // process sum of squared values:
  std::cout << "sum of squared: "
      << std::transform_reduce(coll.cbegin(), coll.cend(),   // range
                               0L,
                               std::plus{},
                               [] (auto v) {
                                 return v * v;
                               })
      << '\n';
}
```

has the following output:

## 23.2 New Numeric STL Algorithms

```
sum of doubles: 60
sum of squared: 146
```

See the motivation for parallel algorithms for a more detailed motivation (see Section 22.6.1 on page 274) for this algorithm and for other examples (see Section 22.6.1 on page 276).

### `std::transform_reduce()` for Two Ranges

```
T
transform_reduce (ExecutionPolicy&& pol,    // optional
                  InputIterator1 beg1, InputIterator1 end1)
                  InputIterator2 beg2,
                  T initVal)
T
transform_reduce (ExecutionPolicy&& pol,    // optional
                  InputIterator1 beg1, InputIterator1 end1)
                  InputIterator2 beg2,
                  T initVal,
                  BinaryOp1 op1, BinaryOp2 op2)
```

- The first form computes and returns the inner product of *initVal* and all elements in the range [*beg*, *end*) multiplied by the elements in the range starting with *beg2*. In particular, it calls the following for all corresponding elements:

    *initVal* = *initVal* + *elem1* * *elem2*

- The second form computes and returns the result of calling *op* for *initVal* and all elements in the range [*beg1*, *end1*) combined with the elements in the range starting with *beg2*. In particular, it calls the following for all corresponding elements:

    *initVal* = *op1*(*initVal*, *op2*(*elem1*, *elem2*))

- Thus, for the values

    a1 a2 a3 ...
    b1 b2 b3 ...

    the forms compute and return either

    *initVal* + (a1 * b1) + (a2 * b2) + (a3 * b3) + ...

    or

    *initVal* *op1* (a1 *op2* b1) *op1* (a2 *op2* b2) *op1* (a3 *op2* b3) *op* ...

    respectively.

- If the range is empty (*beg*==*end*), all forms return *initVal*.
- The caller must ensure that the range starting with *beg2* contains enough elements to overwrite (in fact, at least as many elements as in the range [*beg*, *end*)), or that insert iterators are used.
- *op1* and *op2* must not modify the passed arguments.
- Complexity: linear (*numElems* calls of operator *op1* and *op2*).

- The algorithm is the parallel (see Chapter 22 on page 259) version of std::inner_product() called for associative (see Section 22.6.1 on page 270) operations. If the first optional execution policy (see Section 22.2 on page 265) is passed:
  - There is no guaranteed order for using the operator *op1*, which means that *op1* must be commutative (see Section 22.6.1 on page 270) and associative (see Section 22.6.1 on page 270).
  - It is up to the caller to ensure that parallel calls of the operations do not result in a data race.
  - The iterators must be forward iterators.

For example, the following program:

*lib/transformreduce2.cpp*

```cpp
#include <array>
#include <iostream>
#include <numeric>
#include <string>

int main()
{
  std::array coll1{3, 1, 7, 5, 4, 1, 6, 3};
  std::array coll2{1, 2, 3, 4, 5, 6, 7, 8};

  // process sum of squared values:
  std::cout << "sum of squared:        "
       << std::transform_reduce(coll1.cbegin(), coll1.cend(),  // 1st range
                                coll1.cbegin(),                // 2nd range
                                0L)
       << '\n';

  // process product of differences of corresponding arguments:
  std::cout << "product of differences: "
       << std::transform_reduce(coll1.cbegin(), coll1.cend(),  // 1st range
                                coll2.cbegin(),                // 2nd range
                                1L,
                                std::multiplies{}, std::minus{})
       << '\n';

  // process sum (concatenation) of concatenated digits:
  std::cout << "sum of combined digits: "
       << std::transform_reduce(coll1.cbegin(), coll1.cend(),  // 1st range
                                coll2.cbegin(),                // 2nd range
                                std::string{},
                                std::plus{},
                                [] (auto x, auto y) {
                                  return std::to_string(x) +
                                         std::to_string(y) + " ";
```

## 23.2 New Numeric STL Algorithms

```
                                  })
         << '\n';
}
```

has the following output:

```
sum of squared:         146
product of differences: -200
sum of combined digits: 31 12 73 54 45 16 67 38
```

### 23.2.3 std::inclusive_scan() and std::exclusive_scan()

```
OutputIterator
inclusive_scan (ExecutionPolicy&& pol,     // optional
                InputIterator inBeg, InputIterator inEnd)
                OutputIterator outBeg,
                BinaryOp op,               // optional
                T initVal)                 // optional

OutputIterator
exclusive_scan (ExecutionPolicy&& pol,     // optional
                InputIterator inBeg, InputIterator inEnd)
                OutputIterator outBeg,
                T initVal)                 // mandatory
                BinaryOp op,               // optional
```

- All forms compute the partial results of combining each element in the source range [*beg*, *end*) with all previous elements and write them to the destination range starting with *outBeg*.
- The difference between inclusive_scan() and exclusive_scan() is that exclusive_scan() starts with the initial value and excludes the last input element from the result. Note that the order of the trailing function parameters differs and that for exclusive_scan(), the initial value is mandatory.
- Thus, for the values

    a1 a2 a3 ... aN

  inclusive_scan() computes

    *initVal* op a1, *initVal* op a1 op a2, *initVal* op a1 op a2 op a3, ... aN

  while exclusive_scan() computes

    *initVal*, *initVal* op a1, *initVal* op a1 op a2, ... op aN-1

  This means that for inclusive_scan(), *initVal* serves as an offset for each output value, while for exclusive_scan(), it serves as the first output value (although it is not written if the input range is empty).
- All forms return the position after the last written value in the destination range (the first element that is not overwritten).

- If no *op* is passed, `std::plus` is used, so that the sum of all elements is computed.
- If no *initVal* is passed (`inclusive_scan()` only), no initial value is added. Thus, the first output value is just the first input value.
- If the range is empty (*beg==end*), all forms write no elements.
- The caller must ensure that the range starting with *outBeg* contains enough elements to overwrite (in fact, at least as many elements as in the source range), or that insert iterators are used.
- *op* must not modify the passed arguments.
- Complexity: linear (*numElems* calls of operator *op*).
- The algorithms are provided as the parallel (see Chapter 22 on page 259) version of `std::partial_sum()` called for associative (see Section 22.6.1 on page 270) operations. If the first optional execution policy (see Section 22.2 on page 265) is passed:
  - There is no guaranteed order for using the operator *op1*, which means that *op1* must be commutative (see Section 22.6.1 on page 270) and associative (see Section 22.6.1 on page 270).
  - It is up to the caller to ensure that parallel calls of the operations do not result in a data race.
  - The iterators must be forward iterators.

For example, the following program:

*lib/scan.cpp*

```cpp
#include <numeric>
#include <iostream>
#include <iterator>
#include <array>

int main()
{
  std::array coll{3, 1, 7, 0, 4, 1, 6, 3};

  std::cout << " inclusive_scan():     ";
  std::inclusive_scan(coll.begin(), coll.end(),
                      std::ostream_iterator<int>(std::cout, " "));

  std::cout << "\n exclusive_scan():     ";
  std::exclusive_scan(coll.begin(), coll.end(),
                      std::ostream_iterator<int>(std::cout, " "),
                      0);    // mandatory

  std::cout << "\n exclusive_scan():     ";
  std::exclusive_scan(coll.begin(), coll.end(),
                      std::ostream_iterator<int>(std::cout, " "),
                      100);  // mandatory

  std::cout << "\n inclusive_scan():     ";
  std::inclusive_scan(coll.begin(), coll.end(),
```

## 23.2 New Numeric STL Algorithms

```
                        std::ostream_iterator<int>(std::cout, " "),
                        std::plus{}, 100);

std::cout << "\n exclusive_scan(): ";
std::exclusive_scan(coll.begin(), coll.end(),
                    std::ostream_iterator<int>(std::cout, " "),
                    100, std::plus{});    // note: different order
}
```

has the following output:

```
inclusive_scan():   3   4  11  11  15  16  22  25
exclusive_scan():   0   3   4  11  11  15  16  22
exclusive_scan(): 100 103 104 111 111 115 116 122
inclusive_scan():     103 104 111 111 115 116 122 125
exclusive_scan(): 100 103 104 111 111 115 116 122
```

Note that both algorithms always output the same number of elements that the input range has. However, with `inclusive_scan()`, we start with the value of the first element and end with the sum/combination of all elements (plus any passed initial value used as offset), while with `exclusive_scan()`, we start with the initial value and end with the sum/combination of all but the last element.

### 23.2.4 `std::transform_inclusive_scan()` and `std::transform_exclusive_scan()`

```
OutputIterator
transform_inclusive_scan (ExecutionPolicy&& pol,     // optional
                          InputIterator inBeg, InputIterator inEnd)
                          OutputIterator outBeg,
                          BinaryOp op2,              // mandatory
                          UnaryOp op1,               // mandatory
                          T initVal)                 // optional

OutputIterator
transform_exclusive_scan (ExecutionPolicy&& pol,     // optional
                          InputIterator inBeg, InputIterator inEnd)
                          OutputIterator outBeg,
                          T initVal)                 // mandatory
                          BinaryOp op2,              // mandatory
                          UnaryOp op1)               // mandatory
```

- All forms compute the partial results of combining the transformed value of each element in the source range [*beg*,*end*) with all previous transformed values and write them to the destination range starting with *outBeg*.

- The difference between `transform_inclusive_scan()` and `transform_exclusive_scan()` is that `transform_exclusive_scan()` starts with the initial value and excludes the last input element from the result. Note that the order of the trailing function parameters differs and that for `exclusive_scan()`, the initial value is mandatory.
- Thus, for the values

    a1 a2 a3 ... aN

    `transform_inclusive_scan()` computes

    *initVal op2 op1*(a1), *initVal op2 op1*(a1) *op2 op1*(a2), ... *op2 op1*(aN)

    while `transform_exclusive_scan()` computes

    *initVal*, *initVal op2 op1*(a1), *initVal op2 op1*(a1) *op2 op1*(a2), ... *op2 op1*(aN-1)

    This means that for `inclusive_scan()`, *initVal* serves as an offset for each output value, while for `exclusive_scan()`, it serves as the first element (although it is not written if the input range is empty).
- All forms return the position after the last written value in the destination range (the first element that is not overwritten).
- If no *initVal* is passed (`transform_inclusive_scan()` only), no initial value is added. Thus, the first output value is just the first transformed input value.
- If the range is empty (*beg==end*), all forms write no elements.
- The caller must ensure that the range starting with *outBeg* contains enough elements to overwrite (in fact, at least as many elements as in the source range), or that insert iterators are used.
- *op1* and *op2* must not modify the passed arguments.
- Complexity: linear (*numElems* calls of operator *op1* and *op2*).
- If the first optional execution policy (see Section 22.2 on page 265) is passed:
    - There is no guaranteed order for using the operator *op2*, which means that *op2* must be commutative (see Section 22.6.1 on page 270) and associative (see Section 22.6.1 on page 270).
    - It is up to the caller to ensure that parallel calls of the operations do not result in a data race.
    - The iterators must be forward iterators.

For example, the following program:

*lib/transformscan.cpp*

```
#include <numeric>
#include <algorithm>
#include <iostream>
#include <iterator>
#include <array>

int main()
{
  std::array coll{3, 1, 7, 0, 4, 1, 6, 3};

  auto twice = [] (int v) { return v*2; };
```

```
    std::cout << " source:                          ";
    std::copy(coll.begin(), coll.end(),
              std::ostream_iterator<int>(std::cout, " "));

    std::cout << "\n transform_inclusive_scan():     ";
    std::transform_inclusive_scan(coll.begin(), coll.end(),
                                  std::ostream_iterator<int>(std::cout, " "),
                                  std::plus{}, twice);

    std::cout << "\n transform_inclusive_scan():     ";
    std::transform_inclusive_scan(coll.begin(), coll.end(),
                                  std::ostream_iterator<int>(std::cout, " "),
                                  std::plus{}, twice, 100);

    std::cout << "\n transform_exclusive_scan():     ";
    std::transform_exclusive_scan(coll.begin(), coll.end(),
                                  std::ostream_iterator<int>(std::cout, " "),
                                  100, std::plus{}, twice);  // note the other param order
}
```

has the following output:

```
 source:                        3 1 7 0 4 1 6 3
 transform_inclusive_scan():    6 8 22 22 30 32 44 50
 transform_inclusive_scan():    106 108 122 122 130 132 144 150
 transform_exclusive_scan():    100 106 108 122 122 130 132 144
```

Note that both algorithms always output the same number of elements that the input range has. However, with `transform_inclusive_scan()`, we start with the transferred value of the first element and end with the sum/combination of all transferred element values (plus any passed initial value used as offset), while with `transform_exclusive_scan()`, we start with the initial value and end with the sum/combination of the transferred values of all but the last element.

## 23.3 Afternotes

`for_each_n()`, the ...`reduce()`, and the ...`scan()` algorithms were first proposed with the general proposal of the parallelization of the STL algorithms in 2012 by Jared Hoberock, Michael Garland, Olivier Giroux, Vinod Grover, Ujval Kapasi, and Jaydeep Marathe in `https://wg21.link/n3408`. It became a formal beta standard, the *Technical Specification for C++ Extensions for Parallelism* (see `https://wg21.link/n3850`). Additional `transform...scan()` forms were added by Jared Hoberock, Grant Mercer, Agustin Berge, and Harmut Kaiser in `https://wg21.link/n4276`. With `https://wg21.link/p0024r2`, the *Technical Specification for C++ Extensions for Parallelism* was adopted to the standard library as proposed by Jared Hoberock. The handling of exceptions was accepted as proposed by JF Bastien and Bryce Adelstein Lelbach in `https://wg21.link/p0394r4`.

# Chapter 24
# Substring and Subsequence Searchers

Since C++98, the C++ standard library has provided a search algorithm for finding a subsequence of elements in a range. However, there are also other search algorithms. For example, by pre-computing statistics about the pattern you are searching for, these algorithms can perform significantly better for special tasks such as finding a substring in a large text.

C++17 therefore introduced the Boyer-Moore and Boyer-Moore-Horspool search algorithms and various interfaces for using them. In particular, they are provided for searching for substrings in large texts, but can also make it faster to find subsequences in containers or ranges.

## 24.1 Using Substring Searchers

The new searchers were especially developed to search for strings (e.g., words or phrases) in large texts. So let us first demonstrate how to use them in such a scenario and how you can benefit with them.

### 24.1.1 Using Searchers with `search()`

We now have the following options for searching for a substring sub in a string text:

1. String member `find()`:
   ```
   std::size_type idx = text.find(sub);
   ```
2. Algorithm `search()`:
   ```
   auto pos = std::search(text.begin(), text.end(),
                          sub.begin(), sub.end());
   ```
3. Parallel algorithm (see Chapter 22 on page 259) `search()`:
   ```
   auto pos = std::search(std::execution::par,
                          text.begin(), text.end(),
                          sub.begin(), sub.end());
   ```
4. Using a `default_searcher`:
   ```
   auto pos = std::search(text.begin(), text.end(),
   ```

```
                      std::default_searcher{sub.begin(), sub.end()});
```

5. Using a `boyer_moore_searcher`:
   ```
   auto pos = std::search(text.begin(), text.end(),
                      std::boyer_moore_searcher{sub.begin(), sub.end()});
   ```

6. Using a `boyer_moore_horspool_searcher`:
   ```
   auto pos = std::search(text.begin(), text.end(),
                      std::boyer_moore_horspool_searcher{sub.begin(),
                                                         sub.end()});
   ```

The new searchers are defined in `<functional>`.

The Boyer-Moore and the Boyer-Moore-Horspool searchers are well-known algorithms that pre-compute tables (of hash values) before the search starts to improve the speed of the search if the search covers a text and/or substring of significant size. To use these searchers, the algorithms require random-access iterators (instead of forward iterators, which suffice for a naive `search()`).

In *lib/searcher1.cpp*, you can find a full program demonstrating the use of these different ways to search for a substring.

Note that all applications of `search()` yield an iterator to the first character of a matching subsequence. If there is no matching subsequence, the passed end of the text is returned. This allows us to search for all occurrences of a substring as follows:

```
std::boyer_moore_searcher bmsearch{sub.begin(), sub.end()};
for (auto pos = std::search(text.begin(), text.end(), bmsearch);
     pos != text.end();
     pos = std::search(pos+sub.size(), text.end(), bmsearch)) {
  std::cout << "found '" << sub << "' at index " << pos - text.begin() << '\n';
}
```

## Performance of Searchers

Which is the best way to search for a substring (fastest and/or least memory)? One special aspect of this question is that we can also use the traditional `search()` in parallel mode (see Chapter 22 on page 259) (which is not possible when using the new searchers).

The answer depends on the circumstances:

- Using just (non-parallel) `search()` is usually the slowest approach, because for each character in `text`, we start to find out whether a substring matches.
- Using the `default_searcher` should produce an equivalent result, but I noted a running time of up to a factor of 3 slower.
- Using `find()` might be faster, but this depends on the quality of implementation in the library. With the measurements I did, I noted an improvement in running time of between 20% and a factor of 100 compared to `search()`.
- For texts and substrings of significant size, the `boyer_moore_searcher` should be the fastest approach. Compared to `search()`, I noted an improvement with a factor of 50 or even 100. In large texts with significant substrings, this was always the fastest search.

## 24.1 Using Substring Searchers

- The `boyer_moore_horspool_searcher` trades space for time. It is usually slower than the `boyer_moore_searcher`, but should not use that much memory. The improvement I noted varied a lot from platform to platform. While on one platform it was close to `boyer_moore` (50 times better than `search()`, and 10 times better than `find()`), on other platforms the improvement was a factor of only 2 or 3 compared to `search()` and using `find()` was much faster.
- Where already supported, using the parallel `search()` gave me a factor of 3 compared to the ordinary `search()`, which indicated that using the Boyer-Moore searcher should usually still be much faster.

Therefore, there is only one piece of advice I can give: **Measure!** Test the typical scenarios on your target platforms. It is worth it because you might get an improvement of a factor of 100 (which I got, for example, when searching for a substring of 1000 characters located close to the end of a string with 10 million characters).

The code in *lib/searcher1.cpp* also prints measurements of the different search options so that you can compare the numbers on your platform.

### 24.1.2 Using Searchers Directly

Alternatively, you can use the function-call operator of the searcher, which returns a pair of both the begin and the end of any subsequence found.

The code would look as follows:

```
std::boyer_moore_searcher bmsearch{sub.begin(), sub.end()};
...
for (auto begend = bmsearch(text.begin(), text.end());
     begend.first != text.end();
     begend = bmsearch(begend.second, text.end())) {
  std::cout << "found '" << sub << "' at index "
            << begend.first - text.begin() << '-'
            << begend.second - text.begin() << '\n';
}
```

However, because you can use `std::tie()` to reassign new values to structured bindings (see Section 1.2.3 on page 10) of a `std::pair<>`, you can simplify the code as follows:

```
std::boyer_moore_searcher bmsearch{sub.begin(), sub.end()};
...
for (auto [beg, end] = bmsearch(text.begin(), text.end());
     beg != text.end();
     std::tie(beg,end) = bmsearch(end, text.end())) {
  std::cout << "found '" << sub << "' at index "
            << beg - text.begin() << '-'
            << end - text.begin() << '\n';
}
```

To find the first occurrence of a substring using the searchers directly, you can use `if` with initialization (see Chapter 2 on page 21) and structured bindings (see Chapter 1 on page 3):

```
std::boyer_moore_searcher bmsearch{sub.begin(), sub.end()};
...
```

```
if (auto [beg, end] = bmsearch(text.begin(), text.end()); beg != text.end()) {
  std::cout << "found '" << sub << "' first at index "
            << beg - text.begin() << '-'
            << end - text.begin() << '\n';
}
```

## 24.2 Using General Subsequence Searchers

Boyer-Moore and Boyer-Moore-Horspool were developed as string searchers. However, C++17 adopts them as generic algorithms, which means that you can use them to find a subsequence of elements in a container or range.

That is, you can now implement the following:

```
std::vector<int> coll;
...
std::deque<int> sub{0, 8, 15, ...};
pos = std::search(coll.begin(), coll.end(),
                  std::boyer_moore_searcher{sub.begin(), sub.end()});
```

And again, you can also use the function-call operator of the searcher:

```
std::vector<int> coll;
...
std::deque<int> sub{0, 8, 15, ...};
std::boyer_moore_searcher bm{sub.begin(), sub.end()};
auto [beg, end] = bm(coll.begin(), coll.end());
if (beg != coll.end) {
  std::cout << "found subsequence at " << beg - coll.begin() << '\n';
}
```

To make this possible, it must be possible to use the elements in a hash table (i.e., a default hash function must be provided and comparing two elements with == has to be supported). If this is not the case, you can use predicates (as described below (see Section 24.3 on page 297)):

Again: measure to find out the benefit in performance (speed and memory). I note an even greater variety of factors when trying out some examples. For example, using the `boyer_moore_searcher` could improve the search by a factor of 100 again (which is again much faster than using parallel algorithms). However, using the `boyer_moore_horspool_searcher` could make the search both faster by a factor of 50 but also slower by a factor of 2. Measure!

The code in *lib/searcher2.cpp* demonstrates the different searchers for a subsequence in a vector and also prints measurements of the different search options so that you can compare the numbers on your platform.

## 24.3 Using Searcher Predicates

When using searchers, you can use predicates, which might be necessary for two reasons:

1. You want to define your own way of comparing two elements.
2. You want to provide a hash function, which is necessary for the Boyer-Moore(-Horspool) searchers.

You have to provide the predicates as additional arguments to the constructor of the searchers. For example, here we are searching for a substring case-insensitively:

```
std::boyer_moore_searcher bmic{substr.begin(), substr.end(),
                               [](char c){
                                 return std::hash<char>{}(std::toupper(c));
                               },
                               [](char c1, char c2){
                                 return std::toupper(c1)==std::toupper(c2);
                               }
                              };
auto begend = bmic(sub.begin(), sub.end());
```

Do not forget to call `toupper()` before you hash the value, because otherwise you violate the requirement that the hash value must be the same for all values, where `operator==` yields `true`.

And here, if we have a class `Customer` defined as follows:

```
class Customer {
  ...
  public:
    Customer() = default;
    std::string getID() const {
      return id;
    }
    friend bool operator== (const Customer& c1, const Customer& c2) {
      return c1.id == c2.id;
    }
};
```

we can search for a subsequence of customers in a vector of customers as follows:

```
std::vector<Customer> customers;
...
std::vector<Customer> sub{...};
...
std::boyer_moore_searcher bmcust(sub.begin(), sub.end(),
                                 [](const Customer& c) {
                                   return std::hash<std::string>{}(c.getID());
                                 });
auto pos = bmcust(customers.begin(), customers.end());
if (pos.first != customers.end()) {
  ...
}
```

However, note that using a predicate might create a significant overhead to using searchers, which means that using them is only worth it if you have a huge number of elements and are searching for a subsequence of significant size (e.g., finding a subsequence of 1000 customers in a collection of 1 million customers).

Once again: think big and measure.

## 24.4 Afternotes

The searchers were first proposed by Marshall Clow in `https://wg21.link/n3411` referring to Boost.Algorithm as a reference implementation. They became part of the first Library Fundamentals TS. For C++17 they were then adopted with other components as proposed by Beman Dawes and Alisdair Meredith in `https://wg21.link/p0220r1`, including an interface fix proposed by Marshall Clow in `https://wg21.link/p0253R1`.

# Chapter 25
# Other Utility Functions and Algorithms

C++17 provides a couple of new utility functions and algorithms, which are described in this chapter.

## 25.1 `size()`, `empty()`, and `data()`

To support the flexibility of generic code, the C++ standard library provides three new helper functions: `size()`, `empty()`, and `data()`.

Just like the other global helpers for generic code iterating over ranges and collections, `std::begin()`, `std::end()`, and `std::advance()`, these functions are defined in the header file `<iterator>`.

### 25.1.1 Generic `size()` Function

The generic `std::size()` function allows us to ask for the size of any range as long as it has an iterator interface or is a raw array. With this function you can write code like this:

*lib/last5.hpp*

```
#ifndef LAST5_HPP
#define LAST5_HPP

#include <iterator>
#include <iostream>

template<typename T>
void printLast5(const T& coll)
{
  // compute size:
  auto size{std::size(coll)};
  // advance to the position starting at the last 5 elements
  std::cout << size << " elems: ";
  auto pos{std::begin(coll)};
```

```
    if (size > 5) {
      std::advance(pos, size - 5);
      std::cout << "... ";
    }
    // print remaining elements:
    for ( ; pos != std::end(coll); ++pos) {
      std::cout << *pos << ' ';
    }
    std::cout << '\n';
  }

#endif // LAST5_HPP
```

Here, with

```
auto size{std::size(coll)};
```

we initialize `size` with the size of the passed collection, which either maps to `coll.size()` or to the size of a passed raw array. Thus, if we call:

```
std::array arr{27, 3, 5, 8, 7, 12, 22, 0, 55};
std::vector v{0.0, 8.8, 15.15};
std::initializer_list<std::string> il{"just", "five", "small", "string",
                                      "literals"};
printLast5(arr);
printLast5(v);
printLast5(il);
```

the output is:

```
9 elems: ... 7 12 22 0 55
3 elems: 0 8.8 15.15
5 elems: just five small string literals
```

And because raw C arrays are supported, we can also call

```
printLast5("hello world");
```

which prints:

```
12 elems: ... o r l d
```

Note that this function template therefore replaces the usual way computing the size of an array using `countof` or `ARRAYSIZE` defined as something like:

```
#define ARRAYSIZE(a) (sizeof(a)/sizeof(*(a)))
```

Note also that you cannot pass an inline defined initializer list to `last5<>()`. This is because a template parameter cannot deduce a `std::initializer_list()`. For this, you have to overload `last5()` with the following declaration:

```
template<typename T>
void printLast5(const std::initializer_list<T>& coll)
```

Finally, note that this code does not work for `forward_list<>` because forward lists do not have a member function `size()`. Therefore, if you only want to check whether the collection is empty, the recommendation is to use `std::empty()`, which is discussed below.

## 25.1.2 Generic `empty()` Function

Similar to the new global `size()` (see Section 25.1.1 on page 299), the new generic `std::empty()` allows us to check whether a container, a raw C array, or a `std::initializer_list<>` is empty.

Thus, similar to the example above, you can generically check whether a passed collection is empty:

```
if (std::empty(coll)) {
  return;
}
```

In contrast to `std::size()`, `std::empty()` also works for forward lists.

Note that, according to language rules, raw C arrays cannot have a size of zero. Therefore, `std::empty()` for raw C arrays is specified to always return `false`.[1]

## 25.1.3 Generic `data()` Function

Finally, the new generic `std::data()` function allows us to give access to the raw data of collections (containers that have a `data()` member, raw C arrays, or `std::initializer_list<>`s). For example, the following code prints every second element:

*lib/data.hpp*

```
#ifndef DATA_HPP
#define DATA_HPP

#include <iterator>
#include <iostream>

template<typename T>
void printData(const T& coll)
{
  // print every second element:
  for (std::size_t idx{0}; idx < std::size(coll); ++idx) {
    if (idx % 2 == 0) {
      std::cout << std::data(coll)[idx] << ' ';
    }
  }
  std::cout << '\n';
}
```

---

[1] By default, some compilers (such as gcc or clang) allow empty raw arrays as an extension (which you have to disable with `-pedantic-errors`). However, using `std::empty()` for such an empty C array does not compile.

```
#endif // DATA_HPP
```

Thus, if we call:
```
std::array arr{27, 3, 5, 8, 7, 12, 22, 0, 55};
std::vector v{0.0, 8.8, 15.15};
std::initializer_list<std::string> il{"just", "five", "small", "string",
                                      "literals"};
printData(arr);
printData(v);
printData(il);
printData("hello world");
```
the output is:
```
27 5 7 22 55
0 15.15
just small literals
h l o w r d
```

## 25.2 as_const()

The new helper function `std::as_const()` converts values into the corresponding `const` values without using `static_cast<>` or the `add_const_t<>` type trait.

It allows us to force calling the const overload of a function for a non-const object in case this makes a difference:
```
std::vector<std::string> coll;

foo(coll);                    // prefers a non-const overload
foo(std::as_const(coll));     // forces using a const overload
```
If `foo()` is a function template, this would also force the template to be instantiated for a const type rather than the original non-const type.

### 25.2.1 Capturing by Const Reference

One application of `as_const()` is the ability to capture lambda parameters by `const` reference. For example:
```
std::vector<int> coll {8, 15, 7, 42};

auto printColl = [&coll = std::as_const(coll)] {
                    std::cout << "coll: ";
                    for (int elem : coll) {
                       std::cout << elem << ' ';
```

```
        }
        std::cout << '\n';
    };
```

Now, calling

```
printColl();
```

will print the current state of `coll` without the danger of accidentally modifying its value.

## 25.3 clamp()

C++17 provides a new utility function `clamp()`, which enables you to "clamp" a value between a passed minimum and maximum value. It is a combined call of `min()` and `max()`. For example:

*lib/clamp.cpp*

```
#include <iostream>
#include <algorithm>   // for clamp()

int main()
{
  for (int i : {-7, 0, 8, 15}) {
    std::cout << std::clamp(i, 5, 13) << '\n';
  }
}
```

The call of `clamp(i, 5, 13)` has the same effect as calling `std::min(std::max(i, 5), 13)`, which means that the program has the following output:

```
5
5
8
13
```

Just like for `min()` and `max()`, `clamp()` requires that all arguments that are passed by `const` reference have the same type T:

```
namespace std {
  template<typename T>
  constexpr const T& clamp(const T& value, const T& min, const T& max);
}
```

The return value is a `const` reference to one of the passed arguments.

If you pass arguments with different types, you can explicitly specify the template parameter T:

```
double d{4.3};
int max{13};
...
std::clamp(d, 0, max);            // compile-time ERROR
```

```
std::clamp<double>(d, 0, max);    // OK
```
You can also pass floating-point values provided they do not have the value NaN.

Just like for `min()` and `max()`, you can pass a predicate as a comparison operation. For example:
```
for (int i : {-7, 0, 8, 15}) {
  std::cout << std::clamp(i, 5, 13,
                          [] (auto a, auto b) {
                            return std::abs(a) < std::abs(b);
                          })
            << '\n';
}
```
has the following output:
```
-7
5
8
13
```
Because the absolute value of -7 is between the absolute values of 5 and 13, `clamp()` yields -7 in this case.

There is no overload of `clamp()` taking an initializer list of values (as `min()` and `max()` have).

## 25.4 sample()

With `sample()`, C++17 provides an algorithm that extracts a random subset (*sample*) from a given range of values (the *population*). This is sometimes called *reservoir sampling* or *selection sampling*.

Consider the following example program:

*lib/sample1.cpp*
```
#include <iostream>
#include <vector>
#include <string>
#include <iterator>
#include <algorithm>    // for sample()
#include <random>       // for default_random_engine

int main()
{
  // initialize a vector of 10,000 string values:
  std::vector<std::string> coll;
  for (int i=0; i < 10000; ++i) {
    coll.push_back("value" + std::to_string(i));
  }

  // print 10 randomly selected values of this collection:
  std::sample(coll.begin(), coll.end(),
```

## 25.4 sample()

```
                std::ostream_iterator<std::string>{std::cout, "\n"},
                10,
                std::default_random_engine{});
}
```

After initializing a vector with plenty of string values (value0, value1, ...), we use sample() to extract a random subset of these string values:

```
// print 10 randomly selected values of this collection:
sample(coll.begin(), coll.end(),
       std::ostream_iterator<std::string>{std::cout, "\n"},
       10,
       std::default_random_engine{});
```

We pass:

- Begin and end of the range we extract the subset of values from
- An iterator used to write the extracted values to (here an ostream iterator writing them to standard output)
- The maximum number of values to extract (we may extract fewer values if the range is too small)
- The random engine used to compute the random subset

As a result, we print a random subset of 10 elements of coll. The output might be, for example:

```
value132
value349
value796
value2902
value3267
value3553
value4226
value4820
value5509
value8931
```

As you can see, the order of the elements is stable (matches their order in coll). However, this is only guaranteed if the iterators for the passed range are at least forward iterators.

The algorithm is declared as follows:

```
namespace std {
  template<typename InputIterator, typename OutputIterator,
           typename Distance, typename UniformRandomBitGenerator>
  OutputIterator sample(InputIterator sourceBeg, InputIterator sourceEnd,
                        OutputIterator destBeg,
                        Distance num,
                        UniformRandomBitGenerator&& eng);
}
```

It has the following specification and constraints:

- The iterators for the source range must be at least input iterators and the iterator of the destination range must be at least an output iterator. If the source iterators are not at least forward iterators, the destination iterator must be a random-access iterator.
- As usual, the destination iterator overwrites, which causes undefined behavior if there are not enough elements to overwrite and no inserter is used.
- The algorithm returns the position after the last copied element.
- The destination iterator must not be in the passed source range.
- *num* may have an integral type. If the elements in the source range are not sufficient, all elements in the source range are extracted.
- The order of the extracted elements is stable unless the iterators in the source range are input iterators.

Here is another example that demonstrates the use of `sample()`:

*lib/sample2.cpp*

```cpp
#include <iostream>
#include <vector>
#include <iterator>
#include <algorithm>    // for sample()
#include <random>       // for random devices and engines

int main()
{
  // initialize a vector of 10,000 string values:
  std::vector<std::string> coll;
  for (int i=0; i < 10000; ++i) {
    coll.push_back("value" + std::to_string(i));
  }

  // initialize a Mersenne Twister engine with a random seed:
  std::random_device rd;        // random seed (if supported)
  std::mt19937 eng{rd()};       // Mersenne twister engine

  // initialize destination range (must be big enough for 10 elements):
  std::vector<std::string> subset;
  subset.resize(100);

  // copy 10 randomly selected values from the source range to the destination range:
  auto end = std::sample(coll.begin(), coll.end(),
                         subset.begin(),
                         10,
                         eng);

  // print extracted elements (using return value as new end):
  std::for_each(subset.begin(), end,
                [] (const auto& s) {
```

```
                         std::cout << "random elem: " << s << '\n';
              });
}
```

After initializing a vector with plenty of string values (value0, value1, ...), we initialize a random-number engine initialized with a random seed:

```
// initialize a Mersenne Twister engine with a random seed:
std::random_device rd;      // random seed (if supported)
std::mt19937 eng{rd()};     // Mersenne Twister engine
```

and a destination range:

```
// initialize destination range (must be big enough for 10 elements):
std::vector<std::string> subset;
subset.resize(100);
```

The call to `sample()` now copies (up to) 10 elements of the source range to the destination range:

```
// copy 10 randomly selected values from the source range to the destination range:
auto end = sample(coll.begin(), coll.end(),
                  subset.begin(),
                  10,
                  eng);
```

The return value that end is initialized with contains the position behind the last randomly extracted element, which can be used afterwards to print the extracted elements:

```
// print extracted elements (using return value as new end):
for_each(subset.begin(), end,
         [] (const auto& s) {
           std::cout << "random elem: " << s << '\n';
         });
```

## 25.5 Afternotes

`size()`, `empty()`, and `data()` were first proposed by Riccardo Marcangelo in https://wg21.link/n4017. The finally accepted wording was formulated by Riccardo Marcangelo in https://wg21.link/n4280.

`as_const()` was first proposed by ADAM David Alan Martin and Alisdair Meredith in https://wg21.link/n4380. The finally accepted wording was formulated by ADAM David Alan Martin and Alisdair Meredith in https://wg21.link/p0007r1.

`clamp()` was first proposed by Martin Moene and Niels Dekker in https://wg21.link/n4536. The finally accepted wording was formulated by Martin Moene and Niels Dekker in https://wg21.link/p002501.

`sample()` was first proposed by Walter E. Brown in https://wg21.link/n3842. The finally accepted wording was formulated by Walter E. Brown in https://wg21.link/n3925.

# Chapter 26
# Container and String Extensions

There are a couple of minor or small changes to the standard containers of the C++ standard library, which are described in this chapter.

## 26.1 Node Handles

By introducing the ability to splice a node out of an associative or unordered container, you can easily:
- Modify keys of (unordered) maps or values of (unordered) sets
- Use move semantics in (unordered) sets and maps
- Move elements between (unordered) sets and maps
- Merge elements from one (unordered) set or map into another

### 26.1.1 Modifying a Key

For example, consider the following program:

*lib/nodehandle.cpp*
```
#include <iostream>
#include <string>
#include <map>

int main()
{
  std::map<int, std::string> m{{1, "mango"},
                               {2, "papaya"},
                               {3, "guava"}};

  auto nh = m.extract(2);   // nh has type decltype(m)::node_type
  nh.key() = 4;
```

```
    m.insert(std::move(nh));

    for (const auto& [key, value] : m) {
      std::cout << key << ": " << value << '\n';
    }
}
```

After defining and initializing a map as follows:

```
std::map<int, std::string> m{{1, "mango"},
                             {2, "papaya"},
                             {3, "guava"}};
```

you can modify the element with the key 2 as follows:

```
auto nh = m.extract(2);   // nh has type decltype(m)::node_type
nh.key() = 4;
m.insert(std::move(nh));
```

The code takes the node for the element with the key 2 out of the container, modifies the key, and moves it back as described in Figure 26.1.

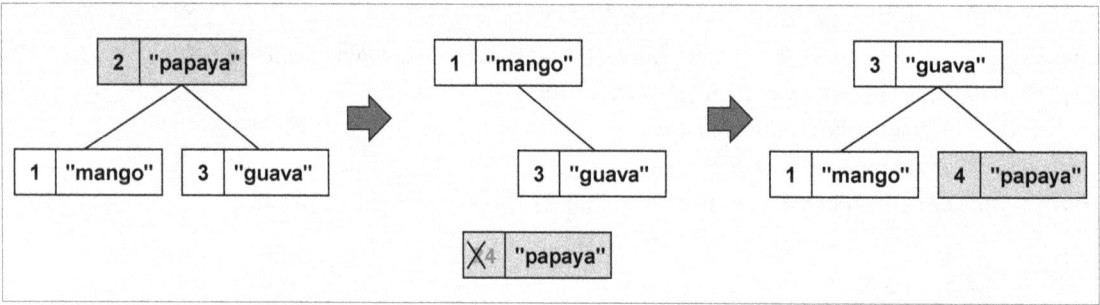

Figure 26.1. Modifying a Key Using Node Handles

Note that before C++17, you could only modify a key by removing the old node and inserting a new one with the same value (keys are `const` because their value is used for the location in the container and must be stable). If we use node handles, no memory (de)allocation is used and pointers and references to the element remain valid. However, using these pointers and references while the element is held in the node handle results in undefined behavior.

The type of a node handle is *container*::node_type. It provides the following members:

- `value()` for all (unordered) set types
- `key()` and `mapped()` for all (unordered) map types

## 26.1.2 Moving Nodes Between Containers

You can also use node handles to move (*splice*) elements from one container to another. The containers can even differ in the following way:
- One supports duplicates while another does not (e.g., you can move elements from a multimap to a map)
- Comparison functions and hash functions might differ

For example, consider the following program:

*lib/nodemove.cpp*

```cpp
#include <iostream>
#include <string>
#include <map>

template<typename T1, typename T2>
void print(const T1& coll1, const T2& coll2)
{
  std::cout << "values:\n";
  for (const auto& [key, value] : coll1) {
    std::cout << "  [" << key << ":" << value << "]";
  }
  std::cout << '\n';
  for (const auto& [key, value] : coll2) {
    std::cout << "  [" << key << ":" << value << "]";
  }
  std::cout << '\n';
}

int main()
{
  std::multimap<double, std::string> src {{1.1, "one"},
                                          {2.2, "two"},
                                          {3.3, "three"}};
  std::map<double, std::string> dst {{3.3, "old data"}};

  print(src, dst);

  // move some elements from multimap src to map dst:
  dst.insert(src.extract(src.find(1.1)));   // splice using an iterator
  dst.insert(src.extract(2.2));             // splice using the key

  print(src, dst);
}
```

We extract an element from `src` twice (once passing the key and once passing an iterator) and insert it into `dst`. Thus, the program has the following output:

```
values:
  [1.1:one]   [2.2:two]   [3.3:three]
  [3.3:old data]
values:
  [3.3:three]
  [1.1:one]   [2.2:two]   [3.3:old data]
```

Note that when no duplicates are allowed (set, map, unordered set, unordered map), the `insert()` member function that takes a node handle returns a structure *container*`::insert_return_type` with three elements (in the following order):

- An iterator **position** of the new element if the insertion was possible (no element with the same key already exists) or to the existing element if the insertion failed.
- A bool **inserted** to signal whether the insertion was successful.
- The *container*`::node_type` **node** with the node handle if the insertion was not possible.

That is, the key information is the second member `inserted`. Using structured bindings (see Chapter 1 on page 3), you might use the return value as follows:

```
auto [pos,done,node] = dst.insert(src.extract(3.3));
if (!done) {
  std::cout << "insert() of node handle failed:"
            << " tried to insert key '" << node.key()
            << "' with value '" << node.mapped()
            << "' but key exists with value '" << pos->second << "'\n";
}
```

If a node is extracted and never inserted, the destructor of a node handle will free the memory allocated for it. Therefore, in this code, there is no memory leak even if the insertion failed.

### 26.1.3 Merging Containers

Based on the node handle API, all associative and unordered containers provide a member function `merge()` now, which allows us to merge all elements from one container to another.

Again, the containers can even differ in the following way:
- One supports duplicates while another does not (e.g., you can merge elements from a multimap to a map)
- Comparison functions and hash functions might differ

If a node cannot be moved because there is already an element with the same key, the element remains in the source container.

For example, the following program:

*lib/nodemerge.cpp*

```
#include <iostream>
#include <string>
#include <map>
```

## 26.1 Node Handles

```cpp
template<typename T1, typename T2>
void print(const T1& coll1, const T2& coll2)
{
  std::cout << "values:\n";
  for (const auto& [key, value] : coll1) {
    std::cout << "  [" << key << ":" << value << "]";
  }
  std::cout << '\n';
  for (const auto& [key, value] : coll2) {
    std::cout << "  [" << key << ":" << value << "]";
  }
  std::cout << '\n';
}

int main()
{
  std::multimap<double, std::string> src {{1.1, "one"},
                                           {2.2, "two"},
                                           {3.3, "three"}};
  std::map<double, std::string> dst {{3.3, "old data"}};

  print(src, dst);

  // merge all elements from src into dst:
  dst.merge(src);

  print(src, dst);
}
```

has the following output:

```
values:
  [1.1:one]  [2.2:two]  [3.3:three]
  [3.3:old data]
values:
  [3.3:three]
  [1.1:one]  [2.2:two]  [3.3:old data]
```

Pointers and references to the merged elements remain valid but change the container they refer to.

## 26.2 Emplace Improvements

### 26.2.1 Return Type of Emplace Functions

For the sequential containers `std::vector<>`, `std::deque<>`, `std::list<>`, and `forward_list<>`, as well as the container adapters `std::queue<>` and `std::stack<>`, the emplace functions now return a reference to the inserted objects (as was already the case for associative containers). This allows us to implement something like:

```
foo(myVector.emplace_back(...));
```

instead of:

```
myVector.emplace_back(...);
foo(myVector.back());
```

### 26.2.2 `try_emplace()` and `insert_or_assign()` for Maps

Two new member functions enable us to write slightly simpler or more optimized code for maps and unordered maps:

- `try_emplace()` emplaces a new value with defined move semantics.
- `insert_or_assign()` is a slightly improved way to insert/update elements.

### 26.2.3 `try_emplace()`

Consider the following code:

```
std::map<int, std::string> m;
m[42] = "hello";
std::string s{"world"};
m.emplace(42, std::move(s));    // might or might not move if 42 already exists
```

There is no definition of whether after this call, `s` still holds its value. The same applies for an `unordered_map` and if `insert()` is used:

```
m.insert({42, std::move(s)});    // might or might not move if 42 already exists
```

Note that this behavior is usually not a problem following the rules of move semantics. With `std::move(s)`, we state only that we are no longer interested in the value of `s`. `std::move()` marks the object as movable and does not move it away. Therefore, it is always the case that after such a call, `s` **might or might not** still have its value.

However, you may be surprised that the value might be moved away even if it was not inserted (which might happen for reasons of implementation details). Sometimes, programmers might want or have to know exactly whether the object was moved or might want or have to make sure that the object is moved only if the insertion actually happened. In particular, this can be the case when move-only types such as threads or unique pointers are used.

For example, the following code is not valid because you have to call `join()` (or `detach()`) for a `std::thread` before its destructor is called:

## 26.2 Emplace Improvements

```
std::map<int, std::thread> m;
std::thread t1{...};
m.insert({42, std::move(t1)});     // might move even without inserting the new value
```

Here, `t1` may be moved away even though it is not inserted, which results in a core dump, because then `t1` is destroyed inside this call without `t1.join()` being called. Instead, you would have to call:

```
auto pos = m.find(42);
if (pos == m.end()) {
  m.insert({42, std::move(t1)});   // insert (and move) if not found
}
```

Not only is this more code; it might perform the lookup for the new element twice.

The new member function `try_emplace()` guarantees to move the passed value only if there is no element yet:

```
m.try_emplace(42, std::move(t1));  // no move if not inserted
```

In fact, it is the short form of:

```
auto pos = m.find(42);
if (pos == m.end()) {
  m.emplace(42, std::move(t1));    // insert
}
```

with the benefit that the position in the map is looked up only once.

As the name implies, `try_emplace()` allows us to pass an arbitrary number of values to initialize a new element in case there is no element, yet:

```
std::map<int, std::string> ms;
ms.try_emplace(42, "hello");       // try to insert element with value "hello"
ms.try_emplace(43, 8, 'a');        // try to insert element with value "aaaaaaaa"
```

However, note that you cannot initialize the elements of a container in this way:

```
std::map<int, std::vector<std::string>> vals;
std::string h{"hello"};
std::string w{"world"};
vals.try_emplace(42, std::vector<std::string>{h, w});  // OK
vals.try_emplace(42, h, w);                            // ERROR
```

An iterator can be passed As an additional first parameter, used as a hint to where the new element should be looked up.

### 26.2.4 `insert_or_assign()`

In addition, the new member function `insert_or_assign()` guarantees to move the value either to a new or an existing argument:

```
m.insert_or_assign(42, std::move(t1));   // will always move
```

The behavior is the short form of:

```
auto pos = m.find(42);
if (pos == m.end()) {
  m.insert({42, std::move(t1)});     // insert
}
else {
  pos->second = std::move(t1);       // update
}
```

which is similar to

```
m[42] = std::move(t1);               // same with value initialization first
```

with the benefit that the position of a new element is looked up only once and the value of a new element is not first initialized with its default value and then overwritten.

Thus, this member function also allows us to insert or update an element when no default constructor can be called.

Note that `insert_or_assign()` takes key and value as separate arguments, while `insert()` takes them as one. Also, an additional first parameter can be passed as a hint to where the new element should be looked up:

```
std::map<int, std::string> m;
...
std::string s1{"s1"};
m.insert({42, std::move(s1)});

std::string s2{"s2"};
auto pos = m.insert_or_assign(42, std::move(s2));

std::string s3{"s3"};
m.insert_or_assign(pos, 42, std::move(s3));
```

## 26.3 Container Support for Incomplete Types

Since C++17, `std::vector`, `std::list`, and `std::forward_list` are required to support incomplete types (see Section A on page 415).

The main motivation for this is described in an article by Matt Austern, entitled *The Standard Librarian: Containers of Incomplete Types*:[1] you can now have a type, which recursively has a member of a container of its type. For example:

```
struct Node
{
  std::string value;
  std::vector<Node> children;     // OK since C++17 (Node is an incomplete type here)
};
```

---

[1] See http://web.archive.org/web/20190305220304/http://www.drdobbs.com/184403814

## 26.3 Container Support for Incomplete Types

This also applies to classes with private members and a public API.
Here is a complete example:

*lib/incomplete.hpp*
```cpp
#ifndef NODE_HPP
#define NODE_HPP

#include <vector>
#include <iostream>
#include <string>

class Node
{
  private:
    std::string value;
    std::vector<Node> children;    // OK since C++17 (Node is an incomplete type here)
  public:
    // create Node with value:
    Node(std::string s) : value{std::move(s)}, children{} {
    }

    // add child node:
    void add(Node n) {
      children.push_back(std::move(n));
    }

    // access child node:
    Node& operator[](std::size_t idx) {
      return children.at(idx);
    }

    // print node tree recursively:
    void print(int indent = 0) const {
      std::cout << std::string(indent, ' ') << value << '\n';
      for (const auto& n : children) {
        n.print(indent+2);
      }
    }
    ...
};

#endif // NODE_HPP
```

You could use this class as follows:

*lib/incomplete.cpp*
```
#include "incomplete.hpp"
#include <iostream>

int main()
{
  // create node tree:
  Node root{"top"};
  root.add(Node{"elem1"});
  root.add(Node{"elem2"});
  root[0].add(Node{"elem1.1"});

  // print node tree:
  root.print();
}
```

The program has the following output:
```
top
  elem1
    elem1.1
  elem2
```

## 26.4 String Improvements

For strings (type `basic_string<>`), C++17 has provided a few improvements:

- For non-const strings, you can now also call `data()` to access the underlying character sequence as a raw C string:
    ```
    std::string mystring{"Hello world"};
    auto cstr = mystring.data();
    cstr[6] = 'W';    // OK since C++17
    ```
    Note that before C++17, the type of `cstr` would be `const char*`, while now the type is `char*`. Before C++17, assigning the return value of `data()` to a `char*` would not compile:
    ```
    std::string mystring{"Hello world"};
    char* cstr = mystring.data();    // OK since C++17
    ```
    As usual, the access to the value returned by `data()` is valid only as long as the `std::string` exists and does not reallocate its memory. Modifying the trailing null terminator of the value returned by `data()` results in undefined behavior.

- An implicit conversion to `std::string_view` is now provided, which, however, might result in some nasty bugs and ambiguities. See the chapter about string views (see Chapter 19 on page 185) for details.

- For strings, polymorphic memory resources are now supported, which means that you can declare:
  ```
  std::pmr::string s1;
  std::pmr::wstring s1;
  std::pmr::u16string s1;
  std::pmr::u32string s1;
  ```
  See the PMR chapter (see Chapter 29 on page 341) for details.

## 26.5 Afternotes

Node handles were first proposed indirectly by Alan Talbot requesting splice operations as library issue `https://wg21.link/lwg839` and by Alisdair Meredith requesting move support for node elements as library issue `https://wg21.link/lwg1041`. The finally accepted wording was formulated by Alan Talbot, Jonathan Wakely, Howard Hinnant, and James Dennett in `https://wg21.link/p0083r3`. The API was slightly clarified as a final version by Howard E. Hinnant in `https://wg21.link/p0508r0`.

The new return value for the emplace member functions was first proposed by Alan Talbot in `https://wg21.link/p0084r0`. The finally accepted wording was formulated by Alan Talbot in `https://wg21.link/p0084r2`.

`insert_or_assign()` and `try_emplace()` for (unordered) maps was first proposed by Thomas Köppe in `https://wg21.link/n3873`. The finally accepted wording was formulated by Thomas Köppe in `https://wg21.link/n4279`.

Container support for incomplete types was first discussed by Matt Austern in `http://drdobbs.com/184403814` and first proposed by Zhihao Yuan in `https://wg21.link/n3890`. The finally accepted wording was formulated by Zhihao Yuan in `https://wg21.link/n4510`.

`data()` for strings was first proposed by Michael Bradshaw as library issue `https://wg21.link/lwg2391`. The finally accepted wording was formulated by David Sankel in `https://wg21.link/p0272r1`.

# Chapter 27
# Multi-Threading and Concurrency

A couple of minor extensions and improvements were introduced in the area of multi-threading and concurrency.

## 27.1 Supplementary Mutexes and Locks

### 27.1.1 `std::scoped_lock`

C++11 introduced a simple `std::lock_guard` to allow a simple RAII-style way for locking a mutex:
- The constructor locks
- The destructor unlocks (which might be caused by an exception)

Unfortunately, this was not standardized as a variadic template to allow multiple mutexes to be locked with a single declaration.

`std::scoped_lock<>` closes this gap. It allows us to lock one or multiple mutexes. The mutexes may have different mutex types.

For example:

```
#include <mutex>
...
std::vector<std::string> allIssues;
std::mutex allIssuesMx;
std::vector<std::string> openIssues;
std::timed_mutex openIssuesMx;

// lock both issue lists:
{
  std::scoped_lock lg(allIssuesMx, openIssuesMx);
    ...   // manipulate both allIssues and openIssues
}
```

Note that due to class template argument deduction (see Chapter 9 on page 77), you do not have to specify the types of the mutexes when declaring lg.

This example usage is equivalent to the following code, which can be called since C++11:

```
// lock both issue lists:
{
  std::lock(allIssuesMx, openIssuesMx);        // lock with deadlock avoidance
  std::lock_guard<std::mutex> lg1(allIssuesMx, std::adopt_lock);
  std::lock_guard<std::mutex> lg2(openIssuesMx, std::adopt_lock);
  ...   // manipulate both allIssues and openIssues
}
```

Thus, if more than one mutex is passed, the constructor of `scoped_lock` uses the variadic convenience function `lock(...)`, which guarantees that the call does not result in a deadlock (the standard notes: *"A deadlock avoidance algorithm such as try-and-back-off must be used, but the specific algorithm is not specified to avoid over-constraining implementations"*).

If only one mutex is passed to the constructor of a `scoped_lock`, it simply locks the mutex. Thus, in a `scoped_lock` with a single constructor, argument acts like a `lock_guard`. It then even defines the member `mutex_type`, which is not defined for multiple mutexes.[1] Therefore, you can replace all uses of `lock_guard` with `scoped_lock`.

If no mutex is passed, the lock guard has no effect.

Note that you can also adopt multiple locks:

```
// lock both issue lists:
{
  std::lock(allIssuesMx, openIssuesMx);        // Note: deadlock avoidance algorithm used
  std::scoped_lock lg{std::adopt_lock, allIssuesMx, openIssuesMx};
  ...   // manipulate both allIssues and openIssues
}
```

However, note that the constructors that adopt the locked mutexes now have the `adopt_lock` argument at the front.[2]

## 27.1.2 `std::shared_mutex`

C++14 added a `std::shared_timed_mutex` to support read/write locks, where multiple threads read a value concurrently, while from time to time a thread might update the value. However, mutexes that do not support timed locks can be implemented more efficiently on some platforms. Therefore, the type `std::shared_mutex` has now been introduced (as `std::mutex` has existed in addition to `std::timed_mutex` since C++11).

`std::shared_mutex` is defined in header `<shared_mutex>` and supports the following operations:

---

[1] The typical implementation is to provide a partial specialization for the case where only a single mutex is passed to the scoped lock.
[2] In the original C++17 standard the `adopt_lock` argument was at the end, which was later fixed with https://wg21.link/p0739r0.

- For exclusive locks: `lock()`, `try_lock()`, `unlock()`
- For shared read-access: `lock_shared()`, `try_lock_shared()`, `unlock_shared()`
- `native_handle()`

That is, unlike type `std::shared_timed_mutex`, type `std::shared_mutex` does not guarantee to support `try_lock_for()`, `try_lock_until()`, `try_lock_shared_for()`, and `try_lock_shared_until()`.

Note that `std::shared_timed_mutex` is the only mutex type not providing the `native_handle()` API.

**Using a shared_mutex**

We use a `shared_mutex` as follows: assume you have a shared vector, which is usually read by multiple threads, but from time to time is modified:

```
#include <shared_mutex>
#include <mutex>
...
std::vector<double> v;         // shared resource
std::shared_mutex vMutex;      // control access to v (shared_timed_mutex in C++14)
```

To have shared read-access (so that multiple readers do not block each other), you use a `shared_lock`, which is a lock guard for shared read access (introduced with C++14). For example:

```
if (std::shared_lock sl(vMutex); v.size() > 0) {
    ...    // (shared) read access to the elements of vector v
}
```

You only use an exclusive lock guard for an exclusive write access. This lock guard might be either a simple `lock_guard`, or a `scoped_lock` (as just introduced (see Section 27.1.1 on page 321)), or a sophisticated `unique_lock`. For example:

```
{
  std::scoped_lock sl(vMutex);
    ...    // exclusive write read access to the vector v
}
```

## 27.2 `is_always_lock_free` for Atomics

You can now use a C++ library feature to check whether a specific atomic type can always be used without locks. For example:

```
if constexpr(std::atomic<int>::is_always_lock_free) {
    ...
}
else {
    ...
}
```

If the `is_always_lock_free()` yields `true` for an atomic type, then `is_lock_free()` yields `true` for any object of this type:

```
if constexpr(atomic<T>::is_always_lock_free) {
  assert(atomic<T>{}.is_lock_free());    // never fails
}
```

The value corresponds to the macro that had to be used before C++17. For example, the value of `std::atomic<int>::is_always_lock_free` is `true` if and only if `ATOMIC_INT_LOCK_FREE` yields 2 (which stands for "always"):

```
if constexpr(std::atomic<int>::is_always_lock_free) {
  // ATOMIC_INT_LOCK_FREE == 2
  ...
}
else {
  // ATOMIC_INT_LOCK_FREE == 0 || ATOMIC_INT_LOCK_FREE == 1
  ...
}
```

The reason for replacing the macro with a static member is to have more type safety and support the use of these checks in complicated generic code (e.g., using SFINAE).

Remember that `std::atomic<>` can also be used for trivially copyable types. Thus, you can also check whether your own structure would need locks if used atomically. For example:

```
template<auto SZ>
struct Data {
  bool set;
  int values[SZ];
  double average;
};

if constexpr(std::atomic<Data<4>>::is_always_lock_free) {
  ...
}
else {
  ...
}
```

## 27.3 Cache Line Sizes

It is sometimes important for a program to deal with cache line sizes:

## 27.3 Cache Line Sizes

- On one hand, it is important for concurrency that different objects accessed by different threads do not belong to the same cache line. Otherwise, the memory of the cache line has to be synchronized between different threads when the objects are accessed concurrently.[3]
- On the other hand, your goal might be to place multiple objects in the same cache line so that accessing the first object gives direct access to the others instead of loading them in the cache.

For this, the C++ standard library introduces two inline variables (see Chapter 3 on page 25) in header `<new>`:

```
namespace std {
  inline constexpr size_t hardware_destructive_interference_size;
  inline constexpr size_t hardware_constructive_interference_size;
}
```

These objects have the following implementation-defined values:

- `hardware_destructive_interference_size` is the recommended minimum offset between two objects that might be accessed by different threads concurrently to avoid worse performance because the same L1 cache line is affected.
- `hardware_constructive_interference_size` is the recommended maximum size of contiguous memory within which two objects are placed in the same L1 cache line.

Both values are only hints because the ideal value might depend on the exact architecture. These constants are the best values a compiler can provide when dealing with the variety of platforms supported by the generated code. Therefore, if you know better, use specific values, but using these values is better than any assumed fixed size for code supporting multiple platforms.

The values are both at least `alignof(std::max_align_t)`. The value is usually the same. However, semantically, they represent different purposes for using different objects, so you should use them accordingly as follows:

- If you want to access two different (atomic) objects with ***different threads***:

  ```
  struct Data {
    alignas(std::hardware_destructive_interference_size) int valueForThreadA;
    alignas(std::hardware_destructive_interference_size) int valueForThreadB;
  };
  ```

- If you want to access two different (atomic) objects with ***the same thread***:

  ```
  struct Data {
    int valueForThreadA;
    int otherValueForTheThreadA;
  };
  ```

  ```
  // double-check we have best performance due to shared cache line:
  static_assert(sizeof(Data) <= std::hardware_constructive_interference_size);

  // ensure objects are properly aligned:
  ```

---

[3] Accessing multiple objects with different threads concurrently is usually safe in C++, but the necessary synchronization might degrade the performance of the program.

```
alignas(sizeof(Data)) Data myDataForAThread;
```

## 27.4 Afternotes

`scoped_lock`s were originally proposed as a modification to make `lock_guard` variadic by Mike Spertus in https://wg21.link/n4470, which was accepted as https://wg21.link/p0156r0. However, because this turned out to be an ABI breakage, the new name `scoped_lock` was introduced by Mike Spertus with https://wg21.link/p0156r2 and finally accepted. Mike Spertus, Walter E. Brown, and Stephan T. Lavavej later changed the order of a constructor as a defect against C++17 with https://wg21.link/p0739r0:

The `shared_mutex` was first proposed together with all other mutexes for C++11 by Howard Hinnant in https://wg21.link/n2406. However, it took time to convince the C++ standards committee that all proposed mutexes are useful. Therefore, the finally accepted wording was formulated for C++17 by Gor Nishanov in https://wg21.link/n4508.

The `std::atomic<>` static member `std::is_always_lock_free` was first proposed by Olivier Giroux, JF Bastien, and Jeff Snyder in https://wg21.link/n4509. The finally accepted wording was also formulated by Olivier Giroux, JF Bastien, and Jeff Snyder in https://wg21.link/p0152r1.

The hardware interference (cache line) sizes were first proposed by JF Bastien and Olivier Giroux in https://wg21.link/n4523. The finally accepted wording was also formulated by JF Bastien and Olivier Giroux in https://wg21.link/p0154r1.

# Chapter 28
# Other Small Library Features and Modifications

There are a couple of minor or small extensions and changes to the C++ standard library, which are described in this chapter.

## 28.1 `std::uncaught_exceptions()`

One key pattern of C++ is *RAII: Resource Acquisition Is Initialization.* As a safe way to deal with a resource that you have to release or clean up, you pass the ownership of the acquired resource to an object so that its destructor automatically releases the resource when the object goes out of scope. The benefit is that the release happens automatically even if the scope is left due to an exception.

However, sometimes the "release" of a resource might depend on whether we left the scope as part of the normal data flow or unexpectedly due to an exception. An example is a transactional resource, where we might *commit* a request at the end of a normal data flow when everything worked fine, but call *rollback* in the event of an exception.

For this, C++11 introduced `std::uncaught_exception()`, which could be used as follows:

```
class Request {
 public:
   ...
   ~Request() {
     if (std::uncaught_exception()) {
       rollback();
     }
     else {
       commit();
     }
   }
};
```

Therefore, when using a `Request`, leaving the scope would either `commit()` or `rollback()` depending on whether or not an exception was thrown:

```
{
  Request r1{...};   // usually destructor calls commit()
  ...
  if (...) {
    throw ...;       // let destructor call rollback()
  }
  ...
}  // calls commit() in the good case and rollback() on exception
```

However, this API did not work for the following use case: if we create a new use `Request` object *while* we are already handling an exception, the request would always `rollback()` even if no (further) exception occurs during its use:

```
try {
  ...
}
catch (...) {
  Request r2{...};
  ...
}  // calls rollback() even if without any additional exception in the catch clause
```

The new standard library function `uncaught_exceptions()` (note the additional s at the end of the name) solves this problem. Instead of returning whether we are handling an exception, it returns how many (nested) exceptions are currently unhandled. This allows us to find out whether (even while handling an exception) an additional exception was raised.

For that, we simply modify the definition of the class `Request` as follows:

```
class Request {
 private:
  ...
  int initialUncaught{std::uncaught_exceptions()};
 public:
  ...
  ~Request() {
    if (std::uncaught_exceptions() > initialUncaught) {
      rollback();
    }
    else {
      commit();
    }
  }
};
```

Now both example scenarios work fine:

```
try {
  Request r1{...};   // usually destructor calls commit()
```

```
  ...
  if (...) {
    throw ... ;        // let destructor call rollback()
  }
  ...
} // calls commit() in the good case and rollback() on exception
catch (...) {
  Request r2{...};
  ...
} // calls commit() if no additional exception
```

Here, the constructor of r2 initializes `initialUncaught` with 1 because we are already handling an exception inside the `catch` clause. However, when the destructor for r2 is called and no additional exception was raised, `initialUncaught` is still 1 and therefore `commit()` is called. `std::uncaught_exceptions()` will only yield 2 if a second unhandled exception is raised inside the `catch` clause. As a consequence, the destructor of r2 will call `rollback()`.

See *lib/uncaught.cpp* for a complete example.

The old API `std::uncaught_exception()` (without the s at the end) is deprecated since C++17 and should no longer be used.

## 28.2 Shared Pointer Improvements

For shared pointers a few improvements were added with C++17.

Note that in addition, the member function `unique()` was deprecated (see Section 35.2.7 on page 412).

### 28.2.1 Special handling for Shared Pointers to Raw C Arrays

Since C++17, you can instantiate shared pointers explicitly for arrays to ensure that `delete[]` is called by the deleter (as was already possible for unique pointers since C++11): You can now simply call:

```
std::shared_ptr<std::string[]> p{new std::string[10]};
```

instead of:

```
std::shared_ptr<std::string> p{new std::string[10],
                               std::default_delete<std::string[]>()};
```

or:

```
std::shared_ptr<std::string> p{new std::string[10],
                               [](std::string* p) {
                                 delete[] p;
                               }};
```

With the instantiation as an array, the API also changes slightly: instead of `operator*`, you have to use `operator[]` (as for unique pointers of raw arrays):

```
std::shared_ptr<std::string> ps{new std::string};
*ps = "hello";      // OK
```

```
ps[0] = "hello";      // ERROR

std::shared_ptr<std::string[]> parr{new std::string[10]};
*parr = "hello";      // ERROR (unspecified behavior)
parr[0] = "hello";    // OK
```

Note that there is no formal specification of whether `operator*` is supported for allocated raw arrays and whether `operator[]` is supported otherwise. However, usually calling these unspecified operations does not compile.

### 28.2.2 `reinterpret_pointer_cast` for Shared Pointers

In addition to `static_pointer_cast`, `dynamic_pointer_cast`, and `const_pointer_cast`, you can now call `reinterpret_pointer_cast` to reinterpret the type of the bits a shared pointer refers to.

### 28.2.3 `weak_type` for Shared Pointers

To support the use of weak pointers in generic code, shared pointers now provide a member `weak_type`. For example:

```
template<typename T>
void observe(T sp)
{
  // initialize weak pointer from passed shared pointer:
  typename T::weak_type wp{sp};
  ...
}
```

### 28.2.4 `weak_from_this` for Shared Pointers

Sometimes you need another shared pointer to an existing object without having access to the existing shared pointer(s). For this problem, C++11 introduced the base class `enable_shared_from_this`, which provides the member function `shared_from_this`:

```
#include <memory>

class Person : public std::enable_shared_from_this<Person>
{
  ...
};

Person* pp = new Person{...};
std::shared_ptr<Person> sp1{pp};                      // sp1 gets owner
std::shared_ptr<Person> sp2{pp};                      // fatal runtime ERROR: sp2 gets independent owners
std::shared_ptr<Person> sp3{pp->shared_from_this()};  // OK: sp1 and sp3 share ownership
```

## 28.2 Shared Pointer Improvements

This feature is needed in particular if a member function of the object shall yield a shared pointer to the object:

```
class Person : public std::enable_shared_from_this<Person>
{
  ...
  std::shared_ptr<Person> sharedPtrTo() {
    return shared_from_this();
  }
};
```

Since C++17, there is an additional helper function to yield a weak pointer to the object:

```
Person* pp = new Person{...};
std::shared_ptr<Person> sp{pp};                        // sp gets ownership
...
std::weak_ptr<Person> wp{pp->weak_from_this()};   // wp observes ownership of what sp owns
```

Before C++17, you could have the same functionality with

```
weak_ptr<Person> wp{pp->shared_from_this()}
```

but `weak_from_this()` achieves the same effect with fewer reference count modifications.

In addition, the behavior of a specific corner case was clarified: If a raw pointer is passed to two different shared pointers (which is valid if only one of them really deletes the associated resource), then `shared_from_this()` and `weak_from_this()` share the ownership with the shared pointer created first. This means that the following is possible:

```
struct Person : public std::enable_shared_from_this<Person>
{
  ...
};

Person* p = new Person;
std::shared_ptr<Person> sp1(p);         // create a first shared pointer

{
  std::shared_ptr<Person> sp2(p,        // create a second shared pointer not sharing ownership
                              [](void*) {
                              });
  auto sp3{p->shared_from_this()};      // sp3 shares ownership with sp1
}

auto sp4{p->shared_from_this()};        // sp4 shares ownership with sp1
```

Before this clarification, some implementations allowed `sp3` and `sp4` to share ownership with the shared pointer created *last*, which threw `std::bad_weak_ptr` when initializing `sp4`.

## 28.3 Numeric Extensions

The following numeric functions were also added with C++17.

### 28.3.1 Greatest Common Divisor and Least Common Multiple

In header `<numeric>`:

- `gcd(x, y)`
  returns the *greatest common divisor* of *x* and *y*
- `lcm(x, y)` returns the *least common multiple* of *x* and *y*

Both arguments have to be of an integral type, except `bool`. The types may differ. In that case, the return value has the common type of both arguments.

For example:

```
#include <numeric>

int i{42};
long l{30};

auto x{std::gcd(i, l)};    // x is long 6
auto y{std::lcm(i, l)};    // y is long 210
```

### 28.3.2 Three-Argument Overloads of `std::hypot()`

In header `<cmath>`:

- `hypot(x, y, z)`
  returns the square root of the square of the passed arguments

As usual for functions in `<cmath>`, this function has overloads to support all floating point types.

These overloads are not provided in `math.h` or outside namespace `std`.

For example:

```
#include <cmath>

// compute distance of two points in 3D space:
auto dist = std::hypot(p2.x - p1.x, p2.y - p1.y, p2.z - p1.z);
```

Before C++17, you had to call something like the following:

```
auto dist = std::hypot(p2.x - p1.x, std::hypot(p2.y - p1.y, p2.z - p1.z));
```

### 28.3.3 Mathematical Special Functions

A collection of table *28.1 Mathematical Special Functions* already standardized in the international standard IS 29124:2010 is now required to be unconditionally available in the C++ standard in header `<cmath>`.

With the original names, the functions take floating-point parameters and declare return values as `double`. All these functions also exist with

## 28.3 Numeric Extensions

| Name | Meaning |
|---|---|
| `assoc_laguerre()` | Associated Laguerre polynomials |
| `assoc_legendre()` | Associated Legendre functions |
| `beta()` | Beta function |
| `comp_ellint_1()` | Complete elliptic integral of the first kind |
| `comp_ellint_2()` | Complete elliptic integral of the second kind |
| `comp_ellint_3()` | Complete elliptic integral of the third kind |
| `cyl_bessel_i()` | Regular modified cylindrical Bessel functions |
| `cyl_bessel_j()` | Cylindrical Bessel functions of the first kind |
| `cyl_bessel_k()` | Irregular modified cylindrical Bessel functions |
| `cyl_neumann()` | Cylindrical Neumann functions (cylindrical Bessel functions of the second kind) |
| `ellint_1()` | Incomplete elliptic integral of the first kind |
| `ellint_2()` | Incomplete elliptic integral of the second kind |
| `ellint_3()` | Incomplete elliptic integral of the third kind |
| `expint()` | Exponential integral |
| `hermite()` | Hermite polynomials |
| `laguerre()` | Laguerre polynomials |
| `legendre()` | Legendre polynomials |
| `riemann_zeta()` | Riemann zeta function |
| `sph_bessel()` | Spherical Bessel functions of the first kind |
| `sph_legendre()` | Spherical associated Legendre functions |
| `sph_neumann()` | Spherical Neumann functions (spherical Bessel functions of the second kind) |

*Table 28.1. Mathematical Special Functions*

- The suffix f for dealing with float as floating-point parameter and return type
- The suffix l for dealing with long double as floating-point parameter and return type

For example:

```
// exponential integral:
double      expint(double x);
float       expintf(float x);
long double expintl(long double x);

// Laguerre polynomials:
double      laguerre(unsigned n, double x);
float       laguerref(unsigned n, float x);
long double laguerrel(unsigned n, long double x);
```

## 28.4 chrono Extensions

C++17 added some extensions to the chrono part of the C++ standard library to make the library easier to use and more consistent.

For durations and time points, new rounding functions were added:
- round(): rounds up or down to the nearest value
- floor(): rounds down towards negative infinity
- ceil(): rounds up towards positive infinity

The rounding modes differ from duration_cast<> and time_point_cast<> (which existed before C++17) in that the new rounding functions do not just truncate towards zero.

In addition, a missing abs() function was added for durations.

The following program demonstrates the behavior for durations:

*lib/chronoext.cpp*

```cpp
#include <chrono>
#include <iostream>

std::ostream& operator<< (std::ostream& strm,
                          const std::chrono::duration<double,std::milli>& dur)
{
  return strm << dur.count() << "ms";
}

template<typename T>
void roundAndAbs(T dur)
{
  using namespace std::chrono;

  std::cout << dur << '\n';
  std::cout << " abs():  " << abs(dur) << '\n';
  std::cout << " cast:   " << duration_cast<std::chrono::seconds>(dur) << '\n';
  std::cout << " floor(): " << floor<std::chrono::seconds>(dur) << '\n';
  std::cout << " ceil():  " << ceil<std::chrono::seconds>(dur) << '\n';
  std::cout << " round(): " << round<std::chrono::seconds>(dur) << '\n';
}

int main()
{
  using namespace std::literals;
  roundAndAbs(3.33s);
  roundAndAbs(3.77s);
  roundAndAbs(-3.77s);
}
```

It has the following output:

```
3330ms
  abs():    3330ms
  cast:     3000ms
  floor():  3000ms
  ceil():   4000ms
  round():  3000ms
3770ms
  abs():    3770ms
  cast:     3000ms
  floor():  3000ms
  ceil():   4000ms
  round():  4000ms
-3770ms
  abs():    3770ms
  cast:     -3000ms
  floor():  -4000ms
  ceil():   -3000ms
  round():  -4000ms
```

## 28.5 `constexpr` Extensions and Fixes

As usual for each new C++ version since C++11, at a couple of places support for `constexpr` was added and/or fixed.

The most important fixes are:
- For `std::array`, the following functions are now `constexpr`:
  - `begin()`, `end()`, `cbegin()`, `cend()`, `rbegin()`, `rend()`, `crbegin()`, and `crend()`
  - `operator[]`, `at()`, `front()`, `back()` also for non-const arrays
  - `data()`
- The generic free-standing functions for range access (`std::begin()`, `std::end()`, (`std::rbegin()`, and `std::rend()`, as well as the helper functions (`std::advance()`, `std::distance()`, (`std::prev()`, and `std::next()`, are also `constexpr` now.
- For classes `std::reverse_iterator` and `std::move_iterator`, all operations are now `constexpr`.
- In the whole chrono part of the C++ standard library (`time_point`, `duration`, clocks, and `ratio`), all operations and variables are `constexpr` now except the clock member functions `now()`, `to_time_t()`, and `from_time_t()`.
- All specializations of `std::char_traits` now have `constexpr` member functions. In particular, this enables us to initialize string views at compile time (see Section 19.4.2 on page 194).

For example, you can now program:

```
constexpr std::array arr{0, 8, 15, 42};
constexpr auto val = arr[2];          // OK
static_assert(val == 15);             // OK and doesn't fail
```

Note that for iterators, we need global or `static` objects because we cannot take the address of objects on the stack at compile time:

```
constexpr static std::array arr{0, 8, 15, 42};
constexpr auto pos = std::next(arr.rbegin());   // OK
static_assert(*pos == 15);                       // OK and doesn't fail
```

## 28.6 `noexcept` Extensions and Fixes

As usual for each new C++ version since C++11, at a couple of places support for `noexcept` was added and/or fixed.

The most important fixes are:

- For `std::vector<>` and `std::string` (`std::basic_string<>`), C++17 guarantees not to throw
  - In the default constructor (provided the default constructor of the allocator does not throw)
  - In the move constructor
  - In the constructor that takes an allocator
- For all containers (including `std::string`/`std::basic_string<>`), C++17 guarantees not to throw
  - In the move assignment operator (provided the allocators are interchangeable)
  - In the `swap()` functions (provided the allocators are interchangeable)

**Consequences for Vector Reallocation**

Note that one of the `noexcept` fixes is very special and remarkable: only vectors and strings now guarantee not to throw in their move constructor. The other containers might still throw.

This has a significant impact if these types are used in a vector, because on reallocation, vectors can only use move semantics if the move constructor of the elements guarantees not to throw.

In other words:

- Reallocating a vector of strings/vectors is now guaranteed to be fast.
- Reallocating a vector of other container types might be slow.

This is yet another good reason to use vectors as the default container unless you have good reason to do otherwise.

## 28.7 Afternotes

The motivation for `std::uncaught_exceptions()` was first raised by Herb Sutter in https://wg21.link/n3614. The finally accepted wording for this feature was formulated by Herb Sutter in https://wg21.link/n4259.

Extending shared pointers for array types and adding `reinterpret_pointer_cast` was first proposed by Peter Dimov in https://wg21.link/n3640. The finally accepted wording for this feature was formulated by Jonathan Wakely in https://wg21.link/p0414r2.

## 28.7 Afternotes

The problem of getting access to the weak pointer type of shared pointers was first raised by Arthur O'Dwyer in `https://wg21.link/n4537`. The finally accepted wording for this feature was formulated by Arthur O'Dwyer in `https://wg21.link/p0163r0`.

`weak_from_this` was first proposed by Jonathan Wakely and Peter Dimov in `https://wg21.link/p0033r0`. The finally accepted wording for this feature was formulated by Jonathan Wakely and Peter Dimov in `https://wg21.link/p0033r1`.

The numeric GCD and LCM functions were first proposed by Walter E. Brown in `https://wg21.link/n3845`. They became part of the first Library Fundamentals TS. For C++17, they were then adopted as proposed by Walter E. Brown in `https://wg21.link/p0295r0`.

The three-argument overloads of `std::hypot()` were first proposed by Benson Ma in `https://wg21.link/p0030r0`. The finally accepted wording for this feature was formulated by Benson Ma in `https://wg21.link/p0030r1`.

Adding special mathematical functions was first proposed in 2003 by Walter E. Brown in `https://wg21.link/n1422`. Making them mandatory in C++17 by adopting the international standard IS 29124:2010 was proposed by Walter E. Brown, Axel Naumann, and Edward Smith-Rowland in `https://wg21.link/p0226r1`.

The chrono extensions were first proposed by Howard Hinnant in `https://wg21.link/p0092r0`. The finally accepted wording for this feature was formulated by Howard Hinnant in `https://wg21.link/p0092r1`.

Adding `constexpr` for chrono was first proposed by Howard Hinnant in `https://wg21.link/p0505r0`. and accepted. The finally accepted wording for this feature was formulated by Howard Hinnant in `https://wg21.link/p0092R1`.

Adding `constexpr` at various other places was accepted as proposed by Antony Polukhin in `https://wg21.link/p0031r0` and in `https://wg21.link/p0426r1`.

The fixes for `noexcept` were first proposed by Nicolai Josuttis in `https://wg21.link/4002`. The finally accepted wording for this modification was formulated by Nicolai Josuttis in `https://wg21.link/n4258`.

# Part V

# Expert Utilities

This part of the book introduces new language and library features that the average application programmer does not usually need to know. It covers features for programmers of foundation libraries and features that might be used to deal with special problems (such as modifying the way heap memory is handled).

# Chapter 29
# Polymorphic Memory Resources (PMR)

Since C++98, the standard library has supported the ability to configure the way classes allocate their internal (heap) memory. Therefore, almost all types in the standard library that allocate memory have an allocator parameter. This allows you to configure the way containers, strings, and other types allocate their internal memory if they need more space than that allocated on the stack.

The default way to allocate this memory is to allocate it from the heap. However, there are different reasons for modifying this default behavior:
- You can use your own way of allocating memory to reduce the number of system calls.
- You can ensure that memory is allocated contiguously to benefit from CPU caching.
- You can place containers and their elements in shared memory available for multiple processes.
- You can even redirect these heap memory calls to use memory allocated earlier on the stack.

Thus, there can be performance and functional reasons for modifying the default behavior.[1]

However, until C++17, using allocators (correctly) was in many ways both tricky and clumsy (due to some flaws, too much complexity, and modifications with backward compatibility).

C++17 now provides a fairly easy-to-use approach for predefined and user-defined ways of memory allocation, which can be used for standard types and user-defined types.

Therefore, this chapter discusses:
- Using standard memory resources (see Section 29.1 on page 342) provided by the standard library
- Defining custom memory resources (see Section 29.2 on page 355)
- Providing memory resource support for custom types (see Section 29.3 on page 360)

This chapter would not have been possible without the significant help of Pablo Halpern, Arthur O'Dwyer, David Sankel, and Jonathan Wakely.

---

[1] The initial reason for allocators was to be able to deal with pointers of different size ("near" and "far" pointers).

## 29.1 Using Standard Memory Resources

This section introduces the standard memory resources and the ways you can use them.

### 29.1.1 Motivating Example

Let us first compare memory consumption with and without standard memory resources.

**Allocating Memory for Containers and Strings**

Assume that in your program, you have a vector of some strings, which you initialize with quite long strings:

*pmr/pmr0.cpp*

```cpp
#include <iostream>
#include <string>
#include <vector>
#include "../lang/tracknew.hpp"

int main()
{
  TrackNew::reset();

  std::vector<std::string> coll;
  for (int i=0; i < 1000; ++i) {
    coll.emplace_back("just a non-SSO string");
  }

  TrackNew::status();
}
```

Note that we track the number of memory allocations using a class that tracks all ::new calls (see Section 30.4 on page 380) performed with the following loop:

```cpp
std::vector<std::string> coll;
for (int i=0; i < 1000; ++i) {
  coll.emplace_back("just a non-SSO string");
}
```

There are a lot of allocations because internally, the vector uses memory to store the elements. In addition, the string elements themselves might allocate memory on the heap to hold their current value (with the usually implemented small string optimization (see Section A on page 416), this typically happens only if the strings have more than 15 characters).

The output of the program might be something like the following:

```
1018 allocations for 134,730 bytes
```

## 29.1 Using Standard Memory Resources

This would mean having one allocation for each element plus 18 allocations for the vector internally, because the vector allocates 18 times (more) memory to hold its elements.[2]

Behavior like this can become critical because memory (re-)allocations take time and in some contexts (such as embedded systems), allocating heap memory at all might be a problem.

We could ask the vector to reserve sufficient memory ahead of time, but in general, you cannot avoid reallocations unless you know the amount of data to be processed ahead of time. If you do not know exactly how much data you process, you always have to find a compromise between avoiding reallocations and not wasting too much memory. And you need at least 1001 allocations (one allocation to hold the elements in the vector and one for each string that does not use the small string optimization (see Section A on page 416)).

**Not Allocating Memory for Containers**

We can easily improve the situation by using a polymorphic allocator. First, we could use a `std::pmr::vector` and allow the vector to allocate its memory on the stack:

*pmr/pmr1.cpp*

```
#include <iostream>
#include <string>
#include <vector>
#include <array>
#include <cstdlib>         // for std::byte
#include <memory_resource>
#include "../lang/tracknew.hpp"

int main()
{
  TrackNew::reset();

  // allocate some memory on the stack:
  std::array<std::byte, 200000> buf;

  // and use it as initial memory pool for a vector:
  std::pmr::monotonic_buffer_resource pool{buf.data(), buf.size()};
  std::pmr::vector<std::string> coll{&pool};

  for (int i=0; i < 1000; ++i) {
    coll.emplace_back("just a non-SSO string");
  }

  TrackNew::status();
}
```

---

[2] The number of reallocations might differ from platform to platform because the algorithms for reallocating more memory differ. If the current memory capacity is exceeded, some implementations enlarge it by 50%, while others double the size of the memory.

First, we allocate our own memory on the stack (using the new type `std::byte` (see Chapter 18 on page 179)):

```
// allocate some memory on the stack:
std::array<std::byte, 200000> buf;
```

Instead of `std::byte` you could also just use `char`.

Then, we initialize a `monotonic_buffer_resource` with this memory, passing its address and its size:

```
std::pmr::monotonic_buffer_resource pool{buf.data(), buf.size()};
```

Finally, we use a `std::pmr::vector`, which takes the memory resource for all its allocations:

```
std::pmr::vector<std::string> coll{&pool};
```

This declaration is just a shortcut for the following:

```
std::vector<std::string,
            std::pmr::polymorphic_allocator<std::string>> coll{&pool};
```

That is, we declare that the vector uses a *polymorphic allocator*, which can switch between different *memory resources* at runtime. The class `monotonic_buffer_resource` is derived from the class `memory_resource` and can therefore be used as a memory resource for a polymorphic allocator. So, by passing the address of our memory resource, we ensure that the vector uses our memory resource as a polymorphic allocator.

If we measure the allocated memory of this program, the output might become:

```
1000 allocations for 32000 bytes
```

The 18 allocations of the vector are no longer performed on the heap. Instead, our initialized buffer `buf` is used.

If the pre-allocated memory of 200,000 bytes is not sufficient, the vector will still allocate more memory on the heap. This happens because the `monotonic_memory_resource` uses the default allocator, which allocates memory with `new` as fallback.

**Not Allocating Memory At All**

We can even avoid using heap memory at all by defining the element type of the `std::pmr::vector` to be `std::pmr::string`:

*pmr/pmr2.cpp*

```
#include <iostream>
#include <string>
#include <vector>
#include <array>
#include <cstdlib>         // for std::byte
#include <memory_resource>
#include "../lang/tracknew.hpp"

int main()
{
  TrackNew::reset();
```

## 29.1 Using Standard Memory Resources

```
  // allocate some memory on the stack:
  std::array<std::byte, 200000> buf;

  // and use it as initial memory pool for a vector and its strings:
  std::pmr::monotonic_buffer_resource pool{buf.data(), buf.size()};
  std::pmr::vector<std::pmr::string> coll{&pool};

  for (int i=0; i < 1000; ++i) {
    coll.emplace_back("just a non-SSO string");
  }

  TrackNew::status();
}
```

Due to the following definition of the vector:

```
std::pmr::vector<std::pmr::string> coll{&pool};
```

the output of the program becomes:

```
0 allocations for 0 bytes
```

This is because a pmr vector tries to propagate its allocator to its elements. This is not successful when the elements do not use a polymorphic allocator, as is the case with type `std::string`. However, by using type `std::pmr::string`, which is a string that uses a polymorphic allocator, the propagation works without any problems.

Again, new memory is allocated by the pool on the heap only when there is no more memory in the buffer. This might happen, for example, with the following modification:

```
for (int i=0; i < 50000; ++i) {
  coll.emplace_back("just a non-SSO string");
}
```

when the output might suddenly become:

```
8 allocations for 14777448 bytes
```

### Reusing Memory Pools

We can even reuse our pool of stack memory. For example:

*pmr/pmr3.cpp*

```
#include <iostream>
#include <string>
#include <vector>
#include <array>
#include <cstdlib>        // for std::byte
#include <memory_resource>
```

```cpp
#include "../lang/tracknew.hpp"

int main()
{
  // allocate some memory on the stack:
  std::array<std::byte, 200000> buf;

  for (int num : {1000, 2000, 500, 2000, 3000, 50000, 1000}) {
    std::cout << "-- check with " << num << " elements:\n";
    TrackNew::reset();

    std::pmr::monotonic_buffer_resource pool{buf.data(), buf.size()};
    std::pmr::vector<std::pmr::string> coll{&pool};
    for (int i=0; i < num; ++i) {
      coll.emplace_back("just a non-SSO string");
    }

    TrackNew::status();
  }
}
```

Here, after allocating the 200,000 bytes on the stack, we use this memory again and again to initialize a new resource pool for the vector and its elements.

The output might become:

```
-- check with 1000 elements:
0 allocations for 0 bytes
-- check with 2000 elements:
1 allocations for 300000 bytes
-- check with 500 elements:
0 allocations for 0 bytes
-- check with 2000 elements:
1 allocations for 300000 bytes
-- check with 3000 elements:
2 allocations for 750000 bytes
-- check with 50000 elements:
8 allocations for 14777448 bytes
-- check with 1000 elements:
0 allocations for 0 bytes
```

Each time the 200,000 bytes are sufficient, we do not need any additional allocation (here, this is the case for up to 1000 elements). The 200,000 bytes are then used and available for the next iteration when the memory pool is destructed.

Each time the memory is exceeded, the pool allocates additional memory on the heap, which is deallocated when the memory pool is destructed.

This way, you can easily program memory pools, where you allocate memory once (either on the stack or on the heap) and reuse this memory with every new task (service request, event, data file to process, and so on).

We will discuss more sophisticated examples for memory pools later on (see Section 29.1.3 on page 353).

### 29.1.2 Standard Memory Resources

To support polymorphic allocators, the C++ standard library provides the memory listed in table *29.1 Standard Memory Resources*.

| Memory Resource | Behavior |
| --- | --- |
| `new_delete_resource()` | Yields a pointer to a memory resource calling `new` and `delete` |
| `synchronized_pool_resource` | Class to create memory resources with little fragmentation, thread-safe |
| `unsynchronized_pool_resource` | Class to create memory resources with little fragmentation, not thread-safe |
| `monotonic_buffer_resource` | Class to create memory resources that never deallocates, optionally using a passed buffer, not thread-safe |
| `null_memory_resource()` | Yields a pointer to a memory resource where each allocation fails |

Table 29.1. *Standard Memory Resources*

`new_delete_resource()` and `null_memory_resource()` are functions that return the pointer to a global memory resource, which is defined as a singleton. The other three memory resources are classes, where you have to create objects and pass pointers to these objects to the polymorphic allocators. Some usage examples:

```
std::pmr::string s1{"my string", std::pmr::new_delete_resource()};

std::pmr::synchronized_pool_resource pool1;
std::pmr::string s2{"my string", &pool1};

std::pmr::monotonic_buffer_resource pool2{...};
std::pmr::string s3{"my string", &pool2};
```

In general, memory resources are passed as pointers. Therefore, it is important that you ensure that the resource objects these pointers refer to exist until the last deallocation is called (this might be later than you expect if you move objects around and memory resources are interchangeable).

**Default Memory Resource**

Polymorphic allocators have a default memory resource that is used if no other memory resource is passed. Table *29.2 Operations for the Default Memory Resource* lists the operations defined for it.

You can get the current default resource with `std::pmr::get_default_resource()`, which is what you can pass to initialize a polymorphic allocator. You can globally set a different default memory resource

| Memory Resource | Behavior |
| --- | --- |
| `get_default_resource()` | Yields a pointer to the current default memory resource |
| `set_default_resource(memresPtr)` | Sets the default memory resource (passing a pointer) and yields a pointer to the previous one |

Table 29.2. Operations for the Default Memory Resource

with `std::pmr::set_default_resource()`. This resource is used as the default in any scope until the next call of `std::pmr::set_default_resource()` is performed. For example:

```
static std::pmr::synchronized_pool_resource myPool;

// set myPool as new default memory resource:
std::pmr::memory_resource* old = std::pmr::set_default_resource(&myPool);
...
// restore old default memory resource as default:
std::pmr::set_default_resource(old);
```

If you create a custom memory resource in your program and use it as the default resource, it is a good approach to create it as a `static` object before anything else in `main()`:

```
int main()
{
  static std::pmr::synchronized_pool_resource myPool;
  ...
}
```

Alternatively, provide a global function that returns your resource as a static object:

```
memory_resource* myResource()
{
  static std::pmr::synchronized_pool_resource myPool;
  return &myPool;
}
```

The return type `memory_resource` is the base class of all memory resources.

Note that a previous default resource might still be used even when it has been replaced. Unless you know (and can ensure) that this is not the case, which means that no static objects are created using the resource, you should have your resource live as long as possible (again, ideally creating it right at the beginning of `main()` so that it is destroyed last).[3]

---

[3] You might still get into trouble if you have other global objects that are destroyed later, which means that good bookkeeping for a proper clean-up of a program that is ending is worthwhile.

## 29.1.3 Standard Memory Resources in Detail

Let us discuss the different standard memory resources in detail.

**`new_delete_resource()`**

`new_delete_resource()` is the default memory resource. It is returned by `get_default_resource()` unless you have defined a different default memory resource by calling `set_default_resource()`. This resource handles allocations in the same way that they are handled when using the default allocator:

- Each allocation calls `new`
- Each deallocation calls `delete`

However, note that a polymorphic allocator with this memory resource is not interchangeable with the default allocator because they simply have different types. Therefore

```
std::string s{"my string with some value"};
std::pmr::string ps{std::move(s), std::pmr::new_delete_resource()};   // copies
```

will not move (pass the allocated memory for `s` to `ps`). Instead, the memory of `s` will be copied to the new memory of `ps` allocated with `new`.

**`(un)synchronized_pool_resource`**

`synchronized_pool_resource` and `unsynchronized_pool_resource` are classes for memory resources that try to locate all memory close to each other. Thus, they force only minimal fragmentation of memory.

The difference is that `synchronized_pool_resource` is thread-safe (which costs more performance), while `unsynchronized_pool_resource` is not. Therefore, if you know that the memory of this pool is handled only by a single thread (or that (de)allocations are synchronized), `unsynchronized_pool_resource` is the better choice.

Both classes still use an underlying memory resource to actually perform the allocations and deallocations. They act only as a wrapper that ensures that these allocations are better clustered. Thus,

```
std::pmr::synchronized_pool_resource myPool;
```

is the same as

```
std::pmr::synchronized_pool_resource myPool{std::pmr::get_default_resource()};
```

In addition, they deallocate all memory when the pool is destroyed.

One major application of these pools is to ensure that elements in a node-based container are located next to each other. This may also increase the performance of the containers significantly, because then the CPU caches load elements together in cache lines. The effect is that after you have accessed one element, accessing other elements becomes very fast because they are already in the cache. However, you should measure, because the performance depends on the implementation of the memory resource. For example, if the memory resource uses a mutex to synchronize memory access, performance might become significantly worse.

Let us look at the effect with a simple example. The following program creates a `map` that maps integral values to strings.

*pmr/pmrsync0.cpp*

```cpp
#include <iostream>
#include <string>
#include <map>

int main()
{
  std::map<long, std::string> coll;

  for (int i=0; i<10; ++i) {
    std::string s{"Customer" + std::to_string(i)};
    coll.emplace(i, s);
  }

  // print element distances:
  for (const auto& elem : coll) {
    static long long lastVal = 0;
    long long val = reinterpret_cast<long long>(&elem);
    std::cout << "diff: " << (val-lastVal) << '\n';
    lastVal = val;
  }
}
```

This data structure is a balanced binary tree, where each node performs its own allocation to store an element. Thus, for each element, an allocation is performed and by default, these allocations allocate memory on the heap (using the standard default allocator).

To see the effect, the program prints the distance between element addresses while iterating over them. An output might look as follows:

```
diff: 1777277585312
diff: -320
diff: 60816
diff: 1120
diff: -400
diff: 80
diff: -2080
diff: -1120
diff: 2720
diff: -3040
```

The elements are not located next to each other. We have distances of 60,000 bytes for 10 elements with a size of around 24 bytes. This fragmentation becomes a lot worse if other memory is allocated between the allocation of the elements.

Now let us run the program with polymorphic allocators using a `synchronized_pool_resource`:

## 29.1 Using Standard Memory Resources

*pmr/pmrsync1.cpp*

```
#include <iostream>
#include <string>
#include <map>
#include <memory_resource>

int main()
{
  std::pmr::synchronized_pool_resource pool;
  std::pmr::map<long, std::pmr::string> coll{&pool};

  for (int i=0; i<10; ++i) {
    std::string s{"Customer" + std::to_string(i)};
    coll.emplace(i, s);
  }

  // print element distances:
  for (const auto& elem : coll) {
    static long long lastVal = 0;
    long long val = reinterpret_cast<long long>(&elem);
    std::cout << "diff: " << (val-lastVal) << '\n';
    lastVal = val;
  }
}
```

As you can see, we simply create the resource and pass it to the constructor of the container as an argument:

```
std::pmr::synchronized_pool_resource pool;
std::pmr::map<long, std::pmr::string> coll{&pool};
```

The output now looks as follows, for example:

```
diff: 2548552461600
diff: 128
diff: 128
diff: 105216
diff: 128
diff: 128
diff: 128
diff: 128
diff: 128
diff: 128
```

As you can see, the elements are now located close to each other. However, they are still not located in one chunk of memory. When the pool finds out that the first chunk is not big enough for all the elements, it allocates more memory for even more elements. Thus, the more memory we allocate, the larger the chunks of memory are, so that more elements are located close to each other. The details of these algorithms are implementation-specific.

Of course, this output is special because we create the elements in the order that they are sorted inside the container. Thus, in practice, if you create objects with random values, the elements will not be located sequentially one after the other (in different chunks of memory). However, they are still located close to each other and that is important for good performance when dealing with the elements of this container.

Note also that we do not look at how memory for the element values is arranged. Here, use of the small string optimization (see Section A on page 416) usually causes no memory to be allocated for the elements. However, as soon as we enlarge the string values, the pool also tries to place those together. Note that the pool manages different chunks of memory for different allocated sizes. That is, in general, the elements are located next to each other and the string values for elements of the same string size are also located close to each other.

### `monotonic_buffer_resource`

The class `monotonic_buffer_resource` also provides the ability to place all memory in big chunks of memory. However, it has two other abilities:
- You can pass a buffer to be used as memory. In particular, this can be memory allocated on the stack.
- The memory resource never deallocates until the resource as a whole is deallocated.

That is, this memory resource is very fast because deallocation is a no-op and you skip the need to track deallocated memory for further use. Whenever there is a request to allocate memory, the resource just returns the next free piece of memory until all memory is exhausted.

Note that objects are still destructed. Only their memory is not freed. If you delete objects, which usually deallocates their memory, the deallocation has no effect.

This resource is recommended if you either have no deletes or if you have enough memory to waste (not reusing memory that was previously used by another object).

We have already seen applications of `monotonic_buffer_resource` in our first motivating examples (see Section 29.1.1 on page 343), where we passed memory allocated on the stack to the pool:

```
std::array<std::byte, 200000> buf;
std::pmr::monotonic_buffer_resource pool{buf.data(), buf.size()};
```

You can also use this pool to allow any memory resource to skip deallocations (optionally passing an initial size). By default, this would apply to the default memory resource, which is `new_delete_resource()` by default. That is, with

```
// use default memory resource but skip deallocations as long as the pool lives:
{
    std::pmr::monotonic_buffer_resource pool;

    std::pmr::vector<std::pmr::string> coll{&pool};
    for (int i=0; i < 100; ++i) {
        coll.emplace_back("just a non-SSO string");
    }
    coll.clear();   // destruction but no deallocation
}   // deallocates all allocated memory
```

## 29.1 Using Standard Memory Resources

From time to time the inner block with the loop will allocate memory for the vector and its elements. Because we are using a pool, allocations are combined into chunks of memory. This might result, for example, in 14 allocations. By calling `coll.reserve(100)` first, this usually becomes only two allocations.

As written, no deallocation is done as long as the pool exists. Thus, if the creation and use of the vector is done in a loop, the memory allocated by the pool will continually rise.

`monotonic_buffer_resource` also allows us to pass an initial size, which it then uses as the minimum size of its first allocation (which is done when the first request for memory occurs). In addition, you can define which underlying memory resource the resource uses to perform the allocations. This allows us to *chain* memory resources to provide more sophisticated memory resources.

Consider the following example:

```
{
    // allocate chunks of memory (starting with 10k) without deallocating:
    std::pmr::monotonic_buffer_resource keepAllocatedPool{10000};
    std::pmr::synchronized_pool_resource pool{&keepAllocatedPool};

    for (int j=0; j < 100; ++j) {
        std::pmr::vector<std::pmr::string> coll{&pool};
        for (int i=0; i < 100; ++i) {
            coll.emplace_back("just a non-SSO string");
        }
    } // deallocations are given back to pool, but not deallocated
    // so far nothing was deallocated
} // deallocates all allocated memory
```

With this code, we first create a pool for all of our memory, which never deallocates as long as it lives and is initialized by starting to allocate 10,000 bytes (allocated using the default memory resource):

```
std::pmr::monotonic_buffer_resource keepAllocatedPool{10000};
```

Then, we create another pool that uses this non-deallocating pool to allocate chunks of memory:

```
std::pmr::synchronized_pool_resource pool{&keepAllocatedPool};
```

The combined effect is that we have a `pool` for all our memory, which starts its allocations for 10,000 bytes, allocates more memory with little fragmentation if necessary, and can be used by all pmr objects that use the `pool`.

The allocated memory, which might be the initial 10,000 bytes plus a few additional allocations for bigger chunks of memory, will all be freed when `keepAllocatedPool` goes out of scope.

What happens here exactly is demonstrated later when we extend this example to track all allocations (see Section 29.2 on page 356) of this nested pool.

### `null_memory_resource()`

`null_memory_resource()` handles allocations such that each allocation throws a `bad_alloc` exception.

The most important application is to ensure that a memory pool that uses memory allocated on the stack does not suddenly allocate additional memory on the heap.

Consider the following example:

*pmr/pmrnull.cpp*

```cpp
#include <iostream>
#include <string>
#include <unordered_map>
#include <array>
#include <cstddef>   // for std::byte
#include <memory_resource>

int main()
{
  // use memory on the stack without fallback on the heap:
  std::array<std::byte, 200000> buf;
  std::pmr::monotonic_buffer_resource pool{buf.data(), buf.size(),
                                    std::pmr::null_memory_resource()};

  // and allocate too much memory:
  std::pmr::unordered_map<long, std::pmr::string> coll {&pool};
  try {
    for (int i=0; i<buf.size(); ++i) {
      std::string s{"Customer" + std::to_string(i)};
      coll.emplace(i, s);
    }
  }
  catch (const std::bad_alloc& e) {
    std::cerr << "BAD ALLOC EXCEPTION: " << e.what() << '\n';
  }
  std::cout << "size: " << coll.size() << '\n';
}
```

We allocate memory on the stack and pass this to a monotonic buffer as a memory resource:

```cpp
std::array<std::byte, 200000> buf;
std::pmr::monotonic_buffer_resource pool{buf.data(), buf.size(),
                                    std::pmr::null_memory_resource()};
```

By also passing `null_memory_resource()` as the fallback memory resource, we ensure that any attempt to allocate more memory throws an exception instead of allocating the memory on the heap.

The effect is that sooner or later the program ends, for example, with the following output:

```
BAD ALLOC EXCEPTION: bad allocation
size: 2048
```

When heap memory allocation is not an option, this helps to get reasonable feedback instead of running into behavior you have to avoid.

## 29.2 Defining Custom Memory Resources

You can provide your custom memory resources. To do this, you have to:
- Derive from `std::pmr::memory_resource`
- Implement the private members
  - `do_allocate()` to allocate memory
  - `do_deallocate()` to deallocate memory
  - `do_is_equal()` to define whether and when your type can interchange memory allocated with another memory resource object

Here is a complete example that simply allows us to track the allocations and deallocations of any other memory resource:

*pmr/tracker.hpp*

```cpp
#include <iostream>
#include <string>
#include <memory_resource>

class Tracker : public std::pmr::memory_resource
{
 private:
  std::pmr::memory_resource* upstream;   // wrapped memory resource
  std::string prefix{};
 public:
  // we wrap the passed or default resource:
  explicit Tracker(std::pmr::memory_resource* us
                   = std::pmr::get_default_resource())
   : upstream{us} {
  }
  explicit Tracker(std::string p,
                   std::pmr::memory_resource* us
                   = std::pmr::get_default_resource())
   : prefix{std::move(p)}, upstream{us} {
  }
 private:
  void* do_allocate(size_t bytes, size_t alignment) override {
    std::cout << prefix << "allocate " << bytes << " Bytes\n";
    void* ret = upstream->allocate(bytes, alignment);
    return ret;
  }
  void do_deallocate(void* ptr, size_t bytes, size_t alignment) override {
    std::cout << prefix << "deallocate " << bytes << " Bytes\n";
    upstream->deallocate(ptr, bytes, alignment);
  }
  bool do_is_equal(const std::pmr::memory_resource& other) const noexcept
```

```
  override {
    // same object?:
    if (this == &other) return true;
    // same type and prefix and equal upstream?:
    auto op = dynamic_cast<const Tracker*>(&other);
    return op != nullptr && op->prefix == prefix
           && upstream->is_equal(other);
  }
};
```

As usual for smart memory resources, we support passing another memory resource (usually called `upstream`) to wrap it or use it as fallback. In addition, we can pass an optional prefix. On each allocation and deallocation, we then trace this call with the optional prefix.

The only other function we have to implement is `do_is_equal()`, which defines when two memory resources are interchangeable (i.e., whether and when one polymorphic memory resource object can deallocate memory allocated by another). In this case, we simply say that any object of this type can deallocate memory allocated from any other object of this type provided the prefix is the same:

```
bool do_is_equal(const std::pmr::memory_resource& other) const noexcept
  override {
    // same object?:
    if (this == &other) return true;
    // same type and prefix and equal upstream?:
    auto op = dynamic_cast<const Tracker*>(&other);
    return op != nullptr && op->prefix == prefix
           && upstream->is_equal(other);
}
```

The first comparison exists only to skip the other more expensive comparisons with the downcast. If we do not use the same tracker, we require that the other memory resource is also a tracker with the same prefix (same in the sense of same value) and an interchangeable underlying memory resource. Otherwise, if we use the tracker with different underlying memory resources, the applications would assume that it is OK to deallocate memory allocated from a totally different memory resource.

Let us use this tracker to understand the behavior of the previously demonstrated nested pools (see Section 29.1.3 on page 353) to allocate chunks of memory without deallocating:

*pmr/tracker.cpp*

```
#include "tracker.hpp"
#include <iostream>
#include <string>
#include <vector>
#include <memory_resource>

int main()
{
  {
```

## 29.2 Defining Custom Memory Resources

```cpp
    // track allocating chunks of memory (starting with 10k) without deallocating:
    Tracker track1{"keeppool:"};
    std::pmr::monotonic_buffer_resource keeppool{10000, &track1};
    {
      Tracker track2{"  syncpool:", &keeppool};
      std::pmr::synchronized_pool_resource pool{&track2};

      for (int j=0; j < 100; ++j) {
        std::pmr::vector<std::pmr::string> coll{&pool};
        coll.reserve(100);
        for (int i=0; i < 100; ++i) {
          coll.emplace_back("just a non-SSO string");
        }
        if (j==2) std::cout << "--- third iteration done\n";
      } // deallocations are given back to pool, but not deallocated
      // so far nothing was allocated
      std::cout << "--- leave scope of pool\n";
    }
    std::cout << "--- leave scope of keeppool\n";
  } // deallocates all allocated memory
}
```

The output might look something like this:

```
  syncpool:allocate 48 Bytes
keeppool:allocate 10000 Bytes
  syncpool:allocate 16440 Bytes
keeppool:allocate 16464 Bytes
  syncpool:allocate 96 Bytes
keeppool:allocate 24696 Bytes
  syncpool:deallocate 48 Bytes
  syncpool:allocate 312 Bytes
  syncpool:allocate 568 Bytes
  syncpool:allocate 1080 Bytes
  syncpool:allocate 2104 Bytes
  syncpool:allocate 4152 Bytes
  syncpool:deallocate 312 Bytes
  syncpool:deallocate 568 Bytes
  syncpool:deallocate 1080 Bytes
  syncpool:deallocate 2104 Bytes
  syncpool:allocate 8248 Bytes
  syncpool:deallocate 4152 Bytes
--- third iteration done
--- leave scope of pool
  syncpool:deallocate 8248 Bytes
  syncpool:deallocate 16440 Bytes
  syncpool:deallocate 96 Bytes
--- leave scope of keeppool
keeppool:deallocate 24696 Bytes
keeppool:deallocate 16464 Bytes
keeppool:deallocate 10000 Bytes
```

The output demonstrates the following:

- With the first allocation by an object, the `syncpool` allocates 48 bytes, which causes the `keeppool` to allocate its initial 10,000 bytes. These 10,000 bytes are allocated on the heap, using the resource from `get_default_resource()` when the `keeppool` was initialized.
- Subsequent objects allocate and deallocate memory, which causes the `syncpool` to allocate more chunks of memory from time to time, but also to deallocate chunks of memory. If the `syncpool` effectively allocates more memory than the `keeppool` has allocated, the `keeppool` again allocates more memory from the heap. That is, only the `keeppool` allocations become (rather expensive) system calls.
- With additional tracing of the end of the third iteration, you can see that all these allocations take place during the first three iterations of the outer loop. The amount of memory (re)used is then stable. Thus, the remaining 97 iterations allocate no memory at all from the operating system.
- The `keeppool` does not deallocate any memory even when the `syncpool` has deallocated all of its memory.
- It is only when the `keeppool` is destroyed that the six allocated chunks of memory are really deallocated, calling `::delete` (or whatever was defined with `set_default_resource()` when the `keeppool` was initialized).

If we introduced a third tracker in this program, we could also track when objects allocate and deallocate memory from the `syncpool`:

```cpp
// track each call, the effect in the sync pool, and the effect in the mono pool:
Tracker track1{"keeppool:"};
std::pmr::monotonic_buffer_resource keepAllocatedPool{10000, &track1};
Tracker track2{"  syncpool:", &keepAllocatedPool};
std::pmr::synchronized_pool_resource syncPool{&track2};
Tracker track3{"    objects:", &syncPool};
...
std::pmr::vector<std::pmr::string> coll{&track3};
```

## 29.2.1 Equality of Memory Resources

Let us briefly discuss `do_is_equal()`, the function that defines when two memory resources are interchangeable. This function requires more thought than first expected.

In our tracker, we have defined that the allocators are interchangeable if they are both of type `Tracker` and use the same prefix:

```cpp
bool do_is_equal(const std::pmr::memory_resource& other) const noexcept
  override {
    // same object?:
    if (this == &other) return true;
    // same type and prefix?:
    auto op = dynamic_cast<const Tracker*>(&other);
    return op != nullptr && op->prefix == prefix;
}
```

## 29.2 Defining Custom Memory Resources

This has the following effect:

```
Tracker track1{"track1:"};
Tracker track2{"track2:"};

std::pmr::string s1{"more than 15 chars", &track1};   // allocates with track1
std::pmr::string s2{std::move(s1), &track1};          // moves (same tracker)
std::pmr::string s3{std::move(s2), &track2};          // copies (different prefix)
std::pmr::string s4{std::move(s3)};                   // moves (allocator copied)
std::string s5{std::move(s4)};                        // copies (other allocator)
```

That is, moves are only performed as moves if the source and destination have interchangeable allocators. This is the case for polymorphic allocated types when the move constructor is used (the new object copied the allocator). However, if a non-interchangeable allocator is required (as with the tracker having a different prefix here) or if a different allocator type is used (as by moving to a `std::string`, which uses the default allocator), the memory is copied. Thus, interchangeability affects the performance of moves.

If we were to make all memory resources of type `Tracker` interchangeable by checking only the type:

```
bool do_is_equal(const std::pmr::memory_resource& other) const noexcept
  override {
    // all Tracker's are interchangeable if they have the same type:
    return this == &other || dynamic_cast<const Tracker*>(&other) != nullptr;
}
```

we would get the following behavior:

```
Tracker track1{"track1:"};
Tracker track2{"track2:"};

std::pmr::string s1{"more than 15 chars", &track1};   // allocates with track1
std::pmr::string s2{std::move(s1), &track1};          // moves (same tracker type)
std::pmr::string s3{std::move(s2), &track2};          // moves (same tracker type)
std::pmr::string s4{std::move(s3)};                   // moves (allocator copied)
std::string s5{std::move(s4)};                        // copies (other allocator)
```

As you can see, the effect would be that the memory allocated with `track1` is passed via `s3` to `s4`, which both use `track2`, so that we get:

```
track1:allocate 32 Bytes
track2:deallocate 32 Bytes
```

This would be a good implementation if our memory resource did not have different states (i.e., did not have the prefix), because this improves the performance of moves.

Therefore, it is worthwhile making memory resources interchangeable because fewer moves convert to copies. However, you should not make them more interchangeable than their purpose needs.

## 29.3 Providing Memory Resource Support for Custom Types

Now that we have introduced standard memory resources and user-defined memory resources, one topic remains: how can we make our custom types polymorphic-allocator-aware so that they can be used like a pmr::string as an element of a pmr container?

### 29.3.1 Definition of a PMR Type

The recipe for supporting polymorphic allocators is surprisingly easy, provided you use pmr members for all data that needs heap memory. You have to:
- Define `allocator_type` as a public member defined as a polymorphic allocator
- Add overloads for all constructors to take the allocator as an additional argument (this includes copy and move constructor)
- Let initializing constructors without an allocator argument to use `allocator_type` (this would *not* apply to the copy and move constructor, if implemented)

Here is a first example:

*pmr/pmrcustomer.hpp*

```cpp
#include <string>
#include <memory_resource>

// Customer as polymorphic-allocator-aware type
// - the allocator is stored in the string member
class PmrCustomer
{
 private:
  std::pmr::string name;   // also used to store the allocator
 public:
  using allocator_type = std::pmr::polymorphic_allocator<char>;

  // initializing constructor(s):
  PmrCustomer(std::pmr::string n, allocator_type alloc = {})
    : name{std::move(n), alloc} {
  }

  // copy/move with allocators:
  PmrCustomer(const PmrCustomer& c, allocator_type alloc)
    : name{c.name, alloc} {
  }
  PmrCustomer(PmrCustomer&& c, allocator_type alloc)
    : name{std::move(c.name), alloc} {
  }

  // setters/getters:
```

## 29.3 Providing Memory Resource Support for Custom Types

```
    void setName(std::pmr::string s) {
      name = std::move(s);
    }
    std::pmr::string getName() const {
      return name;
    }
    std::string getNameAsString() const {
      return std::string{name};
    }
};
```

The first thing to note is that we use a pmr string as member. This not only holds the value (here the name), it also holds the current allocator used:

```
std::pmr::string name;   // also used to store the allocator
```

Then, we have to specify that this type supports polymorphic allocators, which we can do simply by providing a corresponding declaration of type `allocator_type`:

```
using allocator_type = std::pmr::polymorphic_allocator<char>;
```

The type passed to the `polymorphic_allocator` is irrelevant (when it is used the allocator is rebound to the necessary type). You could, for example, also use `std::byte` (see Chapter 18 on page 179) there.[4] Alternatively, you can also use the `allocator_type` of the string member:

```
using allocator_type = decltype(name)::allocator_type;
```

Next we define the usual constructor(s) with an additional optional allocator parameter:

```
PmrCustomer(std::pmr::string n, allocator_type alloc = {})
 : name{std::move(n), alloc} {
}
```

You might think about declaring constructors like this as `explicit`. At least, if you have a default constructor, you should do so to avoid implicit conversions from an allocator to a customer:

```
explicit PmrCustomer(allocator_type alloc = {})
 : name{alloc} {
}
```

Then, we have to provide the copy and move operations that ask for a specific allocator. This is the main interface of pmr containers to ensure that their elements use the allocator of the container:

```
PmrCustomer(const PmrCustomer& c, allocator_type alloc)
 : name{c.name, alloc} {
}
PmrCustomer(PmrCustomer&& c, allocator_type alloc)
 : name{std::move(c.name), alloc} {
}
```

---

[4] https://wg21.link/p0339r0 proposed to also allow the specification of `polymorphic_allocator<void>` or just `polymorphic_allocator<>` here, but that was rejected.

Note that both are not `noexcept`, because even the move constructor might have to copy a passed customer if the required allocator `alloc` is not interchangeable.

Finally, we implement the necessary setters and getters, which are usually:

```
void setName(std::pmr::string s) {
  name = std::move(s);
}
std::pmr::string getName() const {
  return name;
}
```

There is another getter, `getNameAsString()`, which we provide to cheaply return the name as `std::string`. We will discuss this later (see Section 29.3.3 on page 364). For the moment, you could also leave it out.

### 29.3.2 Using a PMR Type

With the definition of `PmrCustomer` above, we can use this type in pmr containers. For example:

*pmr/pmrcustomer1.cpp*

```
#include "pmrcustomer.hpp"
#include "tracker.hpp"
#include <vector>

int main()
{
  Tracker tracker;
  std::pmr::vector<PmrCustomer> coll(&tracker);
  coll.reserve(100);                            // allocates with tracker

  PmrCustomer c1{"Peter, Paul & Mary"};         // allocates with get_default_resource()
  coll.push_back(c1);                           // allocates with vector allocator (tracker)
  coll.push_back(std::move(c1));                // copies (allocators not interchangeable)

  for (const auto& cust : coll) {
    std::cout << cust.getName() << '\n';
  }
}
```

To make what happens visible, we use the `Tracker` (see Section 29.2 on page 355) that tracks all allocations and deallocations:

```
Tracker tracker;
std::pmr::vector<PmrCustomer> coll(&tracker);
```

When we reserve memory for 100 elements, the vector uses our tracker to allocate the necessary data:

```
coll.reserve(100);                              // allocates with tracker
```

## 29.3 Providing Memory Resource Support for Custom Types

The tracker is not used when we create a customer:

```
PmrCustomer c1{"Peter, Paul & Mary"};    // allocates with get_default_resource()
```

However, when we push a copy of the customer into the vector, the vector ensures that all the elements also use its polymorphic allocator. Therefore, the extended copy constructor of the `PmrCustomer` is called with the vector allocator as a second argument so that the element is initialized with the tracker.

```
std::pmr::vector<PmrCustomer> coll(&tracker);
...
PmrCustomer c1{"Peter, Paul & Mary"};    // allocates with get_default_resource()
coll.push_back(c1);                       // allocates with vector allocator (tracker)
```

The same happens if we move the customer into the vector, because the allocator of the vector (the tracker) is not interchangeable with the allocator of the customer (which uses the default resource):

```
std::pmr::vector<PmrCustomer> coll(&tracker);
...
PmrCustomer c1{"Peter, Paul & Mary"};    // allocates with get_default_resource()
...
coll.push_back(std::move(c1));            // copies (allocators not interchangeable)
```

If we also initialized the customer with the tracker, the move would work:

```
std::pmr::vector<PmrCustomer> coll(&tracker);
...
PmrCustomer c1{"Peter, Paul & Mary", &tracker};   // allocates with tracker
...
coll.push_back(std::move(c1));            // moves (same allocator)
```

The same is true if we do not use any tracker at all:

```
std::pmr::vector<PmrCustomer> coll;       // allocates with default resource
...
PmrCustomer c1{"Peter, Paul & Mary"};     // allocates with default resource
...
coll.push_back(std::move(c1));            // moves (same allocator)
```

### 29.3.3 Dealing with the Different Types

While using `PmrCustomer` with pmr types is quite nice, we have a problem: in general, programs use strings of type `std::string`. So how do we deal with using both `std::string` and `std::pmr::string`?

First, there is an explicit but no implicit conversion between different string types:

```
std::string s;
std::pmr::string t1{s};      // OK
std::pmr::string t2 = s;     // ERROR
s = t1;                       // ERROR
s = std::string(t1);          // OK
```

The explicit conversion is supported because any string implicitly converts to a std::string_view (see Chapter 19 on page 185), which has an explicit conversion to any string type. The former is cheap but the latter needs to allocate memory (provided the small string optimization (see Section A on page 416) does not apply).

In our example, this means:

```
std::string s{"Paul Kalkbrenner"};
PmrCustomer c1 = s;                          // ERROR: no implicit conversion
PmrCustomer c2{s};                           // ERROR: no implicit conversion
PmrCustomer c3{std::pmr::string{s}};         // OK (implicitly converts s to string_view)
```

We might want to provide additional constructors but the good thing with not providing them is that programmers are forced to implement the expensive conversion. In addition, if you overload for different string types (`std::string` and `std::pmr::string`), you get additional ambiguities (e.g., taking a `string_view` or a string literal), which means that even more overloads are necessary.

In any case, a getter can return only one type (because we cannot overload on different return types only). Thus, we can provide only one getter, which should usually return the "native" type of the API (here, `std::pmr::string`). This means that if we return a `std::pmr::string` and need the name as `std::string`, again we need an explicit conversion:

```
PmrCustomer c4{"Mr. Paul Kalkbrenner"};           // OK: allocates with default resource
std::string s1 = c4.getName();                    // ERROR: no implicit conversion
std::string s2 = std::string{c4.getName()};       // OOPS: two allocations
```

This is not only less convenient, it is also a performance issue, because in the last statement, two allocations happen:

- First we allocate memory for the return value
- Then the conversion from type `std::pmr::string` to `std::string` needs another allocation

Therefore, it might be a good idea to provide an additional getter `getNameAsString()` (see Section 29.3.1 on page 360) that directly creates and returns the requested type:

```
std::string s3 = c4.getNameAsString();            // OK: one allocation
```

## 29.4 Afternotes

Polymorphic allocators were first proposed by Pablo Halpern in `https://wg21.link/n3525`. This approach was adopted as part of the Library Fundamentals TS as proposed by Pablo Halpern in `https://wg21.link/n3916`. The approach was adopted with other components for C++17 as proposed by Beman Dawes and Alisdair Meredith in `https://wg21.link/p0220r1`.

# Chapter 30
# `new` and `delete` with Over-Aligned Data

Since C++11, you can specify *over-aligned* types, which have a bigger alignment than the default alignment, by using the `alignas` specifier. For example:

```
struct alignas(32) MyType32 {
  int i;
  char c;
  std::string s[4];
};

MyType32 val1;              // 32-byte aligned
alignas(64) MyType32 val2;  // 64-byte aligned
```

Note that the alignment value must be a power of 2 and specifying any value less than the default alignment for the type is an error.[1]

However, ***dynamic/heap allocation*** of over-aligned data is not handled correctly in C++11 and C++14. Using operator `new` for over-aligned types by default ignores the requested alignment, which means that a type that is usually 64-byte aligned might, for example, only be 8-byte or 16-byte aligned.

This gap was closed with C++17. The new behavior provides new overloads with an alignment argument to allow you to provide your own implementations of operator `new` for over-aligned data.

## 30.1 Using `new` with Alignments

By using an over-aligned type such as:

```
struct alignas(32) MyType32 {
  int i;
```

---

[1] Some compilers accept and ignore alignment values less than the default alignment with a warning or even silently.

```
      char c;
      std::string s[4];
};
```

a `new` expression now guarantees that the requested heap memory is aligned as requested (provided over-alignment is supported):

```
MyType32* p = new MyType32;        // since C++17 guaranteed to be 32-byte aligned
...
```

Before C++17, the request was not guaranteed to be 32-byte aligned.[2]

As usual, without any value for initialization, the object is default initialized, which means that available constructors are called but (sub)objects of fundamental types have an undefined value. Therefore, the recommendation is to use *list initialization* (see page xxi) with curly braces to ensure that the (sub)objects have either their default value or 0/`false`/`nullptr`:

```
MyType32* p = new MyType32{};      // aligned and initialized
```

## 30.1.1 Distinct Dynamic/Heap Memory Arenas

Note that the request for aligned memory might result in a call to get the memory from a disjoint memory allocation mechanism. Therefore, a request for aligned memory might require a specific corresponding request to deallocate the aligned data. It is *possible* that the memory is allocated with the C11 function `aligned_alloc()` (which is now also available in C++17). In that case, deallocation with `free()` would still be acceptable, meaning that there is no difference compared to memory allocated with `malloc()`.

However, other implementations of `new` and `delete` are allowed for platforms, which leads to the requirement that different internal functions have to be used to deallocate default-aligned data and over-aligned data. For example, on Windows, `_aligned_malloc()` is usually used, which requires the use of `_aligned_free()` as a counterpart.[3]

In contrast to the C standard, the C++ standard respects this situation and therefore conceptionally assumes that there are two disjoint, non-interoperable *memory arenas*, one for default-aligned data and one for over-aligned data. Compilers generally know how to handle this correctly:

```
std::string* p1 = new std::string;    // using default-aligned memory operations
MyType32* p2 = new MyType32;          // using over-aligned memory operations
...
delete p1;                            // using default-aligned memory operations
delete p2;                            // using over-aligned memory operations
```

However, sometimes the programmer has to do the right thing, as we will see in the remaining sections of this chapter.

---

[2] Compilers/platforms do not have to support over-aligned data. If they do not, a request to over-align should not compile.

[3] This is because the Windows operating systems provide no ability to request aligned storage, which means that the calls over-allocate and align manually. As a consequence, support for `aligned_alloc()` will be unlikely in the near future, because support for the existing Windows platforms will still be required.

## 30.1.2 Passing the Alignment with the `new` Expression

There is also a way to request a specific over-alignment for a specific call of `new`. For example:

```
#include <new>    // for align_val_t
...

std::string* p = new(std::align_val_t{64}) std::string;    // 64-byte aligned
MyType32* p = new(std::align_val_t{64}) MyType32{};        // 64-byte aligned
...
```

The type `std::align_val_t` is defined in header `<new>` as follows:

```
namespace std {
  enum class align_val_t : size_t {
  };
}
```

`std::align_val_t` is provided to allow you to now pass alignment requests to the corresponding implementation of `operator new()`.

**Passing Alignment with `new` Affects `delete`**

Remember that `operator new()` can be implemented in different ways in C++:
- As a **global** function (different overloads are provided by default (see Section 30.3 on page 378), which can be replaced by the programmer)
- As **type-specific** implementations, which can be provided by the programmer (see Section 30.2 on page 370) and have higher priority than the global overloads

Because implementations might differ in that different memory arenas are used,[4] special care has to be taken to deal with them correctly. The problem is that when specifying a special alignment with the `new` expression, the compiler cannot use the type to know whether and which alignment was requested. As a consequence, the programmer has to specify which `delete` to call.[5]

Unfortunately, there is no placement `delete` operator where you can pass an additional argument:

```
delete(std::align_val_t{64}) p;    // ERROR: no placement delete supported
```

Therefore, you have to call the corresponding `operator delete()` directly, which means:
- You have to know which of the multiple overloads are implemented so that you call the right one.
- Before calling `operator delete()`, you have to call the destructor explicitly.

In fact, you have to call the destructor and the global delete if no type-specific delete is defined:

```
std::string* p = new(std::align_val_t{64}) std::string;    // 64-byte aligned
...
```

---

[4] Memory arenas do actually differ. For example, Windows has no over-aligned version of `HeapAlloc()`, which means that they must over-allocate and align inside the returned space.

[5] This is not the first time that the type system is not good enough to call the correct implementation of `delete`. The first example was that it is up to the programmer to ensure that `delete[]` is called instead of `delete` if arrays were allocated.

```
p->~basic_string();                                  // destruct value
::operator delete(p, std::align_val_t{64});          // free memory
```

Note that for `std::string()`, the destructor has the name `~basic_string`.

If a type-specific delete is defined, you have to call it after calling the destructor:

```
MyType32* p = new(std::align_val_t{64}) MyType32{};  // 64-byte aligned
...
p->~MyType32();                                      // destruct value
MyType32::operator delete(p, std::align_val_t{64});  // free memory
```

If you do not know the details of the type, one of the following functions for an object of type T could be called:

```
void T::operator delete(void* ptr, std::size_t size, std::align_val_t align);
void T::operator delete(void* ptr, std::align_val_t align);
void T::operator delete(void* ptr, std::size_t size);
void T::operator delete(void* ptr);
void ::operator delete(void* ptr, std::size_t size, std::align_val_t align);
void ::operator delete(void* ptr, std::align_val_t align);
void ::operator delete(void* ptr, std::size_t size);
void ::operator delete(void* ptr);
```

Yes, it is that complicated and I will explain later in detail (see Section 30.2.2 on page 375) which one is called when. For the moment, I recommend that you stick to the following guidelines:

1. Do not use over-alignment directly in `new` expressions at all. Instead, create your own helper type.
2. Provide implementations of `operator new()` and `operator delete()` that use the same memory arena (so that calling plain `delete` always works).
3. Provide type-specific implementations (see Section 30.2.2 on page 372) of `operator delete()` that match those of `operator new()` and call them directly (see Section 30.2.2 on page 377) instead of using `delete` expressions.

Note that you cannot use a `typedef` or `using` declaration instead:

```
using MyType64 = alignas(64) MyType32;        // ERROR
typedef alignas(64) MyType32 MyType64;        // ERROR
...
MyType64* p = new MyType64;                   // and therefore not possible
```

This is because a `typedef` or `using` declaration is only a new name/alias for the original type and what is requested here is a different type that follows different rules for alignment.

If you want to call an aligned `new` that returns the `nullptr` instead of throwing `std::bad_alloc`, you can do this as follows:

```
// allocate a 64-byte aligned string (nullptr if none):
std::string* p = new(std::align_val_t{64}, std::nothrow) std::string;
if (p != nullptr) {
    ...
}
```

## 30.1 Using new with Alignments

**Implementing Placement `delete`**

If you have to write (generic) code, where you have to use over-alignment in `new` calls and have no idea whether the types have their own operator `delete`, you might want to implement your own placement `delete`.[6]

You can simply implement a type trait that finds out whether an operator `delete` is defined:

*lang/hasdelete.hpp*

```
#include <type_traits>    // for true_type, false_type, and void_t

// primary template:
template<typename, typename = std::void_t<>>
struct HasDelete
  : std::false_type {
};

// partial specialization (may be SFINAE'd away):
template<typename T>
struct HasDelete<T, std::void_t<decltype(T::operator delete(nullptr))>>
  : std::true_type {
};
```

Here, we use `std::void_t<>` (see Section 33.3 on page 403) to SFINAE away the specialization if the expression calling the type-specific operator `delete` is not valid.

By using `std::void_t<>`, we can define our own placement `delete` helper:

```
template<typename TP, typename... Args>
void placementDelete(TP* tp, Args&&... args)
{
  // destruct value:
  tp->~TP();

  // free memory using the right operator delete:
  if constexpr(HasDelete<TP>::value) {
    TP::operator delete(tp, std::forward<Args>(args)...);
  }
  else {
    ::operator delete(tp, std::forward<Args>(args)...);
  }
}
```

and use this helper as follows:

```
std::string* p1 = new(std::align_val_t{64}) std::string;    // 64-byte aligned
MyType32* p2 = new(std::align_val_t{64}) MyType32{};        // 64-byte aligned
```

---

[6] Thanks to Ayaz Salikhov for coming up with this idea.

```
...
placementDelete(p1, std::align_val_t{64});
placementDelete(p2, std::align_val_t{64});
```

## 30.2 Implementing `operator new()` for Aligned Memory

In C++ you can provide your own implementation of allocating and deallocating memory when `new` and `delete` are called. This mechanism now also supports passing an alignment parameter.

### 30.2.1 Implementing Aligned Allocation Before C++17

Globally, C++ provides overloads of `operator new()` and `operator delete()`, which are used unless type-specific implementations are defined. If type-specific implementations of these operators exist, they are used. Note that having one type-specific `operator new()` disables the use of any of the global `operator new()` implementations for that type (the same applies to `delete`, `new[]`, and `delete[]`).

That is, each time you call `new` for a type T, a corresponding call of either a type-specific `T::operator new()` or (if none exists) the global `::operator new()` is called:

```
auto p = new T;    // tries to call a type-specific operator new() (if any)
                   // or, if none exists, tries to call a global ::operator new()
```

In the same way, each time you call `delete` for a type T, a corresponding call of either a type-specific `T::operator delete()` or the global `::operator delete()` is called. If arrays are allocated/deallocated, the corresponding type-specific or global operators `operator new[]()` and `operator delete[]()` are called.

Before C++17, a requested alignment was not automatically passed to these functions and the default mechanisms allocated dynamic memory without considering the alignment. An over-aligned type always needed its own implementations of `operator new()` and `operator delete()` to be correctly aligned on dynamic memory. Even worse, there was no portable way to perform the request for over-aligned dynamic memory.

As a consequence, you had to define something along the lines of following:

*lang/alignednew11.hpp*

```
#include <cstddef>          // for std::size_t
#include <string>
#if __STDC_VERSION >= 201112L
#include <stdlib.h>         // for aligned_alloc()
#else
#include <malloc.h>         // for _aligned_malloc() or memalign()
#endif

struct alignas(32) MyType32 {
  int i;
  char c;
  std::string s[4];
```

## 30.2 Implementing operator new() for Aligned Memory

```
    ...
    static void* operator new (std::size_t size) {
        // allocate memory for requested alignment:
#if __STDC_VERSION >= 201112L
        // use API of C11:
        return aligned_alloc(alignof(MyType32), size);
#else
#ifdef _MSC_VER
        // use API of Windows:
        return _aligned_malloc(size, alignof(MyType32));
#else
        // use API of Linux:
        return memalign(alignof(MyType32), size);
#endif
#endif
    }

    static void operator delete (void* p) {
        // deallocate memory for requested alignment:
#ifdef _MSC_VER
        // use special API of Windows:
        _aligned_free(p);
#else
        // C11/Linux can use the general free():
        free(p);
#endif
    }
    // since C++14:
    static void operator delete (void* p, std::size_t size) {
        MyType32::operator delete(p);   // use the non-sized delete
    }
    ...
    // also for arrays (new[] and delete[])
};
```

Note that since C++14, you can provide a size argument for the delete operator. However, it may be that the size is not available (e.g., when dealing with incomplete types (see Section A on page 415)), and there are cases where platforms can choose whether or not to pass a size argument to operator delete(). Therefore, since C++14, you should always replace both the unsized and the sized overload of operator delete(). Allowing one to call the other usually works.

With this definition, the following code behaves correctly:

*lang/alignednew11.cpp*

```
#include "alignednew11.hpp"
```

```
int main()
{
  auto p = new MyType32;
  ...
  delete p;
}
```

As stated, since C++17, you can skip the overhead of implementing operations to allocate/deallocate aligned data. The example works well even without defining `operator new()` and `operator delete()` for your type:

*lang/alignednew17.cpp*

```
#include <string>

struct alignas(32) MyType32 {
  int i;
  char c;
  std::string s[4];
  ...
};

int main()
{
  auto p = new MyType32;   // allocates 32-byte aligned memory since C++17
  ...
  delete p;
}
```

## 30.2.2 Implementing Type-Specific `operator new()`

If you have to implement your own implementation of `operator new()` and `operator delete()`, there is now support for over-aligned data. In practice, the corresponding code for type-specific implementations since C++17 looks as follows:

*lang/alignednew.hpp*

```
#include <cstddef>   // for std::size_t
#include <new>       // for std::align_val_t
#include <cstdlib>   // for malloc(), aligned_alloc(), free()
#include <string>

struct alignas(32) MyType32 {
  int i;
  char c;
  std::string s[4];
```

## 30.2 Implementing `operator new()` for Aligned Memory

```cpp
  static void* operator new (std::size_t size) {
    // called for default-aligned data:
    std::cout << "MyType32::new() with size " << size << '\n';
    return ::operator new(size);
  }
  static void* operator new (std::size_t size, std::align_val_t align) {
    // called for over-aligned data:
    std::cout << "MyType32::new() with size " << size
              << " and alignment " << static_cast<std::size_t>(align)
              << '\n';
    return ::operator new(size, align);
  }

  static void operator delete (void* p) {
    // called for default-aligned data:
    std::cout << "MyType32::delete() without alignment\n";
    ::operator delete(p);
  }
  static void operator delete (void* p, std::size_t size) {
    MyType32::operator delete(p);         // use the non-sized delete
  }
  static void operator delete (void* p, std::align_val_t align) {
    // called for default-aligned data:
    std::cout << "MyType32::delete() with alignment\n";
    ::operator delete(p, align);
  }
  static void operator delete (void* p, std::size_t size,
                                std::align_val_t align) {
    MyType32::operator delete(p, align);  // use the non-sized delete
  }

  // also for arrays (operator new[] and operator delete[])
  ...
};
```

In principle, we only need the overloads for the additional alignment parameter and to call the functions to allocate and deallocate aligned memory. The most portable way to do this is to call the globally provided functions for over-aligned (de)allocation:

```cpp
static void* operator new (std::size_t size, std::align_val_t align) {
  ...
  return ::operator new(size, align);
}
...
```

```
static void operator delete (void* p, std::align_val_t align) {
  ...
  ::operator delete(p);
}
```

You could also call the C11 functions for aligned allocation directly:

```
static void* operator new (std::size_t size, std::align_val_t align) {
  ...
  return std::aligned_alloc(static_cast<size_t>(align), size);
}
...
static void operator delete (void* p, std::align_val_t align) {
  ...
  std::free(p);
}
```

However, due to the problem Windows has with `aligned_alloc()` (see Section 30.1.1 on page 366), in practice, we then need special handling to be portable:

```
static void* operator new (std::size_t size, std::align_val_t align) {
  ...
#ifdef _MSC_VER
  // Windows-specific API:
  return aligned_malloc(size, static_cast<size_t>(align));
#else
  // standard C++17 API:
  return std::aligned_alloc(static_cast<size_t>(align), size);
#endif
}

static void operator delete (void* p, std::align_val_t align) {
  ...
#ifdef _MSC_VER
  // Windows-specific API:
  _aligned_free(p);
#else
  // standard C++17 API:
  std::free(p);
#endif
}
```

Note that all allocation functions take the alignment parameter as type `size_t`, which means that we have to use the static cast to convert the value from type `std::align_val_t`.

In addition, you should declare the `operator new()` with the `[[nodiscard]]` attribute (see Section 7.1 on page 55):[7]

---

[7] In C++20 the default implementations of `operator new()` will have this attribute.

## 30.2 Implementing `operator new()` for Aligned Memory

```
[[nodiscard]] static void* operator new (std::size_t size) {
  ...
}

[[nodiscard]] static void* operator new (std::size_t size,
                                         std::align_val_t align) {
  ...
}
```

It is rare but (as you can see here) possible to call `operator new()` directly (not using a `new` expression). With `[[nodiscard]]`, compilers will then detect whether the caller forgot to use the return value, which would result in a memory leak.

### When Is `operator new()` Called?

As explained, we now can have two overloads of `operator new()`:

- The version with only the `size` argument, which was also supported before C++17, is generally provided for requests of default-aligned data. However, it can also serve as a fallback if a version for over-aligned data is not provided.
- The version with the additional `align` argument, which is available since C++17, is generally provided for requests of over-aligned data.

Which overload is used does *not* necessarily depend on whether `alignas` is used; it depends instead on the platform-specific definition of over-aligned data.

A compiler switches from default-alignment to over-alignment according to a general alignment value, which you can find in the new preprocessor constant

    `__STDCPP_DEFAULT_NEW_ALIGNMENT__`

That is, with any alignment larger than this constant, a call of `new` switches from trying to call

    `operator new(std::size_t)`

to trying to call

    `operator new(std::size_t, std::align_val_t)`

As a consequence, the output of the following code might vary from platform to platform:

```
struct alignas(32) MyType32 {
  ...
  static void* operator new (std::size_t size) {
    std::cout << "MyType32::new() with size " << size << '\n';
    return ::operator new(size);
  }
  static void* operator new (std::size_t size, std::align_val_t align) {
    std::cout << "MyType32::new() with size " << size
              << " and alignment " << static_cast<std::size_t>(align) << '\n';
    return ::operator new(size, align);
    ::operator delete(p);
  }
```

```
...
};
```

```
auto p = new MyType32;
```

If the default alignment is 32 (or more and the code compiles), the expression new MyType32 will call the first overload of operator new() with only the size parameter, so that the output is something like:[8]

```
MyType32::new() with size 128
```

If the default alignment is less than 32, the second overload of operator new() for two arguments will be called, so that the output becomes something like:

```
MyType32::new() with size 128 and alignment 32
```

**Type-Specific Fallbacks**

If the std::align_val_t overloads are not provided for a type-specific operator new(), the overloads without this argument are used as fallbacks. Thus, a class that (as supported before C++17) provides only operator new() overloads still compiles and has the same behavior (note that for the global operator new() this is not the case):

```
struct NonalignedNewOnly {
  ...
  static void* operator new (std::size_t size) {
    ...
  }
  ...    // no operator new(std::size_t, std::align_val_t align)
};
```

```
auto p = new NonalignedNewOnly;    // OK: operator new(size_t) used
```

The opposite is not true. If a type provides only the overloads with the alignment parameter, any attempt to allocate storage with new using the default alignment will fail:

```
struct AlignedNewOnly {
  ...    // no operator new(std::size_t)
  static void* operator new (std::size_t size, std::align_val_t align) {
    return std::aligned_alloc(static_cast<size_t>(align), size);
  }
};
```

```
auto p = new AlignedNewOnly;    // ERROR: no operator new() for default alignment
```

It would also be an error if an alignment that is (less than) the default alignment is requested for the type.

---

[8] The size might vary depending on how big an int and a std::string are on the platform.

## 30.2 Implementing `operator new()` for Aligned Memory

**Requesting an Alignment in the `new` Expression**

If you pass a requested alignment in the `new` expression, the passed alignment argument is always passed and has to be supported by the `operator new()`. In fact, alignment arguments are handled just like any other additional argument you can pass to `new` expressions: they are passed as they are as additional parameters to `operator new()`.

Thus, a call such as:

```
std::string* p = new(std::align_val_t{64}) std::string;   // 64-byte aligned
```

will *always* try to call:

```
operator new(std::size_t, std::align_val_t)
```

A size-only overload would *not* serve as a fallback here.

If you have a specific alignment request for an over-aligned type, the behavior is even more interesting. If, for example, you call:

```
MyType32* p = new(std::align_val_t{64}) MyType32{};
```

and MyType32 is over-aligned, the compiler first tries to call

```
operator new(std::size_t, std::align_val_t, std::align_val_t)
```

with 32 as the second argument (the general over-alignment of the type) and 64 as the third argument (the requested specific alignment). It is only as a fallback that

```
operator new(std::size_t, std::align_val_t)
```

is called with 64 as the requested specific alignment. In principle, you could provide an overload for the three arguments to implement specific behavior when a specific alignment is requested for over-aligned types.

Again, note that if you need special deallocation functions for over-aligned data, you have to call the correct deallocation function when passing the alignment in the `new` expression (see Section 30.1.2 on page 367):

```
std::string* p1 = new(std::align_val_t{64}) std::string{};
MyType32* p2 = new(std::align_val_t{64}) MyType32{};
...
p1->~basic_string();
::operator delete(p2, std::align_val_t{64});               // !!!
p2->~MyType32();
MyType32::operator delete(p1, std::align_val_t{64});       // !!!
```

This means that the `new` expressions in this example will call

```
operator new(std::size_t size, std::align_val_t align);
```

while the `delete` expressions will call one of the following two operations for default-aligned data:

```
operator delete(void* ptr, std::align_val_t align);
operator delete(void* ptr, std::size_t size, std::align_val_t align);
```

and one of the following four operations for over-aligned data:

```
operator delete(void* ptr, std::align_val_t typealign, std::align_val_t align);
operator delete(void* ptr, std::size_t size, std::align_val_t typealign,
                std::align_val_t align);
```

```
operator delete(void* ptr, std::align_val_t align);
operator delete(void* ptr, std::size_t size, std::align_val_t align);
```
Again, a user-defined placement delete (see Section 30.1.2 on page 369) might help.

## 30.3 Implementing Global `operator new()`

By default, C++ platforms now provide a significant number of global overloads for `operator new()` and `delete()` (including the corresponding array versions):

```
void* ::operator new(std::size_t);
void* ::operator new(std::size_t, std::align_val_t);
void* ::operator new(std::size_t, const std::nothrow_t&) noexcept;
void* ::operator new(std::size_t, std::align_val_t,
                     const std::nothrow_t&) noexcept;

void ::operator delete(void*) noexcept;
void ::operator delete(void*, std::size_t) noexcept;
void ::operator delete(void*, std::align_val_t) noexcept;
void ::operator delete(void*, std::size_t, std::align_val_t) noexcept;
void ::operator delete(void*, const std::nothrow_t&) noexcept;
void ::operator delete(void*, std::align_val_t,
                       const std::nothrow_t&) noexcept;

void* ::operator new[](std::size_t);
void* ::operator new[](std::size_t, std::align_val_t);
void* ::operator new[](std::size_t, const std::nothrow_t&) noexcept;
void* ::operator new[](std::size_t, std::align_val_t,
                       const std::nothrow_t&) noexcept;

void ::operator delete[](void*) noexcept;
void ::operator delete[](void*, std::size_t) noexcept;
void ::operator delete[](void*, std::align_val_t) noexcept;
void ::operator delete[](void*, std::size_t, std::align_val_t) noexcept;
void ::operator delete[](void*, const std::nothrow_t&) noexcept;
void ::operator delete[](void*, std::align_val_t,
                         const std::nothrow_t&) noexcept;
```

If you want to implement your own memory management (e.g., to allow you to debug dynamic memory calls), you do not have to override all of these overloads. It is sufficient to implement the following basic functions because by default, all other functions (including all array versions) call one of these basic functions:

```
void* ::operator new(std::size_t);
void* ::operator new(std::size_t, std::align_val_t);
void ::operator delete(void*) noexcept;
void ::operator delete(void*, std::size_t) noexcept;
```

```
void ::operator delete(void*, std::align_val_t) noexcept;
void ::operator delete(void*, std::size_t, std::align_val_t) noexcept;
```

In principle, the default of the sized versions of `operator delete()` also just call the unsized versions. However, this might change in the future, therefore you must implement both (some compilers issue a warning if you do not do this).

### 30.3.1 Backward Incompatibilities

Note that the behavior of the following program changes silently with C++17:

*lang/alignednewincomp.cpp*

```
#include <cstddef>      // for std::size_t
#include <cstdlib>      // for std::malloc()
#include <cstdio>       // for std::printf()

void* operator new (std::size_t size)
{
  std::printf("::new called with size: %zu\n", size);
  return ::std::malloc(size);
}

int main()
{
  struct alignas(64) S {
    int i;
  };

  S* p = new S;   // calls our operator new only before C++17
}
```

In C++14, the global ::operator new(size_t) overload was called for all new expressions, which meant that the program always had the following output:[9]

```
::new called with size: 64
```

Since C++17, the behavior of this program has changed, because now the default overload for the over-aligned data

```
::operator new(size_t, align_val_t)
```

is called here, which is *not* replaced. As a result, the program will no longer output the line above.[10]

---

[9] There might be additional output for other initializations that allocate memory on the heap.

[10] Some compilers warned about calling new for over-aligned data before C++17, because the alignment was not handled properly before C++17.

Note that this problem applies only to the global `operator new()`. If the type-specific `operator new()` is defined for S, the operator is still also used as a fallback for over-aligned data (see Section 30.2.2 on page 376), which means that such a program behaves in the same way that it did before C++17.

Note also that `printf()` is used intentionally here to avoid an output to `std::cout` allocating memory while we are allocating memory, which might result in nasty errors (core dumps at best).

## 30.4 Tracking All ::new Calls

The following program demonstrates how to use the new `operator new()` overloads in combination with inline variables (see Chapter 3 on page 25) and `[[nodiscard]]` (see Section 7.1 on page 55) to track all calls of ::new simply by including this header file:

*lang/tracknew.hpp*

```cpp
#ifndef TRACKNEW_HPP
#define TRACKNEW_HPP

#include <new>          // for std::align_val_t
#include <cstdio>       // for printf()
#include <cstdlib>      // for malloc() and aligned_alloc()
#ifdef _MSC_VER
#include <malloc.h>     // for _aligned_malloc() and _aligned_free()
#endif

class TrackNew {
 private:
  static inline int numMalloc = 0;       // num malloc calls
  static inline size_t sumSize = 0;      // bytes allocated so far
  static inline bool doTrace = false;    // tracing enabled
  static inline bool inNew = false;      // don't track output inside new overloads
 public:
  static void reset() {                  // reset new/memory counters
    numMalloc = 0;
    sumSize = 0;
  }

  static void trace(bool b) {            // enable/disable tracing
    doTrace = b;
  }

  // implementation of tracked allocation:
  static void* allocate(std::size_t size, std::size_t align,
                        const char* call) {
    // track and trace the allocation:
    ++numMalloc;
```

## 30.4 Tracking All ::new Calls

```cpp
      sumSize += size;
      void* p;
      if (align == 0) {
        p = std::malloc(size);
      }
      else {
#ifdef _MSC_VER
        p = _aligned_malloc(size, align);      // Windows API
#else
        p = std::aligned_alloc(align, size);   // C++17 API
#endif
      }
      if (doTrace) {
        // DON'T use std::cout here because it might allocate memory
        // while we are allocating memory (core dump at best)
        printf("#%d %s ", numMalloc, call);
        printf("(%zu bytes, ", size);
        if (align > 0) {
          printf("%zu-byte aligned) ", align);
        }
        else {
          printf("def-aligned) ");
        }
        printf("=> %p (total: %zu bytes)\n", (void*)p, sumSize);
      }
      return p;
    }

    static void status() {                  // print current state
      printf("%d allocations for %zu bytes\n", numMalloc, sumSize);
    }
};

[[nodiscard]]
void* operator new (std::size_t size) {
  return TrackNew::allocate(size, 0, "::new");
}

[[nodiscard]]
void* operator new (std::size_t size, std::align_val_t align) {
  return TrackNew::allocate(size, static_cast<size_t>(align),
                            "::new aligned");
}

[[nodiscard]]
```

```cpp
void* operator new[] (std::size_t size) {
  return TrackNew::allocate(size, 0, "::new[]");
}

[[nodiscard]]
void* operator new[] (std::size_t size, std::align_val_t align) {
  return TrackNew::allocate(size, static_cast<size_t>(align),
                            "::new[] aligned");
}

// ensure deallocations match:
void operator delete (void* p) noexcept {
  std::free(p);
}
void operator delete (void* p, std::size_t) noexcept {
  ::operator delete(p);
}
void operator delete (void* p, std::align_val_t) noexcept {
#ifdef _MSC_VER
  _aligned_free(p);   // Windows API
#else
  std::free(p);       // C++17 API
#endif
}
void operator delete (void* p, std::size_t,
                              std::align_val_t align) noexcept {
  ::operator delete(p, align);
}

#endif // TRACKNEW_HPP
```

Consider using this header file in the following CPP file:

*lang/tracknew.cpp*

```cpp
#include "tracknew.hpp"
#include <iostream>
#include <string>

int main()
{
  TrackNew::reset();
  TrackNew::trace(true);
  std::string s = "string value with 26 chars";
  auto p1 = new std::string{"an initial value with even 35 chars"};
  auto p2 = new(std::align_val_t{64}) std::string[4];
```

```
    auto p3 = new std::string[4] { "7 chars", "x", "or 11 chars",
                                   "a string value with 28 chars" };
    TrackNew::status();
    ...
    delete p1;
    delete[] p2;
    delete[] p3;
}
```

The output depends on when the tracking is initialized and how many allocations are performed for other initializations. However, it should contain something like the following lines:

```
#1 ::new (27 bytes, def-aligned) => 0x8002ccc0 (total: 27 Bytes)
#2 ::new (24 bytes, def-aligned) => 0x8004cd28 (total: 51 Bytes)
#3 ::new (36 bytes, def-aligned) => 0x8004cd48 (total: 87 Bytes)
#4 ::new[] aligned (100 bytes, 64-byte aligned) => 0x8004cd80 (total: 187 Bytes)
#5 ::new[] (100 bytes, def-aligned) => 0x8004cde8 (total: 287 Bytes)
#6 ::new (29 bytes, def-aligned) => 0x8004ce50 (total: 316 Bytes)
6 allocations for 316 bytes
```

In this example, the first output is to initialize the memory for the value of s. Note that the value might be larger depending on the allocation strategy of the `std::string` class.

The next two lines written are caused by the second request:

```
    auto p1 = new std::string{"an initial value with even 35 chars"};
```

This request allocates 24 bytes for the core string object plus 36 bytes for the initial value of the string (again, the values might differ).

The third call requests a 64-byte aligned array of four strings.

The final call again performs two allocations: one for the array and one for the initial value of the last string. Yes, only for the last string because implementations of the library typically use the *small/short string optimization* (SSO) (see Section A on page 416), which usually stores strings of up to 15 characters in data members instead of allocating heap memory at all. Other implementations might perform five allocations here.

## 30.5 Afternotes

Alignment for heap/dynamic memory allocation was first proposed by Clark Nelson in `https://wg21.link/n3396`. The finally accepted wording was formulated by Clark Nelson in `https://wg21.link/p0035r4`.

# Chapter 31
# `std::to_chars()` and `std::from_chars()`

The C++ standard library provides new low-level functions for converting numeric values into character sequences and vice versa.

## 31.1 Motivation for Low-Level Conversions between Character Sequences and Numeric Values

Converting integral values into character sequences and vice versa has been an issue since C. While C provides `sprintf()` and `sscanf()`, C++ first introduced string streams, which, however, need a lot of resources. With C++11, convenient functions such as `std::to_string` and `std::stoi()` were introduced, which take `std::string` arguments only.

C++17 introduced new elementary string conversion functions with the following abilities (as quoted from the initial proposal):

- No runtime parsing of format strings
- No dynamic memory allocation inherently required by the interface
- No consideration of locales
- No indirection through function pointers required
- Prevention of buffer overruns
- When parsing a string, errors are distinguishable from valid numbers
- When parsing a string, whitespace or decorations are not silently ignored

In addition, for floating-point numbers, this feature will provide a round-trip guarantee that values converted into a character sequence and converted back result in the original value.

The functions are provided in the header file `<charconv>`.[1]

---

[1] Note that the accepted wording for C++17 first added them to `<utility>`, which was changed via a defect report after C++17 was standardized because this created circular dependencies (see `https://wg21.link/p0682r1`).

## 31.2 Example Usage

Two overloaded functions are provided:
- `std::from_chars()` converts a given character sequence into a numeric value.
- `std::to_chars()` converts numeric values into a given character sequence.

### 31.2.1 `from_chars()`

`std::from_chars()` converts a given character sequence into a numeric value. For example:

```
#include <charconv>

const char* str = "12 monkeys";
int value;
std::from_chars_result res = std::from_chars(str, str+10,
                                             value);
```

After a successful parsing, `value` contains the parsed value (12 in this example). The result value is the following structure:[2]

```
struct from_chars_result {
  const char* ptr;
  std::errc ec;
};
```

After the call, `ptr` refers to the first character not parsed as part of the number (or the passed second argument, if all characters were parsed) and `ec` contains an error condition of type `std::errc` or is equal to `std::errc{}` if the conversion was successful. Thus, you can check the result as follows:

```
if (res.ec != std::errc{}) {
  ...  // error handling
}
```

Note that there is no implicit conversion to `bool` for `std::errc`, which means that you cannot check the value as follows:

```
if (res.ec) {     // ERROR: no implicit conversion to bool
```

or:

```
if (!res.ec) {    // ERROR: no operator! defined
```

However, by using structured bindings (see Chapter 1 on page 3) and `if` with initialization (see Section 2.1 on page 21), you can write:

```
if (auto [ptr, ec] = std::from_chars(str, str+10, value); ec != std::errc{}) {
  ...  // error handling
}
```

---

[2] Note that the accepted wording for C++17 declared `ec` as a `std::error_code`, which was changed via a defect report after C++17 was standardized (see https://wg21.link/p0682r1).

## 31.2 Example Usage

For integral values, you can pass a base for the value read as an optional last argument. The base might be between 2 and 26 (inclusive). For example:

```
#include <charconv>

const char* str = "12 monkeys";
int value;
std::from_chars_result res = std::from_chars(str, str+10,   // char sequence to read from
                                              value,         // value to set
                                              16);           // optional base
```

For other examples, see
- The conversion of a bit sequence to a `std::byte` (see Section 18.2.2 on page 184)
- The parsing of a passed string view (see Section 19.3 on page 187)

### 31.2.2 `to_chars()`

`std::to_chars()` converts numeric values into a given character sequence. For example:

```
#include <charconv>

int value = 42;
char str[10];
std::to_chars_result res = std::to_chars(str, str+9,
                                         value);
*res.ptr = '\0';   // ensure a trailing null character is behind
```

After a successful conversion, `str` contains the character sequence that represents the passed value (42 in this example) without a trailing null character.

Again, for integral values, you can pass a base for the value read as an optional last argument. The base might be between 2 and 26 (inclusive). For example:

```
#include <charconv>

int value = 42;
char str[10];
std::to_chars_result res = std::to_chars(str, str+9,   // char sequence to write to
                                         value,         // value to convert
                                         16);           // optional base
*res.ptr = '\0';   // ensure a trailing null character is behind
```

For another example, see the conversion of a `std::byte` to a bit sequence (see Section 18.2.2 on page 183). The result value is the following structure:[3]

```
struct to_chars_result {
  char* ptr;
```

---

[3] Note that the accepted wording for C++17 declared `ec` as a `std::error_code` which was also changed via a defect report after C++17 was standardized (see https://wg21.link/p0682r1).

```
    std::errc ec;
};
```
After the call, `ptr` refers to the character after the last written character and `ec` either contains an error condition of type `std::errc` or, if the conversion was successful, is equal to `std::errc{}`

Thus, you can check the result as follows:
```
if (res.ec != std::errc{}) {
    ...    // error handling
}
else {
    process(str, res.ptr - str);    // pass characters and length
}
```
Note again that there is no implicit conversion to `bool` for `std::errc`, which means that you cannot check the value as follows:
```
if (res.ec) {       // ERROR: no implicit conversion to bool
```
or:
```
if (!res.ec) {      // ERROR: no operator! defined
```
Because a trailing null terminator is not written, you have to ensure that you only use the written characters or add a trailing null character as done in this example using the `ptr` member of the return value:
```
*res.ptr = '\0';    // ensure a trailing null character is behind
```
Again, by using structured bindings (see Chapter 1 on page 3) and `if` with initialization (see Section 2.1 on page 21) you can write:
```
if (auto [ptr, ec] = std::to_chars(str, str+10, value); ec != std::errc{}) {
    ...    // error handling
}
else {
    process(str, ptr - str);    // pass characters and length
}
```
Note that this behavior is safer and easier to implement using the existing `std::to_string()` function. Using `std::to_chars()` makes sense only if further processing needs simply the written character sequence.

## 31.3 Floating-Point Round-Trip Support

If no precision is given, `to_chars()` and `from_chars()` guarantee round-trip support for floating-point values. This means that a value converted into a character sequence and read back has exactly its original value. However, this guarantee applies only when writing and reading on the same implementation.

As a consequence, floating-point values have to be written as a sequence of characters with the finest granularity and the highest precision. Therefore, the character sequence the value is written to might have a significant size.

Consider the following function:

*lib/charconv.hpp*

## 31.3 Floating-Point Round-Trip Support

```cpp
#include <iostream>
#include <charconv>
#include <cassert>

void d2str2d(double value1)
{
  std::cout << "in:  " << value1 << '\n';

  // convert to character sequence:
  char str[1000];
  std::to_chars_result res1 = std::to_chars(str, str+999,
                                            value1);
  *res1.ptr = '\0';  // add trailing null character

  std::cout << "str: " << str << '\n';
  assert(res1.ec == std::errc{});

  // read back from character sequence:
  double value2;
  std::from_chars_result res2 = std::from_chars(str, str+999,
                                                value2);

  std::cout << "out: " << value2 << '\n';
  assert(res2.ec == std::errc{});

  assert(value1 == value2);  // should never fail
}
```

Here we convert a passed `double` value into a character sequence and parse it back. The assertion at the end double-checks that the value is the same.

The following program demonstrates the effect:

*lib/charconv.cpp*

```cpp
#include "charconv.hpp"
#include <iostream>
#include <iomanip>
#include <vector>
#include <numeric>

int main()
{
  std::vector<double> coll{0.1, 0.3, 0.00001};

  // create two slightly different floating-point values:
```

```
    auto sum1 = std::accumulate(coll.begin(), coll.end(),
                                0.0, std::plus<>());
    auto sum2 = std::accumulate(coll.rbegin(), coll.rend(),
                                0.0, std::plus<>());

    // look the same:
    std::cout << "sum1: " << sum1 << '\n';
    std::cout << "sum1: " << sum2 << '\n';

    // but are different:
    std::cout << std::boolalpha << std::setprecision(20);
    std::cout << "equal: " << (sum1==sum2) << '\n';   // false !!
    std::cout << "sum1: " << sum1 << '\n';
    std::cout << "sum1: " << sum2 << '\n';
    std::cout << '\n';

    // check round-trip:
    d2str2d(sum1);
    d2str2d(sum2);
}
```

We accumulate two small floating-point sequences in different order. `sum1` is the sum accumulating from left to right, while `sum2` is the sum accumulating from right to left (using reverse iterators). As a result, the values look the same but they are not:

```
sum1:   0.40001
sum1:   0.40001
equal:  false
sum1:   0.40001000000000003221
sum1:   0.40000999999999997669
```

When passing the values to `d2str2d()`, you can see that the values are stored as different character sequences with the necessary granularity:

```
in:   0.40001000000000003221
str:  0.40001000000000003
out:  0.40001000000000003221

in:   0.40000999999999997669
str:  0.40001
out:  0.40000999999999997669
```

Again, note that the granularity (and therefore the necessary size of the character sequence) depends on the platform.

The round-trip support should work for all floating-point numbers including `NAN` and `INFINITY`. For example, passing `INFINITY` to `d2st2d()` should have the following effect:

```
value1: inf
```

```
str:    inf
value2: inf
```

However, note that the assertion in `d2str2d()` will fail for `NAN` because it never compares to anything, including itself.

## 31.4 Afternotes

Low-level conversions between character sequences and numeric values were first proposed by Jens Maurer in `https://wg21.link/p0067r0`. The finally accepted wording was formulated by Jens Maurer in `https://wg21.link/p0067r5`. However, significant clarifications and a new header file were assigned as a defect report against C++17 by Jens Maurer in `https://wg21.link/p0682r1`.

# Chapter 32
# `std::launder()`

There is a new library function called `std::launder()`, which, as far as I understand and see it, is a workaround of a core problem. that, however, does not really work.

## 32.1 Motivation for `std::launder()`

According to the current standard, the following code results in undefined behavior:
```
struct X {
  const int n;
  double d;
};
X* p = new X{7, 8.8};
new (p) X{42, 9.9};    // request to place a new value into p
int i = p->n;          // undefined behavior (i is probably 7 or 42)
auto d = p->d;         // also undefined behavior (d is probably 8.8 or 9.9)
```
The reason is the current memory model, written in Section `[basic.life]` of the C++ standard, which states roughly:

> If, ..., a new object is created at the storage location which the original object occupied,
> - a pointer that pointed to the original object,
> - a reference that referred to the original object, or
> - the name of the original object
> 
> will automatically refer to the new object ... if:
> - the type of the original object is not `const`-qualified, and, if a class type, does not contain any non-static data member whose type is `const`-qualified or a reference type,
> - ...

This behavior is not new. It was specified with C++03 to enable several compiler optimizations (including similar optimizations when virtual functions are used).

As a consequence of the corresponding wording in the standard, we have to ensure that the return value of placement new is always used with each access to the memory if the objects there have constant or reference members:

```
struct X {
  const int n;
  double d;
};
X* p = new X{7, 8.8};
p = new (p) X{42, 9.9};   // Note: assign return value of placement new to p
int i = p->n;              // OK, i is guaranteed to be 42
auto d = p->d;             // OK, d is guaranteed to be 9.9
```

Unfortunately, this rule is not widely known and used. Even worse, in practice, you cannot always easily use the return value of placement new. You might need additional objects, and the current allocator interface does not support this.

One example where using the return value causes overhead is when the storage is an existing member. That would be the case for std::optional (see Chapter 15 on page 135) and std::variant (see Chapter 16 on page 149).

Here is a simplified example of implementing something like std::optional:

```
template<typename T>
class optional
{
  private:
    T payload;
  public:
    optional(const T& t)
      : payload(t) {
    }

    template<typename... Args>
    void emplace(Args&&... args) {
      payload.~T();
      ::new (&payload) T(std::forward<Args>(args)...);   // *
    }

    const T& operator*() const & {
      return payload;   // OOPS: returns payload not reinitialized
    }
};
```

If here, T is a structure with constant or reference members:

```
struct X {
  const int _i;
  X(int i) : _i(i) {}
  friend std::ostream& operator<< (std::ostream& os, const X& x) {
```

## 32.1 Motivation for `std::launder()`

```
      return os << x._i;
    }
};
```

then the following code results in undefined behavior:

```
optional<X> optStr{42};
optStr.emplace(77);
std::cout << *optStr;      // undefined behavior (probably outputs 42 or 77)
```

This is because the output operation calls `operator*`, which returns `payload`, where placement new (called in `emplace()`) placed a new value without using the return value.

In a class like this, you would have to add an additional pointer member that keeps the return value of placement new and is used whenever the value is needed:

```
template<typename T>
class optional
{
  private:
    T payload;
    T* p;           // to be able to use the return value of placement new
  public:
    optional(const T& t)
      : payload(t) {
        p = &payload;
    }

    template<typename... Args>
    void emplace(Args&&... args) {
      payload.~T();
      p = ::new (&payload) T(std::forward<Args>(args)...);
    }

    const T& operator*() const & {
      return *p;    // don't use payload here!
    }
};
```

There is also a similar problem with allocator-based containers such as `std::vector`, because internally, they use placement new via allocators. For example, a class like `vector` is roughly implemented as follows:

```
template<typename T, typename A = std::allocator<T>>
class vector
{
  public:
    typedef typename std::allocator_traits<A> ATR;
    typedef typename ATR::pointer pointer;
  private:
```

```
    A _alloc;              // current allocator
    pointer _elems;        // array of elements
    size_t _size;          // number of elements
    size_t _capa;          // capacity
  public:
    void push_back(const T& t) {
      if (_capa == _size) {
        reserve((_capa+1)*2);
      }
      ATR::construct(_alloc, _elems+_size, t);   // calls placement new
      ++_size;
    }

    T& operator[] (size_t i){
      return _elems[i];    // UB for replaced elements with constant members
    }
    ...
};
```

Again, note that `ATR::construct()` does not return the return value of the called placement new. Thus, we cannot use this return value instead of `_elems`.

Note that this is a problem only since C++11. Before C++11, using elements with constant members was either not possible (`std::vector`) or not formally supported, because elements had to be CopyConstructible and Assignable (although node-based containers such as lists worked perfectly fine with elements with const members). However, with C++11 introducing move semantics, elements with constant members such as class X above are supported and cause this undefined behavior.

`std::launder()` was introduced with the aim of solving these problems. However, as I will describe below, it turned out that we cannot solve the vector problem with `std::launder()` at all.

## 32.2  How `launder()` Solves the Problem

The core working group of the C++ standards committee decided to solve this problem by introducing `std::launder()` as follows (see https://wg21.link/cwg1776): if you have a pointer where access is undefined behavior because the underlying memory was replaced:

```
struct X {
  const int n;
  double d;
};
X* p = new X{7, 8.8};
new (p) X{42, 9.9};     // request to place a new value into p
int i = p->n;           // undefined behavior (i is probably 7 or 42)
auto d = p->d;          // also undefined behavior (d is probably 8.8 or 9.9)
```

you can call `std::launder()` whenever a pointer is used to ensure that the underlying memory is reevaluated:

## 32.3 Why/When `launder()` Does Not Work

```
int i = std::launder(p)->n;    // OK, i is 42
auto d = std::launder(p)->d;   // OK, d is 9.9
```

Note that `launder()` does not fix the problem when using p afterwards, it only solves the problem for the particular expression it is used in:

```
int i2 = p->n;                 // still undefined behavior
```

You have to use `std::launder()` any time you access data where placement new was called.

This could work in a class like `optional` introduced above as follows:

```
template<typename T>
class optional
{
  private:
    T payload;
  public:
    optional(const T& t)
      : payload(t) {
    }

    template<typename... Args>
    void emplace(Args&&... args) {
      payload.~T();
      ::new (&payload) T(std::forward<Args>(args)...); // *
    }

    const T& operator*() const & {
      return *(std::launder(&payload));   // OK
    }
};
```

Note that we have to ensure that each access to the raw payload has to go through the "whitewashing" of `std::launder()` the way it is done for `operator*` here.

## 32.3 Why/When `launder()` Does Not Work

However, for allocator-based containers like vector, the solution does not work. This is because if we try something like this:

```
template<typename T, typename A = std::allocator<T>>
class vector
{
  public:
    typedef typename std::allocator_traits<A> ATR;
    typedef typename ATR::pointer pointer;
  private:
    A _alloc;                    // current allocator
```

```
      pointer _elems;      // array of elements
      size_t _size;         // number of elements
      size_t _capa;         // capacity
    public:
      void push_back(const T& t) {
        if (_capa == _size) {
          reserve((_capa+1)*2);
        }
        ATR::construct(_alloc, _elems+_size, t);   // calls placement new
        ++_size;
      }

      T& operator[] (size_t i){
        return std::launder(_elems)[i];   // OOPS, still UB
      }
      ...
};
```

the call of `launder()` in `operator[]` does not help because the `pointer` might be a smart pointer (i.e., a class type) and for them, `launder()` has no effect.[1]

Also trying

```
std::launder(this)->_elems[i];
```

does not work because `launder()` works only for pointers to objects for which the lifetime has ended.[2]

Thus, `std::launder()` does not solve the problem of avoiding undefined behavior in allocator-based containers if you have elements with constant/reference members. It appears that a general core fix is necessary (see my paper https://wg21.link/p0532).

## 32.4 Afternotes

`std::launder()` was introduced as a result of a national body comment for C++14 (see https://wg21.link/n3903) and was first discussed as core working group issue 1776 (see https://wg21.link/cwg1776). As a solution, it was first proposed by Richard Smith and Hubert Tong in https://wg21.link/n4303. The finally accepted wording was formulated by Richard Smith in https://wg21.link/p0137r1.

---

[1] Thanks to Jonathan Wakely for pointing this out.
[2] Thanks to Richard Smith for pointing this out.

# Chapter 33
# Improvements for Implementing Generic Code

A couple of helpers were introduced with C++17 to help with the implementation of generic code and libraries.

Note that we already introduced some new type traits features in the chapter *Type Traits Extensions* (see Chapter 21 on page 251).

## 33.1 `std::invoke<>()`

The new utility `std::invoke<>()` is a new helper for writing generic code that calls a callable, regardless of whether it is a function, a lambda, `operator()` for a function object, or a member function.

Here is a simple helper function that demonstrates how to use it:

*tmpl/invoke.hpp*
```
#include <utility>      // for std::invoke()
#include <functional>   // for std::forward()

template<typename Callable, typename... Args>
void call(Callable&& op, Args&&... args)
{
  ...
  std::invoke(std::forward<Callable>(op),        // call passed callable with
              std::forward<Args>(args)...);      // all additional passed args
}
```

Whatever you pass to `call()` as a first argument, it is called with the other additional arguments used as follows:
- If the callable is a pointer to a member, it uses the first additional argument as the object for calling the member function. All remaining additional parameters are just passed as arguments to the callable.
- Otherwise, all additional parameters are just passed as arguments to the callable.

For example:

*tmpl/invoke.cpp*

```cpp
#include "invoke.hpp"
#include <iostream>
#include <vector>

void print(const std::vector<int>& coll)
{
  std::cout << "elems: ";
  for (const auto& elem : coll) {
    std::cout << elem << ' ';
  }
  std::cout << '\n';
}

int main()
{
  std::vector<int> vals{0, 8, 15, 42, 13, -1, 0};

  call([&vals] {
          std::cout << "size: " << vals.size() << '\n';
       });
  call(print, vals);

  call(&decltype(vals)::pop_back, vals);
  call(print, vals);

  call(&decltype(vals)::clear, vals);
  call(print, vals);
}
```

Note that calling an overloaded function is an error if you do not specify which overload to call:

```cpp
call(&decltype(vals)::resize, vals, 5);      // ERROR: resize() overloaded

call<void(decltype(vals)::*)(std::size_t)>(&decltype(vals)::resize,
                                           vals, 5);                       // OK
```

Also note that calling a function template requires explicit instantiation. If `print()` were a template:

```
template<typename T>
void print(const T& coll)
{
  std::cout << "elems: ";
  for (const auto& elem : coll) {
    std::cout << elem << ' ';
  }
  std::cout << '\n';
}
```

then you would have to pass a call to it with explicitly specified template parameters:

```
call(print, vals);                          // ERROR: can't deduce template parameter T

call(print<std::vector<int>>, vals);   // OK
```

Finally, note that according to the rules of move semantics, returning the result of an invocation requires `decltype(auto)` to *perfectly return* the return value to the caller:

```
template<typename Callable, typename... Args>
decltype(auto) call(Callable&& op, Args&&... args)
{
  return std::invoke(std::forward<Callable>(op),    // call passed callable with
                     std::forward<Args>(args)...);  // all additional passed args
}
```

## 33.2  std::bool_constant<>

If traits yield Boolean values, they now use the alias template `bool_constant<>`:

```
namespace std {
    template<bool B>
      using bool_constant = integral_constant<bool, B>;   // since C++17
    using true_type = bool_constant<true>;
    using false_type = bool_constant<false>;
}
```

Before C++17, you had to use `integral_constant<>` directly, which meant that `true_type` and `false_type` were defined as follows:

```
namespace std {
  using true_type = integral_constant<bool, true>;
  using false_type = integral_constant<bool, false>;
}
```

Still, Boolean traits should usually inherit from `std::true_type` if a specific property applies and from `std::false_type` if this is not the case. For example:

```
// primary template: in general T is not a void type
template<typename T>
struct IsVoid : std::false_type {
};

// specialization for type void:
template<>
struct IsVoid<void> : std::true_type {
};
```

However, you can now define your own type trait by deriving from `bool_constant<>` if you can formulate the corresponding compile-time expression as a Boolean condition. For example:

```
template<typename T>
struct IsLargerThanInt
  : std::bool_constant<(sizeof(T) > sizeof(int))> {
}
```

so that you can use such a trait to compile depending on whether a type is larger than an `int`:

```
template<typename T>
void foo(T x)
{
  if constexpr(IsLargerThanInt<T>::value) {
    ...
  }
}
```

By adding the corresponding variable template for suffix `_v` (see Section 21.1 on page 251) as an inline variable (see Chapter 3 on page 25):

```
template<typename T>
inline static constexpr auto IsLargerThanInt_v = IsLargerThanInt<T>::value;
```

you can also shorten the usage of the trait as follows:

```
template<typename T>
void foo(T x)
{
  if constexpr(IsLargerThanInt_v<T>) {
    ...
  }
}
```

As another example, we can define a trait that checks whether the move constructor for a type `T` guarantees not to throw roughly as follows:

```
template<typename T>
struct IsNothrowMoveConstructibleT
  : std::bool_constant<noexcept(T(std::declval<T>()))> {
};
```

## 33.3 std::void_t<>

A small but very useful helper for defining type traits was standardized in C++17: `std::void_t<>`. It is simply defined as follows:

```
namespace std {
  template<typename...> using void_t = void;
}
```

That is, it yields `void` for any variadic list of template parameters. This is helpful where we only want to deal with types solely in an argument list.

The major application is the ability to check for conditions when defining new type traits. The following example demonstrates the application of this helper:

```
#include <utility>      // for declval<>
#include <type_traits>  // for true_type, false_type, and void_t

// primary template:
template<typename, typename = std::void_t<>>
struct HasVarious : std::false_type {
};

// partial specialization (may be SFINAE'd away):
template<typename T>
struct HasVarious<T, std::void_t<decltype(std::declval<T>().begin()),
                                 typename T::difference_type,
                                 typename T::iterator>>
  : std::true_type {
};
```

Here, we define a new type trait `HasVariousT<>`, which checks for three things:

- Does the type have a member function `begin()`?
- Does the type have a type member `difference_type`?
- Does the type have a type member `iterator`?

The partial specialization is used only when all the corresponding expressions are valid for a type T. In that case, it is more specific than the primary template and as we derive from `std::true_type` (see Section 33.2 on page 401), a check against the `value` of this trait yields `true`:

```
if constexpr (HasVarious<T>::value) {
  ...
}
```

If any of the expressions results in invalid code (i.e., T has no `begin()`, or no type member `difference_type`, or no type member `iterator`), the partial specialization is *SFINAE'd away*, which means that it is ignored due to the rule that *substitution failure is not an error*. Then, only the primary template is available, which derives from std::false_type (see Section 33.2 on page 401), which means that a check against the `value` of this trait yields `false`.

In the same way, you can use `std::void_t` to easily define other traits that check for one or multiple conditions, where the existence/ability of a member or operation matters. See `HasDelete<>` (see Section 30.1.2 on page 369) for an example.

## 33.4 Afternotes

`std::invoke<>()` was first proposed by Tomasz Kaminski in `https://wg21.link/n3727`. The finally accepted wording was formulated by Tomasz Kaminski in `https://wg21.link/4169`. Its return type later changed using the `invoke_result<>` type trait (see Section 21.2 on page 255) as proposed by Daniel Krügler, Pablo Halpern, Jonathan Wakely in `https://wg21.link/p0604r0`.

`std::bool_constant<>` was first proposed by Zhihao Yuan in `https://wg21.link/n4334`. The finally accepted wording was formulated by Zhihao Yuan in `https://wg21.link/n4389`.

`std::void_t<>` was adopted as proposed by Walter E. Brown in `https://wg21.link/n3911`.

# Part VI
# Final General Hints

This part of the book introduces some final general hints about C++17 such as the updated compatibility to C and deprecated features.

# Chapter 34

# Common C++17 Settings

This chapter contains a few concluding general aspects of C++17.

## 34.1 Value of __cplusplus

The preprocessor value that signals the current C++ version, `__cplusplus` shall now be defined as 201703L.

However, note that Visual C++ still uses the value 199711 by default in all modes. To activate the correct behavior, use the option `/Zc:__cplusplus`, as it is discussed in:

http://docs.microsoft.com/en-us/cpp/build/reference/zc-cplusplus

## 34.2 Compatibility to C11

C++17 is based on C11 instead of C99, which was the basis for C++14.

In principle, this means that C++17 benefits from and has to honor the modifications C11 introduced. However, there are various constraints:

- The C11 standard introduced several functions and macros for "safer, more secure programming" that shall replace traditional C functions and macros that can be a problem such as overwriting an unlimited amount of memory. Most of them just have the additional suffix `_s`. For example, `strcpy_s()`, `sprintf_s()` were introduced to take an additional size parameter to ensure that they do not overwrite a character sequence that is too short for the operation.

    In C11, these functions are introduced in the header files where the corresponding unsafe versions exist. In the corresponding C++17 header file, they are *not* introduced in namespace `std`. It is implementation-defined whether they are available declared in the global namespace when any C++ header file is included.
- The new C headers `<stdatomic.h>`, `<stdnoreturn.h>`, and `<threads.h>` are all ignored and have no C++ counterparts.
- The use of the header files `<ccomplex>`, `<cstdalign>`, `<cstdbool>`, and `<ctgmath>` is deprecated.

## 34.3 Dealing with Signal Handlers

As a side effect of becoming compatible to C11, C++17 clarifies which calls and functionality are possible in signal handlers.

C++17 introduces the term *signal-safe* evaluation. According to its definition, the following is not allowed in signal handlers:

- Calling any standard library function (unless explicitly specified as signal-safe)
- Calling `new` or `delete` (unless a safe memory allocator is used)
- Using objects that are `thread_local`
- Using `dynamic_cast`
- Throwing an exception or entering a `try` block
- Performing or waiting for the first initialization of a variable with static storage duration

The following functions are signal-safe and can be called:

- `abort()` and `_Exit()`
- `quick_exit()`, if the functions registered with `at_quick_exit()` are signal-safe
- `memcpy()` and `memmove()`
- All member functions of `std::numeric_limits<>`
- All functions for `std::initializer_lists`
- All type traits

## 34.4 Forward Progress Guarantees

C++17 clarifies what it means for a program to "make progress" or "block."

See https://wg21.link/p0072r1 for a motivating discussion of this topic.

## 34.5 Afternotes

C++17 referring to C11 instead of C99 was first proposed by Hans-J. Boehm and Clark Nelson in https://wg21.link/p0063r0 (based on a paper by Thomas Plum that analyzed the situation in https://wg21.link/n3631). The finally accepted wording for this feature was formulated by Clark Nelson and Hans-J. Boehm in https://wg21.link/p0063r3.

The clarification of dealing with signal handlers was first proposed by Hans-J. Boehm in https://wg21.link/p0270r0. The finally accepted wording for this feature was formulated by Hans-J. Boehm in https://wg21.link/p0270r3.

Forward progress guarantees were accepted as proposed by Torvald Riegel in https://wg21.link/p0296r2.

# Chapter 35
# Deprecated and Removed Features

There are a few features that were deprecated in C++17 or finally removed.

Implementations might still provide removed features but you cannot rely on that. Implementations might or might not issue a warning if you use deprecated features.

## 35.1 Deprecated and Removed Core Language Features

### 35.1.1 Throw Specifications

Dynamic exception specifications are no longer supported (they have been deprecated since C++11):

```
void f6() throw(std::bad_alloc);   // ERROR: invalid since C++17
```

The empty throw specification can still be used but is still deprecated:

```
void f5() throw();                  // deprecated since C++11
```

Use noexcept instead (which is now part of the type of a function (see Section 8.7 on page 69)):

```
void f5() noexcept;                 // OK
```

### 35.1.2 Keyword `register`

The keyword register no longer has any standardized semantics but is still reserved:

```
register int x = 42;                // ERROR since C++17
```

```
std::string register;               // still ERROR in all C++ versions
```

One reason why register is still reserved is that it is still a keyword with standardized semantics in C (e.g., it can appear in a function parameter list).

Because the keyword was already deprecated in C++11 and C++14, if a compilation fails due to using register, simply remove the keyword.

### 35.1.3 Disable ++ for `bool`

You can no longer call ++ for objects of type `bool` (calling -- was never allowed):

```
bool b{false};
```

```
++b;    // ERROR since C++17
```

Instead, use:

```
b = true;
```

### 35.1.4 Trigraphs

You can no longer use sequences of three characters that represent special characters (such as ??= representing #).

This feature was introduced to allow the use type writers that did not have a key for the special characters such as #. Supporting this feature is no longer necessary.

### 35.1.5 Definition/Redeclaration of `static constexpr` Members

Because `static constexpr` data members are `inline` now (see Section 3.3 on page 28), a later definition is no longer necessary and is considered to be a redundant redeclaration. Therefore, the definition/redeclaration is now deprecated:

```
struct D {
  static constexpr int n = 5;  // was declaration, now definition
};
```

```
constexpr int D::n;            // was definition, now deprecated
```

## 35.2 Deprecated and Removed Library Features

### 35.2.1 `auto_ptr`

The smart pointer type `std::auto_ptr<>` was finally removed. Standardized in C++98, it tried to provide exclusive ownership move semantics using copy operations, which could cause some unwanted errors or side effects.

Use `std::unique_ptr<>` instead.

### 35.2.2 Algorithm `random_shuffle()`

The C++98 algorithms for randomly shuffling the order of elements, `random_shuffle()`, was finally removed.

Use `std::shuffle()` instead or, if you only need a random subset of a collection, the new algorithm `std::sample()` (see Section 25.4 on page 304).

## 35.2.3 `unary_function` and `binary_function`

The helper types for implementing function objects, `std::unary_function` and `std::binary_function`, were finally removed. They were provided to support a simple, standardized way for type definitions when defining function objects. However, with all the new language features of C++11 (lambdas, `decltype`, ...) they are no longer necessary or are inapplicable in some situations.

Remove the base class and provide the necessary type definitions manually.

## 35.2.4 `ptr_fun()`, `mem_fun()`, and Binders

The binders and the wrappers for creating more sophisticated function call adapters were finally removed:

- Instead of `std::ptr_fun()`, you can now use lambdas, the class template `std::function<>`, and the function template `std::bind()`.
- Instead of `std::mem_fun()` and `std::mem_fun_ref()`, you can now use lambdas and `std::mem_fn()`.
- Instead of `std::bind1st()` and `std::bind2nd()`, you can now use lambdas and the function template `std::bind()`.

## 35.2.5 Allocator Support for `std::function<>`

Originally, the class template `std::function<>` was standardized with allocator support. However, no major compiler implemented the support completely and the specification raised some interesting issues in terms of behavior (see library issues 2385, 2386, 2062, 2370, 2501, 2502).

As a result, allocator support for `std::function<>` was removed with C++17.

## 35.2.6 Deprecated IOStream Aliases

The IOStream aliases for types and functions that were already deprecated in C++98 were finally removed:

- Type `io_state` in `std::ios_base`
- Type `open_mode` in `std::ios_base`
- Type `seek_dir` in `std::ios_base`
- Type `streamoff` in `std::ios_base`
- Type `streampos` in `std::ios_base`
- `stossc()` in `std::std::basic_streambuf<>`
- `clear(io_state)` in `std::basic_ios<>`
- `setstate(io_state)` in `std::basic_ios<>`
- `exceptions(io_state)` in `std::basic_ios<>`
- `pubseekoff(off_type, ios_base::seek_dir, ios_base::open_mode)` in `std::basic_streambuf<>`
- `pubseekpos(pos_type, ios_base::open_mode)` in `std::basic_streambuf<>`
- `open(const char*, ios_base::open_mode)` in `std::basic_filebuf<>`, `std::basic_ifstream<>`, and `std::basic_ofstream<>`

## 35.2.7 Deprecated Library Features

The following library features are deprecated since C++17 and should no longer be used:
- The type trait `result_of<>`.
    Use `invoke_result<>` (see Section 21.2 on page 255) instead.
- The type trait `is_literal_type<>` is deprecated.
- For shared pointers, the member function `unique()` is deprecated.
    Use `use_count()` instead.
- The support for character code conversions (the whole contents of the header file `<codecvt>` and the standard classes `wstring_convert<>` and `wbuffer_convert<>`) are deprecated.
    This functionality was introduced in C++11, but it turned out that the approach is not very helpful in practice and has security flaws. To make room for better support of character encoding in C++20, the whole contents of `<codecvt>` with the standard classes for character type conversions became deprecated in C++17.
- Class `std::iterator<>` is deprecated.
- Class `std::raw_storage_iterator<>` is deprecated.
- `std::get_temporary_buffer()` is deprecated.
- `std::allocator<void>`, the specialization for `void` of the standard allocator, is deprecated.
- The use of the header files `<ccomplex>`, `<cstdalign>`, `<cstdbool>`, and `<ctgmath>` is deprecated.
- The use of `std::uncaught_exception()` is deprecated.
    Use `std::uncaught_exceptions()` (see Section 28.1 on page 327) instead.
- The memory synchronization order `memory_order_consume` is temporarily discouraged. The way it is specified now, it is not useful, but this might be fixed later.
    In the meantime, use `memory_order_acquire` instead.

## 35.3 Afternotes

Removing throw specifications was finally accepted with the wording proposed by Alisdair Meredith in `https://wg21.link/p0003r5`.

Removing the use of the keyword `register` was finally accepted with the wording proposed by Alisdair Meredith in `https://wg21.link/p0001r1`.

Removing `++` and `--` for `bool` was finally accepted with the wording proposed by Alisdair Meredith in `https://wg21.link/p0002r1`.

Removing trigraphs was accepted with the wording proposed by Richard Smith in `https://wg21.link/n4086`.

Removing `auto_ptr<>` was first proposed by Billy Baker in `https://wg21.link/n4168`. The finally accepted wording for this removal was formulated by Stephan T. Lavavej in `https://wg21.link/n4190`.

Removing `random_shuffle()` and the functional helpers for function objects was finally accepted with the wording proposed by Stephan T. Lavavej in `https://wg21.link/n4190`.

Removing allocator support for `std::function<>` was finally accepted with the wording proposed by Jonathan Wakely in `https://wg21.link/p0302r1`.

Removing the deprecated IOStream aliases was finally accepted with the wording proposed by Alisdair Meredith in `https://wg21.link/p0004r1`.

Deprecating `result_of<>` was accepted as proposed by Daniel Krügler, Pablo Halpern, and Jonathan Wakely in `https://wg21.link/p0604r0`.

Deprecating `unique()` for shared pointers was accepted as proposed by Stephan T. Lavavej in `https://wg21.link/p0521r0`.

Deprecating `<codecvt>` was accepted as proposed by Alisdair Meredith in `https://wg21.link/p0618r0`.

Deprecating `is_literal_type(<>, class iterator<>, class raw_storage_iterator<>, get_temporary_buffer(), and std::allocator<void>` was accepted as proposed by Alisdair Meredith in `https://wg21.link/p0174r2`.

Deprecating the use of the header files `<ccomplex>`, `<cstdalign>`, `<cstdbool>`, and `<ctgmath>` was accepted as proposed by Clark Nelson and Hans-J. Boehm in `https://wg21.link/p0063r3`.

Temporarily discouraging `memory_order_consume` was accepted as proposed by Hans-J. Boehm in `https://wg21.link/p0371r1`.

# Glossary

This glossary provides a short definition of the most important non-trivial technical terms used in this book.

## B

**bitmask type**
An integral or scoped enumeration type (`enum class`) for which different values represent different bits. If it is a scoped enumeration type, only the bit operators are defined and you need a `static_cast<>()` to use its integral value or use it as a Boolean value.

## F

**full specialization**
An alternative definition for a (*primary*) template that no longer depends on any template parameter.

## I

**incomplete type**
A class that is declared but not defined, an array of unknown size, an enumeration type without the underlying type defined, `void` (optionally with `const` and/or `volatile`), or an array of incomplete element type.

## P

**partial specialization**
An alternative definition for a (*primary*) template that still depends on one or more template parameters.

# S

**small/short string optimization (SSO)**
An approach to save allocating memory for short strings by always reserving memory for a certain number of characters. A typical value in standard library implementations is to always reserve 16 or 24 bytes of memory so that the string can have 15 or 23 characters (plus 1 byte for the null terminator) without allocating memory. This makes all strings objects larger but usually saves a lot of running time, because in practice, strings are often shorter than 16 or 24 characters and allocating memory on the heap is a pretty expensive operation.

# V

**variable template**
A templified variable. It allows us to define variables or static members by substituting the template parameters with specific types or values.

**variadic template**
A template with a template parameter that represents an arbitrary number of types or values.

# Index

=
    for path   226
. directory   211
.. directory   211
++ for `bool`   410
/= for path   226
!=
    for directory entry   246
    for path   228
+=
    + for path   226
/
    for path   226
<
    for directory entry   246
    for path   228
<<
    for path   221
<=
    for directory entry   246
    for path   228
==
    for directory entry   246
    for path   228
>
    for directory entry   246
    for path   228
>=
    for directory entry   246
    for path   228
>>
    for path   221

## A

AAA   192
about the book   xxi
`abs()`
    for durations   334
`absolute()`
    for path   241
Access Control List   237
`accumulate()`
    parallel   281
ACL   237
add
    `perm_options`   240
aggregate   33
    definition   36
algorithm
    associative   270
    `clamp()`   303
    commutative   270
    `exclusive_scan()`   287
    `for_each_n()`   279
    `inclusive_scan()`   287
    + new in C++17   279
    non-associative   272
    non-commutative   270
    parallel   259
    `reduce()`   269, 281

sample() 304
searcher 293
transform_exclusive_scan() 289
transform_inclusive_scan() 289
transform_reduce() 274, 283
alignas 365
aligned_alloc() 366
_aligned_free() 366
_aligned_malloc() 366
alignment
    with new and delete 365
align_val_t 367
all
    file permission 235
allocation
    over-aligned 365
allocator
    polymorphic 341
allocator_type 360
allocator&lt;void&gt; 412
almost always auto 192
any 171
    in_place_type 175
any_cast&lt;&gt;() 171
append()
    for path 226
argument deduction
    for class templates 77
    with auto 121
array
    deduction guide 90
    number of elements 300
    shared pointers to 329
    structured bindings 9
arrays
    structured bindings 9
ASCII 68
as_const() 302
assign()
    for directory entry 246
    for path 226
associative container
    node handle 309
associative parallel algorithm 270
assoc_laguerre() 332

assoc_legendre() 332
atomic&lt;&gt;
    is_always_lock_free 323
attribute 55
    deprecated 58
    fallthrough 58
    for enumerator 58
    for namespace 58
    maybe_unused 57
    nodiscard 55
    using prefix 58
auto
    almost always 192
    as template parameter 121
    for variable templates 124
    for variadic templates 122
    list initialization 66
auto_ptr&lt;&gt; 410
available
    space_info 243

## B

bad_optional_access 139
basic_string
    improvements 318
begin()
    for directory iterators 245
    for path 218
Bessel functions 332
beta() 332
binary_function 411
bind1st() 411
bind2nd() 411
bindings
    structured 3
bitmask type **415**
block file type 216
bool
    + ++ 410
bool_constant 401
Boyer-Moore 293
Boyer-Moore-Horspool 293
boyer_moore_horspool_searcher 293
boyer_moore_searcher 293

byte 179
    to_integer<>() 180

# C

C 407
cache line sizes 324
canonical()
    for path 241
capacity
    space_info 243
capture
    *this 50
    by const reference 302
case sensitive
    file names 211
<ccomplex> 412
ceil()
    for durations and time points 334
character file type 216
character literals 68
character sequence
    to numeric values 385
character set 68
_Check_return_ 57
chrono
    constexpr 335
    extensions 334
clamp() 303
class
    structured bindings 8
class template argument deduction 77
    for std::variant 155
clear()
    for path 226
<codecvt> 412
collection
    with variant 162
comma operator
    in fold expression 112
commutative parallel algorithm 270
compare()
    for path 228
comp_ellint_1() 332
comp_ellint_2() 332

comp_ellint_3() 332
compile-time if 95
concat()
    for path 226
concurrency 321
conjunction<> 255
const reference
    capture 302
constexpr 335
    CTAD 91
    if 95
    inline 28
    lambdas 47
    string_view 194
container
    deduction guide 90
    subsequence search 296
conversion
    between string types 363
copy()
    for path 237
copy elision 39
copy_file()
    for path 237
copy_options 238
copy_symlink()
    for path 237
copy_symlinks
    copy option 238
__cplusplus 407
create_directories()
    for path 237
create_directory()
    for path 237
create_directory_symlink() 207
    for path 237
create_hard_link()
    for path 237
create_hard_links
    copy option 238
create_symlink()
    for path 237
create_symlinks
    copy option 238
<cstdalign> 412

```
<cstdbool>   412
c_str()
    for path   224
CTAD   77
    constexpr   91
    deduction guide   84
    lambda   80
    make_pair()   83
<ctgmath>   412
curly braces   xxi
current directory   211
current_path()   217
    for path   243
cyl_bessel_i()   332
cyl_bessel_j()   332
cyl_bessel_k()   332
cyl_neumann()   332
```

# D

```
data()
    for strings   318
data() global   301
decay   6
    with deduction guides   85
decltype(auto)   401
    as template parameter   126
deduction
    class template arguments   77
deduction guide   84
    decay   85
    for iterators   90
    for pairs and tuples   89
    std::array   90
default_searcher   293
delete
    placement   369
    user-defined   370
    with alignment   367
deprecated   58
deprecated features   409
directories_only
    copy option   238
directory
    ..   211
    .   211
    current   211
directory_entry   246
directory file type   216
directory_iterator   202, 244
directory iterator range   245
directory_options   245
disjunction<>   255
do_allocate()
    for memory resources   355
do_deallocate()
    for memory resources   355
do_is_equal()
    for memory resources   355, 358
double
    round-trip support   388
dynamic allocation
    over-aligned   365
```

# E

```
EBCDIC   68
elision
    mandatory   39
ellint_1()   332
ellint_2()   332
ellint_3()   332
elliptic integrals   332
email to the authors   xxiii
emplace()
    for any   174
    for containers   314
    for optional<>   139
    for variant<>   153
emplace_back()
    for containers   314
emplace_front()
    for containers   314
empty()
    for path   218
empty() global   301
end()
    for directory iterators   245
    for path   218
enum
```

initialization 65
enumerator
    attributes 58
`equivalent()`
    for path 228, 243
ERROR xxii
`error_code` 215
error handling
    filesystem 214
evaluation order 62
exception
    `filesystem_error` 215
exception handling
    noexcept specifications 69
    parallel algorithms 266
exception specification 409
`exclusive_scan()` 287
execution character set 68
execution policy 260, 265
`exists()`
    for directory entry 246
    for `file_status` 234
    for path 202, 230
`expint()` 332
`extension()`
    for path 218
`extract()`
    for node handles 309

# F

`fallthrough` 58
`false_type` 401
fifo file type 216
file
    other 217
    special 217
`filename()`
    for path 218
`file_size()` 202
    for directory entry 246
    for path 231
filesystem 201
    case sensitive 211
    `error_code` 215
    error handling 214
    `filesystem_error` 215
    file types 216
    functions 213
    normalization 212
    output on Windows 203
    path 201, 211
    performance 213
    permissions 235
`filesystem_error` 209, 215
    `path1()` 215
    `path2()` 215
`file_type` 216
floating-point
    hexadecimal literals 67
    round-trip support 388
`floor()`
    for durations and time points 334
fold expression 107
    comma operator 112
    hash function 113
`follow_directory_symlink` 208
    directory option 245
`for_each()`
    parallel 260
`for_each_n()` 279
forward progress guarantees 408
free
    `space_info` 243
`from_chars()` 386
fs
    namespace 205, 207
`fs` namespace 211
full specialization **415**
function
    noexcept specifications 69
`function<>` 411

# G

`gcd()` 332
generic lambda
    as visitor 159
generic path 211
    conversions 224

```
generic_string()
    for path   224
generic_u16string()
    for path   224
generic_u32string()
    for path   224
generic_u8string()
    for path   224
generic_wstring()
    for path   224
get()
    for variant<>   153
get_default_resource()   347
get_if()
    for variant<>   153
get_temporary_buffer()   412
glossary   415
glvalue   43
greatest common divisor   332
group_all
    file permission   235
group_exec
    file permission   235
group_read
    file permission   235
group_write
    file permission   235
guarantees for forward progress   408
```

# H

```
hard_link_count()
    for directory entry   246
    for path   231
hardware_constructive_interference_size
        324
hardware_destructive_interference_size
        324
has_extension()
    for path   218
has_filename()
    for path   218
hash function   113
hash_value()
    for path   229
```

```
__has_include   73
has_parent_path()
    for path   218
has_relative_path()
    for path   218
has_root_directory()
    for path   218
has_root_name()
    for path   218
has_root_path()
    for path   218
has_stem()
    for path   218
has_unique_object_representations<>
        254
has_value()
    for any   174
    for optional<>   139
heap allocation
    over-aligned   365
hermite()   332
heterogeneous collection
    with variant   162
hexadecimal floating-point literals   67
hexfloat   67
holds_alternative()
    for variant<>   153
hypot()   332
```

# I

```
if
    compile-time   95
    with initialization   21
inclusive_scan()   287
incomplete type   415
    for containers   316
index()
    for variant<>   153
    for variants   150
INFINITY   390
inhomogeneous collection
    with variant   162
initialization   xxi
    of aggregates   33
```

of enumerations  65
   with `auto`  66
   with `if`  21
   with `switch`  23
inline
   `constexpr`  28
   `thread_local`  29
   variable  25
`inner_product()`
   parallel  285, 287
`in_place`
   for `std::optional<>`  140
`in_place_index`
   for `variant<>`  154
`in_place_type`
   for `std::any`  175
   for `variant<>`  154
`insert()`
   for node handles  309
`insert_or_assign()`
   for maps  315
`insert_return_type`  312
`invoke<>()`  399
`invoke_result<>`  255
`is_absolute()`
   for path  218
`is_aggregate<>`  252
`is_always_lock_free`  323
`is_block_file()`
   for directory entry  246
   for `file_status`  234
   for path  230
`is_character_file()`
   for directory entry  246
   for `file_status`  234
   for path  230
`is_directory()`  202
   for directory entry  246
   for `file_status`  234
   for path  230
`is_empty()`
   for path  231
`is_execution_policy<>`  265
`is_fifo()`
   for directory entry  246

   for `file_status`  234
   for path  230
`is_invocable<>`  254
`is_invocable_r<>`  254
`is_literal_type<>`  412
`is_nothrow_invocable<>`  254
`is_nothrow_invocable_r<>`  254
`is_nothrow_swappable<>`  253
`is_nothrow_swappable_with<>`  253
ISO-Latin-1  68
`is_other()`
   for directory entry  246
   for `file_status`  234
   for path  230
`is_regular_file()`  202
   for directory entry  246
   for `file_status`  234
   for path  230
`is_relative()`
   for path  218
`is_socket()`
   for directory entry  246
   for `file_status`  234
   for path  230
`is_swappable<>`  253
`is_swappable_with<>`  253
`is_symlink()`
   for directory entry  246
   for `file_status`  234
   for path  230
iterator
   as range  245
   deduction guide  90
`<iterator>`  299
`iterator<>`  412

## J

junction file type  216

## K

key
   modification  309
`key()`
   for node handles  309

## L

laguerre() 332
lambda
    *this capture 50
    as_const() 302
    as visitor 159
    constexpr 47
    CTAD 80
    overload 129
last_write_time()
    for directory entry 246
    for path 231, 239
Latin-1 68
launder() 393
lcm() 332
least common multiple 332
legendre() 332
lexically_normal()
    for path 221
lexically_proximate()
    for path 221
lexically_relative()
    for path 221
list
    incomplete types 316
list initialization xxi
    of aggregates 33
    with auto 66
literal
    UTF-8 characters 68
literals
    floating-point hexadecimal 67
    sv 194
lock 321
lock_shared() 321, 322
lvalue 42

## M

make_any() 174
make_optional<>() 139
make_pair() 83
map
    extract() 309
    insert() 309
    insert_or_assign() 315
    merge() 312
    node handle 309
    try_emplace() 314
mapped()
    for node handles 309
map-reduce 274
mask
    file permission 235
materialization 39
mathematical special functions 332
maybe_unused 57
mem_func() 411
mem_func_ref() 411
memory_order_consume 412
memory resource 341
    predefined 347
    string types 363
    user-defined 355
    user-defined types 360
memory_resource 348
merge()
    for containers 312
minimum and maximum 303
monostate 151
monotonic_buffer_resource 347, 352
monotonic_memory_resource 343
move constructor
    noexcept 336
multi-threading 321
mutex 321

## N

namespace
    attributes 58
    fs 205, 207, 211
    nested 61
NAN 390
native()
    for path 224
native path 211
    conversions 224
negation<> 255

nested namespace   61
new
    tracking   380
    user-defined   370
    with alignment   365
new_delete_resource()   347, 349
node handle   309
node_type   309
nodiscard   55
noexcept   336
    specifications   69
nofollow
    perm_options   240
none
    copy option   238
    directory option   245
    file permission   235
    file type   216
normalization   212
not_found file type   216
NTBS   185
null_memory_resource()   347, 353
nullopt   139
nullopt_t   139
null terminated byte stream   185
numeric
    to character sequence   385

## O

operator
    comma in fold expression   112
    evaluation order   62
optional   135
    bad_optional_access   139
    in_place   140
    launder()   393
    nullopt   139
optional<>
    value()   142
    value_or()   142
order of evaluation   62
other file   217
others_all
    file permission   235
others_exec
    file permission   235
others_read
    file permission   235
others_write
    file permission   235
over-aligned types   365
overload for lambdas   129
overwrite_existing
    copy option   238
owner_all
    file permission   235
owner_exec
    file permission   235
owner_read
    file permission   235
owner_write
    file permission   235

## P

pair
    deduction guide   89
    structured bindings   10
par   265
    execution policy   260
parallel
    accumulate()   281
    associative   270
    commutative   270
    inner_product()   285, 287
    non-associative   272
    non-commutative   270
parallel algorithms   259
    exception handling   266
    par   260
    sorting   263
    versus no-parallel   266
parallel_policy   265
parallel_unsequenced_policy   265
parameter pack
    fold expression   107
    function calls   112
parent directory   211
parent_path()

for path  218
partial specialization  **415**
`par_unseq`  265
path  201, 211
    conversions  221
    creation  217
    generic conversions  224
    I/O  221
    native conversions  224
    output on Windows  203
    `string_type`  224
    UTF-8  217
`path()`
    for directory entry  246
`path1()`  215
`path2()`  215
permissions
    Access Control List  237
    for files  235
`permissions()`
    for `file_status`  234
    for path  239
`perm_options`  240
perms  235
placeholder type
    as template parameter  121
placement `delete`  367, 369
placement `new`
    `launder()`  393
pmr  341
    `string`  343
    `string` types  363
    user-defined memory resource  355
    user-defined type  360
    `vector`  343
polymorphic allocator  341
`polymorphic_allocator`  343
polymorphism
    with `variant`  162
polynomials  332
population subset  304
preprocessor
    `__cplusplus`  407
    `__has_include`  73
progress guarantees  408

`proximate()`
    for path  241
prvalue  43
`ptr_fun()`  411

# R

RAII
    `uncaught_exceptions()`  327
`random_shuffle()`  410
range of directory iterators  245
`raw_storage_iterator<>`  412
`read_symlink()`
    for path  241
reallocation
    of vectors  336
recursive
    copy option  238
`recursive_directory_iterator`  208, 244, 276
`reduce()`  269, 281
`refresh()`
    for directory entry  246
`register`  409
regular file type  216
`reinterpret_pointer_cast`  329, 330
`relative()`
    for path  241
`relative_path()`
    for path  218
remove
    `perm_options`  240
`remove()`
    for path  237
`remove_all()`
    for path  237
removed features  409
`remove_filename()`
    for path  226
`rename()`
    for path  239
replace
    `perm_options`  240
`replace_extension()`
    for path  226

replace_filename()
    for directory entry  246
    for path  226
reservoir sampling  304
reset()
    for any  174
    for optional<>  139
resize_file()
    for path  239
resources
    polymorphic  341
result_of<>  412
riemann_zeta()  332
root_directory()
    for path  218
root_name()
    for path  218
root_path()
    for path  218
round()
    for chrono  334
    for durations and time points  334
round-trip support
    for floating-points  388
runtime error  xxii
rvalue  42

## S

sample()  304
search()  293
searcher  293
selection sampling  304
seq  265
sequenced_policy  265
set
    extract()  309
    insert()  309
    merge()  312
    node handle  309
set_default_resource()  347
set_gid
    file permission  235
set_uid
    file permission  235

shared_lock  321, 322
shared_mutex  321, 322
shared pointer  329
    reinterpret_pointer_cast  329, 330
    to arrays  329
    unique()  412
    weak_from_this  330
    weak_type  330
shared_ptr
    unique()  412
shared_ptr<>  329
    reinterpret_pointer_cast  330
    to arrays  329
    weak_from_this  330
    weak_type  330
short string optimization  383
signal handler  408
signal-safe  408
size() global  299
skip_existing
    copy option  238
skip_permission_denied
    directory option  245
skip_symlinks
    copy option  238
small/short string optimization (SSO)  **416**
small string optimization  383
socket file type  216
sort()
    with string_view  264
source character set  68
space()
    for path  243
space_info  243
special file  217
sph_bessel()  332
sph_legendre()  332
sph_neumann()  332
splice node handles  311
SSO  383
static_assert  72
status()
    for directory entry  246
    for path  234
__STDCPP_DEFAULT_NEW_ALIGNMENT__  375

stem()
    for path  218
sticky_bit
    file permission  235
STL
    algorithms  279
    parallel  259
    subsequence search  296
string
    as template parameter  119
    different types  363
    find substring  293
    improvements  318
    pmr::string  343
    reallocation  336
    to numeric values  385
    vs. string_view  185
string()
    for path  221
string_type
    for path  224
string_view  185
    classes  192
    constexpr  194
    sort()  264
    sv suffix  194
    vs. string  185
struct
    structured bindings  8
structured bindings  3
    array  9
    class  8
    move semantics  7
    pair  10
    raw arrays  9
    struct  8
    tie()  10
    tuple  10
    tuple-like API  11
subsequence search  296
substring search  293
suffix _v  251
sv suffix  194
swap()
    for path  226

switch
    with initialization  23
symbolic link  217
    creation  207
symlink file type  216
symlink_status()  231
    for directory entry  246
    for path  234
synchronized_pool_resource  347, 349

# T

temp_directory_path()  217
template
    string parameter  119
template parameter
    decltype(auto)  126
temporary
    copy elision  39
terminology  **415**
*this
    capture  50
thread
    forward progress guarantees  408
thread_local
    inline  29
throw()  409
throw specification  409
throw() specification  69
tie()
    for structured bindings  10
Timer  259
to_chars()  387
to_integer<>()
    for byte  180
sort()
    parallel  263
track new  380
traits  251
    bool_constant  401
    suffix _v  251
    void_t  403
transform_exclusive_scan()  289
transform_inclusive_scan()  289
transform_reduce()  274, 283

trigraph   410
true_type   401
try_emplace()   314
    for maps   314
tuple
    deduction guide   89
    structured bindings   10
tuple-like API for structured bindings   11
type()
    for any   174
    for file_status   234
    for optional<>   139
type system
    noexcept specifications   69
type traits   251
    bool_constant   401
    suffix _v   251
    void_t   403

## U

u16string()
    for path   221
u16string_view   192
u32string()
    for path   221
u32string_view   192
u8   68
u8path()   217
u8string()
    for path   221
unary_function   411
uncaught_exception()   412
uncaught_exceptions()   327
uniform initialization   xxi
unique()
    for shared pointers   412
unknown
    file permission   235
unknown file type   216
unordered container
    extract()   309
    hash function   113
    insert()   309
    merge()   312

    node handle   309
unsynchronized_pool_resource   347, 349
update_existing
    copy option   238
using
    extended declarations   129
    for attributes   58
UTF-16
    u16string()   221
UTF-32
    u32string()   221
UTF-8   68, 217
    u8string()   221

## V

_v suffix   251
value()
    for node handles   309
    for optional<>   139, 142
value category   42
valueless_by_exception()   162
    for variant<>   153
value_or()
    for optional<>   139, 142
variable
    inline   25
variable template   **416**
    with auto   124
variadic template   **416**
    fold expression   107
    function calls   112
    with auto   122
variant   149
    class template argument deduction   155
    heterogeneous collection   162
    index()   150
    in_place_index   154
    in_place_type   154
    launder()   393
    monostate   151
    polymorphism   162
    valueless_by_exception()   162
    visitor   157
vector

incomplete types   316
launder()   393
pmr::vector   343
reallocation   336
visit()
   for variant<>   157
visitor
   for variants   157
   generic lambda   159
   return values   160
void_t   403

# W

warn_unused_result   57
wbuffer_convert<>   412

weak_from_this   330
weakly_canonical()
   for path   241
weak_type   330
Windows
   Access Control List   237
   filesystem path handling   203
wstring()
   for path   221
wstring_convert<>   412
wstring_view   192

# X

xvalue   43

CPSIA information can be obtained
at www.ICGtesting.com
Printed in the USA
BVHW060226120122
625983BV00004B/465